Dr. Lee Ann B. Marino, Ph.D., D.Min., D.D.

The Wedding Workbook

Your Four-Month Guide to the Marriage of Your Dreams

The Wedding Workbook

Your Four-Month Guide to the Marriage of Your Dreams

Dr. Lee Ann B. Marino, Ph.D., D.Min., D.D.

Published by:

Righteous Pen Publications

(The righteousness of God shall guide my pen)

www.righteouspenpublications.com

Photos appearing in this book are all in the public domain or the design of the author.

Book Classification: Books > Religion & Spirituality > Christian Books & Bibles > Christian Living > Marriage

ISBN: 1940197309

13-Digit: 978-1-940197-30-2

Printed in the United States of America.

Acknowledgements

I must, first and foremost, thank God for the insight and revelation to write this book. Writing on marriage is never an easy task, and writing on marriage, with its ins and outs, ups and downs, and specifics to couples means that it is that much more challenging. I praise and thank my God, Who revealed Himself so much through this project, and Who I have truly learned so much about belonging to and being married to Him in the pages of this revelation.

Secondly, I thank all those who are a part of my life because He is Lord of it. I thank all of those who are here, and yes, even those who have left, because it is a season of purpose and victory. Here's to all who have made this walk worthwhile, and those who are yet on the horizon who will make it even more worthwhile to come.

Table of Contents

Introduction

I am going to admit that I am not the biggest fan of weddings. I've spent years avoiding them. I am not into the whole "bride" thing. I don't like showers and bachelorette parties, and I think the fuss we have seen in weddings over the past several decades merits insanity. It does not make sense to me to spend thousands of dollars on a party when that money can be put toward a house, a car, or other needs that a couple will incur as part of their lives together.

That, however, is me. I know it's not everyone else. Big, fancy weddings were never something I desired in my life. As a minister, however, I can't deny that people want their weddings. For many individuals, weddings are the peak of human experience. They celebrate everything they feel, want, and desire in that one event. That means that weddings are an important part of human experience for the average individual, and especially for the average churchgoer.

As a result, weddings have become a crazy, booming industry. People will spend years planning their weddings, getting the details just right, and then find themselves divorced within a few years. There are many who speculate on why this is. Having spent so many years counseling individuals as a minister, I don't think there is one answer. I think people get divorced for several reasons. I don't think, contrary to what some might say, that anyone approaches their wedding day with divorce on their minds. People do not enter marriage anticipating the day when the life they have will be divided into "THEIRS" and "THEIRS." Nobody anticipates that their wedding will parade them to a courthouse for custody battles and separation disputes. When it comes time for the wedding, people aren't that cynical.

I want to emphasize that I think it's a good thing that people aren't cynical when it comes time to get married. It makes me happy to know that there are still people out there who believe that they can be happy in marriage and that they anticipate marriage can be a good thing. I don't want to cast a doom-and-gloom approach to weddings, nor to marriage. We should be excited when couples get married and want to give them that hand up as they approach their big day. Instead of having nagging feelings and concerns in the background, we should equip them with tools to make sure that relationship cynicism doesn't become a last resort.

At the same time, it is never a good idea to make such a serious commitment as pertains to marriage without knowing the person you are going to marry. I have seen many relationships fall apart or falter at the last minute because a couple was grossly unprepared for the realities of married life. Those realities were sucked up and buried under wedding preparations and fanciful ideas that would soon surface when life hit them in the face.

Being married can be a great thing, but I think we need to remember that marriage, like anything else, has its difficulties. The reason we are given marriage in this life is not to ride off into the sunset and experience eternal bliss. Marriage has been given to us in order to help us grow and develop into all we can be as we both receive support and give support to another person in a long-term relationship. Through marriage, it is God's desire that we will learn about give and take, about purpose and perspective, and that we will achieve personal balance.

When it comes to weddings, love, and marriage, the goal is for couples to approach their relationship with a balanced and prepared attitude. Couples need to learn how they view things, how to articulate their views, and how to understand and embrace the views of their partner. Couples need to be fully informed about marriage, about the legalities involved in that process, about relationship dynamics, and, ultimately, must learn how to work together as a team. Even though most of the contemporary focus is on how couples feel about each other, we should be focused on growing into love and whether or not a couple will be able to do that as time passes.

That's why I have created this, *The Wedding Workbook*. Many ministers and counselors approach pre-marital counseling with the anticipated goal of getting couples to have spiritually centered relationships. There is nothing wrong with this in and of itself, but the message often given through these programs is that God is the One Who will fix all the problems a couple has in their marriage. We don't prepare couples for all the things that will arise in marriages that are the result of people's personal choices or the things that come up as a part of daily living. When someone is unable to pray away a problem or a change in feeling and status that arises as a part of marriage, they are unable to cope and function through that situation.

Marriages take more than just loving feelings or abstract ideals we might have about relationships. They take more than determination to make things work, or the idea that someone is taking divorce off the table forever. Marriages take true consideration, love and respect for the other partner to survive. It is a daily restart, a willingness to move forward with someone and know that what you have is worth sustaining through the low points as well as the high points. It is, in the end, a decision that married couples must make every day. That decision starts with whether a couple feels that they have what it takes to change their lives and get married, spending out the rest of their days learning how to live with that person.

The Wedding Workbook is so titled because it is ideally used for pre-marital counseling. It can also be used, however, as part of marital counseling or as part of a program in preparation for a wedding anniversary ceremony or vow renewal. It can be of benefit to single people preparing for marriage, couples who are looking to reconcile in a relationship, divorced individuals who are remarrying either their first spouse or someone else, or people who want to learn how to communicate better in relationships.

In order to complete this course, couples need:

- Two copies of *The Wedding Workbook* (one for each)
- Two copies of *Discovering Intimacy: A Journey Through the Song of Solomon* (one for each)
- Two copies of the Bible (any translation, one for each; in this book, I predominately use The Expanded Bible)
- Two journals (one for each)

The minister or counselor facilitating pre-marital counseling needs the following:

- One copy of *The Wedding Workbook*
- One copy of *Discovering Intimacy: A Journey Through the Song of Solomon*

- One copy of *Sacred Ceremonies: The Who, What, Where, When, Why, and How of Christian Ordinances, Rites, and Rituals*
- One copy of the Bible (any translation; in this book I predominately use The Expanded Bible, in *Discovering the Beauty of Intimacy: A Journey Through the Song of Solomon* I predominately use the New International Version, and in the book *Sacred Ceremonies*, I predominantly use the King James Version)

The text and workbook will be handed out at the first session, of which there are no lessons in the workbook. The first short session, which begins prior to the 16 lessons of this course, will be to meet the couple, talk briefly, hand out the books, and then instruct them to get a journal book and complete their first week's reading and assignments as well as begin on the first month's reading and assignments for their next session.

The workbook is divided into four sections, one for each month of pre-marital counseling. Each month focuses on different aspects of relationship building, self-awareness, and communication. Each section is divided into weeks, one lesson per week (16 weeks in total). Each lesson covers important topics that should be read and discussed as part of counseling. At the end of each chapter, there are important assignments for couples to complete. Some of these assignments should be completed individually, while some of them involve couple participation. It's vitally important that couples follow the instructions for each exercise and complete them as directed.

In addition to the exercises and counseling process, couples should be encouraged to talk and share about things they are thinking and feeling. They should be encouraged to continue dating, enjoying each other, meeting one another's families, and preparing to share in their lives.

About midway through the counseling process, there is a special meeting that will involve the main individuals of both families of the couple, to educate and direct them as to the details of the wedding. This gives the future couple a chance to work together, to present their vision for the day as a couple, and to also open the door for familial involvement in the planning. This is also vital for the minister to recognize and acknowledge where problems in the process may be coming from and ways to help empower couples to prepare for their marriage as they plan their wedding.

Notes to couple

- Make sure you each individually complete all reading and all assignments as outlined in the text.

- Select a minister for counseling that you are comfortable with and that you have some semblance of a relationship with. Now is not the time to pick a minister to just perform at a ceremony.

- Talk as a couple outside of counseling. There is no reason to think you need to stop living because you are planning to get married! Continue to express your thoughts and know more about each other in the process.

- Don't feel pressured one way or another. You are taking this to help prepare you for marriage, because your engagement signals that's what you want to do. If you decide that's not what you want to do in this process, speak up!

Notes to counselor or minister

- If a couple does this course for a few weeks or months and then find that they don't want to get married, do not force the issue. Let them make that decision for themselves and pursue other relationship options. Just because a couple is engaged does not mean they have to get married. It is better they decide they don't want to get married before the wedding than find they don't want to be married afterwards.

- Do not judge the couple, regardless of what might come out because of the counseling process. Judgment takes many forms. Make sure that you aren't looking down on one of the partners and are siding with the other. Maintain objectivity to help this couple achieve what they seek to achieve.

- Avoid the temptation to make everything all about the wedding. I know that weddings are stressful, but they can easily become larger than they must be because the wedding becomes about everything but the couple. Encourage the couple to have the wedding they desire, rather than the wedding they may be pressured into having.

- Use this text and the books in this process to help provide a balanced perspective about relationships. Don't just instruct in marriage as a bunch of rules and roles that most people do not follow anymore. Open their world to the possibilities of true partnership and intimacy and encourage them to have nothing less. As a minister facilitating this important counseling, be sure to expand upon the topics presented and the discussions that the couple will have. Add your own questions, provide and expand with your own input, relay your own advice when needed, and offer from your own experience. This is not a static book, but a workbook, an ongoing discussion that helps prepare couples to communicate and engage as they will need to within the beauties of married life. As the minister, you have an awesome opportunity to equip and prepare them. Take this opportunity and help them to become all that they can be.

Month One

GETTING TO KNOW YOU, YOUR SPOUSE, AND YOUR RELATIONSHIP

Reading assignments:

- *Discovering The Beauty of Intimacy: A Journey Through the Song of Solomon*: Author's Note, About the Commentary, Introduction and all of section I (the Song of Solomon Bible text)

Week One

All About You

GOD CAN SEE WHAT IS IN PEOPLE'S HEARTS AND [THE ONE WHO SEARCHES HEARTS] KNOWS WHAT IS IN THE MIND OF THE SPIRIT, BECAUSE THE SPIRIT SPEAKS TO GOD [INTERCEDES; APPEALS] FOR HS PEOPLE [OR HIS HOLY PEOPLE; THE SAINTS] IN THE WAY GOD WANTS [OR IN HARMONY WITH GOD, ACCORDING TO GOD].
(ROMANS 8:27)

<u>Bible reading:</u> Psalm 139:1-24

<u>Journaling assignments for in-session discussion:</u>

- In reading through the Song of Solomon and learning about its history and background, why do you think it was included in the Bible?
- What do you think the Song of Solomon reveals to us about intimate relationships?
- In reading it, do you think anything is blocking you from having that kind of relationship? If so, what is it?

It's easy to think that we know everything there is to know about ourselves. After all, we've lived with ourselves for our entire lives. We are the ones who have constantly been walking with ourselves from the beginning, from our first steps to our school years and then on into adulthood. We've lived, loved, lost, and overcome, time and time again. Who knows us better than we know ourselves? Who could ever fathom that we don't know who we are?

The truth is that, yes, we have been with ourselves since the beginning, and no one has been closer to our life experiences than we have. In marriage, however, we are inviting someone else to become that close to us. We are giving someone else access to our memories, our habits, our jumbled-up thoughts and lives, and the results of our entire life experiences. All those things are wrapped up in our personalities and our personal perspectives on life. Even though it might seem impossible to fathom, when we enter a close relationship with someone (especially that results in marriage), we often learn things about ourselves that we never knew before.

This week, we are going to look at learning about the most basic person you have been in a relationship with: you. Since you have known yourself since birth, you are the perfect person to start talking about! Spend some time this week in prayer, focusing on and realizing who you are, things you never knew, and things that bring you to a blessed place as you prepare to give of yourself in an intimate relationship.

Who are you?

People have been asking the question, "Who am I?" for centuries. No matter how cute we might try to answer this question, it is a serious question that should be taken with sincere thought. Every one of us should ask this question, because asking the question reveals to us, more than anything, where we are and who we want to be.

There are four different ways that many people answer this question:

- You are a product of your identity (male, female, non-binary, agender, transgender, etc.).
- You are a product of your culture (your ethnic make-up and where you were born and how your family lives).
- You are a product of your spirituality (your beliefs as pertain to deeper life things).
- You are a product of your desires (what you want and who

you aspire to be).

All these things are a part of who you are and are, most likely, part of how you identify yourself. They are a part of who you are, but they are not exclusively who you are.

Simply put, you are you.

Who you are is a child of God who is walking through life, doing the best with what has been handled to you. You are not your job, you are not what has happened to you, you are not your relationships, you are not how much money you have, and you are not some ambiguous social status. You are more than these things: you are an individual, unique and precious in the sight of God, and precious and important in the sight of people in your life.

Every single one of us is an individual, with our own thoughts, feelings, ideas, and concepts. Who we are is a product of all those things, plus several more: our thoughts, our ideas, our feelings, our concepts, our personality, our identity, our history, our outlook, our goals, our dreams, and, ultimately, our purpose. When we combine all of these things together, we get the product of who we are. That's why it's so hard to define yourself in one word, or even a sentence or a phrase. Who we are is a big jumble of things, some of those things quite complicated, that make us the human beings that we are.

Even though different people feel different ways about life, life itself is a wonderful thing. We, as human beings, are the product of life. We're the result of all those steps we've taken since day one and we have the unique ability to process what we have experienced as we continue. One of the most exciting things about our lives is relationships with other people. When most of us talk about being in "a relationship," we talk about it in the context of dating or romance. That is a relationship, but that is not the only relationship we are in. Over the course of your life, you have probably interacted with many people in a relationship context. Relationships are our interactions and dynamics with other people. We are in relationships with our parents or primary caregivers, our brothers and sisters (if we have any), our extended family (such as aunts and cousins), our co-workers, our acquaintances, our church family, and our friends. Every single one of these relationships has different boundaries, conditions, and terms, but they all have one thing in common: they teach us how to be social and how to interact with others. They are building blocks to different foundations throughout life.

Human beings are designed for connection. All the way back in the Garden of Eden, it was God Who stated that "It is not good for man to be alone." Even though this has become the worst pick-up line of all time, there is a fundamental truth contained within its words: too much time alone isn't good for any of us. All of us desire to have people in our lives who love us for who we are, who give us a sense of grounding and belonging. Most people have a hard time with total isolation, even if it is temporary. None of us likes to be lonely. God has placed this desire within all of us because it has been His purpose since the beginning to prepare us for His Kingdom, in which we shall dwell forever. His Kingdom is a "social" thing. It's not just a random, distant reality, but a living body of people who seek to give Him glory throughout eternity.

Genesis 2:15-23:

THE LORD GOD [TOOK AND] PUT THE MAN [OR ADAM; 1:27] IN THE GARDEN OF EDEN TO CARE FOR [OR TILL] IT AND WORK [TAKE CARE OF; LOOK AFTER] IT. THE LORD GOD COMMANDED HIM, "YOU MAY EAT THE FRUIT FROM ANY TREE [OR ALL THE TREES] IN THE GARDEN, BUT YOU MUST NOT EAT THE FRUIT FROM THE TREE WHICH GIVES THE [OF THE] KNOWLEDGE OF GOOD AND EVIL [EATING FROM THIS TREE WOULD MAKE ADAM, NOT GOD, THE DETERMINER OF RIGHT AND WRONG]. IF YOU EVER EAT FRUIT FROM THAT TREE, YOU WILL [CERTAINLY] DIE!"

THEN THE LORD GOD SAID, "IT IS NOT GOOD FOR THE MAN TO BE ALONE. I WILL MAKE A HELPER [IN THE SENSE OF A PARTNER OR ALLY; THE WORD DOES NOT IMPLY SUBORDINATE STATUS; SEE PS. 79:9] WHO ·IS RIGHT FOR [IS SUITABLE FOR; CORRESPONDS WITH] HIM."

FROM THE GROUND GOD FORMED EVERY WILD ANIMAL [ANIMAL OF THE FIELD] AND EVERY BIRD IN THE SKY [HEAVENS], AND HE BROUGHT THEM TO THE MAN SO THE MAN COULD NAME THEM [TO SEE WHAT HE WOULD CALL THEM]. WHATEVER THE MAN CALLED EACH LIVING THING, THAT BECAME ITS NAME. THE MAN GAVE NAMES TO ALL THE TAME ANIMALS [BEASTS; LIVESTOCK], TO THE BIRDS IN THE SKY [HEAVENS], AND TO ALL THE WILD ANIMALS [ANIMALS OF THE FIELD]. BUT ADAM [OR THE MAN; 1:27] DID NOT FIND A HELPER THAT WAS RIGHT FOR HIM [2:18]. SO THE LORD GOD

CAUSED THE MAN TO SLEEP VERY DEEPLY [A DEEP SLEEP TO FALL ON THE MAN/ADAM], AND WHILE HE WAS ASLEEP, GOD REMOVED ONE OF THE MAN'S RIBS [OR SIDES]. THEN GOD CLOSED UP THE MAN'S SKIN AT THE PLACE WHERE HE TOOK THE RIB [OR SIDE]. THE LORD GOD USED THE RIB [OR SIDE] FROM THE MAN TO MAKE [BUILD; CONSTRUCT] A WOMAN, AND THEN HE BROUGHT THE WOMAN TO THE MAN.

AND THE MAN SAID,

"NOW, THIS IS SOMEONE WHOSE BONES CAME FROM MY BONES, WHOSE BODY CAME FROM MY BODY [AT LAST, THIS IS BONE OF MY BONES AND FLESH OF MY FLESH]. I WILL CALL HER [SHE WILL BE CALLED] 'WOMAN [HEBREW 'ISHSHAH],' BECAUSE SHE WAS TAKEN OUT OF MAN [HEBREW 'ISH]."

The first relationship God created was with Adam. It is God's desire that our first, and most primary relationship in this life, be with Him. We will talk a little more about that later in this chapter. Right now, we are going to look at the reason you are here, which is the second relationship God created back in the garden, and that was of Adam and Eve. The second relationship God created was that of a spouse, or marital companion. Yes, we know they didn't have marriage licenses back then and there wasn't a lot of competition for Adam and Eve's time, but the second relationship created was for fruitfulness and intimacy. If you're interested in this book, it's because you are either engaged to be married, approaching engagement, interested in a marriage relationship, or are already in one, but are preparing for something else special (such as a vow renewal). That means the relationship that you want to look at is the marriage relationship, or a special relationship created for intimacy and fruitfulness with your partner.

When we come into a relationship with anyone, in any context, that big jumble of things I spoke of a few paragraphs back comes with us. What we often want in a relationship comes from the ideas and concepts we acquired somewhere in our lives, usually at different points in time. This is why relationships are, by nature, so intrinsically complicated. In a relationship, you take one person with their big jumble and another person with their big jumble and try to stick them together. In the process, many things about those two complicated jumbles come to light. Those things may be positive or negative, functional or dysfunctional, seriously problematic or nothing more than a few bumps in the road. This is one of the reasons relationships are so important: they unveil and reveal these things within us, telling us more about who we are and who we should aspire to be.

New creature, old habits, behaviors and memories

I can't talk about the general concept of who you are without talking about some aspects of faith. If you are taking this program, it is highly likely that you are a member of a church somewhere and your pastor or leader has given you this book as a part of your pre-marriage preparation. This means that I am understanding you, as the reader, to be in a place in your faith where the "basics" have been covered. These basics include:

- Water baptism
- Spirit baptism
- Receiving communion as often as it is held
- Participation in your local church or ministry
- Regular contribution to that ministry (tithes and offerings)

If you haven't done any of these or aren't doing them like you should, now is the time to get those things right in your life. Marriage and weddings incur all sorts of unexpected and unplanned events and expenses, and now is the time to straighten things out, while you are still single. It is far easier to merge spiritual living and giving when both parties are doing it prior to marriage than waiting and trying to sort it out when a new life is quickly forming. It's important that you talk to your pastor or leader about these things, and make sure you understand what you have done and what still needs to be done.

2 Corinthians 5:16-18:

[SO; AS A RESULT] FROM THIS TIME [NOW] ON WE DO NOT THINK OF ANYONE AS THE WORLD DOES [OR FROM A MERELY HUMAN PERSPECTIVE; ACCORDING TO THE FLESH]. [ALTHOUGH] IN THE PAST WE THOUGHT OF CHRIST AS THE WORLD THINKS [OR AS NOTHING MORE THAN A MAN;

ACCORDING TO THE FLESH], BUT WE NO LONGER THINK OF HIM IN THAT WAY. IF ANYONE BELONGS TO CHRIST, THERE IS A NEW CREATION [THE NEW CREATION HAS ARRIVED; OR THAT PERSON HAS BECOME A NEW CREATION]. THE OLD THINGS HAVE GONE; [LOOK; BEHOLD] EVERYTHING IS MADE NEW [THE NEW HAS COME]! ALL THIS IS FROM GOD, WHO THROUGH CHRIST MADE PEACE BETWEEN US AND [RECONCILED US TO] HIMSELF, AND GAVE US THE WORK OF TELLING EVERYONE ABOUT THE PEACE WE CAN HAVE WITH HIM [MINISTRY/SERVICE OF RECONCILIATION].

The reason these things are important is simple: you are entering a new phase of your life, a new phase of being a "new creature in Christ." We talk about the new birth as a one-time deal all by itself, and that is only partially correct. As believers, the principle of being "born again" means that we are starting over, starting our lives again, from the very beginning in a spiritual sense. That means we will have spiritual milestones in the same parallel of natural ones: we will learn how to talk spiritually, walk spiritually, run spiritually, go to spiritual school for the first time, learn how to eat spiritual food, and so on and so forth. In marriage, we enter yet another phase of newness: we are becoming one with another person. A lot of people talk about that as nothing more than a physical thing, but that isn't true. Being one means aspiring to one life and one spiritual connection, embracing the other person as a part of a sense of completion. It doesn't mean that we aren't complete by ourselves as individuals, but that we take on a new understanding of what it means to be in a relationship and be a part of somebody's life. Adam and Eve were one, then separated physically, then came back together as one again. Yes, they were good and complete on their own, but they were something incredible together.

It's God's plan that married people become something incredible, new, and great together. The first step to achieving this is being able to become incredible and awesome as individual people. Once we start talking about weddings and marriage, it almost feels as if the "you" portion of that relationship becomes non-existent. Everything starts becoming about "the couple." "What does the couple need?" "Where are you going to live together?" "When do you plan to have children?" "Who is going to provide primary income?" It's great to think that your partner will affirm the "you" that you are...but married life tends to become complicated.

All the fun and early experiences of a relationship get replaced with bills… and children… and responsibilities… and family time… and the "you" that you thought your partner was going to affirm for you gets lost somewhere in that struggle.

You, as a person, without a date, without a partner, without a spouse, are important. Who "you" are is going to change many times throughout your life, with continued shades of who you have always been shining through. Your opinions will change, your perspectives will change, and your feelings about things will change. That's why it is important to be able to know and understand yourself, as much as it is possible, right now – because marriage has a way of swallowing people up, and not in a good way. If you don't have a good sense of yourself now, your marriage isn't going to bring you that perspective identity… it will just get lost. When you come to a place where you can find it again, it is very possible you might not like a lot of things about your life and you may seek a way out of them… including your marriage.

Yes, we are new creatures in Christ, but we are still ourselves, with our old habits, our old dysfunctions, and our old challenges. We may even have issues that we don't know are there because we haven't been in situations that require us to deal with them. Just because we believe in God and start walking as a new creature doesn't mean that all the old things of our past magically disappear. Some people do teach faith like that, but I don't. Belief in God is not a magic wand, nor a land of fairy dust. Faith is here for everyday living, the challenges and choices we have to make on a regular basis. God is here for things just like we are talking about: self-discovery, empowering ourselves, and empowering our relationships. We grow in Him by glory to glory and faith to faith, one step at a time. As we become more like Him, we shed more of our old image.

In marriage, we deliberately put ourselves in situations that demand us to become more Christ-like. We live with someone else; we must learn to live with our "old person" habits and ways as well as their "old person" habits and ways, and we do so with the expectation that we will be able to do this for the rest of our lives. This is why being as spiritually right as is possible is so vital, and so important. Whatever foundations do exist, that's great. Whatever foundations need improvement, improve them now. While you are improving on your own transformation, talk to your partner, and make sure you are both on a path of spiritual transformation in the areas of glory and faith.

Also, make sure the spirituality of your life is not taking a backseat to your wedding and marriage life. If you believe God is the center of your life and you desire Him to be the center of your marriage, make sure you are behaving in a way that reflects that. Life does not stop because someone gets married or wants to get married. Nobody stops working because they get married, so nobody should stop attending church, reading Scripture, praying and meditating, and communicating with God, either. If you have a ministry, it should be understood that your ministry does not stop because you get married, and your ministry should not suffer from neglect due to your impending marriage. Remain centered and focused and understand that if your partner is right for you, they should understand how important spiritual things are for you and for them, too.

Loving yourself

Being single can be a wonderful time in someone's life. Seldom is it spoken of in this way. Most people depict marriage to be far better than the single life, but I think this is a serious misnomer. There are many married people who are miserable, who long for their single days. There are also many single people who are miserable, who wish they were married. If we break it down like that, it's obvious that many people are simply unhappy, whether married or single.

I believe God desires us to reach a state of contentment in life, regardless of whether we are married or single. This means we are at peace and centered in His will, blessed where He has us, no matter what our outside circumstances may be. The way we can achieve this is when we love who we are, as children of God, and as women and men being transformed into His image in a deeper way.

Mark 12:30-31:

LOVE THE LORD YOUR GOD WITH ALL YOUR HEART, ALL YOUR SOUL, ALL YOUR MIND, AND ALL YOUR STRENGTH' [DEUT. 6:4–5; THESE ARE THE OPENING WORDS OF THE SHEMA, THE PRAYER SAID BY PIOUS JEWS TWICE A

DAY]. THE SECOND COMMAND IS THIS: 'LOVE YOUR NEIGHBOR AS YOU LOVE YOURSELF' [LEV. 19:18]. THERE ARE NO COMMANDS MORE IMPORTANT [GREATER] THAN THESE."

The Bible tells us that we are to love our neighbor as we love ourselves. This doesn't mean we should be "in love" with ourselves, so preoccupied with our own being that there is no room for anyone else. I have met people across the board who were like this, and it was obvious because their expectations of a mate were impossible to meet. Loving ourselves does mean that we should care for and esteem other people in the same way we would take the time to care about and esteem ourselves. This is a foundational principle to relationships of all sorts, because it means that we must first accept God's love and image of us into our lives so we can pour that out to other people.

While you are still single, I highly advise you get to know yourself better and come to a greater love of what God is doing in and through your life. There are some awesome revelations that come about when it is just "Him and us," revelations that are harder to come by when we live with someone else. You also have the opportunity to know God in a deeper way, in a different way that will be highly useful when living with someone else. The more you know who you are in Him and the greater your understanding of His love for you, the better you will be as you learn how to navigate a relationship built on intimacy with another person.

While God works love in and through you, it's natural to identify and recognize certain things you want in a mate. Most people can prattle off a long list of traits they expect to see in another person, and they expect their future husband or wife to have those traits. There's nothing wrong with desiring your future mate to have certain characteristics, but there is a problem with not recognizing the characteristics you need to have within yourself to compliment your mate. Whenever we start getting more interested in what our mate can or will do for us than we are interested in what we can do for them, we don't have a relationship, we have a mess.

The single years and single periods of time in between relationships are for developing this love within us. They are an opportunity to be able to know yourself, use spiritual and natural gifts, and develop direction. Being single is not a sin. It doesn't mean you have done something wrong or that you are unlovable. It doesn't mean that you will never meet someone.

Don't be in a relationship for the wrong reasons

Too often we think that we must be married or be in a relationship because we are inadequate on our own. The Bible does not teach that, and I wish the church would stop teaching that. If you are in a relationship to be "completed," to be "whole," to achieve the "next stage of life," or just to have sex, you're in a relationship for the wrong reasons. If you think marriage is going to fix you or save you in some way... don't get married. All you will do is create new complications that are difficult, if not impossible, to overcome. If you are getting married because you just don't want to be single, don't get married. Instead, look at 1 Corinthians 7:7-9 and hear what the Apostle Paul was really trying to tell us:

I WISH THAT EVERYONE WERE LIKE ME [UNMARRIED], BUT EACH PERSON HAS HIS OWN GIFT FROM GOD. ONE HAS ONE GIFT, ANOTHER HAS ANOTHER GIFT. NOW FOR THOSE WHO ARE NOT MARRIED AND FOR THE WIDOWS I SAY THIS: IT IS GOOD FOR THEM TO STAY UNMARRIED AS I AM. BUT IF THEY CANNOT CONTROL THEMSELVES [EXERCISE SELF-CONTROL], THEY SHOULD MARRY. IT IS BETTER TO MARRY THAN TO BURN WITH SEXUAL DESIRE [TO BURN].

I think what the Apostle Paul was trying to point out is that both married life and single life have their own complications, and both can be difficult. Certain benefits and negatives go with single life and with married life. This doesn't make being single a blight on humanity, and it doesn't mean we should get married for the wrong reasons. Every married person was once single, and many single people were once married. Many more single people have been in relationships, some being long-term, and others being single.

Why do you, as a person, who you are, right now, want to get married? What is it about your future spouse that makes you want to give up the benefits of single life? What can they offer you, and what can you offer to them? What is the base of your future marriage relationship?

Never see marriage as "giving up yourself"

One of the reasons why divorce rates are so high today is because the ideas and concepts circulating about marriage in the past century were highly detrimental to family life. Pop culture theories about marriage were that being married required partners to "give up" themselves, becoming a family unit and abandoning their own individual identities. We've all heard stories about people who said they were going out to buy a pack of cigarettes and never returned, or someone who just one day got on a bus, left their home and family, and was never heard from again. The reason these people did this was because they found a conflict between having to give up themselves and being the person that everyone else expected them to be.

In general, the world has a lot of expectations for us. Most of those expectations don't align with modern generations, no matter how we spin it. The general consensus is that you reach a certain age, you should get married, you should have children, and you should live your life according to traditional norms. No matter how well-intentioned some people's questions might be, we are constantly experiencing pressure to do something or be someone other than we are. If you're not married, it's that someone wants to know why or when you're going to do it. If you are married, they want to know when you are going to have children, or when you are going to have more children. If you are divorced, people want to know why, and when you are going to get married again. If we allow ourselves to be consumed by these ideas, the Expectation Train will never leave the station.

It is not God's will for us to approach marriage and life in general through the expectations of other people. It is also not His will for us to abandon ourselves in the pursuit of some vague concept of other people's dreams and desires for us. If you are getting married, the person you are marrying needs to love, esteem, and respect you as a person. It needs to be about more than just thinking you have a great body or even that you might have something valuable to offer spiritually, economically, or personally. The person that you desire to marry needs to have you in their heart, and you in their heart. Rather than giving up yourself, being married should offer you a greater sense of yourself and a greater identity into who you seek to become. Your marriage partner should support your goals and dreams, affirm the interests and desires you have, and be a great advocate, friend, and support in your life. It should never be about becoming someone else, being "changed" into someone else's image of you, and it should never be about transforming to fit into an abstract concept of a wife or a husband.

On the other hand, you need to offer your partner the same things that they should do for you. You should not be marrying someone with the hope or intention to change them, about transforming to fit your ideal husband or wife fantasy, and you too need to support their goals, dreams, interests, and be their advocate, friend, and life-long support. The Song of Solomon 2:6 tells us:

MY LOVER'S LEFT HAND IS UNDER MY HEAD,
AND HIS RIGHT ARM HOLDS ME TIGHT [EMBRACES ME; 8:3].

Above all, couples need to recognize that they are there to support each other on a long-term journey as they discover in deeper ways exactly who God has called them to be.

Learning how to wait

None of us like to wait. In fact, I would dare to say most people are rather impatient, eager to get on with things and hate the idea that they might desire to do something that is not coming to them immediately. We often talk about living in a drive-through society and the issues that people have with instant gratification as a result. We expect things to be done, your way, right away, without any consideration to time factors, quality, and craftsmanship.

God, by His very nature, is a craftsman, because He is the Creator. The point of creation wasn't the number of days it was done in (as to whether they were literal or symbolic). The point was that creation came about by a process, and that God crafted each and every step, each and every point, through the entire process. That same process applies to spiritual things, and that means things that pertain to spirituality don't "speed up" because we live in a different time in history. With God, we often spend much of our spiritual walk waiting and developing an active patience as we continue in our lives.

Should I feel guilty about my past?

SOMETIMES BEING IN A GOOD RELATIONSHIP MAKES US FEEL VERY SELF-CONSCIOUS ABOUT OUR PAST MISTAKES AND OUR PAST RELATIONSHIPS, ESPECIALLY IF THE RELATIONSHIPS WEREN'T VERY GOOD. WE CAN LOOK BACK ON THE THINGS WE DID WHEN WE WERE INVOLVED WITH OTHER PEOPLE AND FEEL LIKE WE COMMITTED A SIN AGAINST OUR SPOUSES OR FUTURE SPOUSES BECAUSE OF WHAT WE DID WITH SOMEONE ELSE. WHETHER IT'S SEX, LIVING WITH SOMEONE, OR EVEN SPENDING TIME ON A RELATIONSHIP THAT JUST WASN'T GOING ANYWHERE, THERE MAY BE A LITTLE VOICE INSIDE THAT SAYS, "WHY DID I DO THAT? WHY DIDN'T I JUST WAIT?"

NONE OF US HAS BEEN PERFECT WHEN IT COMES TO PAST RELATIONSHIPS, AND, HOPEFULLY, WE'VE ALL TAKEN SOMETHING AWAY FROM OUR PAST RELATIONSHIPS FOR US, AS PEOPLE. EVEN IF A RELATIONSHIP DOESN'T WORK OUT, THAT DOESN'T MEAN THE ENTIRE RELATIONSHIP WAS A WASTE. FOR WHATEVER REASON NECESSARY, WALKING THROUGH THAT SITUATION HELPED US TO BECOME BETTER PEOPLE AND SEE MORE CLEARLY WHAT WE WANTED OR NEEDED IN A MATE. RATHER THAN FEEL BAD ABOUT WHAT YOU HAVE DONE PRIOR, RECOGNIZE YOURSELF AS AN OVERCOMER AND KNOW THAT THE THINGS YOU WENT THROUGH IN THE PAST HAVE HELPED TO MAKE YOU WHO YOU ARE, RIGHT NOW.

James 1:4:

[AND] LET YOUR PATIENCE [PERSEVERANCE; ENDURANCE] SHOW ITSELF PERFECTLY IN WHAT YOU DO [HAVE ITS FULL EFFECT; FINISH ITS WORK]. THEN YOU WILL BE PERFECT AND COMPLETE [MATURE AND WHOLE; OR COMPLETELY MATURE] AND WILL HAVE EVERYTHING YOU NEED [LACK NOTHING].

If we are going to endure at this "believer" thing in marriage, there is a very important thing we are going to need, and that's patience. Spouses, children, families, bills, jobs, stress, and life all require that we are patient people, individuals who are willing to grow into all God asks us to be. That means that we must approach everything in our lives with patience... and that includes our spouses. Patience is a real problem when people reach a marrying age and do decide that they want to take the relationship plunge. By the time most people have decided they are ready to get married, they've already dated other people and really feel a settling in their own lives. Because they are eager to settle, they tend to grow very impatient when "the one" they desire to marry does not appear. They are ready, they believe they want it now, and when that person doesn't immediately materialize, it can be frustrating.

Impatience also arises after you have met the person you desire to marry and then you await the time when you've had your wedding, and you are married. The weeks and months leading to a wedding can be a trying and difficult time, and impatience can also result.

Waiting is never easy, but in waiting, God desires us to develop patience. The reason so much waiting surrounds marriage is because in the marriage relationship, we spend a lot of time waiting, and we find ourselves in many situations that require patience. You might have to repeat yourself repeatedly if a spouse is not listening. You might have to wait to get pregnant, which is a special battle for many couples. You will have days when you are waiting for your kids to outgrow certain stages of life, or where you are waiting for them to be grown, period. You may be ready to move ahead with something in the spiritual realm or ready to move on to something new, and you might have to wait for your spouse to catch up. In the waiting, we find maturity and peace. If you have a marriage you want to survive, you will need to learn how to wait and find maturity and peace in your patience.

Looking at your past relationships

In that big jumble of life, we find our past relationships. Most people who desire to get married today have dated in the past, and some have even been married prior. Odds are good that if you are reading this book, you have been involved in another relationship with someone else at some point in time. Whether it was recent, distant, good, bad, serious, or not serious, your past relationships are a part of where you are, right now. That brings us to the question as to just how serious were your past relationships, and how did they influence your approach to relationships today?

2 Corinthians 8:21:

[FOR] WE ARE TRYING HARD TO DO WHAT IS RIGHT, NOT ONLY BEFORE THE LORD BUT ALSO BEFORE PEOPLE [PROV. 3:4].

If we are going to be real and have a relationship that is honorable both before God and other people, we need to come clean about our relationship pasts (or maybe even presents!). Whether we want to admit it or not, living together without being married, having sex with multiple partners that we are not married to, being divorced, experiencing a pregnancy when a couple isn't married, and having children with people we are not married to (even if we once were) all bring a certain amount of baggage to a relationship. I don't feel that these things are insurmountable, nor do I think that we should spend vast amounts of time condemning or berating people for them. They are a part of culture now and good or bad, that means many people are in situations like those listed above. What they do mean, however, is that these things change our outlook on relationships and affect the ways in which we regard those we are involved with.

- **Living together:** When people live together and they are not married, they are basically living together as roommates with a sexual relationship. There are no legal benefits, and this roommate situation demands that both parties contribute a certain amount to the household. People who live together as cohabitating adults both hold down jobs, carry their own insurance, pay for their own bills, and live as two separate people from an economic and social perspective.

  When it comes to marriage, do not expect everything to be magically "different." Many people who live together prior to marriage or who have lived with someone in the past expect their financial and social lives to be quite similar when they tie the knot. They assume life will go on as it always has, in a separate but together mindset, and the relationship will just have legal status now. If you are anticipating marriage to change or shift something in terms of the relationship (you or your partner is going to stop working, finances will be joined, etc.), it is vital that you express these intentions to your partner so you can clearly discuss them. Never assume that marriage is going to change a living together mindset, especially if that is all either one of you know.

- **Sex with multiple partners:** Most people today come into a relationship with a certain level of sexual experience. This is not true for everyone, but it is common enough that it merits discussion. This history often brings expectation into a relationship. In some ways, sexual expectation is not a bad thing. Both partners should expect that their partner cares enough about them to invest time in them as a lover and learn their likes and dislikes. The main issue that many run into is that sex is viewed as all or a crux of a relationship, and that if they feel they are somehow sexually dissatisfied, they think it is as simple as breaking up or finding someone on the side. I do not believe being sexually active before marriage makes someone unfaithful in their marriage, but I do believe being so aware of the options that exist outside of the relationship can challenge fidelity in the wrong person when things don't always turn out the way that someone hopes they would.

It can also make sex a larger aspect of a marriage than it should be. The message we receive throughout our culture is that sex is all about us and our own pleasure. It is true that sex is about us, and it is about our pleasure, but that's not all that it should be about. When we are in serious relationships, we should never treat someone as if they are disposable, neither sexually, or in general. This is especially true in marriage, and it is especially important that marital partners understand bodily changes associated with childbirth, aging, and stress, and the temporary incompatibilities that can arise because of them.

It's also important to mention that sexual needs vary for

partners in a relationship. Not only do hormones, life changes, stress, and other factors impact sexual drives, it's perfectly normal for people to feel differently about a sexual relationship due to asexuality or demisexuality. Knowing and communicating about such with your partner is a must before marriage, rather than hoping things will turn out all right later.

- **Being divorced:** Divorce is a difficult, trying experience, even in the best of circumstances. It's very hard to pick up the pieces of a divorce and move on with life as a single person, let alone deciding to remarry and trying to start over again with someone new. Divorce brings hurt and wounded feelings, some understandable cynicism over relationships and marriage in general, and often financial baggage (such as alimony or child support). If there are children involved, you have the complication of a blended family and pre-existing financial obligations that must be met.

I don't believe the hype that blended families never work. I have met many people who were the product of blended family success stories. I just believe that each situation must be taken individually, and that couples who were either both divorced or one of them were divorced need to take into consideration needed healing, practical steps to make family life work, and all the complications that might arise before marriage takes place.

- **Pregnancy outside of marriage:** I'm not going to get into the debates about pre-marital sex. The reality is, right or wrong, people have sex who are not married, and there are many who do so irresponsibly. I am well aware that birth control is not effective all the time, but I also know the statistics about birth control (I was a clergy educator on these topics for many years) to know that many of the "accidents" that happen are happening without proper use of contraception. One of the biggest complications in a relationship is a child from a prior relationship, especially if the father or mother is still involved in the life of the child.

There's no question children from prior relationships can complicate a marriage. It's not impossible to make it work, but it still raises complications. If people are going to have sex when they are not married, contraception in any of its various forms is a must.

All these different issues relate to an issue of connectedness in a relationship. Some people never have repercussions from these things spill over into their marriages, but many more people do. Whenever we have taken on an intimate relationship that is outside of marriage, we are taking part of marital relationships and stringing them together in a disconnected manner. In other words, people have parts of marriage without having a marriage. It treats relationships today as if they, and the people in them, are disposable. This makes people confused as to just what marriage is and how marriage will be when they finally decide they do want to get married.

In terms of your past relationships, ask yourself: how many have you had? What issues listed above are you bringing to the marriage? What are some things in relationships that you have picked up on, here and there, and then later discarded? Are there other issues that we haven't listed that you are bringing into your marriage? Above all, what are you holding onto from your past relationships that have the potential to hurt your marriage because it is hurting you?

Week 1 Assignments

Answer the following questions by yourself and prepare to discuss them at your next counseling session. If you run out of room in a section, finish the answer to your question in your journal.

1. What is your full name? _____

2. Do you know why you were given your name? Does it have any significance in your family? _____

_____

3. What is the origin and meaning of your name (look online or in a naming book)? _____

_____

4. How old are you? _____

5. What is your ethnic make-up (where is your family's origins from?) _____

_____

6. List some of your general likes and dislikes.

_____

_____

_____

_____

_____

_____

_____

7. How long have you been a Christian? _____

8. Have you been baptized? _____ Have you received the baptism of the Holy Ghost? _____ Have you received communion? _____ Do you participate in your local church? _____ Do you tithe and give offerings regularly? _____ Do you read/study the Scriptures regularly? _____ Do you spend time with God? _____

9. If you answered "no" to any of the questions in #8, what specific steps are you going to take to change these things? _____

_____

_____

_____

10. What is your favorite color? _____ What is your favorite food? _____ Are you a morning person or a night person? _____ Do you prefer the city or the country? _____ What is your favorite flavor ice cream? _____ What is your favorite candy? _____ Who is your best friend? _____

11. Have you reached a place where you can honestly say you have learned how to love yourself? Why or why not? _____

_____

12. Why do you want to get married? _____

_____

_____

_____

_____

13. What is your concept of marriage and being married? _____

_____

_____

_____

_____

_____

14. What do you look for in a spouse? What are some primary characteristics that are important to you? _____

_____

_____

_____

_____

_____

15. Are you a patient person? Why or why not? _____

_____

_____

_____

_____

16. How many relationships have you been in prior to your engagement to your future spouse? _____ Looking at the last section of the chapter, have you been in any relationships that had characteristics mentioned there? _____ What characteristics were they (list them all): _____

_____

_____

_____

_____

17. How do you view relationships in general? How do you feel about your past relationships? _____

_____

_____

_____

_____

_____

18. What do you believe you have to offer to a marriage? _____

_____

_____

_____

_____

_____

19. Looking at the man and the woman in the Song of Solomon, were they aware of who they were and what they had to offer in a relationship? What does this tell you about being in a relationship about yourself? _____

_____

_____

_____

_____

_____

20. In reading Psalm 139:1-24, what does that tell you about the way God regards you? What does it tell you about how you should regard yourself, including in a relationship? _____

_____

_____

_____

_____

_____

21. Find a picture of yourself as a young person that your future spouse has never seen, and bring it to your next counseling session to share. Write the circumstances of the photograph below, so you can re-tell the story behind it. _____

_____

Week Two

All About Your Future Spouse

<u>**Bible reading:**</u> 2 Corinthians 10:12-16

<u>**Journaling assignments for in-session discussion:**</u>

- What knowledge did the couple in the Song of Solomon have of one another?
- Why do you think it's important for couples to know about each other?

When people decide they are going to get married, they typically assume they have been dating for awhile, so they know all there possibly is to know about each other. Based on what they have seen in their dating and then engaged relationship, they assume that their partner is what they have been looking for and that they are perfectly matched.

Once the wedding and honeymoon are over and life settles in, however, couples are often in for a rude awakening as to how difficult married life can be. Some things never came up as a part of the dating situation and couples start to learn other sides of their mates that they never expected to be there. This can put a terrible strain on a marriage and make the difficulties of marriage seem larger-than-life insurmountable.

This week, you are going to learn about your future spouse. We are going to see how much you think you know about them, and next week, you are going to learn how much of it is true. In this vital exercise, you are going to learn about the ins and outs of "perfect matches," the importance of being clear, and ways you might be hurting your relationship (without even realizing it).

How much do you know about your future spouse?

Song of Solomon 6:10-12:

WHO IS THAT YOUNG WOMAN
*   THAT SHINES OUT [LOOKS DOWN] LIKE THE DAWN?*
SHE IS AS PRETTY [BEAUTIFUL] AS THE MOON,
*   AS BRIGHT AS THE SUN,*
AS WONDERFUL AS AN ARMY FLYING FLAGS [AWESOME LIKE AN ARMY
UNDER BANNERS; V. 4].

I WENT DOWN INTO THE ORCHARD [GROVE] OF NUT TREES
*   TO SEE THE BLOSSOMS [NEW GROWTH] OF THE VALLEY,*
TO LOOK FOR BUDS ON THE VINES,
*   TO SEE IF THE POMEGRANATE TREES HAD BLOOMED.*
BEFORE I REALIZED IT, MY DESIRE FOR YOU MADE ME FEEL
*   LIKE A PRINCE IN A CHARIOT [OR PLACED ME IN THE CHARIOTS OF*
AMMINADAB; PERHAPS A WELL-KNOWN LOVER LIKE ROMEO].

Dating is considered a fun, exciting time in someone's life when they have the opportunity to get to know someone else. Couples do social activities, spend time talking and sharing about themselves, and get to know each other's family and friends. When relationships get serious, talk tends to cease in favor of wedding details and plans for the future. It's amazing that the more serious a dating relationship gets, the less couples discuss.

As discussions begin to cease in favor of weddings and marriage, couples start assuming things about one another. For example, the assumption might be made that the opposite partner feels a certain way about a social, political, or spiritual issue. Because the questions are never asked, the truth never comes out, and couples think they know more about each other than they really do.

Silent assumptions are a dangerous enemy to marital relationships, because they don't take into consideration the thoughts and feelings your partner may really have about something. This is one of the reasons why communication is so vital in a relationship, and one of the most difficult aspects of marriage. In marriage, couples are constantly looking for new insight into one another and learning how to respect the changes, opinions, and differences that they have. This means that couples must be able to talk, to share, to express themselves freely, and, above all, be themselves with their partner. We could give a long to-do or to-don't list, or we can just summarize it clearly by stating that you need to love your partner enough to allow them to be themselves, no matter what you think about their feelings and opinions. If something comes up and you don't feel able to do this, it's important to discuss that, and decide from that point forward.

No one is a "perfect match"

Ephesians 4:2-3:

ALWAYS BE [OR BE COMPLETELY] HUMBLE, GENTLE, AND PATIENT, ACCEPTING [PUTTING UP/BEARING WITH] EACH OTHER IN LOVE. MAKE EVERY EFFORT TO PRESERVE THE UNITY OF [PROVIDED BY; AVAILABLE THROUGH] THE SPIRIT IN [THROUGH] THE PEACE THAT JOINS US TOGETHER [BOND OF PEACE].

Growing up, we heard the endless fairy tale stories about the damsel in distress who met the handsome prince. He was quick to run to her rescue when he discovered her plight, a plight from which she was unable to redeem herself. He found her, he kissed her, and they lived happily ever after. We saw them ride off into the sunset and forever there they were, a perfect match in a few minutes or less.

We never heard the rest of the story: how she got tired of having to stay home with the baby while he got to go off and conquer nations, or how she was tired of picking up his socks, or how they

Overcoming relationship games

IF YOU'RE OVER THE AGE OF ABOUT 12 OR 13, YOU'VE ALREADY LEARNED THERE ARE CERTAIN WAYS TO GET ATTENTION, GET WHAT YOU WANT, AND ACQUIRE CERTAIN STATUS, ALL FROM DOING CERTAIN THINGS IN RELATIONSHIPS. BY THE TIME WE ARE OUT OF HIGH SCHOOL, WE HAVE ALREADY EMPLOYED THESE TECHNIQUES IN THE RELATIONSHIPS WE'VE HAD. PEER INVOLVEMENT IN OUR SOCIAL LIVES INSURED THESE TECHNIQUES WOULD LIVE UP TO THEIR REPUTATIONS. ODDS ARE GOOD, WE THOUGHT THEY WERE GOOD THINGS TO DO FOR THE SUCCESS OF OUR DATING AND SOCIAL LIVES.

AS YOU PREPARE TO GET MARRIED, DO YOU FIND THAT THESE TECHNIQUES ARE STILL AS EFFECTIVE WITH YOUR FUTURE SPOUSE? THE ANSWER IS, PROBABLY NOT. PLAYING "HARD TO GET" MIGHT HAVE WORKED A LONG TIME AGO, BUT AS YOU TRY TO WORK TOWARD HAVING A DEEPER CONNECTION, ALL THOSE OLD GAMES AND IDEAS DON'T SEEM TO WORK.

THE TRUTH IS, THE RELATIONSHIP GAMES WE GREW UP PLAYING WERE GREAT AT GETTING US ATTENTION, STATUS, AND SOME OF WHAT WE WANTED, BUT THERE WAS ONE THING THEY WERE NOT GREAT AT CREATING: RELATIONSHIPS. THEY WORKED TO THE EXTENT THAT THEY GOT SOMEONE INTERESTED IN US, BUT THEY COULDN'T KEEP SOMEONE INTERESTED IN US. WHEN IT CAME TIME FOR SOMETHING MORE IN THE RELATIONSHIP, THE RELATIONSHIP DIDN'T MAKE IT. THE GAMES WE'D LEARNED TO PLAY DIDN'T HELP US CONNECT TO OUR PARTNERS IN THE WAY THEY NEEDED TO SO THE RELATIONSHIPS COULD SURVIVE.

EMBRACING A NEW WAY OF RELATIONSHIP DYNAMICS MIGHT SEEM DIFFICULT AT FIRST. YOU MAY NOT KNOW WHAT TO DO OR KNOW HOW TO INTERACT, BECAUSE IT'S ALL NEW. IT MIGHT EVEN SEEM MORE FOREIGN THAN A NEW INTERACTION, BECAUSE IT DOESN'T SEEM LIKE MANY PEOPLE ABIDE BY THESE PRINCIPLES IN THEIR OWN LIVES. IF YOU KNOW THIS RELATIONSHIP IS WORTH PERSEVERING FOR, THEN KEEP PERSEVERING FOR IT AS YOU LEARN NEW THINGS ABOUT YOUR PARTNER AND LEARN WAYS TO COMMUNICATE UNTO LIFE. PUT ASIDE THE CHILDISH GAMES AND LOOK TOWARD A WONDERFUL NEW FUTURE WITH SOMEONE WHO CAN BE THERE FOR YOU THROUGHOUT LIFE.

would argue every time she went to the beauty parlor because her hair color bill was outrageous. We never saw the human side of the people in these fairy tales for one really glaring reason: they weren't human beings! They were story characters, individuals who lived within the confines of a story rather than the reality of everyday life. The problem with this is that while they might have made for great storytelling, as children, we didn't realize these weren't real people. We received the message that when a relationship was "right," everyone rode off into the sunset without a complaint nor issue in sight, and everything was perfect because the two characters were perfectly matched in every way.

It doesn't help that now that we are adults, most romantic comedies, romantically themed books, and romantically themed movies don't really show the "life" side of relationships in them, either. I would agree that there are some movies out there that are more realistic when it comes to relationships than others, but overall, the prince finding the damsel in distress is an underlying theme of all these books and movies. The people in the movies might have serious issues or problems, including some real differences that will not be resolved with a marriage license, but we don't ever see them working out their issues in marriage. We see them get married, and then that's it, as if marriage makes all their problems go away.

What we have done in church is take all these fairy tales, never-really-existed-concepts, and thrust them on God. We now teach that God will give us a perfectly mated match if we are willing to wait it out and have faith for it. We've taken every fairy tale we ever read and tried to super-impose it, as if having a godly relationship will feel like Cinderella or Snow White every step of our lives.

If you look at the Bible, there were no "perfect relationships" (and we will look more at this in-depth on Week Thirteen). If anything, a lot of Biblical couples had some very real problems that were not easily solved. The Bible displays for us a great array of relationships, relationship issues, relationship types, and relationship complications. From all this, we should get the message that marriage is not an easy thing, and it can be even harder if we think it's going to be a dusk ride into the sunset.

Marriage is not a magic wand. If you have issues before you get married, those same issues will still be there after you get married. A marriage license will not make them vanish. If anything, getting married may create and raise new issues between a couple. To avoid the barriers that often create discord for couples, it's important to step back and realize a few things about your mate and about your relationship.

- **Your mate is not perfect:** There's no "Create-A-Mate" toy that you can buy on the internet. We can't build a spouse for our own specifications. Even though you might see your mate as "perfect," your mate is far from perfect. They have flaws, problems, issues, challenges, thoughts, feelings, and ideas that are probably very far from your ideal concept of a mate or a spouse. The sooner you accept your mate is a human being and not a character from a fairy tale book, the better your life with them will be.

- **Your mate does not need "rescuing":** The principle that fairy tales give us about one partner needing to rescue the other is very damaging to relationships. It becomes very dangerous when someone comes into a relationship who is deeply hurting from their past and has the concept that a mate is supposed to "rescue" them out of their past and take them into something better. No human being is God, and our spouses cannot save, nor rescue, nor undo what has been done to us in the past. If people have serious emotional problems, they need help – not a relationship rescue.

- **Your mate does not need someone who needs "rescuing":** Our problems and issues are our own. We should never, ever expect our mate to bear the responsibility of "rescuing" us out of serious situations or emotional problems.

- **There is no such thing as a "perfect match":** No matter how well-suited people might seem for each other, there is no such thing as people who are "perfectly matched." People are imperfect, which means their relationships are going to be imperfect, too. It is unrealistic to think your mate is going to be what you want them to be, all the time, in every situation.

- **Be very wary of programs and instructions that teach on "soul mates.":** Many Christian programs now teach that God creates "soul mates," or one perfect person for every person on this planet. The relationships are custom-designed, perfect, heaven-sent, and have no problems, nor conflicts. They cite Adam and Eve as examples to justify this thinking. Do I have to remind you all how Adam and Eve wound up? Eve had a lengthy discussion with a serpent who led her right into sin, and Adam followed, only to turn around and blame both Eve and God for what he did! Then when a relationship hits the rocks, imagine the disillusionment of the couple: what happened to the God-nature of the relationship? There is no such thing as a relationship that does not take conscious effort, time, and work to make it successful. The soul-mate teaching is just a lazy excuse to try and have a relationship that doesn't require anything of the partners.

Handling your differences

Conventional advice typically tells us if we are going to be successful in a relationship, we should have as much in common as possible. People who want to get married are encouraged to find mates who share the same values, have the same religion, believe the same things politically, and have the same outlook on life. We're given this advice because, on the surface, it sounds like the ideal map for a great relationship.

It sounds great... but the reality is that the world is full of divorced couples who seemed to be "made" for each other. They both came from similar backgrounds, went to the same church, had the same likes and dislikes, adhered to the same political beliefs... and they are now divorced, because their commonalities didn't sustain their relationship.

No matter how much you have in common with someone, you are always going to disagree about something. We've spent so many years trying to find things we agree on with a mate, we haven't looked enough at how to handle the things we don't agree about. It's not how much you have in common that you must look at, but how you handle the disagreements you have.

One of the biggest disagreements couples run into relate to spiritual things. It's very possible to go to the same church with someone but be at totally different spiritual levels. As couples go forward in marriage, it is more than likely that spouses will be at different spiritual places in their relationship. As an example of learning how to disagree, the Apostle Peter in 1 Peter 3:1-7 gives the following advice to married couples:

IN THE SAME WAY [2:18], YOU WIVES SHOULD YIELD [SUBMIT; BE SUBJECT; EPH. 5:21–24; COL. 3:18; PUTTING THE OTHER PERSON'S INTERESTS FIRST] TO YOUR HUSBANDS. THEN, IF SOME HUSBANDS DO NOT OBEY [OR BELIEVE] GOD'S TEACHING [THE WORD/MESSAGE], THEY WILL BE PERSUADED TO BELIEVE [WON OVER; GAINED] WITHOUT ANYONE'S SAYING A WORD TO THEM. THEY WILL BE PERSUADED [WON OVER; GAINED] BY THE WAY THEIR WIVES LIVE [THEIR WIVES' CONDUCT/BEHAVIOR]. YOUR HUSBANDS WILL SEE THE PURE LIVES YOU LIVE WITH YOUR RESPECT FOR GOD [IN REVERENCE/FEAR; FEAR IN THE POSITIVE SENSE OF REVERENCE FOR GOD; PROV. 1:7]. IT IS NOT [EXTERNAL THINGS LIKE] FANCY [BRAIDED; ELABORATE] HAIR, GOLD JEWELRY, OR FINE CLOTHES THAT SHOULD MAKE YOU BEAUTIFUL [BE YOUR ADORNMENT]. NO, YOUR BEAUTY SHOULD COME FROM WITHIN YOU [YOUR INNER SELF; THE HIDDEN/SECRET PERSON OF THE HEART]—THE BEAUTY OF A GENTLE AND QUIET SPIRIT THAT WILL NEVER BE DESTROYED [FADE; PERISH] AND IS VERY PRECIOUS [VERY VALUABLE; OF GREAT WORTH] TO GOD [PROV. 31:30]. IN THIS SAME WAY THE HOLY WOMEN WHO LIVED LONG AGO AND FOLLOWED [PUT THEIR HOPE IN] GOD ·MADE THEMSELVES BEAUTIFUL [ADORNED THEMSELVES], YIELDING [SUBMITTING; SUBJECTING THEMSELVES] TO THEIR OWN HUSBANDS. SARAH OBEYED ABRAHAM, HER HUSBAND, AND CALLED HIM HER MASTER [LORD; GEN. 18:12]. AND YOU WOMEN ARE TRUE CHILDREN OF SARAH IF YOU ALWAYS DO WHAT IS RIGHT [GOOD] AND ARE NOT AFRAID [FEAR NO FEAR/INTIMIDATION].

IN THE SAME WAY [2:18; 3:1], YOU HUSBANDS SHOULD LIVE WITH YOUR WIVES IN AN UNDERSTANDING [CONSIDERATE] WAY [EPH. 5:25–33; COL. 3:19], SINCE THEY ARE WEAKER THAN YOU [THE WEAKER SEX; OR THE LESS EMPOWERED ONE; THE WEAKER VESSEL; WOMEN ARE TYPICALLY PHYSICALLY WEAKER, BUT IN GRECO-ROMAN AND JEWISH SOCIETY, THEY ALSO HAD LESS POWER AND AUTHORITY]. BUT SHOW THEM RESPECT [PAY/GIVE THEM HONOR], BECAUSE GOD GIVES THEM THE SAME BLESSING HE GIVES YOU—[THEY ARE CO-HEIRS OF] THE GRACE THAT GIVES TRUE LIFE [OR GOD'S GIFT OF LIFE; THE GRACE OF LIFE]. DO THIS SO THAT NOTHING WILL STOP [HINDER] YOUR PRAYERS.

There are many ways people interpret this passage, but I believe it is telling us to, above all, yield to the Spirit in times of disagreement. Just because you and your spouse may not see eye-to-eye about things doesn't mean you should go and file for divorce. If anything, we need to be people who continue to love and care about our spouses, showing them character and consideration, in each and every situation in which we find ourselves. Whether the issue is over spiritual differences or some other difference, the principle is the same. We should not be people who behave in one exterior manner toward our spouse and then behave another way in private. We should show the same courtesy, love, and respect to our spouses that we would if they agreed with us. It's called "agreeing to disagree" without any disruption in the relationship.

Relationship games and politics

From the time we are coming up as children, we hear the adage: "He/she mistreats you because he/she likes you." We learned early on to be confused by the messages we received from our peers because other people told us their actions meant something other than what they seemed. When our time came to "like" someone, we played the same confusing games, giving the same confusing messages, implying that our intentions meant something different than our actions.

Relationships are a building block of interaction. That means they can be used in right or wrong ways, and it especially means that they can be manipulated and used for gain. Throughout history, interactions between people have been marred by politics and societal use for personal or professional gains. The result, down to our modern day and age, are certain relationship games and politics that are used by common people to get what they want out of someone else in that relationship. Society tells us that if we want to achieve something in a relationship, we should play certain these established relationship games to get it.

When it comes time for marriage and the hope and prayer we will have godly marriages, all our former games and politics follow right along. We pride ourselves in our ability to chase after a man, woman, or other individual, and we attribute our ability to be in that relationship by how well we are able to play games. Some of these games include:

- Playing "hard to get" (acting like you really don't like someone when you really do)
- Not returning phone calls, texts, or messages (acting indifferent; I'm all for having some self-control and not spending all day returning calls and messages, but don't do it as a statement; do it because you have something else to do)
- Creating jealousy in a relationship (not a good idea, period)
- Living your life at your mate's whim (you still need to have a life; you can't live off love, contrary to what movies and music tell you)
- Being dishonest about likes and dislikes to get someone interested in you (eventually they will find out you hate thimble museums or skydiving... or whatever else it might be)
- "Playing the field" (I agree that if you've been out on one date with someone, they don't own you, but make it clear when the agreement to be exclusive starts)
- Misrepresenting yourself as making more money, being more "relevant," or being something you just are not (really, really bad idea)
- Pretending to be stupider, smarter, richer, or poorer than you are (or any other concoction of dishonest pretend games)
- Using guilt or pulling guilt trips to get your own way (you either believe in forgiveness, or you don't)
- Either starting or facilitating rumors about your significant other (grow up)
- Using sex as a weapon (don't use sex or withholding sex as a pawn to get your own way or to get what you want out of your partner)
- Entrapment (under no circumstances, neither male nor female, should you ever get pregnant or aspire to get your partner pregnant without their consent)

Doing these things in your relationships is antithetical to honesty and to clear communication. If you are doing one thing that conveys one message to your partner, and you expect them to know that you intend the opposite. Then we find couples at odds because their partners don't believe them when they say things or take the things they say seriously. Relationship partners are people, not mind-readers. There isn't some sort of way to decipher what message you intend to give at whatever time. Expecting your mate to figure out and read between the lines whatever you are trying to communicate through negative actions is not going to work, and it is going to create dysfunction in your relationships.

Ephesians 4:25-29:

SO YOU MUST STOP TELLING LIES. TELL EACH OTHER THE TRUTH [LET EACH ONE OF YOU SPEAK TRUTHFULLY TO HIS NEIGHBOR; ZECH. 8:16], BECAUSE WE ALL BELONG TO EACH OTHER IN THE SAME BODY [ARE MEMBERS OF ONE ANOTHER]. WHEN YOU ARE ANGRY, [OR BE ANGRY, AND] DO NOT SIN [PS. 4:4; THERE IS A TIME FOR RIGHTEOUS ANGER, BUT IT MUST NOT RESULT IN SIN], AND BE SURE TO STOP BEING ANGRY BEFORE THE END OF THE DAY [DON'T LET THE SUN SET ON YOUR ANGER]. DO NOT GIVE THE DEVIL A WAY TO DEFEAT YOU [FOOTHOLD; OPPORTUNITY]. THOSE WHO ARE STEALING MUST STOP STEALING AND START WORKING. THEY SHOULD EARN AN HONEST LIVING FOR THEMSELVES [DO SOMETHING GOOD/USEFUL WITH THEIR HANDS]. THEN THEY WILL HAVE SOMETHING TO SHARE WITH THOSE WHO ARE POOR [HAVE NEED]. DON'T SAY ANYTHING THAT WILL HURT OTHERS [LET ANY ROTTEN/UNHEALTHY WORD COME FROM YOUR MOUTH], BUT ONLY SAY WHAT IS HELPFUL [GOOD] TO MAKE OTHERS STRONGER [BUILD OTHERS UP] AND MEET [ACCORDING TO] THEIR NEEDS. THEN WHAT YOU SAY WILL DO GOOD [GIVE GRACE; BE A GIFT] TO THOSE WHO LISTEN TO YOU.

When we seek to speak to anyone or be in any kind of relationship with someone, our first job is to effectively communicate. That means our own politics toward lying, deceiving, manipulating, or trying to control others through our emotions need to stop. This becomes especially important in marriage. Successful relationships are not political ones. They are based on the way that partners treat each other, and they are based on treating each other with love. Love is not a politic. This also means that instead of trying to find relationship advice that encourages traditional "roles" and "relationships" and trying to base your marriage on that, you need to step back and examine your own relationship and the person you are with from the perspective of the two of you. Relationships are not made up of roles, they are made up of people. Together, it is your job as a couple to figure out what is going to work best for you and figure out what you both need from one another and what you need to do to work together as a couple. This is accomplished through effective communication and abandoning behaviors that are designed to control and manipulate.

Respecting your mate for who they are

I once heard an expression: "Men marry women hoping they won't change, and women marry men hoping they will." I don't believe after counseling couples for so many years that it's as simple as one partner wants one thing and the other wants something else. I do believe, however, that the truth in this expression is something more understated: each partner comes into a relationship with their own viewpoint and their own agenda. Whenever a couple gets married, both partners in that mix have their own expectations as to what their partner will do or become.

For example: a woman may note that her fiancé tends to drink too much. He seems to have habits that relate to watching pornography. The issues might have come up a few times, in passing, in a few backhanded comments. Rather than be direct about the issue, the woman begins to think if she marries him, his drinking and his pornography will go away. She expects that, now that they are married, they are settled, he has regular access to sex, and that they are looking to start a family, he will stop watching pornography and will get his drinking under control.

The problem with this expectation sounds obvious to all of us. How in the world can he know his drinking and pornography watching are a problem for her if she doesn't tell him? How can he know how she feels about it if she doesn't say anything? He is going to go on the premise that she knows about those things, she even seems to joke about them (i.e., the backhanded comments), and because she doesn't indicate otherwise, he just assumes it is all right to continue doing them. Even though in listening to that example, we can figure out exactly where the breakdown is and see how problematic it is... all of us have done this in our relationships at some point in time. We have all harbored "unexpected expectations" that are just waiting to come out at the wrong time and explode all over everywhere, becoming a notable source of contention in a relationship.

1 Thessalonians 4:11-12:

DO ALL YOU CAN [... AND TO ASPIRE] TO LIVE A PEACEFUL LIFE. TAKE CARE OF [ATTEND TO; MIND] YOUR OWN BUSINESS, AND DO YOUR OWN WORK [WORK WITH YOUR HANDS] AS WE HAVE ALREADY TOLD [INSTRUCTED; COMMANDED] YOU. IF YOU DO, THEN YOU WILL WIN THE RESPECT OF [OR LIVE A RESPECTABLE/PROPER LIFE BEFORE] UNBELIEVERS [OUTSIDERS], AND YOU WILL NOT HAVE TO DEPEND ON OTHERS FOR WHAT YOU NEED.

Whoever your mate is, that's who they are. Whether or not we want to confront this fact, it is a fact: unless we live in a culture where marriages are arranged (which most do not), we choose our mate. We choose who we want to live with and be with, and we choose to marry all that person, both the good and the bad. If we choose not to address or overlook things that we see in our mate that might be problematic and marry them anyway, that's a choice we make. If those issues were not clear before we got married, it's a little different, but the principle of being direct about the issues remains the same. Sometimes our unspoken expectations are much more subdued than the example I gave: you might not like something in your mate's personal tastes or style, you may dislike a habit they have, you might not like how quiet or loud they are, you might find you don't like their job or some of their verbal skills... whatever it is, there is something very important that you need to look at within yourself. Respect is a two-way street. Surely you desire to be loved, despite the faults you might have. Nobody likes to feel like someone is trying to change who they are. If you are choosing to marry this person, you are choosing to marry all of them. If issues arise that need addressing... address them. Don't have the unvoiced expectation that they should change because you want them to. Respect their right to be an individual in opinion, ideas, thoughts, concepts, and personality. In turn, expect to receive the same from them.

Having the assurance that you are ready to be the "one for them"

Most people have some doubts before they get married. Marriage is, after all, a very big change in someone's life. A lot goes along with marriage, and a lot goes into being married. It's normal to be unsure about some of the details of the dynamics that will commence after the ceremony. What is not within the realm of normal, however, is having overwhelming doubts about the person you are to marry and overwhelming doubts about their fidelity or faithfulness to you.

For example, there shouldn't be a question that your mate is the one you want to be with, and that you are the one they want to be with. There shouldn't be wistful thoughts of "one that got away" constantly between the two of you. It's within the realm of normal to wonder what happened to someone or wonder what someone made of their life, but it's not normal to be with one person and still wish you were with someone else.

Proverbs 5:15-20:

BE FAITHFUL TO YOUR OWN WIFE [DRINK WATER FROM YOUR OWN WELL; SONG 4:10–15],
    JUST AS YOU DRINK [GUSHING] WATER FROM YOUR OWN WELL [CISTERN].
DON'T POUR YOUR WATER IN THE STREETS [LET YOUR FOUNTAINS BURST FORTH OUTSIDE];
    DON'T GIVE YOUR LOVE TO JUST ANY WOMAN [STREAMS OF WATER IN THE PUBLIC SQUARES].
THESE THINGS ARE YOURS ALONE
    AND SHOULDN'T BE SHARED WITH STRANGERS.
BE HAPPY WITH THE WIFE YOU MARRIED WHEN YOU WERE YOUNG [REJOICE IN THE WIFE OF YOUR YOUTH].
    SHE GIVES YOU JOY, AS YOUR FOUNTAIN GIVES YOU WATER [MAY YOUR SPRING BE BLESSED].
SHE IS A LOVELY DEER AND A GRACEFUL DOE.
    LET HER LOVE [OR BREASTS] ALWAYS MAKE YOU HAPPY;
    LET HER LOVE ALWAYS HOLD YOU CAPTIVE [INTOXICATE/INEBRIATE YOU; SONG 4:10].
MY SON, DON'T BE HELD CAPTIVE [WHY SHOULD YOU BE INTOXICATED/INEBRIATED… ?] BY A WOMAN WHO TAKES PART IN ADULTERY [STRANGER].
    DON'T FONDLE THE BOSOM OF A WOMAN WHO IS NOT YOUR WIFE [FOREIGNER].

Marriage is a serious commitment, and I am not just talking about the wedding. Yes, weddings involve money and planning, but marriage also involves life. In many instances, it is the life just not of the couple, but the lives of children, as well. If there are any indications or any doubts that your mate has doubts about you (or you about them), you don't have to live with a ghost of relationships haunt past or feel like this is going to be a mistake for some other reason.

Preparing to love God with someone else

You might be saying to yourself, "What does loving God have to do with my spouse?" The truth is, your marriage, who you choose to marry, and you choose to handle your marriage can have a lot to do with where you find yourself in your relationship with God. This is true in ways you might never expect, and by the time you are aware of it, it can be very difficult to figure out and resolve.

There are many people who can love God by themselves but find it difficult or impossible to love God in the way they need to when they are in a relationship with people or with certain people. Sometimes people don't complement one another in the way they need to in order to accentuate the individual relationship each has with God and nurture the relationship the couple needs to foster with God together.

It's important that couples discuss spiritual matters with each other. You need to find out how each one feels about the beliefs that are important to each of you and figure out if those beliefs can form a solid spiritual life together. When it comes to spirituality, don't assume your mate is exactly where you expect them to be. You need to discuss things that might even seem elementary, such as spiritual gifts, speaking in tongues, baptism, communion, women preachers, five-fold ministry, beliefs on Bible doctrines, and more, to make sure that the spirituality you both have is going to be edified, rather than destroyed, in your relationship. If you don't agree on some of these core things, you need to discuss what you are going to do about them, how you will resolve the issues at hand, and how you will raise any children that will result from your marriage.

In a larger sense, you also need to assess your relationship from a spiritual perspective. Many people think that a proper mate is on your same exact "spiritual level," but the reality is that very few people, if any, are on the exact level you are on. Spiritual levels are very individual things, and depend on the person, whether they are in ministry, their calling, their spiritual insights and gifts, and their length of time walking with the Lord in a deep way.

1 Corinthians 12:4-11:

THERE ARE DIFFERENT KINDS OF GIFTS, BUT THEY ARE ALL FROM THE SAME SPIRIT. THERE ARE DIFFERENT WAYS TO SERVE [MINISTRIES] BUT THE SAME LORD TO SERVE. AND THERE ARE DIFFERENT WAYS THAT GOD WORKS THROUGH PEOPLE [KINDS OF ACTION; ACTIVITIES] BUT THE SAME GOD WORKS IN ALL OF US IN EVERYTHING WE DO [ALL THINGS IN ALL PEOPLE]. SOMETHING FROM THE SPIRIT CAN BE SEEN IN [THE MANIFESTATION/DISCLOSURE OF THE SPIRIT IS GIVEN TO] EACH PERSON, FOR THE COMMON GOOD. THE SPIRIT GIVES ONE PERSON THE ABILITY TO SPEAK WITH WISDOM [MESSAGE/WORD OF WISDOM], AND THE SAME SPIRIT GIVES ANOTHER THE ABILITY TO SPEAK WITH KNOWLEDGE [MESSAGE/WORD OF KNOWLEDGE]. THE SAME SPIRIT GIVES FAITH TO ONE PERSON. AND, TO ANOTHER, THAT ONE SPIRIT GIVES GIFTS OF HEALING. THE SPIRIT GIVES TO ANOTHER PERSON THE POWER TO DO MIRACLES [WORKS OF POWER], TO ANOTHER THE ABILITY TO PROPHESY [PROPHECY]. AND HE GIVES TO ANOTHER THE ABILITY TO KNOW THE DIFFERENCE BETWEEN GOOD AND EVIL [DISCERNMENT/DISTINGUISHING OF] SPIRITS. THE SPIRIT GIVES ONE PERSON THE ABILITY TO SPEAK IN DIFFERENT KINDS OF LANGUAGES [OR ECSTATIC UTTERANCE; TONGUES] AND TO ANOTHER THE ABILITY TO INTERPRET THOSE LANGUAGES [INTERPRETATION OF TONGUES]. ONE SPIRIT, THE SAME SPIRIT, DOES ALL THESE THINGS, AND THE SPIRIT DECIDES WHAT TO GIVE [DISTRIBUTES JUST AS HE WISHES TO] EACH PERSON.

Don't automatically assume that you are incompatible with someone if they see something having to do with God in a different way than you do. We are all given different spiritual gifts, and we are all given different gifts for a reason. The building up of the Body through different gifts does relate to the church, but we can also understand that the same principle applies to godly relationships. Expecting someone to be the same as you doesn't lead to happiness, it leads to misery.

When assessing the spiritual aspect of your relationship, take into consideration your ability to compliment your partner, and your partner compliment you. Can they allow you to develop your relationship with God, no matter where it takes you? Can you do the same for them? Can you love the Spirit at work within them, changing and transforming them, and they for you? Can you both pray for one another and be there for one another? Can you agree to love and respect what God wants to do in both of you?

Don't wait for your wedding to start praying and discussing spiritual things. Pray together, study the Word together, attend church together, talk about these matters now, and see what you find out. Learn to love your future spouse as they are of service to the Lord, an individual that God uses for His work.

Week 2 Assignments

Answer the following questions by yourself (do not ask your future spouse these questions!) and prepare to discuss them at your next counseling session. If you are unsure of an answer, give it your best guess. If you run out of room in a section, finish the answer to your question in your journal.

1. What is your mate's full name? _____

2. Do you know why your mate was given his/her name? Does it have any significance to his/her family? _____

_____

3. What is the origin and meaning of your mate's name (look online or in a naming book)? _____

_____

4. How old is your mate? _____

5. What is your mate's ethnic make-up (where is your mate's family's origins from?) _____

_____

6. List some of your mate's general likes and dislikes. _____

_____

_____

_____

_____

_____

_____

_____

_____

7. How long has your mate been a Christian? _____

8. Have your mate been baptized? _____ Has your mate received the baptism of the Holy Ghost? _____ Have your mate received communion? _____ Do your mate participate in your local church? _____ Does your mate tithe and give offerings regularly? _____ Does your mate read/study the Scriptures regularly? _____ Does your mate spend time with God? _____

9. What is your mate's favorite color? _____ What is your mate's favorite food? _____ Is your mate a morning person or a night person? _____ Does your mate prefer the city or the country? _____ What is your mate's favorite flavor ice cream? _____ What is your mate's favorite candy? _____ Who is your mate's best friend? _____

10. Has your mate reached a place where he/she can honestly say he/she has learned how to love themselves? Why or why not? ____

_____

11. Why does your mate want to get married? _____

_____

_____

_____

_____

12. What is your mate's concept of marriage and being married? __

_____

_____

_____

_____

_____

13. What does your mate look for in a spouse? What are some primary characteristics that are important to them? _____

_____

_____

_____

_____

14. Is your mate a patient person? Why or why not? _____

_____

_____

_____

_____

15. How many relationships has your mate been in prior to your engagement? _____

16. How does your mate view relationships in general? How do they feel about their past relationships? _____

_____

_____

_____

_____

_____

17. What do they believe they have to offer to a marriage? _____

_____

_____

_____

_____

_____

18. The man and woman in the Song of Solomon deeply desired to be together and have time together. Do you feel this in your relationship? Why or why not? _____

_____

_____

_____

_____

19. In reading 2 Corinthians 10:12-16, what principles are introduced to you about relationships? How can you interact better with your future spouse based on some of the concepts outlined there? _____

_____

_____

_____

_____

20. Find one picture of you and your spouse and bring it to your next counseling session to share (both partners should bring the same photo but write individual perspectives on the picture). Write the circumstances of the photograph below, so you can re-tell the story behind it. _____

_____

_____

_____

_____

_____

_____

_____

Week Three

How Well Do You Know Your Future Spouse?

THE WORDS OF THE WISE BRING THEM PRAISE [*OR* FAVOR],
BUT THE WORDS OF A FOOL WILL DESTROY [SWALLOW] THEM.
(ECCLESIASTES 10:12)

Bible reading: Psalm 1:1-6

Journaling assignments for in-session discussion:

- How did the couple in the Song of Solomon speak to each other?
- Do you think how couples talk to each other is important? Why or why not?

You probably noticed by now that last week's workbook activities were very similar to the ones you did the week before. The only difference is you answered the questions based on what you thought you knew about your future spouse, rather than for yourself. How successful were you in answering the questions? Did you sit back and realize you didn't know some of the answers? Do you suspect that you answered some of them wrong?

If you think you got some of the questions wrong or stumbled over some of the answers, do not despair! That is expected in this process. The reason you probably stumbled over some of those questions is because you never thought to ask them before. Some of them you probably answered without a second thought, but some of them you had to think about and were not sure about. There are probably some that you guessed at, and some that you may very well have answered incorrectly.

When we're dating (and later when we are married) we tend to assume we know things about the people we're involved with. The longer we are in a situation, the more we construct assumptions based on the information we already have. We think we know more about our mate than we actually might – and a little bit of assumption can cause a lot of strain on a relationship.

This week, we are going to talk about communication in intimate relationships. Communication is such a vital factor in a relationship, there are no words to express how important it is. Even if you communicate well, we can always communicate better with one another. This week is a journey into the world of communication and the many ways spouses communicate with one another.

Infatuation and marriage

Most people today say they married someone else because they feel (or felt) or have feelings of love for that person. They might find them very physically attractive or be drawn to certain qualities they have. Maybe they loved another attribute they have, such as connections or money (and yes, whether good or bad, there are people who get married for these reasons). Whatever the reason was, they attributed that feeling to love. They believed that loving feeling would carry them through the ups and the downs they would experience in life... or maybe they even believed there wouldn't be any downs. The expectation that feelings of love would last for eternity were the very thing they hinged their relationship on, long-term.

The problem with those feelings of "love" is that they aren't love, they are infatuation and attraction. Without a doubt, they pass in every relationship. As hard as that might be to believe right now, those feelings change. When that change comes, those intense feelings seldom, if ever, return. There will be memories of that intensity, there will be shades of it over time, but that initial response will never be there in the same exact way once it goes away. The question becomes: what replaces those feelings?

1 Peter 4:8:

MOST IMPORTANTLY, LOVE EACH OTHER DEEPLY [EARNESTLY], BECAUSE LOVE WILL CAUSE PEOPLE TO FORGIVE EACH OTHER FOR MANY SINS [COVERS A MULTITUDE OF SINS; PROV. 10:12; LUKE 7:46–47].

What is left is either a combination of good, solid relationship dynamics that evolve into a true love and affection (a deeper relationship) or the relationship will fall apart, with both partners looking for something the other one can't give them. If you are onto the path for good relationship dynamics before you get married, you have a far easier time transitioning to true love and affection than if you don't know how to communicate now. Ideally, the more we learn about our spouse, the more we should love them and develop an intimate connection with them as a human being.

Communication is the key to developing true love in a relationship. As hard as it is to imagine, we do learn how to love our spouses as we interact, talk with, and live with them. We learn how to show them that we love them, and the many unique ways we can show them appreciation.

Learning how to communicate

Believe it or not, we are constantly communicating with other people. I'm not talking about texts, emails, and phone calls, although those are certainly forms of communication. We are always communicating with others through our body language, our attitudes, our tone of voice, and the way we talk. No matter how we may try to appear to feel about something on the outside, we give off signals that indicate how we really feel about things without having to say what we are thinking or feeling.

This is in large contrast to the things we were told when we were growing up. We were probably told to speak a certain way, stand a certain way, and carry ourselves in a certain manner, despite how we might have been feeling. We were led to believe that if we tried hard enough, we could disguise our more negative feelings of disgust or disdain for something if we "acted" good enough. The truth is, if people know us and are paying attention, we can't hide our true feelings about matters from them. Our body, our tone, our words, and our attitude will give away how we really feel about whatever is going on.

In other words, you're not fooling anyone when you are really livid about something, but you try to hold it in. If you are repulsed by something, it shows. If you are sad, no amount of pretending to be happy is going to cover it up… and so on. You might not verbally tell someone how you feel, but how you feel comes out in other ways. This is especially true when it comes to our relationships. We might get away with thinking that we are hiding things from strangers, but it's hard to fool a spouse (especially in a relationship that has been around for awhile). In relationships, our spouse often picks up on our mannerisms very quickly and plays off of those (or does not, depending on what the circumstances may be).

Instead of covering up, lying about, and pretending to act a certain way with our feelings, it's far more effective to learn how to communicate with our spouses about what frustrates us, what we would like to be done differently, and being able to verbalize our thoughts and interests. It is impossible to live with someone who expects you to read their mind (and vice versa). It's not fair to expect that someone understands what you are unwilling to express, and it is unfair to maintain a relationship based on such confusion.

Unfortunately, communication isn't a priority in many programs related to marriage and marital understanding; it's just the opposite. Couples are taught to adopt restrictive attitudes and roles, and think if they maintain those positions, they will have a relationship that doesn't require communication. We are not taught how to communicate, but how to not communicate. Lack of upfront communication leads to all sorts of passive-aggressive behaviors and on-the-side means of communication, through body language, intonation, and annoyance.

Colossians 4:5-6:

BE WISE IN THE WAY YOU ACT WITH [BEHAVE TOWARDS] PEOPLE WHO ARE

NOT BELIEVERS, MAKING THE MOST OF EVERY OPPORTUNITY. WHEN YOU TALK, YOU SHOULD ALWAYS BE KIND [GRACIOUS] AND PLEASANT [WINSOME; ENGAGING; OR WHOLESOME; SEASONED WITH SALT] SO YOU WILL BE ABLE TO ANSWER EVERYONE IN THE WAY YOU SHOULD.

When speaking to your spouse, here are some good guidelines to make sure that communication is effective, rather than ineffective.

- **Know what you want:** Many of us go by the old adage, "I'll know it when I see it." Sometimes this works, but in relationships, people don't tend to try many different things out to see what works. Spouses respond well to knowing what their mate needs, when they need it, and knowing where their mate stands. If you aren't sure about what it is you want or need, then state that, and talk about it with your mate.

- **Be comfortable with voicing needs, wants, concerns, and opinions as needed:** Shying away, lying and saying you "don't care" if you really do, pretending to be coy, and suffering in silence are not the proper ways to do what needs doing. Speak in the form of "I" statements, which means that rather than saying "we" or "you," you speak from your own perspective: "I feel," "I think," etc. Take ownership for your positions! There is no shame in doing that.

- **State what you mean:** If you say one thing and mean something else, how can your spouse figure out what you mean? Be clear in what you mean. State your position or your need in as few words as possible. If that means you must think about your wants, needs, or position for a while before you mention it, then say you need some time to think about it.

- **Set aside emotions:** I do not mean to imply that when it comes to marriage that our feelings do not count. Our feelings absolutely count, and our spouse should take them into consideration when making decisions, saying things, and doing things. I am talking about judging situations through our feelings. If I am really angry about a situation, my opinions and needs may appear to be one way at that moment.

When I am not feeling so angry later, how I am feeling may reflect different needs, wants, and opinions. When opinions are strong, it is best not to speak out of turn and to wait until things are clearer to voice what needs to be said.

- **Don't wait until you are at an explosive point:** Too often we let things pass, when we shouldn't. We notice something that bothers us and instead of saying "That really bothered me," we let it pass. When it happens the next time, we get mad all over again... and again... and again... until we just explode. This is an unhealthy way to live, and it leads to greater miscommunication down the line. State how you feel about something and hear the situation out.

- **Have consideration for your partner's thoughts, feelings, opinions, needs, and wants:** It's important to remember that relationships aren't all about you. While your needs should certainly be affirmed, so should your partner's. It's improbable and unrealistic to think you should be the only one getting without you ever having to give. If you are noticing that your partner is having a hard time with something but doesn't seem able to talk about it, offer the opening for them to do so, and be there for them.

- **Give information when it's needed:** If you are going to do something, buy something, or make some sort of a major life decision, have enough respect for your partner to sit down and talk about it with them. If what you are going to do is going to affect your partner, you need to consider their input and consider if it is a decision that is best for everyone.

- **Watch tone and body language:** Nobody likes feeling disrespected, spoken down to, or like they are being judged or criticized. We are quick to recognize this when we are dealing with those we are not closest to, but we often forget that our spouses are not children and do not deserve to be treated as such. Watch how you speak to your spouse, and make sure it doesn't echo of patronization or disrespect. Make sure when you speak to your spouse, you are speaking on an issue and not putting them down. Be equally aware of your body language and what it is saying when you talk to them. Make sure your attitude is not shining through.

- **Be open to talking:** I completely understand not being really comfortable with small talk or being someone who wants to go over endless opinions about stuff all the time, especially when things don't matter. I am not real comfortable with small talk, no matter who I am talking with. What I am talking about is the opposite of this. Don't fill your hours with meaningless talk or meaningless silence, because both are extremes. Don't spend all your time talking about money and bills and children. Be open to having meaningful discussions with your spouse. Be comfortable sharing about long-term dreams and visions, about spiritual things, about things that are important to you, and while sharing, make sure you are listening to what is important to them, as well.

Affirmation in marriage

Hebrews 3:13:

BUT ENCOURAGE EACH OTHER EVERY DAY WHILE IT IS "TODAY" [MEANING THE TIME OF OPPORTUNITY TO BE SAVED; V. 7]. HELP [ENCOURAGE] EACH OTHER SO NONE OF YOU WILL BECOME HARDENED BECAUSE SIN HAS TRICKED YOU [BY SIN'S DECEPTION].

Hebrews 10:24:

LET US THINK ABOUT EACH OTHER AND HELP EACH OTHER [OR HOW TO PROVOKE/ROUSE/ENCOURAGE EACH ANOTHER] TO SHOW LOVE AND DO GOOD DEEDS.

To "affirm" means to declare that something is true. In the context of marriage, when you affirm your spouse or your spouse affirms you, you are declaring the truth in your promises to love, cherish, and respect them. You are also declaring the truth within them: that they are an individual loved by God, loved by you, and that they are important and unique. These are messages that everyone needs to hear from someone in their life, and they are especially important in marriage. Too often, spouses allow the negatives in their partners to overshadow the positives in their relationship, and instead of affirming the good things that they see in each other, everything is reduced to nitpicking. Having someone constantly pick at little things without any sort of encouragement is grating, no matter who you are, and no matter how long you have been married.

Obviously, if there is a serious negative in your spouse or your marriage, that needs to be clearly discussed using effective communication techniques. What we are talking about here are little things that sometimes become larger than life because we are angry about something else. People argue about subjects, but issues lie beneath them. If there is something larger than life, nagging and nitpicking is not the way to address it. Problems do not get addressed when we try to deal with them through something else. If there is something that is causing you to feel unappreciated in your marriage, then you need to talk about that – not everything else.

When it comes to specific ways to affirm and be affirmed in marriage, every couple is different. The major issue arises when people try to affirm someone else through the methods and ways they heard work best for someone else. It is true that there are some things that all people appreciate, but some things mean more to others than they might to you or your spouse. The best way you can affirm your spouse is to know who they are, what they love, and what is important to them, as a person.

Some examples of ways people affirm one another include:

- **Providing verbal words of affirmation:** Thank your spouse when they do something for you that is appreciated, and praise them when they do something that is good. Celebrate their accomplishments by telling them they did a good job, and you are proud of them. In failures, reassure them that sometimes setbacks come, and that they need to learn from what has happened. More than anything, a spouse who has incurred a setback needs to know you are still with them and that you still love and respect them.

- **Show respect:** Listen when your partner is talking. Make eye contact when they are speaking to you, and you to them.

Don't always be so distracted that you are looking at your phone and computer when they are speaking. Show interest in them as a person. You don't have to be interested in the things they are interested in and want to take them up yourself (or even participate in them) but have the courtesy to hear what interests them, and expect to receive the same, yourself.

- **Watch your complaining negativity**: In terms of complaints and being negative, I am not just talking about your complaints that pertain to your spouse or marriage. I'm talking here about all your complaints and negative remarks, especially as pertain to life, your job, social commentaries and politics, and the little offhanded remarks that we often make without thinking about them. It is overwhelming to note how negative we are and how much complaining we do on a regular basis, especially if we take the time to pay attention and note just how much of it we do. Being around someone who is chronically negative and always complaining is a serious drain and drag, and it makes it so you don't want to be around that person. One of the surest ways to cut off communication and affirmation in a marriage is to be negative and complain, all the time.

- **Be of service**: For too long, households have been divided into "men's chores" and "women's chores." If you are a part of a household and something needs doing, step up and do it. Don't sit back and think that it's "not your job." We do not live in an era where a chore belongs all to one person and not at all to another. Make sure you take an interest in household chores and responsibilities and that you are appreciative of the things your spouse does to help keep your household running.

- **Spend (some of) your money on your spouse**: Life should never be all about rent and bills. If all your money is spent on those things, you are over-extending your budget. You should have money to spend on little things from time to time both for yourself and for your spouse. It doesn't have to be something big or a huge, expensive gesture, but something that lets your spouse know that you care about them and appreciate them.

- **Do something for your spouse that is just for them:** There are so many ways we can show people that we love and care about them, if we only take the time to do so. Do something for them that you know they like, cook a favorite meal, pick up a favorite flower, go to a favorite restaurant, see a movie, whatever it is – do it just for them, to show them that you appreciate them.

Displays of affection

Some people are very comfortable with being physically affectionate in public, and some are not. Some levels of public displays of affection should be reserved for private settings, period. I think it's important for us to realize that we don't have to display our relationship in front of other people to prove something about it. Just because a couple is all over each other in public does not mean they have a good relationship. If anything, being so overly physical in public tends to mean that a couple is deliberately trying to give a certain impression about a relationship that is, most likely, not even true. Even though being all over each other in public is not appropriate, it is still important to display affection for each other in the form of touch.

Proverbs 5:18-19:

LET THY FOUNTAIN BE BLESSED: AND REJOICE WITH THE WIFE OF THY YOUTH.
LET HER BE AS THE LOVING HIND AND PLEASANT ROE; LET HER BREASTS SATISFY THEE AT ALL TIMES; AND BE THOU RAVISHED ALWAYS WITH HER LOVE. (KJV)

Many marital and pre-marital programs emphasize the importance of sex in a marriage. Sex is an important component of many marriages, but it is not the only way that couples show appreciation and physical affection (or in some cases, how they show it at all). There will be points in your marriage where sex, for whatever reason, will not be an option. One or both partners might be sick or somehow physically incapacitated, and there will be plenty of days when one or both partners are tired. It is impossible to rely upon sex as the sole source of affection in your marriage, and it is often deeply important that partners know how to show affection outside of sex.

Physical displays of affection include hugging and kissing (even if it is something quick, on the cheek, or forehead), holding hands or leaning on one another while watching television, a gentle touch on the hand or other body part, and displaying other levels of closeness through touch and contact. Couples need to refrain from physical displays that do not imply affection, that imply abuse or physical mistreatment, because these speak the opposite of affection.

Spending time together

It's not a secret that this increase in the demand for our attention is something newer to the scene. In past generations, families and couples ate dinner together, every night. "Family time" was not a specially scheduled event that happened during certain hours on Saturday afternoons. Life moved at a slower pace and people believed in the importance of being together rather than specifically making time to be together. Togetherness was just something that happened because people lived together, spent time together, or did things together. It was not scheduled, and it was not so planned out.

Today we often expect things to fall into place and plan at the convenience of our availability. People are far busier with activities than they were in years past, but the activities they are doing are often not important or relevant. We spend more time in traffic, in transit, working overtime so someone else can make a lot of money, or taking kids to different activities that they often did in generations past on their own, without parents spending money and kids needing the organizational aspect of it.

We live in a busy, busy world. It seems as if everyone we know and everyone in our lives is always vying for our attention. Whether the phone is ringing, social media is calling, children need picking up or dropping off at events, church services, the job expects you to put in overtime, and extended family members seem to attack you with drama, it seems like there is no time left to eat or sleep, let alone spend time with your spouse.

There is nothing wrong with having a full life or being busy. I believe one of the major problems some people have today is not having enough to do. There are some people who whittle their lives and days away on social media sites and television, never really accomplishing much. The issue, however, is about being busy with productive things. If your entire life is all about running here and there and not really accomplishing much, it's time to step back and look at why you have so much to do. Ecclesiastes 6:3 calls us to look the way we spend our time, and how much we are getting out of it:

A MAN MIGHT HAVE A HUNDRED CHILDREN AND LIVE A LONG TIME [MANY YEARS], BUT WHAT GOOD IS IT IF HE CAN'T ENJOY THE GOOD GOD GIVES HIM [IS NOT SATISFIED WITH THE GOOD THINGS HE HAS] OR HAVE A PROPER BURIAL? I SAY A BABY BORN DEAD [STILLBORN] IS BETTER OFF THAN HE IS.

Couples require time to spend together. I think it's great to schedule a regular date night or something along those lines, but I think it's also important to have unscheduled time together. Couples need to know how to be together, to just have a nice meal, or watch something on television, or do something casual. It needs to be about being able to interact, just as people, and enjoy each other's company rather than forcing what other people define as "relationship" all the time.

Spending time apart

Married life is a daily concoction of two people living together in one life. We know that they need to spend time together, but as individuals, couples also need to spend time apart. I am not talking about moving out of the house and not speaking for an extended period of time, I am talking about each individual in the couple having time by themselves to rest or pursue personal interests.

When we get married, we should never feel forced to abandon personal interests or hobbies because our spouse doesn't share them. On the contrary, one of the things your partner should love about you is your interest and diversity in different things. There should never be a push to get so busy or so wrapped up in your relationship that you start abandoning interests you have as a human being.

Song of Solomon 3:9-11:

KING SOLOMON HAD A COUCH [LITTER; V. 7] MADE FOR HIMSELF

OF WOOD FROM LEBANON.
HE MADE ITS POSTS OF SILVER
   AND ITS BRACES [CANOPY] OF GOLD.
THE SEAT WAS COVERED WITH PURPLE [THE COLOR OF ROYALTY] CLOTH
   THAT THE WOMEN [DAUGHTERS] OF JERUSALEM [1:5] WOVE [INLAID ITS INTERIOR] WITH LOVE.
WOMEN [DAUGHTERS] OF JERUSALEM [ZION; 1:5], GO OUT AND SEE KING SOLOMON.
   HE IS WEARING THE CROWN HIS MOTHER PUT ON HIS HEAD
ON HIS WEDDING DAY,
   WHEN HIS HEART WAS HAPPY!

A particularly striking facet about this passage found in the Song of Solomon is that it shows people doing different things at different times. In a book about togetherness, we see Solomon having one task done, and the women doing their own part, on their own. He didn't expect the women to stand there and hand him tools, or to be engaged in something that really didn't interest them. It is good for a relationship for people to maintain their individuality and uniqueness. As people, we all need space and time from the stress of life and time to think. We also need to make sure that as we maintain our own individual space through activities or restful interests, we also take time for God and take time to continue to develop our relationship with Him.

Spending time with friends

Proverbs 27:9-10:

THE SWEET SMELL OF PERFUME AND OILS IS PLEASANT, AND SO IS GOOD ADVICE FROM A FRIEND.

DON'T FORGET [ABANDON] YOUR FRIEND OR YOUR PARENT'S FRIEND.
DON'T ALWAYS GO TO YOUR FAMILY FOR HELP [BROTHER] WHEN TROUBLE COMES. A NEIGHBOR CLOSE BY IS BETTER THAN A FAMILY [BROTHER] FAR AWAY.

Proverbs 27:17:

AS IRON SHARPENS IRON, SO PEOPLE CAN IMPROVE EACH OTHER [SHARPEN THEIR FRIENDS].

Being married also does not mean that we should abandon our friends. While it goes without saying that married couples should not engage in social behaviors that will negatively affect their marriage or discourage fidelity (friends should understand and respect your marriage), there is no reason that couples cannot spend time with friends, both as a couple and as individuals. Friendships help keep us through difficult times, and the support that we all receive from friends helps keep us going.

Learning how to disagree

Now, let's tie together all the things we have discussed as we've talked about principles involved in getting to know your future spouse. We all like to feel that our opinions are correct (we create dividing lines between right and wrong ideas) and we like it when other people agree with us. There is a reason we select the friends that we do, and we like having people around us who reflect our own values. As single people, we have the option to create circles that are around us when we want them to be around, and that we remove ourselves from when we don't want to be around them anymore. Marriage, however, is not that simple. We can't just jump in one day and then out the next, and this is one of the reasons why people have such a hard time with married life. It's not like being single, and your spouse is not going to conveniently reflect the values and ideas you have, all the time.

In marriage, it is important to agree about things. It's great to have shared values, goals, and aspirations. No matter how much you agree on things, you are going to hit that inevitable wall where you disagree about something. In over 20 years' of ministry (having counseled individuals through most of that), I have yet to see couples who don't hit the wall of disagreement. Sometimes the disagreements may not seem serious to me as a minister or to someone else, but they seem larger than life to that couple (or one individual in the couple) who can't see the other person's perspective.

In our modern times, social issues tend to be serious dividing points for couples. Whether it's that your politics don't align (one is a Democrat and one is a Republican or something else), or that you disagree on something that the other considers a matter of life or death (gay marriage, abortion, birth control, sex before marriage, corporal punishment for children, women ministers, women preaching, women in the workplace, single parents, gays and lesbians adopting children, racial issues, foreign policy, gun control, etc.). To many people in the world, these are issues that they take seriously and have staunch views about. When they come up in a marriage, they can divide partners, who feel betrayed that their views are not shared by someone else.

Your partner is still a person and is still entitled to feel however they feel about social or political issues. How they feel about these issues should not affect your relationship, because you don't marry someone based on how they feel about current events. As quickly as all these issues become national news, they can pass from national headlines. Things that are important today may not be tomorrow, and as passing generations come and go, what is important to one generation changes as a new one takes over.

Romans 14:1-4:

ACCEPT INTO YOUR GROUP [WELCOME; RECEIVE] SOMEONE WHO IS WEAK IN FAITH [OR CONVICTIONS; ON DEBATABLE ISSUES], AND DO NOT ARGUE ABOUT OPINIONS [DOUBTFUL/DEBATABLE ISSUES]. ONE PERSON BELIEVES IT IS RIGHT TO EAT ALL KINDS OF FOOD. BUT ANOTHER, WHO IS WEAK, BELIEVES IT IS RIGHT TO EAT ONLY VEGETABLES [POSSIBLY THE ISSUE OF WHETHER TO KEEP THE OT DIETARY LAWS, AND/OR WHETHER TO AVOID FOOD SACRIFICED TO IDOLS (SEE 1 COR. 8—10)]. THE ONE WHO KNOWS THAT IT IS RIGHT TO EAT ANY KIND OF FOOD [EATS; V. 14; SEE MARK 7:18–19] MUST NOT REJECT [DESPISE; LOOK DOWN ON] THE ONE WHO EATS ONLY VEGETABLES [DOES NOT EAT]. AND THE PERSON WHO EATS ONLY VEGETABLES [DOES NOT EAT] MUST NOT THINK THAT THE ONE WHO EATS ALL FOODS IS WRONG [JUDGE THE ONE WHO EATS], BECAUSE GOD HAS ACCEPTED THAT PERSON. YOU CANNOT [WHO ARE YOU TO... ?] JUDGE ANOTHER PERSON'S SERVANT. THE MASTER DECIDES IF THE SERVANT IS DOING WELL OR NOT [BEFORE HIS OWN LORD/MASTER HE STANDS OR FALLS]. AND THE LORD'S SERVANT WILL DO WELL [STAND] BECAUSE THE LORD HELPS HIM DO WELL [CAN MAKE HIM STAND].

Social issues should not divide couples. As a couple, you need to learn how to disagree about matters and apply these same principles to other people who feel differently about things in life. If it means you cannot talk about the issues with each other, then don't discuss them. Life is an abundance of things outside of your thoughts and viewpoints on one specific subject.

More importantly, learn the value in respecting each other's opinions and differences. Marriage is a great training ground to gain the perspective that your opinion is not always right, nor is it relevant much of the time. It is simply something that you feel, a viewpoint that you have, that does not have to be voiced to the detriment of your marriage or other relationships that you might have. Learn to quiet yourself, to discipline yourself, and to realize that oftentimes respect means humbling yourself, not having to have that last word.

Week 3 Assignments

Answer the following questions based on discussions you have had with your spouse in counseling this week and additionally on your own time and prepare to discuss them at your next counseling session. If you run out of room in a section, finish the answer to your question in your journal.

1. Have you and your future spouse discussed current events and issues? _____

2. Do you feel you know where your mate stands on major news stories? _____

3. How do you feel about your mate's position? _____

_____

4. Do you find the two of you often fighting over social or current events as a couple? _____

5. What social issue is most important to you? Why is it most important? _____

_____

_____

_____

_____

6. What social issue is most important to your mate? Why is it important? _____

_____

_____

_____

_____

7. What do you think in life has caused you to form the opinions that you have and hold dear? _____

_____

_____

_____

_____

8. Are you for, against, or neutral for: gay marriage _____ gun control _____ women in the workplace _____ women in ministry/women preachers _____ abortion _____ birth control _____ sex outside of marriage _____ gay rights _____ corporal punishment _____ gay and lesbian adoption _____ overpopulation _____ global warming _____ racial equality _____

9. Is your mate for, against, or neutral for: gay marriage _____ gun control _____ women in the workplace _____ women in ministry/women preachers _____ abortion _____ birth control _____ sex outside of marriage _____ gay rights _____ corporal punishment _____ gay and lesbian adoption _____ overpopulation _____ global warming _____ racial equality _____

10. How does learning these things cause you to feel about your relationship? Why? _____

_____

_____

_____

11. What are some of your interests that you intend to continue to maintain after your marriage? _____

_____

12. What do you believe are the most important aspects of communication in a relationship? _____

_____

13. How can someone best affirm who you are? What actions help you to feel loved and appreciated by someone else? _____

_____

_____

_____

_____

14. How does your mate find affirmation? What actions help them to feel loved and appreciated by someone else? _____

_____

_____

_____

_____

15. What do you enjoy doing with your mate? What does your mate enjoy doing with you? What activities do you both enjoy equally? _____

_____

_____

_____

_____

16. What activities do you like doing with friends? _____

_____

_____

_____

_____

17. Having done the first exercises this week followed by the latter ones, what is most important to you about your mate? How can you better display that through a) communication and b) in disagreements? _____

_____

_____

_____

_____

18. How do you think the man and woman in the Song of Solomon would have handled their disagreements? _____

_____

_____

_____

_____

19. In reading Psalm 1:1-6, what characteristics are introduced that can be used to better a relationship? How can these characteristics help foster better communication? _____

_____

_____

_____

_____

20. What is something you learned about your mate in this process that you didn't know before? _____

_____

_____

_____

_____

Week Four

All About Families

SO [PAUL BEGINS AGAIN THE PRAYER HE STARTED IN V. 1] I BOW IN PRAYER [KNEEL] BEFORE THE FATHER FROM WHOM EVERY [OR THE WHOLE] FAMILY [A PLAY ON WORDS, SINCE THE WORDS "FATHER" AND "FAMILY" ARE RELATED] IN HEAVEN AND ON EARTH GETS ITS TRUE NAME.
(EPHESIANS 3:14-15)

Bible reading: Ephesians 2:11-22

Journaling assignments for in-session discussion:

- What kind of family life can be seen in the Song of Solomon?
- Are married couples a family by themselves, if they have no children? Why or why not?

Some people recount their childhoods with wistful tears full of joy and hope from a bygone era. There are people who have nothing bad to say about their parents, nothing angry to say about their siblings, and who spent summer days with their upstanding, moral grandparents. They had a solid, two-parent family that stayed together long enough to see a fortieth and fiftieth wedding anniversary surrounded by children and grandchildren. They love to talk about the wonder they experienced as children and staunchly want to re-create that kind of life for their own children.

Then... there's the rest of us who had less-than-ideal childhoods in one form or another: an abusive parent or other abusive figure in our lives, terrible siblings that we never learned how to get along with, divorced parents, parents who fought all the time and "stayed together for the kids" (do the kids a favor and just get divorced!), relatives with drug and alcohol problems, family alienations that might have existed long before you were born, poverty... and so on and so forth. In modern times, childhoods often sound a lot more like what I just described than the idealistic world we were all taught was "perfect" and we should want, regardless of the fact that it seldom, if ever, existed.

Families have problems, because families are composed of people. Down to the present day, most families have thrived on many generations of issues, dysfunctions, negative cycles and issues. Even the families that seemed the most perfect had their problems; they were just better at hiding them. Contrary to what pop psychology may want us to believe, no matter what your childhood was like, there are things within you and within your viewpoints that have affected your views on relationships and family life. Whether you acquired them from your own family or from viewing the world around you, there are things about life that affect your view of family.

Married couples, whether they have children or not, are a family unit. That means the way a couple views family life will often affect their relationship. This week, you will be looking at your views and your partner's views on family and see how you can grow in your perspectives on family to have a better and stronger relationship.

Incorrectly applying the "family" thing

I have long argued that the way we view family in church is hurting the church's mission, as a whole. The way in which we approach family in church is in alignment with most modern societal views of it: parents with young children who are encouraged to be involved become the focus, because it is the best "looking" to outsiders. It's a lot nicer and more appealing for a family to come into church, everyone neatly dressed, with a few young children in tow, than it is to welcome a single mother with four or five screaming children from multiple fathers. Church today, whether we want to admit it or not, is very image-based. Every church wants to attract people who won't be full of drama and will present a nice image in pictures and on paper. This means that, when it comes to marketing church, church is marketed to two-parent families, who have never been divorced prior, with young children.

The problem with this becomes, what do we do with everyone else? What happens to single parents, or blended families, or couples without children, or single people, or divorced people, or widowed people, or people who are living together and aren't legally married? There are many people who report feeling downright unwelcome at church because they do not fit the desired profile of churchgoers... and that means they don't attend church. What is even worse is the way in which these people feel marginalized, as if there is something wrong with them because they just didn't have or don't have what everyone thinks they should.

This also causes a lack of proper healing and hope for people who come from different families or have unique family situations. Instead of feeling like they can come to church and learn how to have good relationships that defy their odds of origin or find hope for the situation they might be in, they feel rejected, like they won't ever measure up because all that matters is a vague, ideal concept of "family."

Matthew 12:46-50:

WHILE JESUS WAS TALKING TO THE PEOPLE [CROWDS], [LOOK; BEHOLD] HIS MOTHER AND BROTHERS [OR BROTHERS AND SISTERS; THE GREEK WORD CAN MEAN "SIBLINGS"] STOOD OUTSIDE, TRYING TO FIND A WAY [SEEKING; ASKING] TO TALK TO HIM. SOMEONE TOLD JESUS, "[LOOK; BEHOLD] YOUR MOTHER AND BROTHERS [AND SISTERS] ARE STANDING OUTSIDE, ·AND THEY WANT [SEEKING; ASKING] TO TALK TO YOU."

HE ANSWERED, "WHO IS MY MOTHER? WHO ARE MY BROTHERS [AND SISTERS]?" THEN HE POINTED TO [OR STRETCHED OUT HIS HAND TOWARD] HIS FOLLOWERS [DISCIPLES] AND SAID, "HERE ARE [LOOK; BEHOLD] MY MOTHER AND MY BROTHERS. MY TRUE BROTHER AND SISTER AND MOTHER ARE THOSE WHO DO WHAT MY FATHER IN HEAVEN WANTS [THE WILL OF MY FATHER IN HEAVEN]."

The Bible teaches us that "family" is far more than just parents with young children. "Family" extends to the entire church, to all people who call upon Christ as Savior and do the Father's will. This applies beyond traditional bloodline, and creates bonds that are stronger than blood, because they are born in Spirit. If we are in Christ, we are family, no matter who we are, what our family lives were like growing up, what our family life is like right now, and no matter where we are. As a church, we need to expand our concept of family to recognize that we are family, we are the family that so many people seek and need. As the church embraces this perspective, it makes it much easier for us to foster a healthy idea of family and help couples to embrace it in their own marriages.

All kinds of families

Mark 3:20-21:

THEN JESUS WENT HOME [INTO A HOUSE], BUT AGAIN A CROWD GATHERED. THERE WERE SO MANY PEOPLE THAT JESUS AND HIS FOLLOWERS COULD NOT EAT. WHEN HIS FAMILY [OWN PEOPLE] HEARD THIS, THEY WENT TO GET [SEIZE; TAKE CHARGE OF] HIM BECAUSE THEY THOUGHT HE WAS OUT OF HIS MIND.

What we define as "family" today came into play in the 1950s. It is what is known as the "nuclear" family. It is understood to be one generation of parents living with their children in housing by themselves, without extended family or other relatives living with them. This concept of family is relatively new to familial understanding. It emerged after World War II, as couples desired to move away from their extended families and live on their own. Prior to this time, families typically lived in the same area where several generations had been born, and many generations of families lived together under one roof. A family house might have included grandparents or older aunts or uncles, sometimes cousins, and sometimes more than one generation of children. Families lived like this because it made survival easier, especially as generations passed and younger members of the family could take over "the family farm" because they had worked on it for so many years prior.

In more recent times, we see the "blended family" (which is really not a new idea, either) gaining speed, where couples have been married prior and bring children from previous relationships into their current marriage. I know a significant number of people who were raised by their grandparents or by their extended family members (such as an aunt or cousin). I also know stories of people who, whether one agrees with the life or not, lived with gay or lesbian parents. There are still many people who lived in foster care or were adopted. No matter how you spin it, family takes on many forms and isn't just about biology or the comfortable concept of a nuclear family. Our family consists of the people who love and support us, who help us to be who we are to be and help us to aspire to greater things. When it comes to "family," there is no one singular definition.

If you didn't have an "ideal" family, the family that everyone told you that you should have had, don't sweat it. The person who told you that probably didn't have an ideal family, either! They just heard from someone else that that's what was or is "normal" and they reiterated that. There's nothing wrong with having a crazy, messed up family, a family that was moderately crazy, or even a family that had their crazy under control. There's nothing wrong with having a different family. Whatever kind of family you came from, something wonderful came out of it, and that's you. No matter what kind of issues you might have personally, know you would have some kind of an issue, no matter what kind of family you came from.

All this said: after you get married, you and your spouse are going to introduce a new kind of family into your life. The two of you are going to be responsible for your own household, your own concept of "family," and your own ability to love, support, be who you are, and help each other to aspire to greater things. Embrace this concept and recognize that the two of you are about to embark on creating your own "new kind of family."

It's OK to not be OK

In connection with what I spoke of earlier about church image, we have gotten the message in church that it's not all right to be anything but "OK." If we are going through a difficult time or experiencing pressures or stress, we are always pushed to "be OK," even if the way we behave is a complete and total farce. This message of being OK has marred our entire image of ourselves and our ability to interact with others. If something about our lives, or our childhoods hurt us, or our adulthoods hurt us, or something, somewhere, has caused us hurt, we get the message that we are so screwed up, we will never be able to be in a good relationship or have healthy relationships because we are not "OK."

Take a deep breath and receive the words that will probably help your entire life: it's perfectly OK to not be OK. Everyone, at some point in their lives, is not OK. If anything, we probably have several periods of our lives where we aren't doing well and aren't feeling good about doing well. It doesn't mean you will never feel good again, nor does it mean you will forever be marked for life. People have had relationships for generations and done so as completely screwed up, not OK individuals. Just because you've had problems or you have issues now doesn't mean your relationships are doomed. It also doesn't mean you are unlovable or hopeless. It just means you have had or are having a bad time.

In the Song of Solomon 1:5-6, the woman makes the following declaration about herself:

I'M DARK BUT [OR AND] LOVELY [BEAUTIFUL; SHE WAS OUT IN THE SUN BECAUSE HER BROTHERS FORCED HER TO WORK THE FIELDS; V. 6],
   WOMEN [DAUGHTERS] OF JERUSALEM [HER FRIENDS WHOM SHE IS INSTRUCTING ABOUT LOVE],
   DARK LIKE THE TENTS OF KEDAR [DESERT NOMADS; GEN. 25:13; JER. 49:28–29],
   LIKE THE CURTAINS OF SOLOMON [OR SALMA; SOUTH ARABIAN DESERT NOMADS].
DON'T LOOK AT HOW DARK [SWARTHY] I AM,
   AT HOW DARK THE SUN HAS MADE ME [BECAUSE THE SUN SCORCHED ME].
MY BROTHERS [MOTHER'S SONS] WERE ANGRY WITH ME
  AND MADE ME TEND [OR GUARD] THE VINEYARDS,
   SO I HAVEN'T TENDED [OR GUARDED] MY OWN VINEYARD [REFERRING TO HER BODY]!

In ancient times, sun-darkened skin was associated with manual labor and servitude. It meant you were not wealthy, and you had to live your life doing hard work for the benefit of the rich. To say that she was "dark, but lovely" acknowledged the scars that she had. She had to live with the memories of being forced into hard work because her own blended family, her stepbrothers, forced her into it. That was a wound she carried in her life; it was something that made her "not feel OK." It was a constant reminder that she had been mistreated by someone else and had to live with the results.

Her family did that to her. It wasn't done by a stranger or a random person on the street, it was done by those who were supposed to care about her and have her best interests at heart. The Bible does make it clear that families, especially those of origin, don't always do what they are supposed to do and can leave us in situations where we have issues and concepts that we need to change as we get older and start our own lives.

At the same time, the woman declares herself, "Dark, but lovely." In other words, her wounds were a part of her, and she was still beautiful. Even though she had something notable that made it obvious to everyone what had happened to her, she did not accept what happened to her as her entire identity. She was dark, but beautiful, and part of her beauty came from her experience.

You don't have to feel OK about what has happened to you in your life, even after you have experienced the process of forgiveness. Some things are never right, no matter how we come to reconciliation with them in our lives. Our experiences are a part of us, but they aren't all of us. They don't have to define how we are going to act, behave, interact with others, and see ourselves throughout our lives. It's perfectly fine to have areas in our lives that leave us "dark," but do not forget that you are "lovely," too. Rather than feeling bad, realize that you survived through things that would have knocked someone else out of the game. You are here and you are a survivor. Sometimes survivors have scars, but survivors are always, in the end, lovely.

Looking back

In order to have a new family, we have to deconstruct our concepts about the old one we have. As I have already stated through this chapter, we've already grown-up hearing concepts about what "family" is supposed to be. This has led many people to think they don't want a family, to be a part of family, or to have anything to do with family. They think family means dysfunction, or it means abuse or mistreatment, or it means being surrounded by people who don't really love or care about them.

There are very, very few people I have met in my life who I would really describe as true "loners." Most people, no matter how much they might protest to the contrary, like to have people around them that care about them and that they can also, in turn, care about. God has created us to be social people, and in being social, we like to be with others. In Psalm 68:6, God says:

GOD SETS THE LONELY IN FAMILIES, HE LEADS FORTH THE PRISONERS WITH SINGING; BUT THE REBELLIOUS LIVE IN A SUN-SCORCHED LAND. (NIV)

The answer to loneliness is connection. Not just being around other people to be around them, but to have people around you who are connected, who care, and who are engaged in things in life. The answer to loneliness, feeling lost and isolated, is to have a genuine connection to people in life, and to be "set in" a family, a true family.

The problem is not family; it's the concept of family that many people have. This is something that is completely understandable and takes time to work through. Whatever concept of family that we have, it needs to change so that we can embrace the new family you are starting and becoming.

- **Dysfunction:** Dysfunction is when certain abnormal patterns of interaction become the normal way that people function and thrive. I am of the belief that all families have some level of dysfunction because all families consist of people and all people have some level of interaction in their lives that is not perfect and is not within the realm of what it should be. I don't care for the word "normal," because I don't necessarily agree with the belief that everything "normal" is healthy or right in interaction. For hundreds of years, it was "normal" to enslave people based on their race and for thousands of years, has been "normal" to treat women with disrespect and with disdain. These are not healthy behaviors, but for a long time, they were considered "normal." This means that dysfunction can easily be "normal," especially when culture condones or conforms to it.

Dysfunction is overcome when we learn that our unhealthy "normal" needs to change. Don't think that doing so doesn't take effort, however. When we realize our function needs to change, that means we become aware of how intensely dysfunctional the world around us is. Everyone who thrives on your dysfunctional environment may very well not make the changes and may not support your decision to do so. When the time comes to walk away from dysfunction, you may have to walk away from people, to choose some new patterns of behavior and find a whole new family, especially if dysfunction has run deep for many generations.

- **Fantasy:** If you have nothing but stellar, ideal things to say about your childhood... we must step back and question your level of reality when it comes to your past. Nobody had a perfect childhood. Even if things were reasonably stable at home, something, somewhere at time happened that was less than perfect: either at school, with friends, with siblings, or with other relatives. The reason I know this is because encountering adversities and dealing with people who are unpleasant, unfriendly, or exclusive is just a part of life.

Coming to terms with the fact that not everything in life always went your way and that you have feelings about it is perfectly acceptable. It is perfectly all right to feel different ways about things that happened, and it is perfectly acceptable to be realistic about them. Remembering things from a realistic standpoint and being able to talk about them in a way that does not elicit so much over-emotion and upset doesn't mean that you didn't feel the way that you did or that you think what happened now is right, but it does acknowledge that some things in life cause us to feel some sort of way... and that is within the realm of healthy living.

- **Abuse/mistreatment:** People today disagree about what "abuse" and "mistreatment" are. When I was growing up, corporal punishment wasn't regarded as abusive behavior. It was considered "corporal punishment." Then, as kids got hurt due to unnecessary force, such behavior became identified as abusive. News stories abounded of people who were over-disciplined and either died or were seriously injured in the process. Nowadays, there are very vocal people who are in favor of corporal disciplinary punishment, who think that spanking and hitting children is not abuse, and that we have gotten too lenient with children in bribing or talking to them about issues.

I think that in our endless debating over who is wrong or right about corporal punishment, we are missing the point about abuse and mistreatment and ignoring the fact that it exists in families who use all sorts of disciplinary measures. Being spanked or beaten with an object to the point where physical markings are left on a child's body or their bodies are injured or damaged is abuse, or when a child is somehow handled in a sexual manner, or when they are verbally or emotionally treated in a manner that is demoralizing. Abuse and mistreatment within a family dynamic is also detrimental to children, even if they are not the ones who are being physically, emotionally, sexually, or verbally harmed.

If you were abused when you were growing up or even as an adult in an intimate relationship, it is hard to live with those memories and the feelings that come from them. It's also hard growing up, seeing other people abused and having feelings about that abuse, especially when you are not able to do much to help the victims. Abuse and mistreatment are dysfunctional behavior patterns that we learn to live with and then often spend many years trying to avoid and overcome, only to fall into them again with other people. When we are in situations that are not abusive, we can create chaos or not know how to handle calm and serene situations.

- **Divorce:** Being a child of divorce is not an easy thing, but it is easier than feeling like you are the reason your parents are staying together in misery. That having been said, having people knowing all your business, feeling like things that were once familiar to you are falling apart, and feeling like you don't understand what is happening are hard to live with. Like all things, children do eventually adjust to divorce situations. The thing that never gets easier to handle is the stigma and the way in which people respond to the issue. Long into adulthood, children of divorce have people pity them, look down on them, treat them as if they missed something in their lives, and "handled" by people who think that being the child of a divorce is something to scorn or shame.

There is also so much propaganda against divorce today, people who grew up with divorced parents are almost forced into a position to think and feel like they will never become anything or able to handle things. They think they can't have happy marriages or relationships because the "experts" tell them they won't be able to do so. They think that they are never going to be good at achieving things, because that's what they are constantly told. They are told they are angry (when maybe they are not) or that they have feelings that they may not even have, as people try to crawl in their heads and make their own selves feel superior based on this one fact.

I don't think people should stay in unhappy marriages because their children will have to deal with judgmental people as adults. That's not the solution to the problem, because we can't live our lives worrying about what judgmental people will say or do. I also strongly disagree with the concept that the children of divorced parents are permanently screwed up. Let's not forget that living in disastrous homes where people have problems they can't fix can also screw up lives, but we don't ever talk much about that. What it does mean, however, is that if someone grows up living with that constant concept that there is something wrong with them that can't be fixed, it can negatively affect their relationships.

As a society, we need to stop using situations that do not fall into our leading definitions of "normal" to judge other people. We spend so much time praying for marriage as an institution,

Singles giving marital advice?

THERE ARE MANY WHO FEEL IT IS UNADVISABLE TO HAVE A SINGLE OR DIVORCED PASTOR OR CHURCH LEADER GIVING ADVICE ABOUT MARRIAGE TO THEIR CONGREGATION. SOME GO AS FAR AS TO SAY THAT SINGLE PASTORS SHOULDN'T EVEN COUNSEL MARRIED COUPLES. WHILE, ON THE SURFACE, THIS ALMOST SOUNDS WISE — HOW IN THE WORLD CAN SOMEONE WHO HAS NEVER EXPERIENCED MARRIAGE GIVE ADVICE ON IT? — IS IT THE ATTITUDE GOD WANTS US TO HAVE ABOUT MARRIAGE?

WELL, THE MAJORITY OF WORDS ON MARRIAGE IN THE NEW TESTAMENT WERE WRITTEN BY SINGLE MEN — JESUS AND THE APOSTLE PAUL. MORE THAN ANY OTHER TWO NEW TESTAMENT FIGURES, WE TRY TO UPHOLD (OFTEN WITHOUT PROPER UNDERSTANDING) THEIR OWN TEACHINGS ON MARRIAGE AND MARITAL ADVICE. WHEN MARRIED PASTORS AND OTHER LEADERS START QUOTING MARRIAGE ADVICE FROM THE NEW TESTAMENT, THEY ARE QUOTING TWO SINGLE PEOPLE, WHO FROM THE RECORDS WE HAVE, NEVER, AT ANY POINT IN THEIR LIVES, LIVED WITH A SPOUSE.

WHAT DOES THIS TELL US? IT PROVES THAT GOD CAN REVEAL TRUTHS ABOUT SITUATIONS TO PEOPLE WHO HAVE NOT NECESSARILY LIVED THEM. WHILE IT IS A GREAT THING TO BE MARRIED AND BEING MARRIED CAN OBVIOUSLY PROVIDE EXPERIENCE TO MARRIAGE, THAT DOESN'T MEAN THAT SOMEONE HAS INSIGHT INTO MARRIAGE OR THAT THEIR EXPERIENCE IS ADEQUATE TO PROVIDE REVELATION OR ADVICE ON THE SUBJECT. THERE ARE LOTS OF PEOPLE WHO, WHILE WELL-INTENTIONED, GIVE ADVICE THROUGH THEIR OWN SITUATIONS AND DON'T REALLY ATTEND TO THE NEEDS OF THE PEOPLE THEY ARE SUPPOSED TO BE HELPING.

WHEN SEEKING COUNSELING ADVICE OR HELP FROM A MINISTER, WATCH TO SEE IF THEY SEEM EMBITTERED AGAINST MARRIAGE AND IF THEY ARE SENSITIVE TO RELATIONSHIP ISSUES. JUST BECAUSE MARRIAGE MIGHT NOT BE FOR OR NOT WORKING FOR YOUR LEADER DOESN'T MEAN THEY SHOULD ENCOURAGE YOU TO SWEAR OFF OF IT ALL TOGETHER. LOOK FOR OBJECTIVITY AND UNDERSTANDING, AS WELL AS A GOOD HEAD TO ENCOURAGE YOU TO COMMUNICATE AS A COUPLE.

we have stopped praying for individuals who are in marriages. We don't consider what a difficult situation a divorce is for a married couple, especially when children are involved, and we uphold institution rather than what is best for the people. As a church, we need to stop making people pay for mistakes and for things they did that they cannot make right. We especially need to stop treating children of divorce as if they are a special, doomed, and damnable case. Why? In the pursuit of trying to save an institution, we are causing more people dysfunction and helping more people to get divorced.

I am going to tell you something right now that will change your entire life if you are the adult child of divorced parents: you are not a problem. You can have successful relationships. Your parents' divorce showed you that being unhealthy in a relationship is a bad thing and you learned from that how important being healthy is in your relationships. You might not always understand how to behave in a good relationship, but that's not because your parents got divorced. It's because when we have spent our lives in relationships that don't go anywhere, we aren't always sure how to respond to a relationship that does move forward. You are not any less than anyone else, and no, just because your parents were divorced, it doesn't mean you have the problems that other people think you have. You can start a new family; you can start a new pattern of relationships. You should never be ashamed of what other people think, because they didn't live through what you did.

Looking at single life

1 Corinthians 7:8-9:

NOW FOR THOSE WHO ARE NOT MARRIED AND FOR THE WIDOWS I SAY THIS: IT IS GOOD FOR THEM TO STAY UNMARRIED AS I AM. BUT IF THEY CANNOT CONTROL THEMSELVES [EXERCISE SELF-CONTROL], THEY SHOULD MARRY. IT IS BETTER TO MARRY THAN TO BURN WITH SEXUAL DESIRE [TO BURN].

In church, we talk a lot about people being "called" to live their lives in certain relationship contexts (usually either married or single). I do believe that there are some people who are "called" (if we want to use that word) to live their lives as single men and women who never marry. The who, what, when, why, and how, I can't answer, because it isn't my decision and it isn't my desire that is put within them. The message we do give is that if you are not called to be single, then you need to get married. We don't consider timing or the way that marriage is often flaunted hurts those who are single, or makes married life seem like something it just is not.

It also means that most single people who desire to get married don't give single life much of a chance. They spend most of their single life waiting to be married, bouncing from relationship to relationship, hoping that they will find "the one" they can marry. If watching most single people is any sort of indication, most people who are single spend their time unhappy, lonely, and frustrated. They feel like they are missing out on something special in their lives and wonder what is wrong with them, because so many other people have it, and they do not.

Then we have the opposite extreme: people who seem very comfortable in the single life, with no interest or haste to settle down. Regardless of gender, they may enjoy "playing the field," dating many people, and the social aspects of dating without commitment or marital connection. Others aren't especially interested in dating, but enjoy being single, without the bounds of marriage. They seem to be the best "single people," never lonely or doubtful of their lifestyles. People who are like this are seen as empty or void, because they don't seem to want to settle in or live like other people want to.

Some people like being single, some people don't. Some people like the idea of having a relationship and keeping it on a certain level, and other people don't. Some people are the best "swinging" bachelors and bachelorettes, and other people aren't. Some people settle into married life well, and other people miss single life and long for the independence and freedom they feel they forsook in favor of a spouse. There isn't one type of single or married person, just like there isn't one type of person, period. While there is no call for wild or immoral behavior, some people gravitate to it without any void or feeling like they are missing anything in their lives.

It's obvious that we aren't teaching people a balanced perspective on "calling" and both single and married life. The reality of life is that, whether "called" to marriage or not, everyone spends some portion of their lives as single people. Then, for those who do get married, many find themselves living as "single" people again, either as the result of divorce or the death of a spouse. In other words, it's important that we, as human beings, learn how to be single and how to be content as single people. It doesn't mean that we must be engaged in wild lifestyles or always happy about being single, but it does mean that we should be able to be contented people when we must live on our own, not feeling inferior or incomplete.

It also means that when we are considering a spouse, we should aspire to marry someone for the right reasons. We should not be getting married because we just don't like being single or don't feel like we fit in well with the single lifestyle. There needs to be a true connection and the ability to form family relationships among couples, especially as their marriages grow and change. If that connection is lacking, the relationship will, most likely, be unfulfilling or dissolve at some point in time.

Being a two-person family

When a couple decides to get married, they establish their own family based on their own foundations. They join their immediate biological relatives and distant relatives together and create a new family, with the two of them as the solid base. This means that newly married couples need to know how to be a two-person family.

Colossians 3:18-19:

WIVES, YIELD TO THE AUTHORITY OF [SUBMIT TO] YOUR HUSBANDS, BECAUSE THIS IS THE RIGHT THING TO DO [APPROPRIATE; FITTING] IN THE LORD [EPH. 5:22–24; 1 PET. 3:1–6].

HUSBANDS, LOVE YOUR WIVES AND BE GENTLE WITH [DON'T BE HARSH TOWARD/EMBITTERED AGAINST] THEM [EPH. 5:25–33; 1 PET. 3:7].

Some people say that you aren't a real family until you have children, but this is not anywhere near the truth. As is evident above, husbands and wives can love and interact as family even if it is just the two of them. Families are about connections, not numbers of children. When you and your spouse marry, you will be a family. You will share every aspect of your life together, you will make decisions together, you will divide up household chores, you will sort through problems together, you will argue, you will make up, and you will create a powerful bond that will help you endure the ups and downs of life.

It is vital couples understand and maintain the balance of being a two-person family and know that they are family, with or without kids. Eventually kids grow up and leave home, and then the couple will become a two-person family again. Some couples are unable to have children or opt not to have them, and they are not any less a family than those who do have them.

Even if you are coming into marriage with children from other relationships or from before you were married, you still need to learn how to be a two-person family. It becomes more difficult to find that time, but it becomes no less relevant. Couples need to know how to interact as "just them," partnering and helping each other out with things and learning how to be a unit together.

Family expansion

1 Samuel 1:1-2:

THERE WAS A [CERTAIN] MAN NAMED ELKANAH SON OF JEROHAM FROM RAMATHAIM [RAMAH; JUST NORTH OF JERUSALEM] IN THE MOUNTAINS [HILL COUNTRY] OF EPHRAIM. ELKANAH WAS FROM THE FAMILY [OR REGION] OF ZUPH. (JEROHAM WAS ELIHU'S SON. ELIHU WAS TOHU'S SON, AND TOHU WAS THE SON OF ZUPH FROM THE FAMILY GROUP OF EPHRAIM [AN EPHRAIMITE].) ELKANAH HAD TWO WIVES NAMED HANNAH AND PENINNAH. PENINNAH HAD CHILDREN, BUT HANNAH HAD NONE [CHILDLESSNESS CARRIED A SERIOUS SOCIAL STIGMA].

Many people decide that they do want to have children at some point in their marriage. Before marriage vows are exchanged and wedding arrangements are planned, couples need to sit down and discuss the issue of children in their marriage relationship. The following questions need to be asked, answered, and discussed by both parties:

- Do you want to have children?
- How many children do you want to have?
- Do you want to have children right away, or do you want to wait?
- What does "right away" or "wait" mean to you?
- How would you feel if having your own biological children was not an option in this relationship?
- How would you feel about your mate if they are, for whatever reason, unable to have children?
- If infertility arises, what do you think is the best way to handle it?
- How do you feel about fertility treatments?
- How do you feel about adoption?
- How do you feel about child rearing? Do you believe someone should stay home with the children after they are born? If so, for how long and who do you think it should be?
- What would you do if you had a child with developmental or physical disabilities?
- How do you feel about child discipline and what methods do you believe should be used?

It is vitally important that you take the results of this discussion into account before getting married. Do not think that your mate is going to change their mind about wanting or not wanting children – or any of the details as pertain to this issue. It's a wonderful concept to think that the two of you will align on these things after the wedding, but if you don't agree with them beforehand, you are not going to agree on them after, either. Children and raising your own family are prime subjects that must be discussed prior to a wedding.

Another note on this topic: be honest with each other. If you really don't want to have children or it's something you don't want to do right away, say so. If you want them right away and it's important that you have children in your life, then say that. Whatever it is, say it! Don't think that your partner already knows, because they may very well be going on assumptions rather than facts. Don't lead someone into thinking you are on the same page about something and then harbor anger or attitude about the results of your own deception.

If you desire to have children, you need to start planning now for your future with them. The reason this discussion is so important is because if you want to have children at any point in time, regardless of how many years away you are planning to do so, you need to consider the finances involved in pre-natal care, pregnancy, delivery, and child raising. If you decide that you would like to adopt or are interested in fertility treatments, you need to consider the cost of those, as well, because all processes involving parenthood cost money. Choosing to have a child and raise that child to adulthood is a serious, long process that is financially expensive, emotionally taxing, and sometimes a strain on a marriage. There is no question that rewards are involved in parenting and that parenting can enrich a marriage and enrich one's life, but parenting is also something that must be carefully considered and seriously handled. Rather than running into parenthood as if it is going to be an opportunity to mold a life or create another human being, parenthood should be viewed as a responsibility, something to think about and to do when you are ready as a couple. That may mean you take a few years as a couple and spend time travelling, or building up your careers, or doing whatever it is that you want to do. If you want to have children right away, make sure that you can financially afford parenthood and that you are prepared to provide for the needs and wants of the child.

Family planning

If you are not ready to have children, then responsible family planning is in order to prevent unexpected or unplanned pregnancy. While it is true that all pregnancy prevention methods have a certain margin of error, many are well over 96% effective at preventing pregnancy when they are used correctly and as directed.

1 Peter 4:10:

EACH OF YOU HAS RECEIVED A GIFT TO USE TO SERVE OTHERS. BE GOOD SERVANTS [STEWARDS; MANAGERS] OF GOD'S VARIOUS GIFTS OF GRACE [ROM. 5:15–16; 6:23].

There is nothing morally, nor Biblically reprehensible about using family planning methods. Even though there are some fringe groups who teach against its use, we need to remember that God calls us to be responsible human beings and good stewards with the resources that we have. Birth control and family planning are a part of responsible stewardship, because they take into consideration that a couple does not want to bring a child into this world when they are unprepared to take care of them. If measures to prevent pregnancy are available to a couple who does not desire to have children, does not desire to have them right away, or has already had a certain number of children and does not desire to have any more children, birth control is a moral and responsible option.

There are many different forms of birth control available, including Natural Family Planning which does not involve the use of medications or drugs, over-the-counter methods, such as condoms or female condoms, and prescription birth control, such as diaphragms or birth control pills. If you are seeking birth control options, it is best to visit a doctor or a clinic that specializes in women's services. Some birth control methods do have side effects, so it is important that, when using family planning methods, that you learn your options in order to make the best decision for your situation.

Infertility

1 Samuel 1:4-8:

WHEN [ON THE DAY] ELKANAH OFFERED SACRIFICES, HE ALWAYS GAVE A SHARE OF THE MEAT [PORTIONS] TO HIS WIFE PENINNAH AND TO ALL HER SONS AND DAUGHTERS. BUT ELKANAH ALWAYS GAVE HANNAH A DOUBLE PORTION OF THE MEAT BECAUSE HE LOVED HER AND THE LORD HAD KEPT HER FROM HAVING CHILDREN [OR ONLY ONE PORTION OF THE MEAT EVEN THOUGH HE LOVED HER, BECAUSE THE LORD HAD KEPT HER FROM HAVING CHILDREN; ONLY ONE PORTION WOULD BE NEEDED SINCE THERE WAS NO CHILD TO FEED]. PENINNAH [HER RIVAL/FOE] WOULD TEASE [TAUNT] HANNAH AND UPSET [PROVOKE; IRRITATE; MAKE FUN OF] HER, BECAUSE THE LORD HAD MADE HER UNABLE TO HAVE CHILDREN [CLOSED HER WOMB]. THIS HAPPENED EVERY YEAR [YEAR AFTER YEAR] WHEN [WHENEVER] THEY WENT UP TO THE HOUSE OF THE LORD AT SHILOH [1:3]. PENINNAH WOULD UPSET [TAUNT; PROVOKE] HANNAH UNTIL HANNAH WOULD CRY AND NOT EAT ANYTHING. HER HUSBAND ELKANAH WOULD

SAY TO HER, "HANNAH, WHY ARE YOU CRYING AND WHY WON'T YOU EAT? WHY ARE YOU SAD [DOWNHEARTED]? DON'T I MEAN MORE [OR AM I NOT BETTER] TO YOU THAN TEN SONS?"

One of the most difficult scenarios for couples who desire children is a situation that involves infertility. Infertility is when a couple is unable to have a child on their own, without some sort of medical intervention. Whether infertility is the result of one partner or both, the inability to have a child when a child is wanted is often one of the most painful experiences a couple can encounter.

There can be many reasons why infertility exists. Some things that are known to affect fertility include:

- Genetics
- Congenital abnormalities
- Poor diet
- Lack of exercise
- Side-affects from medications
- Drug and alcohol abuse
- Disease, especially chronic disease (such as Diabetes)
- Illness
- Physical disability
- Sexually Transmitted Infections

There are also times when infertility just happens, and no one knows why or understands it. Sometimes life just happens, and people are unable to conceive. There are stories where the doctors thought couples had no chance of infertility who struggled to have children, and stories where doctors thought couples were completely infertile who went on to have a child. When it comes to matters of infertility and conception, there are still a lot of things doctors don't know and cannot explain. That having been said, when a couple is confronted with infertility, they need to consider all their options. These options include:

- Remaining childless
- Adoption
- Fertility treatments

All options have setbacks and both adoption and fertility treatments can be expensive. The next question that comes up will be how long to pursue these avenues before they become financially exhausting or unfeasible. Many people want to adopt infants or try different fertility methods, but there are other things that can be considered that are less expensive and still result in care for a child. There are many older children who need adopting, and sometimes even multiple siblings in a family who do not desire to be separated. Looking for love, a home, a family, and a group identity, these children would love the opportunity to be a part of a loving home. There is also the world of foster parenting, which can also be a rewarding opportunity to take care of children who need immediate placement either temporarily or open the door to adoption.

Miscarriage

Exodus 21:22:

SUPPOSE TWO MEN ARE FIGHTING AND HIT [INJURE] A PREGNANT WOMAN, CAUSING THE BABY TO COME OUT [OR A MISCARRIAGE; THE HEBREW IS NOT CLEAR WHETHER DEAD OR ALIVE]. IF THERE IS NO FURTHER INJURY [HARM], THE MAN WHO CAUSED THE ACCIDENT MUST PAY MONEY— WHATEVER AMOUNT THE WOMAN'S HUSBAND SAYS AND THE COURT ALLOWS.

A painful and difficult loss for many couples is that of miscarriage, when, for whatever reason, a fetus is not viable to term and the result is a loss of pregnancy. Miscarriages can be physically painful for the woman as well as emotionally painful for the couple, as it represents a loss in their lives.

When a couple goes through a miscarriage, they need the time to grieve the loss, and the support of family, friends, and church. They need to know that this is not the end of everything good in their lives and marriage, and that they can support and comfort one another rather than blame each other. Miscarriage is something that just happens. It's not anyone's fault, and there is hope for newness of life and a new beginning after the period of pain and loss passes.

Being a part of extended family life

Once you are married (and especially after you have children, if you decide to do so), you have now extended your family beyond the borders of what you grew up identifying as "family" (those in your household). Now having a life that includes your biological family, you also have your spouse and their family. You probably also both have friends that you regard as family, people who will be a part of your life after you are married. This can all seem overwhelming, and especially at first, it can be difficult to keep track of who is who. It can also feel like you don't fit in, because you don't know anyone and feel uncomfortable interacting with this group of new people. The discomfort often comes because people expect to fit in with a family like they fit in with their significant other, who they have already gotten to somewhat know and are already comfortable with. Don't expect too much too soon. Take into consideration that families already have certain dynamics within their units, and it takes time to become included within those dynamics. Also, know your limits. Stand back and observe rather than trying to jump in uninvited. Some things are not your business, and some things are not your place to be involved. Let their own family matters be their own, and instead, show yourself polite, friendly, and courteous.

Just as within your own family, refrain from becoming a part of family drama. Do not closely involve yourself nor engage yourself with extended family members that are given to alcohol or drugs, and do not expose yourself to such in your own lifestyle. If someone is given to abuse or abusive conduct, keep your distance. If you are uncomfortable with someone who repeatedly solicits, mistreats, or abuses you, state your case to your future spouse and make it clear that while you have every regard for their right to be involved with different members of his/her family, you do not want to be involved with this member, and state why. If you are in this position, respect their decision and make it clear that you do not love him or her any less because of this.

Your own family members are also a part of this "extended family," because after marriage, you will not have the exact same relationship with them that you had before. Rather than running home to get away from problems all the time, it's important you try to work things out with your spouse directly (as much as is possible). You will probably also see your parents and older married relatives differently, because you will begin to understand the sacrifices and experiences they had as adults, as married people, throughout their lives. You will probably seek out their wisdom and experience as you go through things, and will learn to regard them as parents, grandparents, aunts, uncles, and married people, individuals who help you to grow and develop as you grow and change.

Job 1:4-5:

JOB'S SONS TOOK TURNS HOLDING FEASTS [ON THEIR DAY; PERHAPS BIRTHDAY CELEBRATIONS] IN THEIR HOMES AND INVITED THEIR SISTERS TO EAT AND DRINK WITH THEM. AFTER A FEAST WAS OVER, JOB WOULD SEND AND HAVE THEM MADE CLEAN [CONSECRATED; MADE HOLY]. EARLY IN THE MORNING JOB WOULD OFFER A BURNT OFFERING [AN ATONEMENT OFFERING; LEV. 1:1–17] FOR EACH OF THEM, BECAUSE HE THOUGHT, "MY CHILDREN MAY HAVE SINNED AND CURSED [BLESSED; A EUPHEMISM FOR "CURSED"] GOD IN THEIR HEARTS." JOB DID THIS EVERY TIME.

There will be great times when the extended family has a chance to be together, such as holidays (if you observe them), celebrations of life (such as the birth of a baby), Sunday or special family dinners (if you are close enough for this on a regular basis), and birthdays. Married couples who have two families that desire their time and celebration should set up a schedule in advance as to how they will divide their time and how they will celebrate events in a way that will be a blessing not just to their families, but to themselves, as well. Some people divide up the holidays (rotating between family members) or days around the holidays, while others prefer to hold events themselves and invite the relatives. Sometimes families rotate who host holidays or special events. However you decide to do this, do what is best for you and what gives all of you the opportunity to see and love your extended family.

Keeping your head with family advice

I am a big advocate in embracing familial advice, especially when it comes to older generations educating younger generations in family life and in their relationships. Older family members who have been through more and experienced more than younger ones often have a lot of wisdom and life experience that can assist in the bumps and uncertainties of married life. As you go through new phases and experiences in your marriage, you will most likely encounter things that you aren't prepared for or certain how to handle, and you will want to hear from other family members what you should or should not do.

Proverbs 12:15:

FOOLS THINK THEY ARE DOING RIGHT [THE PATH OF FOOLS IS VIRTUOUS/RIGHT IN THEIR OWN EYES],
BUT THE WISE LISTEN TO ADVICE.

Proverbs 13:1:

WISE CHILDREN TAKE THEIR PARENTS' ADVICE [SONS LISTEN TO THEIR FATHER'S DISCIPLINE/INSTRUCTION],
BUT WHOEVER MAKES FUN OF WISDOM [MOCKERS] WON'T LISTEN TO CORRECTION [A REBUKE].

Proverbs 13:10:

PRIDE ONLY LEADS TO ARGUMENTS [OR THE EMPTY-HEADED CAUSE ARGUMENTS OUT OF PRIDE],
BUT THOSE WHO TAKE ADVICE ARE WISE.

I think that as with all things, we need to keep a balanced approach when it comes to giving and receiving advice. I do not mean this in any sort of contradiction to what I just stated above. Family members with experience have a lot to offer and it's great to hear from generations of experience. They are there to listen and there to guide us and encourage us to not only be the best we can be as people, but as married adults, as well.

When it comes to receiving family advice, make sure that the intent of the advice is not to cause trouble in your marriage. This is a discernment call, and something that is usually read over time. Sometimes a relative just doesn't like your spouse, for whatever reason. Meddling parents and grandparents who just want to be overly involved are not going to be helpful; they are going to cause trouble. If advice or involvement is going beyond question or care, individuals need to be told that they need to mind their own business.

It's also important to remember that as adults, sometimes we should not need so much advice. In marriage and in parenting alike, sometimes we have situations that we just need to figure out on our own. It's great to know that someone is there to help us if we need it, but we should feel good about handling matters ourselves and being able to communicate with our spouses. If we rely too much on the advice of our relatives, that shows that we're not looking enough at our own ability to discern and read our relationship. If a relationship has grown so problematic that discernment is growing troublesome, it is time to look at the whole of the relationship rather than looking at immediate issues that seem to arise here and there.

Family members also need to respect the boundaries and limits in a marriage. They need to respect the fact that as a marital couple, you are going to need to have privacy, space, and the right to make your own decisions. Sometimes older advice, no matter how well-intentioned it might be, may not apply to issues of your own day and age. It's important to keep limits on offers of unsolicited advice and make sure that you aren't revealing too many private or situational details about your marriage to everyone else in your life. Within limits and boundaries, you show respect to both your elders and your spouse by keeping some things private, some opinions in perspective, and following solid and wise counsel.

Working together as a team

Ecclesiastes 4:9:

TWO PEOPLE ARE BETTER THAN ONE,
BECAUSE THEY GET MORE DONE BY WORKING TOGETHER [A GOOD RETURN FOR THEIR HARD WORK/TOIL].

1 Corinthians 3:9:

WE ARE GOD'S WORKERS, WORKING TOGETHER [COWORKERS BELONGING TO GOD; COWORKERS IN GOD'S SERVICE]; YOU ARE GOD'S FARM [FIELD], GOD'S BUILDING.

There are many different theories out there about what makes a marriage work and what kind of relationship a couple should have to make a marriage successful. The different advice ranges from the traditional to the modern, all coupled together with the personal perspectives of the person who is giving that advice. It's no wonder when, looking at things like this, why people are so confused about marriage and what really works in a marriage. People are quick to provide their testimony as to what they feel works for them, but if we truly look at the range of marital statistics, it is literally impossible to believe that what is presented really works for the average couple. In modern society, most couples cite being stressed out, under pressure, at odds, fighting, angry, and disillusioned with the entire marriage relationship. High numbers of couples' report infidelity and many more report wishing they had never gotten married. One partner is always angry about how they must cover bills, one is always angry about chores, and still yet there are frustrations regarding family interference or childcare.

There are problems in marriage today because we are all too fixated on who is the "boss" and who is going to do what the "boss says." Marriage was never created to be this competitive, mean-spirited competition where men dominate women and women feel the need to fight back. We need to step back and remember that we call spouses in marriage "partners" for a reason. The term "partner" represents a participation in the relationship in a supportive and helping capacity. Some people take grave issue with that concept, especially when it is applied to both a husband and a wife, but if people are in a marital relationship, they need to be partners. Marriage is a team effort, with neither the husband nor the wife as the "boss" or the team coach. The team coach of a true Christian marriage should be Jesus. Both should be making every effort to live the Christian life and display their genuine Christian affection and love for their spouse. That means both roll up their sleeves and do what needs to be done when it needs doing. Both do housework, both are attentive and interested in each other, both take care of children (if they have children) and both are productive. They need to be working together for the good of the relationship and to the end of its benefit. Rather than fixating on roles, if something needs to be done, somebody should do it, not bark orders at the other person. Marriage is not the place for an attitude.

Beyond marriage, if there are children in the home, they should imitate and follow the same rules that we are talking about for marriage partners. Children are a part of the family team, and should never, ever think that they are running the show in a house. They should have chores, know about the value of earning money, and respect the fact that if their parents must work, that means they have to pitch in and help, too. All of us grew up doing chores and none of us died from it. If anything, it helped us to be responsible individuals. Children today still need this structure and to learn the mindset that they are a part of a bigger unit, starting with their families, and that they need the structure and discipline to be productive people through chores and helping their parents out around the house.

Being involved in your church family

Some people stop going to church after marriage. Even though they might have been very disciplined Christians prior to marriage, serious and dedicated about Jesus and believing God for their lives, something about being married leads them away from their dedication to the Lord. Whether it's the concept that they were only seeking God to find a spouse, or they weren't seeking God right for themselves from the beginning, people who fall away from church after they get married need to fall back into church immediately, if not sooner.

It is not possible for your spouse to meet all the needs you have as a person. I don't care what pop psychology or even some preachers might have to say to the contrary. Marriage is not meant to isolate a couple from the larger world and larger society. If anything, marriage is meant to be a socializing factor that helps us to learn how to better interact with other people. Being in a marriage should help to give us the grounding to endure the ups and downs of life, and should inspire us to be more interested and involved in things that pertain to life, such as church.

Let's never forget Hebrews 10:25:

YOU SHOULD NOT STAY AWAY FROM [NEGLECT; FORSAKE] THE CHURCH MEETINGS [MEETING TOGETHER], AS SOME ARE DOING [SOME WERE

*ABANDONING CHRISTIANITY AND RETURNING TO JUDAISM], BUT YOU
SHOULD ENCOURAGE EACH OTHER [TO STAY FAITHFUL TO CHRIST AND TO
OTHER BELIEVERS], AND EVEN MORE SO AS YOU SEE THE DAY COMING [THE
DAY OF THE LORD, WHEN CHRIST WILL RETURN].*

Couples should attend church together. If attending together is not
an option due to work or other issues, then couples should attend
separately when needed, and together when it is an option. Both
husbands and wives should participate in men's and women's
events, continue to build up friendships, and continue to fellowship
with the body of believers. Marriage is a type of the relationship
that Christ has with the Church, which means we should always
and, in all things, keep in mind that participating in church is a part
of living the reality of our marital shadow. As we walk out our
relationship with God in our marriage, we need to recognize that
marriage is bigger than we are, and a true marriage will grow and
develop into all things that Christ truly desires it to be.

Week 4 Assignments

Answer the following questions based on discussions you have had with your spouse in counseling this week and additionally on your own time, and prepare to discuss them at your next counseling session. If you run out of room in a section, finish the answer to your question in your journal.

1. How would you describe your family life growing up? _____

_____

_____

_____

_____

2. What are some things have happened to you in your life to cause you to feel "dark, but lovely?" _____

_____

_____

_____

_____

3. What kind of a family did you have growing up? _____

_____

_____

_____

_____

4. How do you feel about single life? What kind of a single person would you describe yourself as being? _____

_____

_____

_____

_____

5. How do you feel about being a "two-person family?" _____

_____

6. Do you want children? _____ If so, how many do you want to have? _____

7. Is having children important to you? Why or why not? _____

_____

_____

8. Do you want to have children right away, or do you want to wait? What does "right away" or "wait" mean to you? _____

_____

_____

9. How would you feel if having your own biological children was not an option in this relationship? _____

_____

_____

10. How would you feel about your mate if they are, for whatever reason, unable to have children? _____

_____

_____

11. If infertility arises, what do you think is the best way to handle it? _____

_____

12. How do you feel about fertility treatments? _____

_____

_____

13. How do you feel about child rearing? Do you believe someone should stay home with the children after they are born? If so, for how long and who do you think it should be? _____

_____

_____

_____

_____

14. What would you do if you had a child with developmental or physical disabilities? _____

_____

_____

15. How do you feel about child discipline and what methods do you believe should be used? _____

_____

_____

_____

_____

16. How do you feel about family planning? _____

_____

_____

17. How do you feel about receiving advice from family members? What are some topics that would be "off limits" to them? _____

_____

_____

_____

_____

18. How do you think the couple in the Song of Solomon felt about family? How do you think they handled family matters? _____

_____

_____

_____

_____

19. In reading Ephesians 2:11-22, how does it change your perception of family and what family is? How can you better

participate in God's family as a part of your own family that you are preparing to start? _____

_____

_____

_____

_____

20. Get together with your future spouse and discuss how you will spend your special events (holidays, etc.) with your families. How can you best divide and share time between the two of them? _____

_____

_____

_____

_____

Month Two

GETTING TO KNOW YOUR WEDDING

Reading assignments:

- *Discovering The Beauty of Intimacy: A Journey Through the Song of Solomon*: Chapter 1 (Beyond the Superficial) and Chapter 2 (Women and Men)

Week Five

Planning Your Wedding, Part 1

I WILL REJOICE [DELIGHT] GREATLY IN THE LORD; ALL THAT I AM [MY SOUL] REJOICES [EXULTS] IN MY GOD. HE HAS COVERED ME WITH CLOTHES [GARMENTS] OF SALVATION AND WRAPPED ME WITH A COAT [ROBE] OF GOODNESS [RIGHTEOUSNESS], LIKE A BRIDEGROOM DRESSED FOR HIS WEDDING [OR WHO ADORNS HIMSELF WITH A HEADDRESS LIKE A PRIEST], LIKE A BRIDE DRESSED IN [ADORNS HERSELF WITH] JEWELS.
(ISAIAH 61:10)

<u>Bible reading:</u> John 2:1-11

<u>Journaling assignments for in-session discussion:</u>

- What component does intimacy play in a good marriage?
- How does intimacy make for a good wedding experience?

When Prince Charles and Princess Diana got married in 1981, the world stopped as it watched the royal wedding. The elaborate dresses, the pomp and circumstance, the cute flower girls and bridesmaids and the hope of a fairy-tale romance was alive and well in Charles and Diana. Even long after the marriage failed, the wedding was still infamous as the wedding of the century.

People are, as a rule, in love with the idea of being in love. They love the whole concept of weddings, of true love coming together in the form of a wedding, and they love the formality of the occasion. In a world that frequently seeks to buck tradition and break with it at every turn, weddings are a part of the past that we fully embrace. Families love the idea of passing down wedding dresses, celebrating with the bride and the groom, toasting the happy couple, and dancing the night away. Weddings are seen as the ultimate celebration of love, embracing great things and looking forward to future promises.

Weddings should be celebrations of love, not merely big social affairs or parties. If you have a relationship that is set right for marriage, then your wedding day will be an incredible expression of the love and joy you share as a couple. In the hustle of planning the wedding, that love should never be lost.

This week, we are going to look at the information you need to start planning your wedding and put together every needed detail to make your wedding exactly what you hope and pray it will be.

The components of a wedding

John 2:2:

AND JESUS AND HIS FOLLOWERS [DISCIPLES] WERE ALSO INVITED TO THE WEDDING.

Each wedding typically consists of three parts:

- **The rehearsal dinner**, which is the afternoon or night before the wedding ceremony. This wedding tradition gives everyone the opportunity to know what they will do during the ceremony, where they will stand, how they will walk in, and how they will dismiss. After the rehearsal dinner, the wedding party and the families of the bride and groom have an informal dinner, to relax and enjoy themselves, prior to the wedding day itself.

- **The wedding ceremony**, which is the formal ceremony in which the bride and groom are married.

- **The wedding reception**, which is the party or formal dinner celebrating the wedding of the bride and groom. It is typically open to either all who are invited to attend the ceremony or to those who are specifically invited to the reception.

The wedding you want

Romans 13:14:

BUT CLOTHE YOURSELVES WITH THE LORD JESUS CHRIST AND FORGET ABOUT SATISFYING [OR GIVE NO OPPORTUNITY TO THE DESIRES OF; OR DON'T THINK ABOUT WAYS TO GRATIFY] YOUR SINFUL SELF [THE SINFUL NATURE; THE FLESH].

There is no one way for someone to want a wedding, although most people do enjoy a celebration along with a ceremony. From the time people are young, they likely think, from time to time, about the wedding that they would like to have. Sometimes little kids play "getting married" where they pretend to marry each other, and sometimes boys or girls might play with dolls (especially the wedding set dolls) and pretend to "get married" through their dolls. The concept of fancy attire, formal settings, having all your friends and family gathered, and celebrating such a special occasion is something cherished, from the time kids are old enough to understand that a wedding is a time where the bride and groom are celebrated.

You might want the type of wedding you spent years thinking about, with many bridesmaids in pink dresses, a big, white wedding gown, many flowers, handsome groomsmen and the groom in elegant tuxedos, in a large, old church with a huge reception to follow. The dream wedding you always thought of may very well be the wedding you desire.

You might also want a more subdued, small event: something that is more minimal, that focuses more on you and your spouse with a small gathering of family or friends. Still, yet, you might not want much of a ceremony, just something that legalizes your relationship.

Whatever type of wedding you desire, there are several things that you need to consider in the process. These things include the wedding you can feasibly have, the wedding that won't distract from your relationship, and the wedding that glorifies God.

The wedding you can have

We just finished talking about the wedding you want to have. Whatever type of wedding you desire to have, you need to look at its financial feasibility and its practicality in line with the other things you desire to achieve and accomplish within your lifetime. There should be no question on anyone's mind that weddings can be very expensive. The bigger they are, the more expensive they become. Larger weddings also involve more people, require more planning, and more know-how to pull them off.

Proverbs 1:7:

KNOWLEDGE BEGINS WITH RESPECT [FEAR; AWE] FOR THE LORD, BUT FOOLS HATE [DESPISE] WISDOM AND DISCIPLINE [SELF-CONTROL; INSTRUCTION].

Large weddings do not necessarily equate to happy marriages, and they also do not necessarily equate to a better day. It is very important to assess your circumstances and have a wedding that will be practical for budget, for planning, and for accessibility. It is perfectly possible to have a beautiful wedding within a budget, and to have a ceremony that is both committed and celebrates the relationship you share with your future spouse.

The first thing that you need to do is objectively budget what you can afford with a wedding. Depending on whoever is going to absorb the cost, a discussion must be held about what is feasible for the wedding. This needs to be a mature discussion, handled in a mature fashion and without immaturity or tantrums. Married life is for adults, not for children. The first step of married life is a wedding, and in keeping with that, the budget of a wedding is an adult responsibility. It should never be assumed that someone else will cover the bill, so the wedding can be as outrageous as one person might desire. On the contrary, it should be approached with moderation and maturity and budgeted within what is most feasible.

The wedding that won't distract from your relationship

Sometimes people get so caught up in their weddings, they stop working on the essential relationship building that needs to occur right before a couple gets married. The relationship becomes all about the wedding, wedding planning, events, happenings, people, places, and things. It doesn't help when the wedding is a gigantic strain on the couple's resources, and they are unable to interact normally with one another.

Proverbs 2:20:

BUT WISDOM WILL HELP YOU BE GOOD [OR STAY ON THE PATH OF GOOD PEOPLE]
AND DO WHAT IS RIGHT [GUARD THE ROAD OF THE RIGHTEOUS].

If your wedding is so big or so unreasonable that you are ignoring your relationship as a couple, then the wedding is distracting from your relationship. This is the opposite of what weddings are supposed to be about. Your wedding is not all about you, but about your relationship with your partner. If too much of the wedding becomes about you or your partner exclusively, finding finances you do not have to fund it, or making a big fuss so other people will take notice of you or the other, then the wedding distracts you from your relationship, and it needs to be immediately scaled back.

The wedding that glorifies God

Weddings also need to be considered an act of worship before God, a submission of a couple before Him. When we talk about weddings, we often focus on the bride and the groom. The truth is that God's relationship with His people is always spoken of as a marital agreement. This means that whenever two people decide to get married, they need to recognize that what they are doing reflects their regard and relationship with God, as well.

This means that all our Christian principles, beliefs, and lifestyles should reflect in the wedding that we have and that we desire to have. Rather than being a prima donna or diva affair, weddings should be a celebration of life and love before God. A wedding or the suggestion of one should not send anyone on a collision course where their conduct and attitude becomes anything less than that which glorifies God and centers on Him.

Matthew 5:14-16:

YOU ARE THE LIGHT THAT GIVES LIGHT TO [FOR; OF] THE WORLD. A CITY THAT IS BUILT [STANDS; IS SET] ON A HILL CANNOT BE HIDDEN. AND PEOPLE DON'T LIGHT A LAMP AND THEN HIDE IT UNDER A BOWL [OR BASKET]. THEY PUT IT ON A LAMPSTAND SO THE LIGHT SHINES FOR ALL THE PEOPLE IN THE HOUSE. IN THE SAME WAY LET YOUR LIGHT SHINE BEFORE OTHERS [FOR PEOPLE TO SEE], SO THAT THEY WILL SEE THE GOOD THINGS YOU DO [YOUR GOOD DEEDS/WORKS] AND WILL PRAISE [GLORIFY; GIVE HONOR TO] YOUR FATHER IN HEAVEN.

Your wedding also should not distract you from Him, nor other people from Him. It should never be an excuse to stop fellowshipping with the saints, to stop going to church, or to cut back on your volunteer or financial responsibilities to the ministry. While it is understandable that a new couple needs some time to themselves after they get married, being married or having a wedding are not excuses for forsaking your relationship with God. It is still expected that, in marriage, you will spend time with God in worship and praise and remain a part of your church family. Abandoning God or deciding that you don't have time for Him proves a wedding or a spouse to be an idol... and we all know what the Scriptures teach about idols!

How you treat people

In the last section, I tapped a little bit into the issue of being a Christian and having or planning a wedding. We all know that as Christians, our relationship with God extends far beyond our personal devotional time or the time we spend at church. When planning a wedding, most people interact with many different people, including wedding professionals, family, friends, and church staff members. The experience that people have as pertain to your wedding does not begin and end on the wedding day, but in the planning process. So many forget that planning a wedding or being married does not nullify you from being and behaving like a

Christian. There are certain behaviors that, no matter how excited you may be to get married, are never, ever acceptable:

- Being rude or impatient with staff for the wedding
- Acting like a "diva" or a "don"
- Behaving in a negative way and then blaming it on the fact that having a wedding means "it's your day"
- Flashing your engagement ring or the status of your engagement in other people's faces in a flashy manner
- Throwing tantrums when you don't get your way
- Retaliating against people who are unable to attend the wedding
- Acting unseemly toward those who do not send a gift or money
- Expecting special treatment for weeks on end because your wedding is approaching
- Dismissing people from the wedding because you have suddenly started finding faults with them
- Rubbing your impending marriage in the face of those who are unmarried.

Galatians 5:22:

BUT THE SPIRIT PRODUCES THE FRUIT OF [FRUIT OF THE SPIRIT IS] LOVE, JOY, PEACE, PATIENCE, KINDNESS, GOODNESS, FAITHFULNESS [OR FAITH], GENTLENESS, SELF-CONTROL.

Even though society has justified and even glorified such behavior with television shows and merchandising, being a nightmare bride or groom is not a proper way to behave for a Christian. The Scriptures teach us that our conduct is to be love, joy, peace, patience, kindness, goodness, faithfulness, gentleness, and self-control. That applies just as much when it is time to have a wedding as it does after the wedding. Don't make the mistake of thinking that your pre-wedding conduct has no effect on your marriage. How you act, interact, and relate to others as well as your soon-to-be spouse has a lot to do with the way your spouse will perceive you once the wedding is over. If you want to have a good marriage, you need to make sure that your pre-wedding character reflects the way you want your spouse to perceive you after marriage.

Sorting out payment

Ecclesiastes 7:11-12:

WISDOM IS BETTER WHEN IT COMES WITH MONEY [AN INHERITANCE].
  THEY BOTH HELP THOSE WHO ARE ALIVE [IT IS AN ADVANTAGE TO THOSE WHO SEE THE SUN].
WISDOM IS LIKE MONEY:
  THEY BOTH HELP [THE PROTECTION/SHADE OF WISDOM IS IN/OR LIKE THE PROTECTION/SHADE OF MONEY].
BUT WISDOM IS BETTER,
  BECAUSE IT CAN SAVE [GIVE LIFE TO] WHOEVER HAS IT.

The traditional stipulations for weddings revolved around a dowry, or a large sum of money that was paid by a future groom to a future bride's father or her parents. It was typically done in the form of money or goods. As a part of the deal, and often using part of the dowry, the father would pay, in full, for the wedding. The purpose of the wedding was to solidify the business deal, the sale of the daughter for the dowry price.

Yes, you heard me right, the groom bought the bride. That's why fathers paid for their daughters' weddings, and why they were traditionally so eager to get rid of their girls. As part of the tradition, women changed their last names to their husband's family name, because they went from being the property of the father to the property of their husband. Girls were not going to be able to inherit family property or continue it in their family names and were not going to be eligible for other land inheritances or property transfers. This meant that parents often wanted to get rid of their daughters as quickly as possible. Weddings and marriages were often arranged between families, sometimes without the consent of either party (and most usually without the female's consent), and done to represent alliances between families.

All of this becomes relevant because we don't live in times where we recognize weddings as being business exchanges or property transfers between families. As a rule, most people in developed nations select their own spouses, and many live together prior to marriage, thus already having pre-established households.

Even those who don't live together often have employment, income, and the ability to pay for things on their own. We don't live in a world anymore where children are mere extensions of their parents, or dependents on their family for expenses. Individuals are, likewise, far older than they were in ancient times when it comes to marriage. In the days of old, girls were married off as soon as they had their first period, usually somewhere between twelve to fourteen years old. This is not the case anymore, which means that marriage, as we understand it in our modern contexts, is different than in ancient times.

This requires an examination for us when it comes to planning a wedding. If we aren't getting married to uphold ancient customs, we shouldn't expect the financing to fall within ancient parameters.

Therefore, wedding financing should be discussed upon engagement with both families, and an arrangement should be made that accommodates everyone. The following things should be considered when determining who is going to finance the wedding:

- If the couple is living together and not married, the parents on either side are under no financial obligation to cover the wedding, but have the option to do so, if they want to participate.
- If the groom's family wants to be involved in the wedding and in paying, then the groom's family and bride's family should cover equal parts of the wedding.
- Out of courtesy, the couple should also contribute to part of the wedding, if that is an option, and if it is agreeable to all parties.
- The couple also has the option to, regardless of the circumstances, cover the financial issues related to the wedding, to ensure the wedding they desire to have is done according to specifications.
- The more that someone pays for the wedding, the more say they expect to have in the event, and the more they expect to be able to use the wedding as a social medium as they see fit.

Within the wedding itself, the following costs need to be assessed:

- Invitations

- Rehearsal dinner venue
- Ceremony venue
- Reception venue
- Reception menu
- Decorations
- Flowers
- Reception entertainment (band, etc.)
- Cake
- Gifts for people in the wedding party
- Transportation for wedding party (from ceremony to reception)
- Attire for the wedding party
- Offering for minister/presider of ceremony
- Honeymoon destination and cost
- Any additional expenses that may occur

The three main questions of any wedding experience

Proverbs 16:3:

DEPEND ON THE LORD IN WHATEVER YOU DO [COMMIT YOUR ACTS/DEEDS TO THE LORD],
AND YOUR PLANS WILL SUCCEED [BE ESTABLISHED].

Once the issues related to finances are settled, planning needs to begin for the wedding itself. There will be numerous issues to be solved and decided, and to consider those issues, there are three key things that must be established prior to anything else:

- What size wedding do you desire to have?
- Where do you desire to have the wedding?
- When do you plan on having the ceremony?

This wedding workbook is designed to handle issues within four months of your established wedding ceremony date. That does not mean, however, that you must hold off on planning details of your wedding until four or five months before your wedding. Obviously, if you are getting married within the next four months, you probably have some semblance of a date, the kind of wedding you want to have, and where you plan on having the ceremony. These issues are important, because wedding venues often require booking months, if not years, in advance.

To pick the venue, you need to know how large you intend your wedding to be. Weddings are typically sized as follows:

- 75 guests or less: small wedding
- 75-150 guests: medium wedding
- 150 guests or more: large wedding

Wedding size is often determined by budget. The larger a wedding is, naturally, the more expensive it becomes. Large weddings are often regarded as social events, gatherings that are designed to generate social notoriety and help promote careers and professional networking. Smaller weddings are often more about the couple and their immediate friends and family, attending and celebrating with those that they are closest to and associated with. Medium weddings are somewhere in the middle, incorporating both factors into the guest list and event feel.

The size of the event often determines where you desire to have your wedding. Keep in mind that large weddings require large spaces to hold the ceremony and even larger ones for the wedding reception after the ceremony. Some people desire to have the wedding at a church they attend, or a church where relatives got married, and some still desire more secular places, such as museums, hotels, cruises, or other destination wedding locations. Some people have the reception where they have the wedding, and others divide things up and have them in multiple locations. Some people get married where they live, others in their hometown or somewhere else, still. Make sure location is clarified to guests, and require RSVPs from all invited guests to determine an exact number of guests

The "when" of the wedding often comes about because of availability for venues. Most places request a couple provide three dates for a wedding and coordinating the "when" if you are dealing with separate places for the ceremony and the reception can often require booking months in advance. When you decide where you want to have your wedding, call that location, giving plenty of advanced notice, to find out what the requirement is and how long of a waiting list they have.

Some general advice when planning the venue, date, and size of the wedding:

- **Make sure you can accommodate your guests**: If the venue only holds so many people, don't invite more people than the venue holds. Whether large or small, people notice when shortcuts are taken, and needs are overlooked. Make sure that, within the bounds of the budget, all your guests can be fed, served, and comfortable throughout the experience.

- **Don't feel like you must do what everyone else does to have a great wedding**: If you don't want to have a big reception, a big ceremony, or something that requires so many people involved, don't feel like you must do it. Do what works for you, because this is your wedding.

- **You know what you can handle... don't exceed that**: Even if someone else is offering to pay for your wedding, that doesn't exclude you from involvement. I highly recommend that you do not allow the wedding to go beyond the boundaries of your own comfort, no matter who is paying for it. If it becomes an issue, then take over the financial aspect of the wedding yourself. Don't let your wedding turn into something stressful and unpleasant.

The guest list

Matthew 22:2-3:

THE KINGDOM OF HEAVEN IS LIKE A KING WHO PREPARED A WEDDING FEAST [BANQUET] FOR HIS SON. WHEN THE FEAST [BANQUET] WAS READY, THE KING SENT HIS SERVANTS TO TELL [INFORM; CALL] THE PEOPLE WHO HAD BEEN INVITED, BUT THEY REFUSED TO COME.

A wedding guest list is just what it sounds like – the list of the people who will be invited to attend the wedding ceremony and the reception, if you are having one, the other, or both. If you are going to have invited guests, both the bride and groom should contribute to that list (dividing it up as needed, typically half each between both sides of the family), to share the special day with friends and relatives.

There are a few things to consider when it comes to the guest list. Once you have settled on the number of people at the wedding, you need to decide if you want people to attend the ceremony, the reception, or both. Sometimes people desire a more intimate ceremony and a large party, or vice versa. If you want certain people at one part of the event, or both parts, or even none of the parts of the wedding, you need to consider that carefully.

Second, you need to clarify if you will allow children to attend the ceremony or reception. It is completely acceptable to state that you do not want children at either, for whatever the reason, unless they are in the wedding party.

Third, you need to expect that not everyone you invite will be able to attend the wedding. Every invitation should require an RSVP date and expect that individuals will notify you either way if they are able to attend the wedding, or not.

Fourth and most important, start by inviting those you truly want to attend, and then work outwards. Don't randomly invite a bunch of people whose presence doesn't matter.

Next week, we are going to look at who you want in your wedding, and why. Having settled these major issues, you are able to focus more on the more intimate details of the wedding and make sure that anyone you want involved is able to participate with you.

Week 5 Assignments

Answer the following questions based on discussions you have had with your future spouse in counseling this week and additionally on your own time and prepare to discuss them at your next counseling session. If you run out of room in a section, finish the answer to your question in your journal.

1. What are the three components of a wedding and which ones do you desire to have in your own wedding experience? _____

_____

_____

_____

_____

2. What kind of wedding do you want? Describe it in detail. _____

_____

_____

_____

_____

3. Is this wedding feasible for you to have? Why or why not? _____

_____

_____

_____

_____

4. Is there anything about the wedding that you want that will distract you from God or is already distracting you from God? _____

_____

_____

_____

_____

5. Is there anything about the wedding that is distracting you from your future spouse? _____

_____

_____

_____

_____

6. If you answered "yes" and explained what they are above, what can you do to change the wedding to help with these issues? _____

_____

_____

_____

_____

7. How are you treating people since you got engaged? How can you treat people better, reflecting better Christian character, in this process? _____

_____

_____

_____

_____

7. How will you handle payment of your wedding? _____

_____

8. Why is this the way you want to handle the finances of your wedding? _____

_____

9. What size wedding do you desire to have? _____

10. Where do you desire to have the ceremony? _____

11. When do you plan on having the ceremony? _____

12. Will you be able to accommodate your guests? How can you make sure that this is possible? _____

_____

_____

_____

_____

13. Will you be able to handle the wedding you are planning on having? _____

14. What are some specific ways you will be able to combat and handle the stress that will come from wedding planning? _____

_____

_____

_____

15. How do you intend to sort out the guest list? Who are five people that you know you definitely want at your wedding (aside from the wedding party)? _____

_____

_____

_____

16. How do you intend to handle communication about wedding issues with your future spouse and your family? _____

_____

_____

_____

17. What do you look forward to most in your wedding? _____

_____

_____

_____

18. How do you think the couple in the Song of Solomon planned their wedding? Do you think of them as being a traditional or a non-traditional couple? Why? _____

_____

_____

_____

_____

19. In reading John 2:1-11, why do you think Jesus chose a wedding to perform His first miracle? What does this tell you about weddings and wedding parties? How can you make sure that Jesus wants to be a guest at your wedding? _____

_____

_____

_____

_____

20. Get together with your future spouse and your families and decide how you are going to sort through the finances, guest list, venue, and date for your wedding. What conclusions have you come to? _____

_____

_____

_____

_____

Week Six

Planning Your Wedding, Part 2

THE SUN COMES OUT LIKE A BRIDEGROOM FROM HIS BEDROOM [WEDDING CHAMBER]. IT REJOICES LIKE AN ATHLETE [STRONG MAN] EAGER TO RUN A RACE.
(PSALM 19:5)

<u>Bible reading:</u> Matthew 22:1-12

<u>Journaling assignments for in-session discussion:</u>

- How can a wedding reflect the intimacy of a couple?
- What are some of the barriers to intimacy, and how can solid pre-wedding preparation help avoid those barriers in a marriage?

Last week, we talked about the most essential aspects of wedding planning: finances, venue, size of wedding, and guest list. Those are things that many people do not consider before they go into a wedding experience, and as a result, they often overspend on the wedding or wind up in extremely stressful situations that they are unable to handle. It is not God's desire that weddings turn into such difficult and uncomfortable situations. God calls us to do all things decently and in order, and that includes our weddings. Starting with such foundational aspects of the wedding will make sure that the wedding is reasonable, able to be properly executed, and well-handled by those involved in it.

Wedding planning doesn't end there, however. There are still many, many details to cover as pertain to the wedding, and we are going to talk about the majors of these details this week. After we conclude this week, many of the main decisions of the wedding should be covered. There will still probably be many minor details that will need ironing out, and that you will need to discuss, as they arise. After this week, however, most essential details will be sorted out, and you will have a great point to go forward with as you plan the rest of your special experience.

The wedding industry

1 Kings 9:16:

(IN THE PAST PHARAOH, KING OF EGYPT HAD ATTACKED AND CAPTURED GEZER. AFTER BURNING IT, HE KILLED THE CANAANITES WHO LIVED THERE. THEN HE GAVE IT AS A WEDDING PRESENT [DOWRY] TO HIS DAUGHTER, WHO MARRIED SOLOMON.

My mom often tells me stories of weddings she attended as a child in the 1940s. Back then, weddings were done completely between the families, from the decorating, to the venue, to the dress, to the food and catering. Weddings were small affairs (unless done involving royalty or political figures), with people the bride and groom knew personally, and their extended families.

If we fast-forward to today, weddings are far grander for the average person than they were even 70 years ago. The reason for this is simple: the subsequent generations have been exposed to many high-powered and elaborate weddings through television, movies, Hollywood, and the grand schemes through the rich and famous. The more we've seen these weddings, the more we think that we should have them, too. The result: Weddings have become an industry. Gone are the days when weddings were simple, as my mother described to me from her childhood. Now weddings require big venues, planners, elaborate meals, and expensive entertainment. The expectations people have about weddings are now manifest in an entire money-making industry that centers around weddings: planning them, having them, and working them.

What we don't often consider is that no matter how much we might like to believe the contrary, celebrities and very wealthy individuals aren't like the rest of us. They have more money, they don't follow the same rules that the rest of society follows, and they are able to get away with and do things that most people would never be able to imagine. By blindly following the trends that the lifestyles of the rich and famous can start, many have gotten in over their heads when it comes to weddings.

The flip side of this is that the wedding industry can make your wedding planning much easier than it might have been at another time. Even though the drive for such has caused weddings to become very expensive, the wedding industry has made it relatively easy. If you have the money, the wedding industry can match your unique interests and needs with any of their various options.

One of the standard aspects of the wedding industry is the wedding planner (sometimes called wedding coordinator). Wedding planners do exactly what it sounds like they do: they plan weddings. The wedding planner meets with the couple, gets the general idea of what they are looking for, and orchestrates the wedding from start to finish. If you can't afford a wedding planner, do not despair. There are plenty of things you can do, on your own, that can handle the job without having to consult an outside professional.

The wedding's "inner circle"

Proverbs 1:31:

SO YOU WILL GET WHAT YOU DESERVE [EAT FROM THE FRUIT OF YOUR PATH];
YOU WILL GET WHAT YOU PLANNED FOR OTHERS [OR BE SATISFIED WITH YOUR OWN COUNSEL].

We usually use the term "inner circle" to denote those who are closest to us and are our most trusted companions. When it comes to your wedding, there should be three to four people who are there to help you execute this wedding, especially if you are not hiring a wedding planner. They should be:

- Your mom or another trusted, close, female relative (sister, aunt, etc.) who can be involved in the process.

- The maid-of-honor
- The best man
- One other individual who can help to bring the wedding to fruition.

This inner circle consists of your wedding decision-makers. They are the people that you discuss what you want done and how you want it done and can trust that if you give them a task, they can make the decisions needed to handle that task within the bounds of your instructions. Beyond your wedding's inner circle, there may be many people who participate in the wedding, offering various help or volunteering to assist. That's fine, and they are more than welcome to help. This does not mean, however, that these people should be given decision-making power, as those in your inner circle are. You can have many people who help, but you need to make sure that those who are given the ability to make and execute decisions are people you can trust and who understand the general theme and work of the wedding. A true inner circle will report what they have done and execute it exactly as stated, so make sure that the duties and responsibilities are clear. Knowing you have people you can trust, and you can rely on will make all the difference as you move forward with your wedding plans.

The wedding party

Psalm 45:14:

IN HER BEAUTIFUL [EMBROIDERED] CLOTHES SHE IS BROUGHT TO THE KING.
HER BRIDESMAIDS [VIRGINS] FOLLOW BEHIND HER,
AND THEY ARE ALSO BROUGHT TO HIM [HER FRIENDS FOLLOW].

Your wedding party consists of the people who will be involved in the wedding ceremony. They consist of:

- The minister/civil agent for the ceremony
- Bride
- Groom
- Mother of the Bride

- Father of the Bride
- Mother of the Groom
- Father of the Groom
- Maid of Honor
- Bridesmaids
- Best Man
- Groomsmen
- Ring bearer
- Flower girl

Aside from these main players in the wedding, you may also be required to provide individuals who perform the following duties:

- Usher
- Decorating crew
- Clean-up crew
- Dressing attendants

Deciding who will be in your wedding party decides on the size of your wedding. Some people opt to have their ceremonies without a large party, just consisting of the bride, the groom, and the minister. Other people prefer only a maid of honor and best man, while others might desire to have a few people involved in the wedding but keep it small. Keep in mind that it's your wedding, and who you want in the wedding is who should be in the wedding. It's not a time to return many favors and try to keep up with everyone else. Have the size wedding you know you can have and know that you will be blessed in the joy of your experience.

Selecting people is often hard for couples. The best way to determine who should be in your wedding party is to start by deciding who the most important people are in your life. Who are the people you want to share this moment with? Who do you want involved? Family members and friends are obvious choices, as are sisters and brothers in the Lord. Selecting those who mean the most, and who being involved will mean something to, too.

Who traditionally does what in a wedding

2 Chronicles 35:4:

PREPARE YOURSELVES BY YOUR FAMILY GROUPS [DIVISIONS] FOR SERVICE, AND DO THE JOBS THAT KING DAVID AND HIS SON SOLOMON GAVE [WROTE DOWN FOR] YOU TO DO.

Even though there aren't a lot of rules nowadays about who is allowed to do things in a wedding, many like to know the traditional roles people played in a wedding to figure out who will do what in their wedding.

- **Maid of honor:** Handles parties and showers for the bride, adjusts the bride's train at the altar, signs the marriage license, holds the bride's bouquet during the wedding vows, collects monetary gifts for the couple, holds onto the groom's wedding ring, and helps the bride prepare for the ceremony.

- **Best man:** Makes sure groom is at the ceremony on time, pays the minister, signs as a witness for a marriage license, and holds onto the bride's wedding ring.

- **Bridesmaids:** Assists with wedding duties and plans parties for the bride.

- **Groomsmen:** Assists best man with planning parties for the groom. Sometimes they also do the work of ushers in a wedding ceremony.

- **Mothers of the bride and groom:** The mothers of the bride and groom are given ceremonial positions of honor in weddings. Traditionally, it was the mother of the bride who did most of the "wedding planner" duties and was the reception hostess. The mother of the groom often got involved and participated in some capacity, especially attending the bridal shower and rehearsal dinner along with the rest of the family.

- **Flower girl:** Throws flower petals or carries a small bouquet down the aisle before anyone else walks down it.

- **Ring bearer;** A young boy who carries a small pillow with wedding rings on it. Nowadays this role is usually ceremonial, using fake rings, so the real ones do not fall or turn up lost.

- **Train bearers:** Young children who carry an extra-long train down the aisle.

- **Toasts:** Father of the bride, groom, best man, bride, and chief bridesmaid

Colors

Song of Solomon 7:5:

YOUR HEAD IS LIKE MOUNT CARMEL [A PROMINENT, ROUNDED, AND ATTRACTIVE MOUNTAIN],
    AND YOUR HAIR IS LIKE PURPLE CLOTH [A ROYAL COLOR];
    THE KING IS CAPTURED [ENSNARED] IN ITS FOLDS.

Most weddings have "colors," or theme colors that will be used for attire and decorations. The bride and groom typically select two or three colors that will be used for accents, flowers, ribbons, accessories, dresses, drapery, place settings, ties, vests, and other touches that make the wedding unique.

Colors aren't typically selected based on sentimental or traditional reasons. Usually, they are factored by availability of material or items in specific colors and by the colors people like or favor. Sometimes colors are selected based on time of year (for example, a winter wedding might be silver and blue, while a Christmas wedding might be red and gold) or on location (a beach wedding might have seafoam and tan while a church wedding might have ivory and dark blue). Also, make a point to pick colors that will accentuate people who wear them, rather than picking the stereotypically awful colors (such as swamp green or hot pink) that nobody looks good in. Whatever colors you pick, know they are going to permeate your wedding, so make sure they are colors you like and can both agree on.

Flowers

Song of Solomon 1:14:

MY LOVER IS LIKE A BUNCH [CLUSTER] OF FLOWERS [HENNA BLOSSOMS; PLEASANT SMELLING AND USED TO DYE HAIR RED] FROM THE VINEYARDS AT EN GEDI [A ROMANTIC LOCATION WITH A WATERFALL NEAR THE DEAD SEA].

Flowers are typically selected to match the wedding's theme colors. They are usually selected for sentimental value as well as a liking that flower. Flowers may also be considered due to the time of year (poinsettias at Christmas, lilies in the spring, roses in the summer) or location of event (tropical for a cruise wedding, garden flowers for a garden wedding).

Attire

Matthew 22:11-14:

"[BUT] WHEN THE KING CAME IN TO SEE THE GUESTS, HE SAW A MAN WHO WAS NOT DRESSED FOR A WEDDING [IN WEDDING CLOTHES]. THE KING SAID, 'FRIEND, HOW WERE YOU ALLOWED TO COME IN HERE? YOU ARE NOT DRESSED FOR A WEDDING.' BUT THE MAN SAID NOTHING [WAS SPEECHLESS/SILENT]. SO THE KING TOLD SOME SERVANTS, 'TIE THIS MAN'S HANDS AND FEET. THROW HIM OUT INTO THE DARKNESS [DARKNESS OUTSIDE; OR OUTERMOST DARKNESS], WHERE PEOPLE WILL CRY AND GRIND THEIR TEETH WITH PAIN [THERE WILL BE WEEPING AND GNASHING OF TEETH; SYMBOLS OF AGONY AND TORMENT].'

"YES [FOR], MANY ARE INVITED [CALLED], BUT ONLY A FEW ARE CHOSEN."

Wedding attire is a big, booming business. Between the wedding dress, dresses for the wedding party, and tuxedos for the groom and the groomsmen, formal wear for weddings can run thousands of dollars. Next to the venue and entertainment, clothing is often the most expensive aspect of a wedding.

How "Christian" should I be in my marriage?

BEING EXCESSIVELY DEMANDING AND BOSSY WITH YOUR SPOUSE. TREATING YOUR PARTNER AS IF THEY ARE YOUR SLAVE. IGNORING HOUSEHOLD CHORES. STRIPPER POLES IN THE BEDROOM. PRETENDING YOUR SPOUSE IS A PROSTITUTE. ALL OF THESE THINGS HAVE SOMETHING IN COMMON (AND NO, IT'S PROBABLY NOT WHAT YOU ARE THINKING). ALL OF THESE TOPICS RELATE TO ATTITUDES AND CONCEPTS THAT PEOPLE HAVE ABOUT MARRIAGE, AND ADVICE THEY GIVE AS PERTAINS TO MARRIAGE. THERE ARE PEOPLE WHO THINK THAT, IN MARRIAGE, IT IS COMPLETELY ACCEPTABLE TO TREAT YOUR SPOUSE ANY WAY YOU WANT, TO BE DEMANDING OR DEMORALIZING, FROM THE TABLE TO THE BEDROOM. THEY FEEL THAT ONCE YOU ARE MARRIED, THERE ARE NO PERSONAL BOUNDARIES, AND THAT ANYTHING – AND EVERYTHING – GOES FOR THAT COUPLE.

WHEN YOU ARE MARRIED, YOU ARE STILL A CHRISTIAN, AND YOU ARE STILL CALLED TO RESPECT THE PERSONAL BOUNDARIES AND DIGNITY OF YOUR PARTNER. THAT MEANS NO BARKING ORDERS AT YOUR SPOUSE, NO TREATING ANYONE AS IF THEY ARE A SLAVE, NO IGNORING HOUSEHOLD CHORES, AND NOT TREATING YOUR SPOUSE AS IF THEY ARE A STRIPPER OR A PROSTITUTE. IF YOU ARE A CHRISTIAN, YOU ARE STILL ONE IN YOUR MARRIAGE, AND YOU ARE STILL CALLED TO CONSIDER YOUR SPOUSE AS A HUMAN BEING. THAT DOESN'T STOP BECAUSE YOU GET MARRIED!

I don't have much advice to give on picking out clothing for a wedding. I believe that people's tastes are different, and the way a person desires to dress for their wedding should reflect their tastes. Beyond this, selecting wedding attire should fall into the same category as picking out any formal clothing. Good judgment and sense should still apply, and clothing should not be inappropriately fitting, immodest, uncomfortable or improper. Wedding clothing should be, for all purposes, something you would be comfortable wearing to church.

Attire should also match the venue. If you are having a beach wedding, the clothing should be different from that worn in a church wedding, and so on and so forth. Make sure everything goes together, and that guests are informed of appropriate attire for the venue.

Rings

Genesis 24:22:

AFTER THE CAMELS HAD FINISHED DRINKING, HE GAVE REBEKAH A GOLD RING [NOSE-RING; OR EARRING] WEIGHING ONE-FIFTH OF AN OUNCE [ONE HALF SHEKEL] AND TWO GOLD ARM BRACELETS WEIGHING ABOUT FOUR OUNCES [TEN SHEKELS] EACH.

In most societies, married couples wear wedding rings as a symbol of their commitment to one another. The circular nature of the wedding ring represents eternity, symbolizing a love that never ends.

Not all couples choose to wear wedding rings, for any variety of reasons. This doesn't make them any less married, nor any less committed to one another. However, many couples do choose to wear the wedding ring, and most select their rings in advance of their wedding.

How wedding rings are selected depend on the couple. Some match their wedding rings around the engagement ring, some select certain metals or designs, and others like certain stones. If you decide to have wedding rings, make sure they are purchased and in your possession prior to your wedding ceremony date.

The wedding reception

Matthew 22:8-10:

AFTER THAT, THE KING SAID TO HIS SERVANTS, 'THE WEDDING FEAST [BANQUET] IS READY. I INVITED THOSE PEOPLE, BUT THEY WERE NOT WORTHY [DO NOT DESERVE] TO COME. SO GO TO THE STREET CORNERS [CROSSROADS; OR MAIN ROADS] AND INVITE EVERYONE YOU FIND TO COME TO MY FEAST [BANQUET].' SO THE SERVANTS WENT INTO THE STREETS AND GATHERED ALL THE PEOPLE THEY COULD FIND, BOTH GOOD AND BAD

[EVIL]. AND THE WEDDING HALL WAS FILLED WITH GUESTS.

If you are planning on having a wedding reception, a good amount of your wedding plans will go into this aspect of your wedding experience. A wedding reception is usually the party or celebratory aspect of a wedding, held after the wedding ceremony.

Wedding receptions range from simple, intimate dinners to large, wild affairs. Typical elements of a wedding reception include:

- **Dinner** (or some type of food served; some serve appetizers and *hors d'oevures* as well as the meal, and sometimes the formal meal is skipped)
- **Music**
- **Dancing** (father of the bride/bridal dance, mother of the groom/groom dance, first dance of the bride and groom)

The honeymoon

Deuteronomy 24:5:

A MAN WHO HAS JUST MARRIED MUST NOT BE SENT TO WAR [WITH THE ARMY] OR BE GIVEN ANY OTHER DUTY. HE SHOULD BE FREE TO STAY HOME FOR A YEAR TO MAKE HIS NEW WIFE HAPPY [20:7].

The last major detail that is nowadays considered a part of the wedding package is the honeymoon. Traditionally a honeymoon trip was an opportunity for a new couple to spend time alone together and relax after their wedding. In modern times, honeymoons are often opportunities to take trips, because the honeymoon trip is often a gift given to the bride and groom as part of the wedding. Even though this is not always the case and not all couples go on honeymoons, couples often do take the time to enjoy each other in some form or another after their wedding.

If you plan to take a honeymoon trip, this planning should run concurrently with wedding plans, so all is handled prior to the wedding. The honeymoon should also be budgeted and considered as a wedding detail.

Special details

1 Corinthians 14:33:

[FOR] GOD IS NOT A GOD OF CONFUSION [DISORDER] BUT A GOD OF PEACE.

Many weddings contain unique elements that place the couple's unique touch on the experience. Some desire to have special food served as part of their reception, or have special songs played at the ceremony or reception or have someone sing a song. Whatever your "special details" are, let those be known so your wedding day can be as special and unique as your relationship.

Other details

1 Corinthians 14:40:

BUT LET EVERYTHING BE DONE IN A RIGHT [PROPER; FITTING] AND ORDERLY WAY.

You can add, subtract, or reform any of the standard wedding procedures as you desire, because this is your wedding. If you want a traditional element or a not-so-traditional one, remember, this is your wedding, and any way you desire to handle this is optional. Incorporate what is important to you, represents your relationship, and celebrates your lives together, any way you desire to do so.

Week 6 Assignments

Answer the following questions based on discussions you have had with your future spouse in counseling this week and additionally on your own time, and prepare to discuss them at your next counseling session. If you run out of room in a section, finish the answer to your question in your journal.

1. Do you intend to have a wedding coordinator? How will you work out the details of your wedding, either way? _____

_____

_____

_____

_____

2. Who will be in your wedding's "inner circle?" _____

_____

_____

_____

3. What are some of the things you will have your "inner circle" handle in your wedding preparations? _____

_____

_____

_____

_____

4. What are your wedding colors going to be? _____

5. What are your wedding flowers going to be? _____

6. Who will be the people involved in your wedding party, and what will they do? _____

_____

_____

_____

_____

7. Will you have to provide individuals to serve in additional duties? If so, who will they be and what will they do? _____

_____

_____

_____

_____

8. What made you decide to select the people that you selected for service in your wedding? _____

_____

_____

_____

_____

9. Who is going to do what in your wedding? Are you going to follow traditional format, or start a new tradition? _____

_____

_____

_____

_____

10. Do you have clothing already picked out for the wedding? What are people going to wear (styles, colors)? _____

_____

_____

_____

_____

11. Are you going to wear wedding rings as a married couple? Why or why not? If so, what style wedding ring will you be purchasing?

_____

_____

_____

_____

12. What kind of a wedding reception do you plan on having (if any)? _____

_____

_____

_____

13. What kind of food do you plan on having at the reception? _____

_____

_____

_____

_____

14. What kind of music will you have at the reception? Will you have a band? _____

_____

15. Will there be dancing at your wedding? What about other forms of entertainment? _____

_____

16. What are you planning for a honeymoon? How can this trip help your relationship with your future spouse? _____

_____

_____

17. What are some special elements you would like incorporated into your wedding ceremony and reception? _____

_____

_____

_____

18. How do you think the couple in the Song of Solomon selected their wedding party? Why do you think the people they chose were special to them? _____

_____

_____

_____

_____

19. In reading Matthew 22:1-2, why do you think a wedding banquet is used to symbolize such an important detail about the Kingdom of God? What message do you hear, as someone planning a wedding, in that parable? _____

_____

_____

_____

_____

20. Get together with your spouse and your "inner wedding circle" to discuss the details you have laid out in your workbook this week. How did that meeting go? When are you planning to meet again?

_____

_____

_____

_____

_____

Week Seven

Your Wedding Ceremony

<u>Bible reading:</u> Luke 14:7-11

<u>Journaling assignments for in-session discussion:</u>

- How do weddings reflect our humility before God, and each other?
- How do intimacy and humility relate to each other?

We've spent a good part of the second phase of pre-marital counseling looking at the details of the wedding itself, in its entirety. Parts of planning have probably been tiresome and intense as every little detail is explored and scoured to be complete. Sometimes it can be hard to negotiate details (especially when you have been envisioning something for your entire life) with many other people involved. It can also be frustrating if a wedding vision must be scaled back or changed due to limited resources.

The good news: you have covered many of the details, and your date is approaching! This week, we are going to look at an aspect of the wedding that is often a lot of fun for couples, and that is the wedding ceremony. Because the wedding ceremony is typically associated with tradition, many don't realize you can shake up and change portions of the ceremony to explore your own unique style and expressions as a couple.

Wedding ceremonies don't have to be stiff, formal, or traditional. You can incorporate as many traditional elements into a wedding, along with contemporary ones, if the legal aspects of a wedding ceremony are fulfilled. This week, it's time to get with your minister and find out just what you would like to have at your wedding ceremony to make it uniquely yours.

What makes someone "legally married?"

Ecclesiastes 8:4:

WHAT THE KING SAYS IS LAW [SUPREME]; NO ONE TELLS HIM WHAT TO DO [SAYS TO HIM, "WHAT ARE YOU DOING?].

To understand the wedding ceremony, we must first understand the legalities of weddings and what actually makes people married from a legal perspective. In modern times, being married is about more than just living with someone or even sharing a life with someone. Being married is also a legal status, which entitles couples to certain rights and legal benefits.

Believe it or not, the thing that gives married couples those legal rights and status is not the ceremony itself, nor the party after, but a document that is signed and then filed with the state or county where one resides. This document is known as a marriage license, and it is a legal form that is filled out with essential information about the couple and their marital status, which enables them to be recognized as a legal entity.

Each state does have its own unique requirements as pertaining to filings for marriage licenses, so prior to your wedding ceremony, make sure you speak with your minister about the legalities in the state where you reside. Some states have requirements about waiting periods, blood tests, and required documentation. Make sure that all information is acknowledged and provided so that the wedding can go forward as planned, all within the specified period.

For a marriage license to be valid, it must contain the following elements:

- Both individuals must be of legal age (usually 18 in most jurisdictions), or have their parents' consent if underage
- Couples cannot be closely related
- Neither person can be married to another person at the time of licensure
- The names of both persons who desire to be married
- The signature of the officiate of the ceremony
- The signature of two witnesses

This means the ceremony, while a traditional expression and a spiritual solemnity to mark the occasion, is not the very thing that declares a marriage legal in the eyes of the law. There are two ways people look at this. The first is to think that ceremonies are unnecessary. This type of couple goes to city hall and gets married on a lunch break or in a very small, legal sealing that often has two witnesses present, and no more. There is nothing wrong with wanting to skip out on the ceremony, if that is how you feel about your wedding. There is another way to view the ceremony, however, if you are interested in having one. If the legality is out of the way, that makes the wedding ceremony an opportunity to do something really unique and special that marks your own relationship. It's a chance to show something spiritual and purposeful, that is all your own, and to display your own relationship with God as two individuals becoming a couple.

Have weddings always been legal?

The marriage license, as we understand it today, is a newer element in the legality of weddings. Weddings have always been legal ceremonies, however, even though they did not involve formal documentation. Weddings were, prior to modern times, a celebration of property transference. The woman became the property of her husband, bought by him and his family, and sold by her father. The wedding, thus, became a "deal sealing" between all the parties, and signified the alliances made through marriage between the families. Even though the process might not have involved paperwork, the process was considered legally binding, legally valid, the wedding was a bridge between the bride's former life and her adult life. An example of this can be seen in Matthew 1:18-19:

THIS IS HOW THE BIRTH OF JESUS CHRIST [THE MESSIAH] CAME ABOUT. HIS MOTHER MARY WAS ENGAGED [PLEDGED; BETROTHED; A FORMAL AGREEMENT BETWEEN FAMILIES THAT REQUIRED A "DIVORCE" TO ANNUL] TO MARRY JOSEPH, BUT BEFORE THEY MARRIED [CAME TO LIVE TOGETHER], SHE LEARNED SHE WAS [OR WAS FOUND/DISCOVERED TO BE] PREGNANT [WITH CHILD] BY THE POWER OF [THROUGH] THE HOLY SPIRIT. BECAUSE MARY'S HUSBAND, JOSEPH, WAS A GOOD [RIGHTEOUS] MAN, HE DID NOT WANT TO DISGRACE HER IN PUBLIC, SO HE PLANNED TO DIVORCE HER [END THE ENGAGEMENT] SECRETLY [PRIVATELY; QUIETLY].

What identified marriage in past times was co-habitation. If the man and the woman were living together after a wedding celebration, they were considered "married." The woman became a part of his family and his life, and if he were to die, especially without giving birth to a son, it would send her own life into a state of chaos. Because there was no paperwork and inheritances often fell through paternal lines, the rights of inheritance and property were not clearly defined for couples. The main goal of marriage was seen as procreation, especially to bear a male heir. Marriage sealed paternal lines, ensured that offspring were a part of that family, and that property would transfer from father to son. This entire deal was solidified by the wedding, where a young girl was escorted from her father's house to her husband's home, in an elaborate ceremony.

Who can perform a marriage ceremony?

Haggai 2:11:

THIS IS WHAT THE LORD ALL-POWERFUL [ALMIGHTY; OF HEAVEN'S ARMIES; OF HOSTS] SAYS: 'ASK THE PRIESTS FOR A TEACHING [ABOUT THE LAW; FOR GUIDANCE/INSTRUCTION].

If you are reading this book, you most likely already have a pastor, apostle, or other spiritual leader in your life, and they will probably perform your ceremony. If for some reason your immediate spiritual leader is not performing your ceremony, wedding ceremonies must be performed by the same "officiator" who signs your marriage license. If it is a minister, they must be validly licensed and ordained, with certificates to prove their legality to the ministry. Otherwise, a ceremony is performed by a secular justice of the peace, judge, magistrate, or other civil servant who can legally sign and officiate for the rite.

Communicating about the ceremony

Genesis 29:27:

BUT COMPLETE THE FULL WEEK OF THE MARRIAGE CEREMONY WITH LEAH [THIS ONE], AND I WILL GIVE YOU RACHEL [THE OTHER ONE] TO MARRY ALSO. BUT YOU MUST SERVE ME ANOTHER SEVEN YEARS."

Most ministers are open to the idea of incorporating new and different elements into a wedding ceremony, if they are not in any way blasphemous or disruptive to the spiritual atmosphere of the wedding. As a rule, they also have a standard format or basic wedding outline they follow, which can be modified or added to. Don't be afraid to speak up! The minister who officiates your ceremony needs to hear your feedback and learn what you want and are thinking about. If you are unsure of something or need some suggestions, that's what he or she is there for.

Compensating the officiator

It's easy to assume that a spiritual leader is doing the wedding ceremony for you and it's an easy job, but if you have someone who is taking the time to do pre-marital counseling, iron out details, and establish a spiritual foundation for the two of you as a couple, that involves doing much, much more than just performing a ceremony. Most of the time, leaders don't ask for a specified amount when so involved with a wedding, especially if the couple is a part of the church. Performing a wedding is outside of the normal bounds of tithes and does require a special offering. Even if you aren't asked, you need to set aside money in your wedding budget to compensate the minister who takes the time to officiate, because they are making an extra investment within you.

2 Corinthians 9:7:

EACH OF YOU SHOULD GIVE AS YOU HAVE DECIDED IN YOUR HEART TO GIVE. YOU SHOULD NOT BE SAD WHEN YOU GIVE [OR GIVE RELUCTANTLY], AND YOU SHOULD NOT GIVE BECAUSE YOU FEEL FORCED TO GIVE [OUT OF COMPULSION]. [FOR] GOD LOVES THE PERSON WHO GIVES HAPPILY [CHEERFULLY].

Do not, I repeat, do not skimp on your offering to the minister. Ministers take time, expense, and effort to make sure you have the wedding you desire. If you can find the money for thousands of dollars to have your wedding, you can give a financial gift to the minister. To calculate your investment, consider doing a tithe on the budget for your wedding to provide an offering to the officiator. If your wedding costs $10,000, then you should give an offering of $1,000 to the minister. Whatever the total is, figure out a tithe from it, and give that to whoever is sowing into your life spiritually and officiating your wedding throughout this process.

In addition, it is generally understood that the officiator is also a guest and should be invited to the wedding reception and treated like any other guest there. They should be provided with a meal and can spend time with the bride and groom's family and friends, like any other guest.

Standard elements of a wedding ceremony

Jeremiah 2:2:

GO AND SPEAK TO THE PEOPLE OF JERUSALEM [ANNOUNCE/PROCLAIM IN THE EARS OF JERUSALEM], SAYING: THIS IS WHAT THE LORD SAYS:

I REMEMBER HOW FAITHFUL YOU WERE TO ME WHEN YOU WERE A YOUNG NATION [YOUR LOYALTY/DEVOTION AS A YOUTH/GIRL/CHILD].
    YOU LOVED ME LIKE A YOUNG BRIDE.

YOU FOLLOWED [WENT AFTER] ME THROUGH THE DESERT [WILDERNESS; AS THEY TRAVELED FROM EGYPT TO THE PROMISED LAND], A LAND THAT HAD NEVER BEEN PLANTED [SOWN].

Each wedding has the option to be different, so you may find you want all these elements or some of them and might want to mix your own thoughts and ideas into the ceremony.

- **Processional:** The wedding party enters the church
- **Introductory remarks:** The minister invites everyone to the ceremony, talks a little bit about marriage, and identifies the couple by name
- **Giving away of the bride:** The bride is given to the groom by her father (or another male relative) or her parents, and the opportunity is made for anyone who has objection to the wedding to speak
- **Prayer:** Minister offers prayer
- **Sermon:** Minister offers sermon
- **Special selection selected by bride and groom:** Can be a song, a Scripture reading, a poem, something they would like to say, or someone they would like to do those things for or with them as part of the ceremony
- **Wedding vows:** Couple either reads vows they wrote themselves while incorporating traditional vows into the ceremony, or the couple responds to traditional vows with "I do"
- **Ring vows:** Rings are presented to and exchanged by the couple
- **Unity candle ceremony:** A candle symbolizing unity is presented and lit from two smaller candles by the couple
- **Communion:** Communion ceremony is held
- **Pronouncement:** Couple is proclaimed as married
- **Embrace:** Groom kisses bride
- **Pronouncement:** Minister presents couple as husband and wife
- **Closing prayer:** Minister prays
- **Recessional:** Wedding party leaves the church

Suggestions on making the ceremony unique

John 3:29:

THE BRIDE BELONGS ONLY TO THE BRIDEGROOM. BUT THE FRIEND WHO HELPS THE BRIDEGROOM [OR THE BEST MAN] STANDS BY AND LISTENS TO HIM. HE IS THRILLED [REJOICES GREATLY] THAT HE GETS TO HEAR THE BRIDEGROOM'S VOICE. IN THE SAME WAY, I AM REALLY HAPPY [MY JOY IS FULFILLED; IN THIS ANALOGY, JOHN IS THE BEST MAN AND JESUS IS THE BRIDEGROOM].

- **If you're not real traditional, eliminate the section where the bride is given away:** Many people opt out of this portion of the marriage ceremony because it denotes the bride as property and that she is not consenting to the marriage of her own free will and volition. Because the custom has so many connections to ancient practices that are opposite of modern sensibilities, not to mention because it doesn't fit within the theme of many queer wedding ceremonies, many people opt to remove this portion of the service or somehow reword it to be about expanding family rather than buying and selling a person.

- **Write your own vows:** One of the best ways to make a ceremony your own is to write your own vows. In writing vows, just write a few lines that speak your true heart about your relationship and your hopes for the future of your relationship. The only condition: the other person can't see or hear them before the wedding!

- **Have a short tribute to your family (even your church family) and friends who helped to make you the people you are:** It doesn't have to be long, a skit, something drawn out, or something intense, but a few words that thanks family and friends, spoken from your own mouths, can really add a personal touch to an event.

- **When it is time for "special selection," mix it up a bit:** Don't think you can only do one thing. It is generally understood the service shouldn't be extensively long, but there is enough time in a wedding ceremony to include a Bible passage selection, a special song sung by someone who is close to you, and a few remarks. Pick a few short things to make your ceremony "pop."

- **Don't rush through the ceremony:** Sometimes people are so stressed on account of a wedding, they want to hurry it along and get it over with. Enjoy the ceremony as much as you enjoy any other part of your wedding experience.

Week 7 Assignments

Answer the following questions based on discussions you have had with your future spouse in counseling this week and additionally on your own time and prepare to discuss them at your next counseling session. If you run out of room in a section, finish the answer to your question in your journal.

1. What are the requirements for legal marriage in the state where you reside? _____

_____

_____

_____

_____

2. Are you prepared to file for legal marriage? What steps do you have to take? _____

_____

_____

_____

_____

3. How do you feel about wedding ceremonies? Do you desire to have one? Why or why not? _____

_____

_____

_____

4. What kind of a ceremony do you want to have (traditional, non-traditional, somewhere in the middle)? _____

5. How do you envision your wedding ceremony? _____

_____

_____

_____

_____

6. Who will your minister be?_____

7. Does your minister have the proper credentials to perform your ceremony? _____ If not, will they by the time the wedding date arrives? _____

8. How did you select your minister for the ceremony? Why are they important to you in this process? _____

_____

_____

_____

9. What are some things you want your minister to know about the wedding ceremony? _____

_____

_____

_____

_____

10. How much of an offering will you make to the minister who is presiding over your wedding? _____

11. Do you believe compensating the minister who does your wedding is important? Why or why not? _____

_____

_____

12. What standard elements of the wedding do you desire in your own ceremony? _____

_____

_____

_____

_____

13. What are some non-traditional elements that you desire in your wedding? _____

_____

_____

_____

_____

14. Will you be writing your own vows? Why or why not? _____

_____

_____

_____

15. What kind of special selection would you like in your wedding?

_____

_____

_____

16. Will you read or desire Bible passages to be read? If so, which ones? _____

_____

17. Will a song be played or someone singing a song? If so, what song, and who will sing it? _____

_____

18. Do you believe it is important to have communion at the ceremony? Why or why not? _____

_____

19. In reading Luke 14:7-11, why do you think God used a wedding banquet to teach on humility? _____

_____

_____

_____

_____

20. Get together with your spouse and minister to discuss the details you have laid out in your workbook this week. How do you feel it went? How do you feel about your planned wedding ceremony? __

_____

_____

_____

_____

_____

Week Eight

Keeping God in Your Wedding

LET US REJOICE AND BE HAPPY [EXULT] AND GIVE GOD [HIM] GLORY [HONOR],
BECAUSE THE WEDDING [MARRIAGE] OF THE LAMB HAS COME, AND THE
LAMB'S BRIDE HAS MADE HERSELF READY.
(REVELATION 19:7)

Bible reading: Matthew 25:1-13

Journaling assignment for in-session discussion:

- Why is wedding imagery frequently used to describe the time before Jesus returns?

We've spent this entire month looking at the details of your wedding. Now we want to spend this last week of the month looking at the most important component of any wedding and, ultimately, any marriage: God. A couple of weeks back, we discussed a little bit about having a wedding that glorifies God, and now we are going to talk more in-depth about keeping God center in your wedding. Yes, God is the forgotten component of so many relationships, we can't rightly say we have a wedding without involving God. Every good dynamic present in relationships comes from God Himself, Who is love. If we try to talk about weddings and marriages without God, we lose the essential component of love that talks and teaches us about relationships and what they are really about.

Jeremiah 2:32:

A YOUNG WOMAN DOES NOT [DOES A VIRGIN… ?] FORGET HER JEWELRY [ORNAMENTS],
AND A BRIDE DOES NOT [DOES A BRIDE… ?] FORGET THE DECORATIONS FOR HER DRESS.
BUT MY PEOPLE HAVE FORGOTTEN ME
FOR MORE DAYS THAN CAN BE COUNTED.

The wedding imagery has been used throughout the Bible to teach us certain spiritual things that we need to know and prepare ourselves for, because they are soon to come. That means every time we have a wedding or go to a wedding, we should be looking at that experience as a type, or shadow, pointing us to something else. We should be looking at God's truth every time talk of a wedding comes up. Since we are talking about your own wedding, this is an interesting time to look at the types present in weddings and how you can, as a couple, accentuate these themes in your own wedding experience.

What is a "type" or a "shadow?"

Hebrews 10:1:

THE LAW IS ONLY AN UNCLEAR PICTURE [SHADOW] OF THE GOOD THINGS COMING IN THE FUTURE; IT IS NOT THE REAL THING [REALITY ITSELF; TRUE IMAGE OF THEM]. THE PEOPLE UNDER THE LAW OFFER THE SAME SACRIFICES EVERY YEAR, BUT THESE SACRIFICES CAN NEVER MAKE PERFECT THOSE WHO COME NEAR TO WORSHIP GOD.

All of us have walked around on a sunny day and seen the long, black image cast of us along the sidewalk. That black image is a shadow, and it is created when the sun hits something that is not transparent (the sun can't shine through it). That shadow points to the fact that something is there, but it is not actually that thing. It is nature's way of pointing out that an object is present, it is not transparent, and if you are walking in the bright sun, you need to make sure that you don't run into it.

Spiritual shadows, or types, as they are sometimes called, do the same thing, only on a spiritual level. Spiritual types and shadows point us to realities and prove that those realities are there, but they are not, in and of themselves, those exact things. They remind us that God is with us, and working for us, even though we can't see Him and we can't always see His plan. I often call types and shadows as little bits and pieces of God at work, revealing Himself to us, as we look around and see the types that point us to greater realities.

Romans 5:14:

BUT FROM THE TIME OF ADAM TO THE TIME OF MOSES, EVERYONE HAD TO DIE [DEATH REIGNED/RULED], EVEN THOSE WHO HAD NOT SINNED BY BREAKING A COMMAND, AS ADAM HAD [IN THE LIKENESS OF ADAM'S DISOBEDIENCE/TRANSGRESSION]. ADAM WAS LIKE [A TYPE/PATTERN/PREFIGUREMENT OF] THE ONE WHO WAS COMING IN THE FUTURE.

Colossians 2:17:

THESE THINGS WERE LIKE [ARE] A SHADOW OF WHAT WAS TO COME. BUT WHAT IS TRUE AND REAL HAS COME AND IS FOUND IN CHRIST [OR THE REALITY/SUBSTANCE BELONGS TO CHRIST; THE BODY (IS) OF CHRIST].

Hebrews 8:5:

THE WORK THEY DO AS PRIESTS [OR THE SANCTUARY IN WHICH THEY SERVE] IS ONLY A COPY [MODEL; PROTOTYPE] AND A SHADOW OF WHAT IS IN HEAVEN. THIS IS WHY GOD WARNED MOSES WHEN HE WAS READY TO BUILD THE HOLY TENT [TABERNACLE]: "BE VERY CAREFUL TO MAKE EVERYTHING BY THE PLAN [PATTERN; DESIGN] I SHOWED YOU ON THE MOUNTAIN [EX. 25:40]."

Most typology courses focus on different types and shadows present in the Old Testament that point to Jesus. They look at things, such as the water in the rock, the Passover lamb, the manna from heaven, and the person of Moses. What we don't often consider is that there are types and shadows of all sorts of things in the Old Testament that are revealed in the new, and not all those types and shadows have to do with Jesus. There are types and shadows of the Ephesians 4:11 ministry, of the church, of issues in the church, and even of things that are still to come. Types are all around us; they are seen in nature, in nurture, and in many of the spiritual things we do in our everyday lives.

In the context of this book, weddings are spiritual types of the ultimate Marriage Supper of the Lamb. We have often been taught that the wedding banquet of the Lamb will be held at the very end of time, and this is not incorrect if we look at things very literally. I think, though, that we need to consider the Marriage Supper of the Lamb is ongoing, with communion as a part of that supper. Daily people are added to the Kingdom, which means daily we are being prepared and purposed to meet and participate in that powerful meal. Every time a soul comes to Christ, there is a spiritual "wedding" of sorts. We are united with God, and He with us, and the Wedding Supper of the Lamb is the ultimate reception banquet celebrating that union with Him. In the meantime, we have plenty of rehearsal dinners, celebratory moments, ceremonial experiences, and opportunities to love our Lord and celebrate with Him. Thus, every wedding we go to and experience should point us to this powerful and purposed reality.

As you prepare for your wedding, you should always keep in mind that your wedding is a type of our relationship with God and that your banquet is preparing others to receive and learn about the wedding supper of the Lamb. It's not just an experience that is all about you, but points to something else that is very powerful and important. Your wedding can be something that helps inspire people in their own spiritual walk, illustrate important truths, and guide people into the ultimate reality that God wants us to be committed to Him out of love, as He is committed to us.

Weddings in Bible times

Luke 1:26-28:

DURING ELIZABETH'S SIXTH MONTH OF PREGNANCY, GOD SENT THE ANGEL GABRIEL [1:19] TO NAZARETH, A TOWN IN GALILEE, TO A VIRGIN. SHE WAS ENGAGED TO MARRY [PLEDGED TO; ENGAGEMENT WAS A BINDING

CONTRACT BETWEEN TWO FAMILIES AND COULD ONLY BE BROKEN BY DIVORCE] A MAN NAMED JOSEPH FROM THE FAMILY [A DESCENDENT; FROM THE HOUSE] OF DAVID. HER [THE VIRGIN'S] NAME WAS MARY. THE ANGEL CAME TO HER AND SAID, "GREETINGS [HELLO; REJOICE; A COMMON GREETING]! THE LORD HAS BLESSED YOU AND IS WITH YOU [OR … FAVORED ONE, THE LORD IS WITH YOU]."

Weddings in Bible times were as I spoke of in an earlier chapter. They signified business deals (passing the daughter as property to her husband), familial alliances, political alliances, and celebrations of life. Marriages were arranged and engagements were typically long (usually a year or more) in order to give young brides a chance to adjust to the idea of married life. Marriages were announced after a girl went through her first menstrual cycle, and women were not given any choice in who they were going to marry. Grooms were usually a good deal older than their brides (at least ten years), which doesn't sound like a lot, until we consider the bride was somewhere around twelve to fourteen years old. The entire purpose of life was survival and continuation of family lines, and marriage was an essential part of that purpose.

The period that transpired between acceptance of the dowry and the actual wedding was much more official in Biblical times. Once the bridal price had been paid, there was no legal way to escape the ceremony without formal divorce paperwork filed. This period was known as "betrothal," and many couples went through a trial period, of sorts. There were many instances where the woman would live with the future husband and his family, for the sake of an adjustment period, prior to the wedding. The relationship remained unconsummated and would remain as such until after the formal wedding took place (obviously an existing variation in customs). During the betrothal period in New Testament times, the future bride would be offered something of expense, such as a gold ring, symbolizing the "signet" or official nature of the relationship. Prior to the wedding, the bride would be returned to her father's house to prepare, with the bridegroom coming to formally escort her to his family's house, followed by celebration, joy, gladness, and prayers for the couple to be fruitful and purposeful, and covered by God's provision and love.

Should we be polygamous (or polyamorous) today?

IN 1843, JOSEPH SMITH, THE LEADER OF THE MORMON CHURCH (MORE COMMONLY KNOWN AS THE CHURCH OF JESUS CHRIST OF LATTER-DAY SAINTS) SHOCKED MOST OF MAINLINE SOCIETY BY WRITING A DOCTRINE OF "PLURAL MARRIAGE" INTO HIS CHURCH'S ESSENTIAL CODES. HE TAUGHT THAT THEIR DEITY WAS MARRIED TO AN INFINITE NUMBER OF SPIRIT WIVES, SO FOR THE MEN OF HIS CHURCH TO ALSO BECOME GODS, THEY HAD TO BE MARRIED TO MULTIPLE WOMEN. EVEN THOUGH THIS DOCTRINE SOUNDS ABSURD TO THE MAJORITY OF CHRISTIANS (AND WE WOULD NEVER THINK PEOPLE OF MAINLINE DENOMINATIONS WOULD DO SUCH A THING), WOULD YOU BE SHOCKED TO LEARN THAT THERE ARE SMALL SUBGROUPS OF BAPTISTS, NON-DENOMINATIONALS, AND EVEN MESSIANIC AND HEBREW ROOTS ADHERENTS WHO ALSO EMBRACE ONE FORM OF POLYGAMY OR ANOTHER? THEY ALL HAVE DIFFERENT REASONS FOR DOING SO, AND MANY ARE PARTICULARLY DEFENSIVE OF THIS DOCTRINE, FEELING THAT IT IS A RIGHT PROTECTED UNDER AMERICAN LAW AS WELL AS BIBLICALLY BASED.

THERE IS NO QUESTION THAT POLYGAMY WAS AN ANCIENT PRACTICE EMPLOYED BY PEOPLE WHO LIVED IN BIBLE TIMES. THERE IS ALSO NO QUESTION THAT POLYGAMY WAS PRACTICED BY MANY KEY OLD TESTAMENT FIGURES. BY THE TIME OF THE NEW TESTAMENT, POLYGAMY WAS STILL PRACTICED BY A GOOD PORTION OF JEWS, AND IN PART BY SOME GREEKS AND ROMANS (ALTHOUGH ROMAN CULTURE WAS LARGELY MONOGAMOUS). THERE ARE EVEN PARTS OF THE WORLD WHERE POLYGAMY STILL EXISTS, AND IN MORE MODERN WESTERN CULTURE, WE NOW SEE THE TREND OF POLYAMORY, OR A RELATIONSHIP CONSTRUCT WHERE A MARRIED PARTNER OR INVOLVED INDIVIDUAL HAS THE OPTION TO HAVE SEXUAL OR INTIMATE RELATIONSHIPS WITH MORE THAN ONE PARTNER AT A TIME (NOT NECESSARILY ONLY THE MALE, AS IN THE CASE OF POLYGAMY). EVEN THOUGH POLYGAMY IS, FOR THE MOST PART, ILLEGAL IN THE WESTERN WORLD, THAT IS NOT STOPPING PEOPLE FROM FINDING WAYS TO PURSUE MULTIPLE SEXUAL PARTNERS AND RELATIONSHIPS OUTSIDE OF LEGAL ENTITIES.

POLYGAMY EXISTED IN THE BIBLE TO SHOW IT AS A CULTURE OF THE TIMES. IT PROVED THAT EVEN THOUGH PEOPLE WERE NOT PERFECT AND ADHERED TO THE CULTURE OF THEIR DAY, GOD STILL USED THEM AND MOVED IN THEIR LIVES. IF WE LOOK AT THE STORIES OF POLYGAMOUS RELATIONSHIPS, HOWEVER, NONE OF THEM WERE PARTICULARLY SUCCESSFUL. IF ANYTHING, THEY WERE QUITE COMPLICATED, COMPLEX, AND DISASTROUS. WE SEE POLYGAMY IN THE BIBLE TO PROVE THAT THESE RELATIONSHIPS SHOULD NOT EXIST, AND DO NOT LEAD TO LIFE. GIVEN POLYGAMY WAS NEVER INTENDED TO BE A PART OF GOD'S LAW (IT WAS SOMETHING ADAPTED BY CULTURE) AND IT DOES NOT COINCIDE WITH OUR CULTURAL LAWS TODAY, IT IS NOT SOMETHING CHRISTIANS SHOULD PRACTICE.

This is a basic principle of weddings and entering marriage as was present in the ancient world. Wedding customs also changed greatly between Genesis and Revelation. Isaac's wedding experience when he married Rebecca was completely different than Mary's experience when she married Joseph in New Testament times. Ruth and Boaz had a completely non-traditional experience surrounding their engagement and wedding. If there is one thing where we see change in the Bible, it is in the interactions surrounding weddings. The Bible shows us the entire expanse of relationship options: couples, polygamy, concubines, incest, divorce, adultery, prostitution, large families, small families, infertility, single people, widows, and widowers. To say that there is only one form of Biblical marriage, family, or relationship is highly incorrect.

So, the question remains: why does the Bible show us so many different types of weddings, marriages, and relationships? There are many who believe such is a justification for any and all types of relationships, but I don't believe that's the case. God has set us order in our relationships, and our goal in them is to glorify Him. I believe God showed us the bad along with the good to show us that disordered relationships don't work. Even in the best of relationships and most ideal circumstances, the Bible still shows us that people are people, and they don't always do right by their mates or in their relationship settings. God shows us that there is a human side to every relationship, and that means people make their own choices to pursue relationships that are harmful, unhealthy, or against His own precepts. It also shows us the reality that relationships, even under the best of circumstances, are hard. While weddings can be joyous, they don't predict people's future behaviors, trials, or issues.

God wanted us to be fully prepared for what would lie ahead in our relationships, so instead of being full of fairy tales, we see realistic couples, realistic weddings, and realistic marriages. That's God's gift to us: the gift of reality. Wedding customs, the details surrounding weddings, have changed since Genesis and will change further, until Jesus comes back.

What weddings in the Bible teach us

In the covers of the Bible, we hear hints of weddings, but we only have experiences recounted from a few of them. Even though the

Bible often tells us people got married or had a wedding ceremony, we don't hear much about it. People in Biblical times knew the different wedding customs, so the implications therein went along with the story they told. That makes the weddings we do see in the Bible very special and very important and very revealing to us about important things pertaining to weddings.

- **Jacob, Leah, and Rachel (Genesis 29:13-30):** Although not the most ideal wedding circumstances by any stretch of the imagination, the story of Jacob's wedding to Leah gives us insight into weddings of ancient times and how they were arranged. Jacob, the ultimate deceiver, was deceived by Laban, receiving Leah in marriage rather than Rachel. The thick veil covering Leah's face during the ceremony, the arrangements that only involved Jacob and Laban (rather than Rachel or Leah), and the great feast all give us a cultural idea about how weddings and marital arrangements were handled. In this story, God illustrates to us how important consent is in relationships and that all who are involved in a wedding do so of their own choice. Jacob, Leah, and Rachel paid for this deception throughout the rest of their marriage.

- **Wedding at Cana (John 2:1-12):** The wedding feast at Cana was the first public miracle of Jesus. The reason why such a venue was chosen for such a poignant miracle was simple: not only were many people present, but it was also a perfect opportunity to "type" the relationship present between God and the church, and to prepare the church for the wedding of the church and Christ. It proves that God is interested in every aspect of our lives, even our relationships and the mundane things like whether we can be hospitable to our guests, and that He loves us enough to make however much we have enough, as we are transformed by Him.

- **Parable of the Wedding Banquet (Matthew 22:1-14 and Luke 14:15-23):** More than once, Jesus used the example of a wedding to teach a spiritual lesson. One of the greatest spiritual examples is the Parable of the Wedding Banquet, where we find a man inviting many people to his son's wedding, but the people who were invited refused to come for a vast number of reasons (all of which boil down to claiming to be "too busy). This was despite the fact that turning down an invitation to a wedding was considered a great insult. He tries again, only to find his servants mistreated and killed by the people who were invited to come to the wedding. Instead of having those people, who might have looked right on paper but were clearly unworthy of the honor attend the banquet, they went out and found anyone they could find come to the wedding. The poor, the unpopular, anyone who was there – was able to come in. When someone was found dressed improperly, he was thrown out – reminding us that many are called, but few are chosen.

This parable tells us that at the Wedding Supper of the Lamb, there are now and will be a lot of people who we don't consider the "first" or "best choice" to be there. There are plenty of people who might seem like the right choice to be there, who won't attend. They have all sorts of reasons why they can't come, but the bottom line is they just don't want to be there and it is not important enough to them to show up. The "second string" might not be our first choice, but it is who God intends and believes needs to be there. We are also reminded of the importance in showing up properly and with order. Everyone knew about proper attire when it came time for weddings, and there was no excuse for coming in a manner that was not in accord with the guidelines. We, too, all need to remember protocol and come before the Lord in all things, decently and in order, with respect to the One Who invites us and with excitement and haste, realizing nothing is more important than being present at God's Table.

- **Wise and Foolish Virgins (Matthew 25:1-13):** We've all heard the story of the wise and foolish virgins, but many of us overlook the fact that this parable takes place at a wedding. The "virgins" in the story were young women who were attendants of the bride, awaiting the bridegroom to come and escort the bride to his home. The wise virgins brought extra oil for their lamps in case the bridegroom was late, while the foolish virgins didn't bring any extra and expected the wise to "help" them out at the last minute. Obviously a story to teach us about being ready and prepared for the second coming of Christ, the fact that it happened during a wedding – and that we have so much discussion about the Wedding or Marriage Supper of the Lamb – tells us that the time when we are forever with the Lord in the Second coming is our wedding with Him, as a church.

- **Admonition to watchfulness (Luke 12:35-40):** A parallel to the command to be watchful as found in Matthew 25:1-13, Jesus' admonition to watchfulness is compared, once again, to a wedding and to waiting for the bridegroom's arrival.

- **Marriage Supper of the Lamb (Revelation 19:6-10):** The Wedding Supper of the Lamb is typed throughout the New Testament, as you can see from the other wedding examples we have seen. This wedding banquet, or wedding supper, follows Jesus' return and restoration of all things after the fall of Babylon. It is a celebration of the church's union with Christ and of the fact that we shall be together with the Lord, describing the bride as the church, and Christ as the groom. This is an ultimate promise, to be included in this eternal celebration and song, throughout time and eternity.

Every wedding that we have in this realm is preparing us for that wedding banquet. Every wedding we experience, every type in marriage, should be pointing us to that great spiritual reality to come after Jesus returns. No wedding should be just about the bride and groom, but about glorifying God and seeking Him in a deeper way as we seek Him in everything – including weddings and marriages – that we do.

Our position before God

Matthew 25:21:

THE MASTER ANSWERED, 'YOU DID WELL. YOU ARE A GOOD AND LOYAL [FAITHFUL] SERVANT. BECAUSE YOU WERE LOYAL [FAITHFUL] WITH SMALL

[A FEW] THINGS, I WILL LET YOU CARE FOR [PUT YOU IN CHARGE OF] MUCH GREATER [MANY] THINGS. COME AND SHARE MY JOY WITH ME [ENTER INTO THE JOY OF YOUR MASTER].'

Weddings should cause us to look in a deeper way at our relationship and our positioning before Him. As with all things spiritual, God desires that we look at ourselves first before we start looking around at other people. Over the years, I am sure you have been to a wedding or heard about a wedding that did not bless God and did not point people toward Him. There might have been things about it that were tacky, out of order, messy, or disgraceful. You have also probably been to or heard about a wedding that was amazing, well-done, tasteful and elegant. Which would you rather attend? Bring to life the wedding that can be done well, on the budget you have, and with the abilities that you have. Make a point to keep God in your wedding and allow that important type to shine through on your special day.

Week 8 Assignments

Answer the following questions based on discussions you have had with your future spouse in counseling this week and additionally on your own time and prepare to discuss them at your next counseling session. If you run out of room in a section, finish the answer to your question in your journal.

1. What did you learn about types and shadows? _____

_____

_____

_____

_____

2. How do you understand types and shadows to apply to your own marriage? _____

_____

_____

_____

_____

3. What are the weddings we have here a type or shadow of? _____

_____

_____

_____

_____

4. How does learning this information about types and shadows help you in your marriage preparation? _____

_____

_____

_____

5. What would you desire your guests to experience spiritually when they come to your wedding? _____

_____

_____

_____

6. What did you learn that you formerly did not know about weddings in Bible times? _____

_____

_____

_____

7. How did learning about weddings in Bible times bring revelation about your own relationship and your own wedding? _____

_____

_____

_____

_____

8. Why do you think God shows us so many different types of
relationships in the Bible? _____

_____

_____

_____

_____

9. What did you learn looking at the wedding situation of Jacob,
Leah and Rachel? _____

_____

_____

_____

_____

10. What did you learn by looking at the wedding feast at Cana? __

_____

_____

_____

_____

11. What did you learn by looking at the Parable of the Wedding
Banquet? _____

_____

_____

_____

_____

12. What did you learn by looking at the wise and foolish virgins?
_____

_____

_____

_____

13. What did you learn in the admonition of watchfulness? _____
_____

_____

_____

_____

14. What did you learn in the Marriage Supper of the Lamb? _____
_____

_____

_____

_____

15. What is every wedding that we attend preparing us for? _____

_____

16. What should weddings cause us to examine in a deeper way?

_____

_____

_____

_____

17. How can you make sure that your wedding honors God? _____

_____

_____

_____

18. How do you think the couple in the Song of Solomon viewed their own wedding ceremony? _____

_____

_____

_____

19. In reading Matthew 25:1-13, why do you think God used a wedding banquet to teach us about wisdom and faithfulness to Jesus in His second coming? _____

_____

_____

_____

_____

20. Get together with your spouse and minister to prepare for the wedding family meeting, which is coming up next. What do you want to tell your families? How has your focus changed since beginning this program? _____

_____

_____

_____

_____

Marking the Half-Way Point of Your Program

The Wedding Family Meeting

The wedding family meeting is a group session designed to bring in those who are closest to this wedding to discuss with them any remaining details, issues, or thoughts about the wedding planning process.

It's likely that, by this point in time, the family probably already has a general idea of what is going on in the wedding process. That is not always the case, however. Sometimes family members and friends, no matter how well-intentioned, become an intense stress factor in the process. This can happen for a few reasons:

- Having many thoughts and ideas of their own, they desire to voice their opinions and shape the wedding according to their own ideas and visions
- Trying to be too helpful to the point of taking over
- Trying to use the wedding for their own networking or connected purpose
- Lording financial control over the event
- Refusing to execute the couple's wishes as would pertain to the wedding
- Constantly adding more details to the event (such as more guests, more fanfare, etc.)
- Unsure of the direction of the event

As a result of the wedding workbook, we have had couples change their perspective on the wedding, change what they want, or more deeply solidify the goals and visions they had for the wedding, all along. No matter what the case is, this meeting is to help the couple clearly state their desires and interests for the wedding in a safe, comfortable atmosphere. The minister who has been a part of the pre-marital counseling process will be there to help preside and help facilitate the experience so the bride and groom can clarify whatever they desire to state as pertains to their wedding experience.

We call this a "family meeting" because, in most instances, the family is directly involved in the wedding planning. It does not have to be exclusively family, however. Anyone who is directly involved in the wedding or has any influence over what is going on needs to be involved in this meeting. There is also no assumption that the stress factors mentioned earlier are, in any way, necessarily present and of issue in the counseling process. From the sessions and many of the questions and exercises that have been done up to this point, it is probably easy to identify much of what the couple will want to say, and why it is important that they state it.

The session should start and end with prayer and prepare for the session to run approximately one hour.

Month Three

GETTING TO KNOW MARRIAGE

Reading assignments:

- *Discovering The Beauty of Intimacy: A Journey Through the Song of Solomon*: Chapter 3 (Desire and Sex) and Chapter 4 (Sensuality and Experience)

Week Nine

Preparing to Live With Another Person

FOR BY THE SPIRIT AND THROUGH FAITH WE WAIT EAGERLY FOR A RIGHT
RELATIONSHIP WITH GOD [RIGHTEOUSNESS]—THE OBJECT OF OUR HOPE.
(GALATIANS 5:5)

Bible reading: Psalm 133:1-3

Journaling assignments for in-session discussion:

- How does intimacy relate to unity?
- Why is unity important in marriage?

We spent all last month looking at your wedding, what kind of wedding you want to have, the details, and what your wedding should shadow in its ultimate execution. As of right now, you are exactly halfway through your pre-marital counseling program, with only eight weeks left to complete. We will be spending the remainder of this program preparing you for the ins and outs of marriage, including difficulties of marriage and the depth of real relationship.

It is our prayer that, by completing this program, you will be better equipped to handle the difficulties that often come with married life. Many people get married expecting it to be something specific. They have had their dream wedding, they have had their great honeymoon, and they expect the rest of their lives to follow those same precepts. Nobody thinks about the arguments they will have, or the trials they will face, or the complications that arise in the course of daily life. It's almost as if many have forgotten their experiences growing up, watching their parents work things out or watching them face the inevitable demise of their own marriage.

It's great to hope and plan that your marriage will be better than your parents' marriage, or the marriages you saw growing up, or even the marriages you see around you, right now. That's a great aspiration, but the problem with it is that for your marriage to be different, you must do different things within it. It's easy to fall into patterns that we have seen or are comfortable with, especially if that's what we have seen throughout our lives. To have a different marriage, one that works as a true principle, both partners in the relationship need to forsake the fairy tale concepts of marriage and put on a principle of unity that encourages teamwork. This means working together beyond just living in a household or splitting bills, but being a unified front that knows what to allow in – and what to keep out.

Candidates for marriage

Genesis 24:34-41:

HE SAID, "I AM ABRAHAM'S SERVANT. THE LORD HAS GREATLY BLESSED MY MASTER IN EVERYTHING [12:3], AND HE HAS BECOME A RICH MAN. THE LORD HAS GIVEN HIM MANY FLOCKS OF SHEEP, HERDS OF CATTLE, SILVER AND GOLD, MALE AND FEMALE SERVANTS, CAMELS, AND HORSES. SARAH, MY MASTER'S WIFE, GAVE BIRTH TO A SON WHEN SHE WAS OLD [21:1–7], AND MY MASTER HAS GIVEN EVERYTHING HE OWNS TO THAT SON. MY MASTER HAD ME MAKE A PROMISE TO HIM [SWEAR] AND SAID, 'DON'T GET A WIFE FOR MY SON FROM THE CANAANITE GIRLS [DAUGHTERS] ·WHO LIVE AROUND HERE [IN WHOSE LAND I LIVE]. INSTEAD, YOU MUST GO TO MY FATHER'S PEOPLE [HOUSE] AND TO MY FAMILY. THERE YOU MUST GET [TAKE] A WIFE FOR MY SON.' I SAID TO MY MASTER, 'WHAT IF THE WOMAN WILL NOT COME BACK WITH ME?' BUT HE SAID, 'I SERVE [WALK BEFORE] THE LORD, WHO WILL SEND HIS ANGEL [OR MESSENGER] WITH YOU AND WILL HELP YOU [MAKE YOUR WAY SUCCESSFUL]. YOU WILL GET [TAKE] A WIFE FOR MY SON FROM MY FAMILY AND MY FATHER'S PEOPLE [HOUSE].

THEN YOU WILL BE FREE [INNOCENT] FROM THE PROMISE [MY OATH]. BUT IF THEY WILL NOT GIVE YOU A WIFE FOR MY SON, YOU WILL BE FREE [INNOCENT] FROM THIS PROMISE [MY OATH].'

In my book, *Sacred Ceremonies: The Who, What, Where, When, Why, and How of Christian Ordinances, Rites, and Rituals*, I outline the following guidelines as individuals who are candidates for marriage:

- **Of legal age:** Christian churches of all sorts should consistently refuse to marry persons under the age of 18, even when parental consent is involved. State laws pertaining to statutory rape vary, and a church or minister endorsing the marriage of minors can find itself in a very difficult legal situation.

- **Consenting:** Marriages should not be forced or arranged in modern culture. We do not live in a day and age where a female should be forced to marry a male due to pregnancy if they do not desire to get married. Parents should not meddle in their children's relationships, forcing them to marry someone against their will. For a marriage to be valid, both male and female need to consent to the relationship and agree to the marriage.

- **Not married to anyone else:** Even though polygamy is getting a lot of press these days, polygamous marriage is incompatible with Christian belief, life, and understanding. For a Christian to enter a marriage with another believer, both parties must be legally able to marry (i.e., either never married or legally divorced).

- **Mature:** Maturity does not necessarily come with age. Someone who wants to marry at 21 may be just as prepared to marry as someone who is 31 or older. Signs of maturity include:

  o Knows what they want and seek out of life.

o A desire to do as the Lord has commanded them, and are willing to uphold that, whether married or not.
o Has obtained adequate education to participate in participating in the provision for a household.
o Has a proper understanding of marriage and a realistic idea of what married life will be like.
o Has enough understanding of themselves to recognize their flaws and imperfections.
o Knows the flaws and imperfections of their potential husband or wife.
o A good sense of responsibility and of the requirements of being an adult.

- **Stable in belief:** Getting married to try and work out issues with God is a good way to wind up away from God or in a very difficult spot spiritually. Marriage can enhance our faith in God when we are stable in Him.

- **Willing to follow wedding preparation procedure:** If someone is bucking against wedding regulations, the odds are good they aren't ready for formal marriage. One of the surest signs of a readiness for marriage is the willingness to follow the proper authorized procedure for wedding preparation.

The reason I outline these things as essential in a marriage candidate is because being married requires two people who are ready, willing, and able to unite in marriage. Marriage is not an end goal, but one that begins a lifetime of different goals, visions, hopes and dreams, and the individuals who decide to get married need to be purposed and prepared to live their lives together, in unity. Individuals who don't meet the criteria laid out above aren't prepared, nor ready, to try and live with another person for the rest of their lives, in a committed, unified household.

Marriage and marital unity are big commitments with lots of long-standing expectations and scrutiny. If for any reason someone doesn't have the ability to be committed fully, unity will not result, and the marriage will face serious difficulties that will not be easily overcome.

Unity in marriage

Unity in marriage is often exclusively spoken of in a sexual context, but to do so is incorrect on many theological levels. Being married is not just about sex; it's about the entire expanse of life and sharing a life with someone else. Life, as we know it, is often very difficult and takes us to many different places that we never expected nor considered we would ever go. This means that as life hands us things we might not be prepared to handle, our marriage relationship will also experience changes, bumps, and differences as we either go with the flow of change or try to stop and fight against it.

When we talk about unity, everyone loves the idea of it, in theory. We love the idea of being more than just ourselves and of working together with someone else. Whether it's in marriage or in church, mention the word "unity" and watch many people grow very excited at the prospect, nodding in agreement and holding forth in theory. The problem with unity is that it must be more than just an ideal musing, something that we say. We don't talk about how unity works or what unity does, just that we like the concept and we need to have it.

Ephesians 4:2-4:

ALWAYS BE [OR BE COMPLETELY] HUMBLE, GENTLE, AND PATIENT, ACCEPTING [PUTTING UP/BEARING WITH] EACH OTHER IN LOVE. MAKE EVERY EFFORT TO PRESERVE THE UNITY OF [PROVIDED BY; AVAILABLE THROUGH] THE SPIRIT IN [THROUGH] THE PEACE THAT JOINS US TOGETHER [BOND OF PEACE]. THERE IS ONE BODY AND ONE SPIRIT, AND GOD CALLED YOU TO HAVE ONE HOPE [ONE HOPE OF YOUR CALLING].

Unity is about putting ourselves aside because we trust the others involved in what we are doing enough to know that our best interests will be kept at heart. It happens when everyone regards everyone else in a situation enough to be able to work together toward a common goal and common purpose in the love and grace of Jesus Christ. In terms of the Kingdom, we are unified because the Gospel is to be preached to the ends of the earth. In terms of marriage, marital partners are not united for and unto the end of their marriage. They are united unto the end of holiness, encouraging and supporting their mate to do and become all that God has for them to be, no matter where that takes one another. Unity requires the sacrifice of the self on the part of both marriage partners and requires that as they strive to become "we," they do not alienate nor demean the "I" that remains in both people. Rather than demean someone else, unity helps to lift that up, so all people can benefit from that end goal.

Unity doesn't require perfection, but it does require firm resolve and solid communication. It requires that both marital partners consider the good of their partner and the good of the entire family. It also requires that partners resist the temptation to sabotage their relationship by giving in to temptations that are going to be harmful to the entire unit. Unity isn't blind to another's faults or failings, but it recognizes the principle that God is at the center of this relationship and both partners need to put aside their selfish natures to make decisions and ideals that are best for everyone involved.

Moving from a living together mindset to a married mindset

Whether or not you have lived together prior to marriage, the concept of unity that I spoke of above is radically different from the concepts people have about living with another person. Marriage is not about splitting the bills, everything being 50/50 even all the time, looking over your shoulder to make sure you aren't being taken advantage of, and feeling like you must keep things maintained in some sense of an "equal" ideal. Society's comfort with living together without marriage has created this concept that both people in a relationship must be doing the exact same thing, or someone else is being taken advantage of. This has led to countless relationship headaches and problems caused by the simple fact that one or both partners are coming into a relationship with a "ME" mindset rather than a united ideal about helping and growing a relationship and a household.

It's great to think that you are going to go into a relationship and everything is going to be "equal" all the time. We have grown to equate "equal" with sameness, and sameness with importance in a relationship. If things aren't divided right down the middle, it seems like someone, somewhere, always thinks they are being slighted or taken advantage of. The problem with this is that relationships aren't always "equal." Couples are going to have times where one partner needs more emotionally than the other, or where one is stronger than the other, or where one makes more money, or is more competent at their job, or where one is better at something in the household than the other. It's not based on gender, and it's not based on expectation; it's just the way life flows sometimes. Very seldom do couples have exactly equal time, with perfect jobs and the exact same interests or needs. Unity is about that needed flexibility that enables a couple to do and be what is needed in that moment for the other person.

2 Corinthians 13:11:

NOW [FINALLY], BROTHERS AND SISTERS, I SAY GOOD-BYE [OR BE JOYFUL; REJOICE; A COMMON GREETING AND FAREWELL]. LIVE IN HARMONY [SEEK RESTORATION; OR MEND YOUR WAYS]. DO WHAT I HAVE ASKED YOU TO DO [FOLLOW MY EXHORTATION; OR ENCOURAGE/EXHORT ONE ANOTHER]. AGREE WITH EACH OTHER [LIVE IN UNITY], AND LIVE IN PEACE. THEN THE GOD OF LOVE AND PEACE WILL BE WITH YOU.

Let's erase these concepts of "sameness" and instead, look at true unity. For unity to work, not everyone is able to do the same exact thing in the same exact way all the time. That's true in church unity, and it's true at home, as well. There is more than one way to contribute to a household; it's not all about money. There may come a time when one partner (either husband or wife) may feel called to stay at home with a growing child or even work from home. One partner may be called into ministry and called to leave the workforce, and the other not. Just because there isn't an "equal" distribution of money doesn't mean that the partner isn't contributing to the household or that the other one is being taken advantage of. Just like there is more than one way to contribute to a household, there is more than one way to be involved. Likewise, there is more than one circumstance that a couple can have in their home and still be united. There are lots of stay-at-home moms and dads who recognize the other spouse as the "primary breadwinner." There are lots of couples who try to balance ministry with family, or who try to balance important hobbies with families. Some husbands are great cooks, while their wives are great at tending to the yard or are great at fixing things. In many households, chores are done when they need doing, and husbands and wives aren't keeping tabs on who does how many chores at what time. Sometimes husbands are stronger, sometimes wives are stronger, sometimes one is there for the other, and sometimes they are there for each other at the same time. These are all signs of unity, and the reality is that if we want to be unified, we must stop keeping score and do what needs to be done, supporting and caring about our spouses more than we care about things appearing or seeming to be a certain way.

"Two become one"

We love the passage in Genesis 2:24 which reads:

SO A MAN WILL LEAVE HIS FATHER AND MOTHER [IN THE SENSE OF A NEW PRIMARY LOYALTY] AND BE UNITED WITH HIS WIFE, AND THE TWO WILL BECOME ONE BODY [FLESH].

We hear about it, people use it as a weapon against divorced people, and we hear about it often in the context of sacrificing yourself for your marriage. We hear about it in every conceivable way except the true context of becoming united in marriage and of the spiritual principle involved in unity.

As much as we love this passage and the romantic ideas it promotes, there are a few things we need to recognize about it to make it become something reasonable in a marriage today, especially as a principle of unity. Let's start by looking at the passage:

Genesis 2:18-25:

THEN THE LORD GOD SAID, "IT IS NOT GOOD FOR THE MAN TO BE ALONE. I WILL MAKE A HELPER [IN THE SENSE OF A PARTNER OR ALLY; THE WORD DOES NOT IMPLY SUBORDINATE STATUS; SEE PS. 79:9] WHO IS RIGHT FOR [IS SUITABLE FOR; CORRESPONDS WITH] HIM."

FROM THE GROUND GOD FORMED EVERY WILD ANIMAL [ANIMAL OF THE FIELD] AND EVERY BIRD IN THE SKY [HEAVENS], AND HE BROUGHT THEM TO THE MAN SO THE MAN COULD NAME THEM [TO SEE WHAT HE WOULD CALL THEM]. WHATEVER THE MAN CALLED EACH LIVING THING, THAT

BECAME ITS NAME. THE MAN GAVE NAMES TO ALL THE TAME ANIMALS [BEASTS; LIVESTOCK], TO THE BIRDS IN THE SKY [HEAVENS], AND TO ALL THE WILD ANIMALS [ANIMALS OF THE FIELD]. BUT ADAM [OR THE MAN; 1:27] DID NOT FIND A HELPER THAT WAS RIGHT FOR HIM [2:18]. SO THE LORD GOD CAUSED THE MAN TO SLEEP VERY DEEPLY [A DEEP SLEEP TO FALL ON THE MAN/ADAM], AND WHILE HE WAS ASLEEP, GOD REMOVED ONE OF THE MAN'S RIBS [OR SIDES]. THEN GOD CLOSED UP THE MAN'S SKIN AT THE PLACE WHERE HE TOOK THE RIB [OR SIDE]. THE LORD GOD USED THE RIB [OR SIDE] FROM THE MAN TO MAKE [BUILD; CONSTRUCT] A WOMAN, AND THEN HE BROUGHT THE WOMAN TO THE MAN.

AND THE MAN SAID,

"NOW, THIS IS SOMEONE WHOSE BONES CAME FROM MY BONES,
   WHOSE BODY CAME FROM MY BODY [AT LAST, THIS IS BONE OF MY BONES AND FLESH OF MY FLESH].
I WILL CALL HER [SHE WILL BE CALLED] 'WOMAN [HEBREW 'ISHSHAH],'
   BECAUSE SHE WAS TAKEN OUT OF MAN [HEBREW 'ISH]."

SO A MAN WILL LEAVE HIS FATHER AND MOTHER [IN THE SENSE OF A NEW PRIMARY LOYALTY] AND BE UNITED WITH HIS WIFE, AND THE TWO WILL BECOME ONE BODY [FLESH].

THE MAN AND HIS WIFE WERE NAKED, BUT THEY WERE NOT ASHAMED.

There are three things that should jump out at us immediately that we often overlook. Those three things are:

- This passage is from before the fall of man, and
- Adam and Eve were physically created as one being, and
- Adam and Eve did not become a strange, weird, enmeshed creature after God established their relationship.

The first of those three obvious facts, that the passage speaks of the relationship between Adam and Eve before the fall of humankind into sin, needs to strike us the hardest. We aren't living in a time when relationships are simple and uncomplicated, because sin has now entered the world. We live in a world that feels the effects of sin on a regular basis, and the fact that sin has entered every facet of human existence – including marriage – changes the game substantially. It's great and glorious to talk of married couples as being "one," but we also state that with a great amount of naivety, not considering just what we are talking about and how much effort it takes for a couple to be "one" in a world of sin. The fact that Adam and Eve were spoken of as being one prior to the fall means that what we experience in marriage, although we can experience a semblance of oneness, will not be exactly the same as Adam and Eve experienced before sin entered the world.

The second of the obvious facts is that Adam and Eve were literally created as one physical being before they were separated. I hear so many people running around, saying that they are looking for their "rib" or their "side," without giving any credibility to the fact that people aren't created that way now, and haven't been created that way since the beginning of time (unless they are a conjoined twin). It sounds poetic, it sounds romantic, it sounds... odd. Adam and Eve were literally one, and then they were separated, and then in their relationship, they came back together physically as a united couple, as one in their purpose and care for each other.

The third obvious fact is that Adam and Eve didn't become a strange, weird, enmeshed creature after God established their relationship. If anything, they came to a place where they found more of themselves and were able to compliment and care about each other better than they did before they were separated physically. Adam and Eve didn't get married and stop being the people they were. They didn't stop being themselves, and they didn't become something that was so attached or dependent upon their spouse that they couldn't survive without each other.

These three very important facts tell us that as romantic of a notion that we have made unity to be, it is a choice. It is not something that we do beyond our control, nor is it something that we do against our will. It doesn't mean we stop being ourselves (or the person that our spouse fell in love with in the first place), or that we become something strange and otherworldly. Being married means being able to stand as two imperfect people, ready and willing to live with and work through the differences they must walk through life together. It is literally choosing to walk together and be agreed on that path.

Marriage partners aren't perfect

Every marriage partner will face the temptation to stray from the relationship at some point in time. Some people resist the temptation, and others give into it – but all face it, especially when they are finding their relationship difficult or unpleasant. There are many books out there to try and "affair-proof" your marriage, but if you follow statistics on marriage and relationships, it's obvious that the standard advice given on these issues doesn't hold up when people are confronted with temptations... and this becomes obvious, the more we look at the world we are in and the reasons why people give for being in such situations that present themselves.

I think that people find the concept of making a relationship immune to temptation very, very appealing. People like the idea that if they do a few simple things, the issues that surround relationship temptations will vanish and disappear. They won't have to worry about their partner, or themselves, straying, and as a result, they let many signs, symptoms, and little things go, here and there, until those issues mount and become so big that the temptation is larger than life for them.

Matthew 26:41:

STAY AWAKE [KEEP WATCH] AND PRAY FOR STRENGTH AGAINST TEMPTATION [OR NOT TO FAIL THE TEST]. THE SPIRIT WANTS TO DO WHAT IS RIGHT [IS WILLING], BUT THE BODY [OR HUMAN NATURE; THE FLESH] IS WEAK.

I am using the issue of temptation here to illustrate the point that marriage partners aren't perfect, and the issue of "straying" in a relationship happens long before someone decides to engage in a relationship outside of the marriage. Any time a marriage situation grows to where the imperfections of one partner are more than the other can happen, the grass appears greener with someone else who doesn't have the same imperfections and issues.

If marriage is to be successful and things like infidelity are to be prayerfully avoided, the first thing to do is erase the idea in your mind that there is such a thing as a "perfect marriage. "All those marriages that you see around you and exalt in your mind have problems of their own behind closed doors, but they have recognized a basic thing: marriage partners are not perfect. They are going to deal with temptations, they are going to deal with trials, one or both are going to make bad choices and that is going to affect the way that the other one feels about them, and they have accepted that this is a part of life and a part of living with someone else. Instead of trying to remove the concept of temptation, they focus on the relevance and importance of overcoming temptation by not giving into it.

No marriage is perfect, because marriages consist of two very imperfect people. It's impossible to cover every single thing that will come up in a marriage, because there is no way to predict all the problems and temptations that will arise from living with someone else who is very, very imperfect. What this does tell us is that if we want to be successful in marriage, we need to recognize their imperfections so we know where there temptations will lie.

Using sinful behaviors and temptations against the relationship

If we want to learn how to stand against sin and temptations unto principles of unity, we need to be able to have a place of trust in the relationship. The reason that things such as affairs and other matters come into play is because, somewhere in the relationship, a trust has been violated that gives the message that going off and doing something like that will not do harm to the relationship. It doesn't matter where the message comes from, whether it's from the person themselves, relationship breakdown, or something they learned somewhere in their lives. The truth is that, on one party or both parties in the relationship, there has, most likely, been an inclination toward temptation that already did damage somewhere in time – but nobody took the time to notice the inclination toward temptation.

Job 20:20-22:

EVIL PEOPLE NEVER LACK AN APPETITE [EXPERIENCE EASE/COMFORT IN THEIR BELLIES],
    AND NOTHING ESCAPES THEIR SELFISHNESS [THEY COVET ESCAPES THEM].
BUT NOTHING WILL BE LEFT FOR THEM TO EAT [OR AFTER THEY EAT];

THEIR RICHES WILL NOT CONTINUE.

Philippians 2:3:

When you do things, do not let selfishness [rivalry; selfish ambition] or pride be your guide. Instead, be humble and give more honor [regard; value] to others than to yourselves.

Sin and temptation to do things are not just about sex or affairs, they're about being tempted to do something wrong in someone's life that leads into sin. Sin, as we all know, affects other people, not just one individual, much of the time. In marriages, there is always the temptation to be selfish, or to divide. This form of temptation often infiltrates marriages in ways we don't consider, because as I have said many times, we can't force people to be decent human beings. As a church, we tend to only care about marriages when they are on the brink of failure or when someone has done something notably wrong. God, on the other hand, cares about the people in that marriage, and desires that they overcome the temptations to hurt and marginalize one another with selfish behaviors that cause the other to feel as if they don't matter or are unimportant.

Some examples of these behaviors are:

- Taking money from the marriage and using it for something selfish or personal without considering or discussing the matter with the other person
- Controlling the money in the marriage, treating one of the spouses as if they are a child when it comes to financial matters (limiting access, requiring explanation, etc.)
- Doing whatever one wants to do in the relationship, without considering the other
- Expecting the other partner to make constant compromises or sacrifices so that one can have their own way in all matters
- Refusing to listen; constantly ignoring the other partner when they are talking or speaking
- Not considering the other's feelings or thoughts
- Behaving with a demanding or condescending attitude
- Using physical, emotional, financial, spiritual, sexual, or

economic control to dominate one's will in a relationship

None of these things contribute to the unity of a marriage. In fact, they drive permanent wedges in a relationship to the point where resolve in a marriage weakens. If we want to have good marriages, partners should reflect the following characteristics when interacting with their spouses:

- Attentiveness
- Listening
- Equal access to finances and financial information
- Partnership
- Mutual sacrifice
- Respect and honor
- Individuality

Being married to flaws as much as to strengths

We are often attracted to other people because of the characteristics we see in them that we could classify as "strengths." When dating or even engaged, we might not see the flaws in our partner at all, or we might not pay attention to them like we should. The fun and excitement of the relationship seems plausible... right until the fun and excitement is replaced with real life. When living with other people, their flaws and imperfections have a way of shining through, larger than life, in ways we can't defy, nor ignore.

Proverbs 14:1:

A WISE WOMAN STRENGTHENS HER FAMILY [BUILDS HER HOUSE], BUT A FOOLISH WOMAN DESTROYS HERS BY WHAT SHE DOES [TEARS HERS DOWN WITH HER OWN HANDS].

Don't be blind to the flaws that your future spouse has, and don't ignore them. It is one thing to not recognize they are there, but it is another thing entirely to refuse to acknowledge them. When you get married, you are going to be married to his or her flaws as much as his or her strengths and living with those flaws is what causes a whole new door of temptation to open in your married life.

Recognizing flaws gives you the opportunity to decide if you can live with them or not, and to respect the person you marry for who they are, rather than a vague image or concept of who you desire them to be.

Patience

Long-term relationships of any sort do not survive without patience. This is especially true in marriage. Living with someone intimately, day in and day out, sounds like fun... right until you start doing it. You see your partner's weird habits, their idiosyncrasies, the things about them that aren't so godly or attractive, and their stubborn attitudes. The things they need to work on as people, with God, become quite obvious. The fact that they don't want to work on them also becomes obvious, and that they don't get immediately delivered... well... that can work nerves, even under the best of circumstances.

Proverbs 16:32:

PATIENCE IS BETTER THAN STRENGTH [OR A PATIENT PERSON IS BETTER THAN A WARRIOR]. CONTROLLING YOUR TEMPER IS BETTER THAN CAPTURING A CITY.

Proverbs 25:15:

WITH PATIENCE YOU CAN CONVINCE A RULER, AND A GENTLE [TENDER] WORD CAN GET THROUGH TO THE HARD-HEADED [BREAKS BONE].

Romans 5:4:

AND PATIENCE [ENDURANCE] PRODUCES [TESTED AND PROVEN] CHARACTER, AND [TESTED AND PROVEN] CHARACTER PRODUCES HOPE.

Romans 15:4:

[FOR] EVERYTHING THAT WAS WRITTEN IN THE PAST WAS WRITTEN TO TEACH US. THE SCRIPTURES GIVE US PATIENCE [ENDURANCE] AND ENCOURAGEMENT SO THAT WE CAN HAVE HOPE.

2 Corinthians 6:6-7:

WE SHOW WE ARE SERVANTS OF GOD BY OUR PURE LIVES [... IN/BY PURITY; PAUL CONTINUES THE SAME LIST, BUT MOVES TO POSITIVE CHARACTER TRAITS], OUR UNDERSTANDING [... IN/BY KNOWLEDGE], PATIENCE, AND KINDNESS, BY THE HOLY SPIRIT, BY TRUE [SINCERE; UNHYPOCRITICAL] LOVE, BY SPEAKING THE TRUTH [OR THE MESSAGE/WORD OF TRUTH; THE GOSPEL], AND BY GOD'S POWER. WE USE OUR RIGHT LIVING [... WITH WEAPONS OF RIGHTEOUSNESS] TO DEFEND OURSELVES AGAINST EVERYTHING [OR BOTH TO ATTACK (WITH A SWORD) AND DEFEND (WITH A SHIELD); IN OUR RIGHT HANDS AND IN OUR LEFT].

The Bible has important things to say about patience, and it reveals much to us about why it is important as a characteristic that we develop in our lives. Long taught to be about everything except what it is truly about, patience is about developing persistence and active participation in process with God while we wait. It's not so much about doing nothing as about continuing in the things we know we are supposed to be doing while we trust and believe that other things are on their way, preparing to happen.

In the context of marriage, patience is about being a productive, spiritually busy person, no matter what is going on in your relationship with your spouse. So many people say that they aren't moving forward or doing anything because they are waiting on their spouse to "move" or waiting for their spouse to take the initiative. Patience proves that our faith life with God is still up to us – not our spouse or some other person. If you are believing God to do things in your life or even in your marriage, you still need to do whatever it is you know God is telling you to do, regardless of what your spouse decides to do. Sometimes God asks us to go first, and in patience, we are given the ability to do what we know is right, regardless of what might be going on around us.

That means we are called to be consistent in prayer, praying for our spouses and believing God for them, if we know God has called us to do that. We should seek the best for them and seek to be an encouragement and inspiration in their lives. If He has called us to do something for the Kingdom, we should not hesitate to do it but be an example for our spouse in the way that God moves and works in lives. In each and everything we do, including marriage, we should do it with steady and consistent endurance. That is what makes marriage call for patience: the entirety of it requires virtue to succeed.

It definitely seems that all of us can benefit from a good dose of patience... especially those of us who are married or are preparing for marriage.

Week 9 Assignments

Answer the following questions based on discussions you have had with your future spouse in counseling this week and additionally on your own time and prepare to discuss them at your next counseling session. If you run out of room in a section, finish the answer to your question in your journal.

1. What are the six signs of a candidate for marriage? _____

_____

_____

_____

_____

2. How do these different signs interact together in order to create a solid candidate for marriage? _____

_____

_____

_____

_____

3. Is marriage an end goal? What is the end goal of marriage? _____

_____

_____

_____

_____

4. Why do you think everyone likes the idea of unity in theory, but has such a difficult time with it in application? _____

_____

_____

_____

_____

5. What is unity about? _____

_____

_____

_____

_____

6. Does unity require perfection? Why or why not? _____

_____

_____

_____

_____

7. Is marriage always "50/50?" Why or why not? _____

_____

_____

_____

8. How does unity apply in a situation where people have different needs and different circumstances? _____

_____

_____

_____

_____

9. What are some practical ways you can overcome "ME" mentality when approaching marriage? _____

_____

_____

_____

_____

10. What are some things that you learned about the Genesis account of Adam and Eve's relationship that you never considered before? _____

_____

_____

_____

_____

11. Why is looking at the passage of Adam and Eve with new eyes important for marriage preparation? _____

_____

_____

_____

_____

12. Are marriage partners perfect? Does this mean marriages are imperfect? Why are these realizations important? _____

_____

_____

_____

_____

13. Does every marriage partner face temptations? How do temptations arise? _____

_____

_____

_____

_____

14. What are some ways that people use sin and temptations against a relationship? _____

_____

_____

_____

15. What are specific examples that people bring harm into a relationship? _____

_____

_____

_____

16. What are some of your mate's strengths? What are some of your mate's weaknesses? _____

_____

_____

_____

17. Why do you believe patience is important in a marriage? _____

_____

_____

_____

18. What do you think everyday life was like for the couple in the Song of Solomon? _____

_____

_____

_____

_____

19. In reading Psalm 133:1-3, how do you think the benefits and blessings of marriage relate to Biblical teachings on unity? _____

_____

_____

_____

_____

20. Do some individual thinking about yourself and your life. What things exist in your life that could hinder marital unity? What can you do to change them? _____

_____

_____

_____

_____

Week Ten

R-E-S-P-E-C-T

SHOW RESPECT FOR [HONOR] ALL PEOPLE: LOVE THE BROTHERS AND SISTERS
OF GOD'S FAMILY [COMMUNITY OF BELIEVERS; BROTHERHOOD], RESPECT
[FEAR] GOD [PROV. 1:7], HONOR THE KING [OR EMPEROR; ROM. 13:1].
(1 PETER 2:17)

Bible reading: Matthew 5:43-48

Journaling assignments for in-session discussion:

- Why is respect one of the most important components in a marriage?
- How can married couples show respect toward one another?

I once saw a commercial for the television show, *Mad About You*, called "*The Mad About You* Guide to Respect." In the very short clip, Jamie (played by Helen Hunt) comes out of the bathroom and says, "Watch me" to her husband, Paul (played by Paul Reiser), who is sitting with their dog. She then precedes to take the empty toilet paper roll off the toilet paper holder, puts a new roll of toilet paper on the holder, and says, "Voila!" while holding out her hands in demonstration of how easy it is to do. By picking on an age-old adage, the show pointed out how something so small could become such a mundane annoyance when presented in the context of respect and disrespect.

Respect is a big word when it comes to marriage. We can tell other people that we love them all day long, but love is shown in respect. Respect gives both partners the ability to perceive the love their spouse feels for them, especially in the context of the little, everyday interactions that make marriage work. Even though we only tend to pay attention when big things happen, little things happen in relationships all the time that determine where that relationship will be somewhere, down the line.

A marriage will not survive and thrive without respect. Here we are going to delve into just what respect is and how it manifests, so that it can be recognized when it is there, as well as when it is not.

Respect is earned, not magically granted

1 Peter 3:7:

IN THE SAME WAY [2:18; 3:1], YOU HUSBANDS SHOULD LIVE WITH YOUR WIVES IN AN UNDERSTANDING [CONSIDERATE] WAY [EPH. 5:25–33; COL. 3:19], SINCE THEY ARE WEAKER THAN YOU [THE WEAKER SEX; OR THE LESS EMPOWERED ONE; THE WEAKER VESSEL; WOMEN ARE TYPICALLY PHYSICALLY WEAKER, BUT IN GRECO-ROMAN AND JEWISH SOCIETY, THEY ALSO HAD LESS POWER AND AUTHORITY]. BUT SHOW THEM RESPECT [PAY/GIVE THEM HONOR], BECAUSE GOD GIVES THEM THE SAME BLESSING HE GIVES YOU—[THEY ARE CO-HEIRS OF] THE GRACE THAT GIVES TRUE LIFE [OR GOD'S GIFT OF LIFE; THE GRACE OF LIFE]. DO THIS SO THAT NOTHING WILL STOP [HINDER] YOUR PRAYERS.

I have read many different things over the years that state wives have to respect their husbands, whether they deserve it, or not. Some go as far as to say this is true of all marriage partners, regardless of gender. This is a distortion of what God was trying to teach us about marriage, and about respect. Spouses should both be respected in their marriages, and they should also both be respectable. It's not something that is immediately granted, nor given at whim. It is something that we earn in a relationship because we have proven ourselves trustworthy and faithful – and worthy of respect.

Respect, however, is something that we should have when we enter our marriage. We should already respect our future spouses,

Who should get their way in a fight?

EVERY MARRIAGE IS HOST TO A FEW FIGHTS OVER THE YEARS. SOME ARE LARGE AND SOME ARE SMALL, AND SOME ARE EASIER TO RESOLVE THAN OTHERS. THERE ARE ALSO FIGHTS THAT DON'T EVER SEEM TO GET RESOLVED, NO MATTER HOW DEDICATED A COUPLE MIGHT BE TO WORK THE SITUATION OUT. SOME MARRIAGE PROGRAMS BELIEVE THAT ONE PARTNER SHOULD ALWAYS DEFER TO THE OTHER WHEN THEY FIGHT, AND OTHER PEOPLE BELIEVE THAT FIGHTING IS HEALTHY AND ENCOURAGES COMMUNICATION. ARE EITHER OF THESE PROPER PERSPECTIVES FOR MARRIAGE COMMUNICATION AND RESOLVING FIGHTS?

NOT REALLY. THEY REPRESENT EXTREMES: ONE PARTNER BEING STIFLED AND TWO PARTNERS SCREAMING SO LOUDLY, NOTHING GETS RESOLVED. IF YOU ARE MARRIED, IT IS IMPORTANT THAT YOU CAN STATE YOUR THOUGHTS, FEELINGS, AND VIEWPOINTS WITHOUT HAVING TO SCREAM AT EACH OTHER. IT'S ALSO IMPORTANT THAT BOTH PARTNERS OFFER SOLUTIONS OR THOUGHTS ON SITUATIONS INSTEAD OF ONE PARTNER ALWAYS DEFERRING TO THE OTHER.

WHEN IT COMES TO FIGHTING, IT SHOULD NEVER BE ABOUT ONE PERSON GETTING THEIR WAY IN THE FIGHT, BUT ABOUT GETTING PAST THE EMOTION AND ANGER IN THE RELATIONSHIP SO THAT A TRUE SOLUTION CAN BE FOUND IN A MARRIAGE, INVOLVING BOTH PARTIES. RATHER THAN BEING ABOUT WINNING, MARRIAGE SHOULD BE ABOUT DOING WHAT IS BEST FOR EVERYONE, AND BOTH PARTNERS LEARNING TO PUT THEIR HARSH EMOTIONS ASIDE FOR THE BETTERMENT OF THE FAMILY.

before we ever get married. The attributes needed to be respectable, and respectful people should be within them, and we should carry that through after the wedding. Respect is an important and vital leveling ground in a marriage that affirms the worth and dignity of both partners, in an equal and purposed way, so that the relationship can flourish and move forward in all things.

Equality in marriage

We have already discussed that not everything in a marriage is always equal in our concept of equal all the time. This is different, however, from considering both marriage partners as equal in the marriage. What I was talking about earlier is that there is more than one way to contribute, it is not always the same, but that does not mean that both partners in that marriage are not of equal value. Everything is not always equal in sameness, but that does not mean both partners are not equal, of equal status, of equal importance and with an equal say, over what happens in their relationship.

Matthew 7:12:

[SO ALWAYS; SO IN EVERYTHING] DO TO OTHERS WHAT [TREAT OTHERS AS] YOU WANT THEM TO DO TO [TREAT] YOU. THIS IS [SUMS UP; IS THE ESSENCE OF] THE MEANING OF THE LAW OF MOSES AND THE TEACHING OF THE PROPHETS [LAW AND THE PROPHETS; REFERRING TO THE OT].

The world abounds with detrimental marriage advice, same as the church does. We hear about unity, we hear about a need for unity, we hear about our call to "love our neighbor as ourselves," but we don't apply those words in ways that will change and transform our lives for the better. The command to love our neighbor as ourselves is an equalizing command. It means that we recognize we aren't any better, nor any superior, to anyone else. Jesus' command to treat others as you would like to be treated is also a humbling, equalizing viewpoint. If we treat other people the way that we would desire to be treated, then we keep in mind that we are not better than other people.

We seem to (sort of, maybe not really) understand these principles when interacting with other people. The place we do not seem to understand them is in marriage. The second it comes to marriage; we start setting up superiors and subordinates and bottom-lining our relationships. The immediate defense is "Well, what if something comes up and a decision needs to be made and it needs to be made, firm, because there is a disagreement?" Instead of encouraging couples to talk, to discuss, to work out the issue in a manner that is fair for the entire family, couples are encouraged to take an unequal position and allow one partner to "bottom-line" the other. There's a big danger in bottom-lining decisions, and in encouraging such behavior before the problem even arises. In a marriage, neither partner should feel marginalized or like they are being told what they are going to do. Partners should feel free to communicate and decisions that are reached should be for the good of all, not just what one person may want to do. There are numerous facets in a relationship that determine decision-making and many points to consider... and it is quite possible that your spouse has a viewpoint that needs to be heard before a decision is made. Instead of assuming that someone's right to be heard is a threat to authority, consider the fact that what they have to say is, most likely, valid... and hear it out. If possible, come to a compromise, change a perspective, or work out a new option... but don't treat your spouse like they don't have any valid perspective or voice in the marriage.

Treating your spouse like they are an adult

It may seem strange to mention it, but one of the most destructive dynamics in a relationship comes into play when a husband or wife takes on a parental role with their spouse. It's not uncommon to meet partners who, in at least one aspect of their marriage, have adopted a parent-child relationship. This may emerge out of control or emerge out of a sense of needed discipline to structure some portion of life that might be out-of-control (such as spending or buying). Whatever the reason is for its presence, the parent-child relationship in a marriage is very damaging. All people know when they are being treated as if they are inferior or need supervision. Marriage is not intended to be a parent-child relationship, where either spouse is treated by the other as if they need some sort of super-disciplining.

I have long argued that one of the basic problems in society is the assumption that women and men cannot take care of themselves. We talk so much about "needing" a spouse and "needing" each other that we forget most people today are quite capable of taking care of themselves, with or without a spouse. We all have issues, and we all have baggage, but that is no reason to treat your spouse like they are a child. Adults are not children, and they should not ever, ever be treated as such.

Romans 15:1:

We who are strong in faith [strong] should help [bear with; be patient with] the weak with their weaknesses [failings; struggles], and not please only ourselves.

Don't take advantage of the weaknesses or difficulties in your partner's personality or life. Make sure that you aren't demeaning or demoralizing your spouse in the name of control. If issues arise that relate to improper habits, spending, or other behaviors, address them as an adult, not as a parent disciplining an adult child. Your spouse is your spouse, not a baby.

Treating your spouse like they are an individual person

Colossians 3:14:

Even more than all this [above all], clothe yourself in love, which holds you all together in perfect unity [or binds everything together; is the bond of perfection/completeness].

Just because you got married doesn't mean you stop being individual people. Unity and oneness are both choices, not things that automatically come about because someone signed some paperwork. Just because the two of you get married and strive to have one life together doesn't mean that the two of you stop having your own ideas and thoughts. You are still two people, working on the same team, with your own ideas and concepts about how to get to the best place possible.

This means that, in a marriage, spouses have the right to the following things:

- **Their own privacy:** Some people advocate that spouses should have instant, granted access to each other's online accounts, phones, and private documents. I don't advocate this. In marriage, there should be a certain level of trust, and that means that you respect your spouse's private accounts, documents, phones, and personal space. Marriage doesn't give each spouse the right to suspicion.

- **Their own friends:** Unless you have warrant to suspect something inappropriate is going on with a friend of theirs (I'm not just talking about affairs here, I am talking about anything illegal or otherwise inappropriate), your spouse has the right to their friends, whether you like them or not, whether you are friends with them or not. This also applies to friendships. People do have self-control, and sex is not a dynamic in every relationship between friends who are married. Unless suspicion warrants... lay off the detective act.

- **Their family time:** Before you ever came into your future spouse's life, they had a family. No matter how much they might complain about their family, they are going to want to, most likely, spend time with them. Some of that time might be without you. Accepting this is a part of accepting who your spouse is as a person.

- **Their own space:** Sometimes people need space, plain and simple. Sometimes as much as you might like or love someone, you need time away from them to think and gather your own personal thoughts. If your spouse needs space, let them have it. Don't pester or nag them to spend time with you.

- **Their own thoughts:** Just because the two of you are married doesn't mean you have to share one thought between you. Spouses have every right to disagree with each other and expect that the other will respect their opinion, even if it is opposite what they may feel or think.

- **Their own devotional/spiritual time:** I think praying together as a couple is wonderful. I think spending spiritual time together as a couple is also wonderful. That having been said, your spouse is still a person with their own relationship with God and there may very well be many, many times when they need to be on their face, before God, without you watching, commenting, or involved.

- **Their own access to money:** However you want to set it up is your own jurisdiction as a couple (two separate accounts and one joint account, or just a joint account, or some other setup), but both marital partners need to have access to money, both for household purposes and for personal ones, as well.

- **Their right to growth:** The most successful marriages are the ones where both partners have the option to grow and change in the relationship without their mate feeling threatened. Your future spouse has the right to become all God has for them to be with your full support and approval.

Admiring accomplishments

The bottom line of this chapter is that no matter whether your spouse is male or female, they are an individual person who needs to know you care and appreciate them as a human being, not just a husband or wife. It is a concept that transcends our marriages, because all people that we reach and touch with the Gospel want to know, too, that they are cared about and appreciated as people, not just numbers on a church roster. People want to see the respect we claim to have, not watch us talk about respect and ignore it. If we learn how to do it in marriage, it is a lot easier to do it with anyone we encounter in our lives.

Most people like accomplishing things. Very, very few people desire to be people who slide or coast through life with no goals or desires. When we accomplish things, it helps us embrace God's principle of good stewardship and participate in creation and process with our Creator.

Isaiah 26:12:

LORD, ALL OUR SUCCESS IS [ACCOMPLISHMENTS/WORKS ARE] BECAUSE OF WHAT YOU HAVE DONE, SO GIVE US PEACE [OR AND YOU GIVE US PEACE/SECURITY].

One way that we can show respect in marriage is by admiring the accomplishments of our spouse. Accomplishments are important to us as individual people, because they represent milestones and purposefulness in our lives. Showing admiration when your spouse accomplishes something validates them as a person and encourages them as someone who wants to bring forth something beautiful and important. It proves their life is meaningful to you.

Repeatedly ignoring, not listening, not attending ceremonies, or clearly not being interested in things is disrespectful. If you choose to marry this person, you choose to participate and celebrate them in life. It doesn't matter if you aren't really interested in their job or in this aspect of their lives, because you should, as a spouse, be interested in them. If this is important to them, and they are important to you, then this milestone is important to you, too.

Attentiveness and interest

Nehemiah 8:3:

AT THE SQUARE BY THE WATER GATE EZRA READ THE TEACHINGS [LAWS; INSTRUCTIONS; TORAH] OUT LOUD FROM EARLY MORNING UNTIL NOON TO THE MEN, WOMEN, AND EVERYONE WHO COULD LISTEN AND UNDERSTAND [UNDERSTAND WHAT THEY HEARD; PRESUMABLY OLDER CHILDREN]. ALL THE PEOPLE LISTENED CAREFULLY [ATTENTIVELY; EAGERLY] TO THE BOOK [SCROLL] OF THE TEACHINGS [LAWS; INSTRUCTIONS; TORAH].

If there is one thing that drives me crazy as a person, it is talking and knowing the other person is not listening. We've given both marriage partners permission over the years to treat their spouse's words as if they are dismissible, and this is perhaps some of the worst marriage advice ever given. When your spouse is talking to you, you should be listening. If it's not a good time or you aren't able to give your attention at that moment, then say so and wait until things calm down. There is nothing wrong with saying I am unavailable right now, but there is something wrong with not listening, period.

If you can see that your spouse is occupied and unable to give you their attention and you demand it anyway, you are setting them up, and that's not fair. That shows disrespect to the time and attention your partner needs to invest in whatever they are doing at that moment. If you see your partner is busy, then wait until they are done with what they are doing. It's fine to mention you have something to talk about but wait until a better time to expect their attention. One of the things we learn as we go along in marriage is that no one can demand anyone's attention all the time. This should make us grateful for the time we do have with someone, and for the attention that they give us.

Money

There is one thing couples fight about more than anything else. It's something that represents a good portion of people's thoughts and preoccupations. People strive to have it, long for it, love it, and never seem to have enough of it. This thing that couples fight about more than anything else is not sex, children, or chores… it is money. As much as the so-called experts seem to recognize this fact, they don't seem to offer much help into the "why" it is such an issue for couples. Have we ever considered why money is such a decisive factor in a marriage? What is it about it that seems to cause marriages to easily fall awry due to money?

We don't deal with underlying issues that relate to and are represented by money in people's minds. Money represents power and control, and the ability to do whatever one wants. If one has all the money, then one has all the power. If one has all the power, they have all the control, and can shape and form things however they desire, as they wish, whenever they want. This understanding of equating money with power and control has led not only to a love of money, but to a serious distortion in our relationship with it, especially as pertains to our intimate relationships. Whether we like to think of it this way or not, every single one of us has a relationship with money. Money is a necessity to live, cover expenses, and to handle our day-to-day living. If we are in business or ministry, money is a requirement to offer both. If we view money as a means for power, our approach and need for money will reach the points of gluttony and greed, and we will mishandle our finances in every situation.

In marriages, money represents power and control. We've adapted this mindset from the world. That means how the money is spent, who controls it, and who has the most of it, even in a marriage, has the upper hand in the relationship. Unfortunately, money is used this way in many marriages, thus the reality is that it is a source of deep contention and upset in most relationships.

Let's remember the words of 1 Timothy 6:9-10:

THOSE WHO WANT TO BECOME RICH BRING TEMPTATION TO THEMSELVES [FALL INTO TEMPTATION] AND ARE CAUGHT IN A TRAP. THEY WANT [DESIRE] MANY FOOLISH AND HARMFUL THINGS THAT RUIN AND DESTROY PEOPLE [PLUNGE PEOPLE INTO RUIN AND DESTRUCTION]. [FOR] THE LOVE OF MONEY CAUSES [IS THE ROOT OF] ALL KINDS OF EVIL. SOME PEOPLE HAVE LEFT [STRAYED/WANDERED FROM] THE FAITH, BECAUSE THEY WANTED TO GET MORE MONEY [IT], BUT THEY HAVE CAUSED THEMSELVES MUCH SORROW [AND HAVE PIERCED THEMSELVES WITH MANY PAINS].

- If you are married and you are fighting about money and constantly trying to outdo your spouse through money, you have the love of money.
- If you are married and you can't agree on how to budget your household, you have the love of money.
- If you are married and trying to amass a great number of material things all the time, you have the love of money.
- If you are married and amassing credit card debt, you have the love of money.
- If you are married and constantly trying to "keep up with the Joneses," then you have the love of money.
- If you can't live within your means, then you have the love of money.
- If every thought you have revolves around getting more money, having more money, or the dreaded, "If I only had more money…" then you have the love of money.

How can we take the "sting" out of money in a household? The best way to do it is changing the relationship both partners have with money. If money is no longer seen as a force for power and control, it will no longer be used to try and dominate a relationship. Ways to help avoid these issues with money include:

- **Have a household budget that both partners understand and agree to abide by:** Budgeting is simply an assessment of the monthly income and outgo in a household, monitored by bills that need to be paid and income that comes in. Both partners in the household should be adult enough and mature enough to recognize that unlimited spending is simply not an option in any household, no matter how much money you have. Priorities need to be set (food, rent/mortgage, clothing, hygiene, electricity, gas, paying of debt, etc.) and need to be set in stone. Couples also need to make sure that money goes away for savings, retirement, and if they have children, college funds.

- **Have separate money for each partner:** We talked earlier about the fact that each spouse has the right to their own money. Nobody, whether in a relationship or not, has the right to take someone else's money or tell them how to spend it. In marriage, it is mutually understood that both parties need to share the funds they have and make sure that basic needs are covered, but one party does not have the right to take, nor seize funds from the other. Each partner is entitled to have some of their own money to do with what they desire.

- **Discuss money:** Talking about money should not be the theme of every discussion you have, nor should it be the same whiny "I never have enough money" conversation that people typically have. Rather, you should talk about your goals and hopes as a couple. You should talk about what is most important, and how you can better spend your money. If you are seeking to buy a house or a better apartment, find ways to reduce debt. If you want to take a trip, find ways to do so without it costing an arm and a leg. Recognize that talking about money doesn't mean anyone has the bottom line in the discussion, and that discovering how each of you feels and what each of you wants to come makes it so that both of you are a part of the financial decision-making in the household.

- **Set priorities:** There should be some priorities that are priorities without saying such, such as food, rent, mortgage, and electricity. There are other priorities, however, that are personal priorities: they are important to the individual as a person. For example, if someone is in ministry, making sure they have adequate funds to do their ministry would be a priority of theirs. If someone desires to own their own home, that would be a priority of theirs. As a couple, the priorities of both partners should be relevant, and should both be given the necessary consideration and encouragement when financially planning.

- **Work together as a team:** Cease the financial strife by working together, as a team, to bring all your goals, dreams, and visions to pass. Stop making it about how much one has or doesn't have. Work together and be willing to compromise and help each other out.

The "little foxes"

In our central Biblical text for this marriage preparation project, we find a verse that many overlook. It is Song of Solomon 2:15:

CATCH [GRAB] THE FOXES FOR US— THE LITTLE FOXES THAT RUIN THE VINEYARDS WHILE THEY ARE IN BLOSSOM [THREATS TO THE RELATIONSHIP].

We are quick to talk about the "big things" that affect relationships: affairs, adultery, secret lives, etc. Those are things people want to keep themselves safe from and guard against securely and tightly. What people don't talk about and don't consider are all the little things that come our way and try to affect our lives negatively, every day and in every way, or the way we can respond to them that will either be helpful or harmful.

Even though we want to focus on big things, this verse is trying to teach us that the little things matter. If something small can ruin something big, then something small can also make a world of difference.

There are so many "little foxes" in a relationship that are obvious to partners when they genuinely care for and seek to work together in a relationship. The little things, little gifts, little moments, little expressions of care, and the little moments of affection that really show someone else care and love. If you are listening to your partner and paying attention to the things they like and the things that are important to them, then the "little foxes" shouldn't be hard to pick up. Some examples include:

- A special, unplanned lunch or dinner date
- Treating someone to a special dessert treat (such as ice cream)
- Making coffee just the way they like it
- Breakfast in bed
- A special gift (such as jewelry or an intimate gift such as lingerie)
- A special book or Bible
- Bringing home their favorite cologne or perfume
- A favorite candy
- A favorite flower or flowers
- Taking care of an errand or chore
- Offering to watch the kids so they can have a day to themselves

In keeping with principles of respect, next we will be looking at communion – and the important role it plays in marriage. Keep in mind all you have learned about respect, because it is going to be very important as we consider the essence of communion and its heart of respect!

Week 10 Assignments

Answer the following questions based on discussions you have had with your future spouse in counseling this week and additionally on your own time and prepare to discuss them at your next counseling session. If you run out of room in a section, finish the answer to your question in your journal.

1. How is love shown in respect? _____

_____

_____

_____

_____

2. Why do you think a marriage cannot survive without respect?

_____

_____

_____

_____

3. Is respect automatically granted or is it earned? Why do you feel this way? _____

_____

_____

_____

_____

4. Should couples enter into marriage with a sense of respect for one another? Why is this important? _____

_____

_____

_____

_____

5. Are marriage partners equal in the marriage? How is this different from everything being "equal" all the time? _____

_____

_____

_____

_____

6. How does "loving our neighbor as we love ourselves" and "treat others the way you want to be treated" apply in our marriage situations? _____

_____

_____

_____

_____

7. Instead of "bottom-lining" decisions, how should couples handle issues that arise in their marriages? _____

_____

_____

_____

_____

8. Should partners in a marriage ever feel marginalized? Why is this feeling so detrimental to marriages? _____

_____

_____

_____

_____

9. Why are parent-child dynamics so dangerous in a marriage? How can they be overcome? _____

_____

_____

_____

_____

10. How can you avoid taking advantage of your partner's weaknesses and failings? _____

_____

_____

_____

_____

11. What eight things does every spouse have the right to? _____

_____

_____

_____

_____

12. Why is acknowledging accomplishments an important thing in a marriage? _____

_____

_____

_____

_____

13. What are some ways people show disrespect to each other in marriage? _____

_____

_____

_____

_____

14. If you need to talk to your spouse and they are busy, what is the best way to handle that situation? _____

_____

_____

_____

_____

15. Why do you think that money is such a source of conflict in so many marriages? _____

_____

_____

_____

_____

16. What are some ways you can avoid conflicts over money? What would you say are financial priorities for you as a person?

_____

_____

_____

_____

_____

17. What are some small things you intend to do for your spouse once you get married? _____

_____

_____

_____

_____

18. Do you think the couple in the Song of Solomon had respect for each other? Why or why not? _____

_____

_____

_____

_____

19. In reading Matthew 5:43-48, how do you think Jesus' command to love our neighbor, pray for our neighbor, and do good to our neighbor applies to marriage? _____

_____

_____

_____

_____

20. Talk with your future spouse about moments in your relationship when you felt loved and respected by one another and share those stories here. _____

_____

_____

_____

_____

Week Eleven

Marriage and Communion

WE GIVE THANKS FOR THE CUP OF BLESSING [USED IN THE LORD'S SUPPER], WHICH IS [IS THIS NOT...?] A SHARING [PARTICIPATION; FELLOWSHIP] IN THE BLOOD OF CHRIST. AND THE BREAD THAT WE BREAK IS [IS IT NOT...?] A SHARING [PARTICIPATION; FELLOWSHIP] IN THE BODY OF CHRIST. BECAUSE THERE IS ONE LOAF OF BREAD, WE WHO ARE MANY ARE ONE BODY, BECAUSE WE ALL SHARE THAT ONE LOAF.
(1 CORINTHIANS 10:16-17)

Bible reading: 1 Corinthians 11:17-34

Journaling assignments for in-session discussion:

- How does the communion of married couples relate to the communion of the Body of Christ?
- Why are communion and marriage connected?

Communion is one of those aspects of church we don't hear about much these days. It used to be something that we spoke about in very serious terms, preparing the church for and examining ourselves for, because we were warned against taking it unworthily. Partaking of Communion was considered a big deal, and it was an honor to be able to eat at the table of the Lord. We weren't just eating little pieces of bread or wafers and having some grape juice; we were partaking in something with God, coming and receiving a revelation of Christ and His sacrifice for us that we could not get in another way. By participating in communion, we expressed our union with Him, and with one another, for those of us who were also in Him.

In the last two chapters, we talked about unity and respect. Now we are talking about communion in marriage. Even though it might not seem like it, respect, unity, and communion all relate to each other, and are very, very important components of marriage. This is because the communion that a couple has in marriage is both a type of the communion we have with Christ, and the union we have with our fellow brothers and sisters in Christ when we come together in the rite of Communion. There are many ways it is expressed, and many more ways that we can come to understand it as we live, move, and have our being with Him as married people.

Holy Communion

Luke 22:14-20:

WHEN THE TIME [HOUR] CAME, JESUS AND THE APOSTLES WERE SITTING AT THE TABLE [RECLINED; THE POSTURE AT A FORMAL MEAL; SEE 7:36]. HE SAID TO THEM, "I WANTED VERY MUCH TO EAT THIS PASSOVER MEAL WITH YOU BEFORE I SUFFER. [FOR I TELL YOU] I WILL NOT EAT ANOTHER PASSOVER MEAL UNTIL IT IS GIVEN ITS TRUE MEANING [FULFILLED] IN THE KINGDOM OF GOD."

THEN JESUS TOOK A CUP, GAVE THANKS, AND SAID, "TAKE THIS CUP AND SHARE IT AMONG YOURSELVES. [FOR I TELL YOU] I WILL NOT DRINK AGAIN FROM THE FRUIT OF THE VINE [WINE] UNTIL GOD'S KINGDOM COMES."

THEN JESUS TOOK SOME BREAD, GAVE THANKS, BROKE IT, AND GAVE IT TO THE APOSTLES, SAYING, "THIS IS MY BODY, WHICH I AM GIVING FOR YOU. DO THIS TO REMEMBER [AS A MEMORIAL TO; IN REMEMBRANCE OF] ME." IN THE SAME WAY, AFTER SUPPER [THEY HAD EATEN], JESUS TOOK THE CUP AND SAID, "THIS CUP [OR THIS CUP THAT IS POURED OUT...] IS THE NEW AGREEMENT [COVENANT; A BINDING RELATIONSHIP BETWEEN GOD AND HIS PEOPLE; JER. 31:31–34] THAT BEGINS WITH [THAT IS ESTABLISHED BY; OR THAT IS SEALED WITH; IN] MY BLOOD, WHICH IS POURED OUT FOR YOU [INTERPRETERS DIFFER AS TO WHETHER IT IS THE "CUP" OR THE "BLOOD" THAT JESUS SAYS IS "POURED OUT"].

Since this book is not specifically about the rite of Holy Communion, I am not going to devote much time to discussion on exactly what it is. It's understood that if you are in church, you most likely have heard teachings on communion and have learned about it in preaching, Sunday School, and Bible study. If you haven't, I suggest you talk to your spiritual leader about learning more about it. If you would like to learn more about it and need a good textual reference, I recommend my book, *Sacred Ceremonies: The Who, What, When, Where, Why, and How of Christian Ordinances, Rites, and Rituals.* In there, I devote an entire chapter to the ordinance of communion and its ins and outs. Here, we are going to go over a very brief overview of Holy Communion and what it is:

- Holy Communion is the memorial of Jesus' death. We find record of it in the Gospels as occurring during the Passover, on the night before Jesus died. At the end of the Passover meal, Jesus took unleavened bread and wine, both of which were on the table, and offered them up, telling the disciples at the table to take and eat and drink, because they represented His body and blood.
- We are instructed that inasmuch as we do this same rite, to do it in memory of Him.
- Most churches use unleavened bread in the form of matzo crackers or wafers and grape juice (so as to invite all to the table, including those with substance abuse histories and children) in communion services.
- We have no indication of how often to hold Communion, except that every time we do it, we should do it in memory of Him.
- We are called to examine ourselves prior to partaking Communion, to make sure we do not receive unworthily, mocking or disregarding God or His Body in the church.
- Communion is not snack-time, or an excuse to be glutinous.
- Communion teaches us basic principles about unity and connectedness in the Body.
- Many Communion services also include a foot washing service, which reenacts Jesus' washing the disciples' feet in John 13 and reminds us of our call to serve the Lord as we

serve one another.

- Most churches hold Communion service either monthly or quarterly, and most also handle Communion with the utmost reverence.

In preparation for your marriage, I encourage both of you to take an active participation in the Communion ministry prior to your wedding. Talk with your leader about ways you can be more involved, whether by preparing elements, distributing them, cleaning up after service, or preparing items for a foot washing ceremony.

Unity and Communion

Jesus' death on the cross was an act of atonement for sin. That act of atonement wasn't just to make sin go away and make it so we can reach our full human potential, like many preachers teach. Jesus' act of atonement was one of unity, one that gave human beings the ability to unite again with God and to commune with Him: to celebrate a state of being that reflects unity and purpose with Him. When we come to God through Christ, we are able to rest in Him and share our lives with Him in a way that was impossible before Christ's death on the cross. That is why communion is a memorial of His death: Jesus' death was a communing act, something that brought about a unity between God and human beings. Communion reminds us of that sacrifice, and of Jesus' true willingness to lay Himself down and become the reparation for sin.

Communion didn't just unite each of us with God; it also unites us as a body of believers, the church. Communion shows that each of us are in union with God, and that we are working together, here on earth, to proclaim the Gospel and make His Kingdom known.

Romans 12:4-5:

[FOR JUST AS] EACH ONE OF US HAS A [ONE] BODY WITH MANY PARTS, AND THESE PARTS ALL HAVE DIFFERENT USES [FUNCTIONS]. IN THE SAME WAY, WE ARE MANY, BUT IN CHRIST WE ARE ALL ONE BODY, AND EACH PART BELONGS TO ALL THE OTHER PARTS [MEMBERS].

These same principles apply to us in marriage, as well. Marriage is an agreement of covenant, a union, that we agree to live and dwell together as spouses and proclaim the Kingdom of God. As marriage is a type of the relationship between Christ and the church, so too marriage shows the union between Christ, His church, and the church members as sisters and brothers. Marriage is a form of unity, a depth of teamwork and agreement, working together through a lifetime bond of covenantal love.

We can't be in communion rightly and worthily if we are not in unity with God and with our brothers and sisters in Christ. We can't be in marriage if we are not in communion with one another. If we desire to have healthy, Christ-centered marriages, we must see communion as an important, essential element of our union with one another... and with God.

Respect and Communion

In many churches, the table on which Communion elements are displayed is never touched. On Communion Sundays, it is covered with a pure, white linen cloth. Communion elements are brought out in the finest trays, and those who handle and distribute Communion wear white gloves in the process. Ministers are expected to attire themselves in full civic attire, and church mothers and ministers-in-training usually wear white. Even people in the congregation are required to come to the Communion table in certain attire, and are warned about receiving Communion "unworthily."

1 Corinthians 11:27-30:

SO A PERSON WHO EATS THE BREAD OR DRINKS THE CUP OF THE LORD IN A WAY THAT IS NOT WORTHY OF IT [OR AN INAPPROPRIATE MANNER] WILL BE GUILTY OF SINNING AGAINST [OR HELD RESPONSIBLE FOR; LIABLE FOR; GUILTY OF] THE BODY AND THE BLOOD OF THE LORD. LOOK INTO YOUR OWN HEARTS [LET A PERSON EXAMINE HIMSELF] BEFORE YOU EAT THE BREAD AND DRINK THE CUP, BECAUSE ALL WHO EAT THE BREAD AND DRINK THE CUP WITHOUT RECOGNIZING [DISCERNING; CAREFUL REGARD FOR] THE BODY EAT AND DRINK JUDGMENT AGAINST THEMSELVES. THAT IS WHY MANY IN YOUR GROUP ARE SICK AND WEAK, AND SOME [A NUMBER] OF YOU HAVE DIED [FALLEN ASLEEP; A EUPHEMISM FOR DEATH].

All these things are signs of respect for the Lord in our Communion supper. No matter what our specific doctrines may be as pertain to Communion, we do not want to take the risk of disrespecting the Lord's sacrifice in our remembrance of Him in Communion. Communion is a time to show respect and honor for what God has done for us through Christ, and it is our place to extend that respect in the things we do and the way we treat the communion elements.

We don't want to offend Christ by approaching His sacrifice with disrespect. The same principle applies in marriage. If we are married or are going to be married, we should apply principles of respect so we can show our spouse that we respect and honor them. As marriage partners, we should be careful how we approach, treat, and handle matters as pertain to our spouses. It should not be a situation where anything goes and any approach is acceptable but we should always be careful to merit a certain level of respect and appropriateness in every situation. If we maintain Christian relationships where we believe that God has allowed us the honor of living with our mate, then that means God can take our mate from us at any time. Respecting our mate is not merely respecting a vessel, but the creation of God and the honor that God has given us to live with and share our lives with this person in marriage.

Communion and marriage are not designed to end

In our relationship with God, our communion with Him should never end. It is something ongoing, symbolized in Holy Communion. Whether it should end or not, sometimes it does, for a variety of reasons. The same applies to marriage. In an ideal and sinless world, there would be no divorce. We acknowledge it exists and happens, but it's not something that ideally should have to exist. At the same time, it is something that is designed to be ongoing. Marriage is designed to take us throughout life, through highs, lows, complications, challenges, joys, and concerns. At the end of every day of marriage, there's a table, a living room, a bedroom, or other private place where we can commune together, sharing with our spouse – much as we do with God.

Keeping the "spark" in marriage

THERE ARE ENDLESS BOOKS, TIPS, AND TEACHINGS ABOUT KEEPING THE "SPARK" IN MARRIAGE. IF WE LISTEN TO THE WORLD, MAKING SURE THAT YOUR RELATIONSHIP IS SATISFYING IN THE BEDROOM IS THE ULTIMATE ANSWER TO KEEPING A MARRIAGE TOGETHER. IS THIS TRUE?

IT IS TRUE THAT PROBLEMS RELATING TO SEX ARE USUALLY AN INDICATOR THAT SOMETHING ELSE IS WRONG IN A MARRIAGE, BUT THIS IS NOT ALWAYS THE CASE. THERE CAN BE MEDICALLY RELATED OR EMOTIONALLY RELATED ISSUES THAT AFFECT A COUPLE'S SEX LIFE THAT HAVE NOTHING TO DO WITH WHERE THEIR RELATIONSHIP IS. AT THE SAME TIME, FOR MANY COUPLES, IF SEX STARTS TO TAPER OFF, BECOME LESS AND LESS OF A PRIORITY, OR UNENJOYABLE FOR ONE OR BOTH PARTNERS, THERE IS PROBABLY AN ISSUE SOMEWHERE ELSE IN A MARRIAGE. IT USUALLY RELATES TO A COUPLE'S LEVEL OF CONNECTION, WHICH SOMEWHERE, AT SOME POINT IN TIME, STARTED TO SUFFER FROM DISCONNECTION.

THE BEST WAY TO KEEP A SPARK ALIVE IN A MARRIAGE IS TO KEEP COMMUNICATION OPEN AND TO FEEL COMFORTABLE WITH YOUR PARTNER. IF ONE PARTNER BECOMES OVERLY DEMANDING OR CRITICAL, IT CAUSES THE OTHER PARTNER TO FEEL LIKE THEY ARE UNIMPORTANT AND THEIR NEEDS ARE NOT GOING TO BE MET. THIS DOESN'T JUST RELATE TO THINGS ABOUT SEX, BUT ANY SORT OF PROBLEM OR ISSUE THAT GOES ON IN THE RELATIONSHIP. IF ONE PARTNER (OR BOTH) FEEL THAT THEY ARE NOT A PRIORITY IN THE RELATIONSHIP, HAS TOO MANY RESPONSIBILITIES OR FEELS BURDENED, THEY ARE GOING TO FIND THEMSELVES MORE AND MORE DISINTERESTED IN SEX AND PHYSICAL INTERACTION WITH THEIR PARTNER.

COUPLES SHOULD SPEND TIME TOGETHER, SEPARATE FROM THEIR RESPONSIBILITIES, CHORES, AND FAMILIES. THEY SHOULD ALSO REMEMBER THE VALUE IN TAKING CARE OF THEMSELVES AND IN PAMPERING ONE ANOTHER. LIFE SHOULD NOT BE RESPONSIBILITIES ALL THE TIME OR DUTIES ALL THE TIME, BUT THE FREEDOM TO LOVE AND ENJOY ONE ANOTHER AS PEOPLE, REMEMBERING THAT THEY ARE, AS INDIVIDUALS AND A COUPLE, IMPORTANT, TOO.

Psalm 23:5-6:

YOU PREPARE A MEAL [TABLE] FOR ME

IN FRONT [THE PRESENCE] OF MY ENEMIES.
YOU POUR OIL OF BLESSING ON MY HEAD [ANOINT MY HEAD WITH OIL; OIL
WAS A MEANS OF REFRESHMENT IN A HOT, DRY ENVIRONMENT];
   YOU FILL MY CUP TO OVERFLOWING [MAKE MY CUP OVERFLOW; A CUP
OF BLESSING].
SURELY YOUR GOODNESS AND LOVE [LOYALTY; MERCY] WILL BE WITH
[PURSUE; FOLLOW] ME
   ALL MY LIFE,
AND I WILL LIVE IN THE HOUSE OF THE LORD FOREVER [FOR LENGTH OF
DAYS].

Weddings are great, wonderful, exciting events in people's lives. They represent milestones, new beginnings, and new lives. They also end. One day, the wedding you have been planning for ages will be over, and a new event will begin: your marriage. Unlike your wedding, your marriage is, ideally, not set to end in this lifetime. Like communion with God, we should continue to be in fellowship and relationship with our spouse until the end of our lives. This echoes communion, which doesn't end when Communion Sunday's service concludes.

Receiving the different rites, rituals, and ordinances in the church

Titus 3:7:

BEING [... SO THAT HAVING BEEN] MADE RIGHT WITH GOD [JUSTIFIED; DECLARED RIGHTEOUS] BY HIS GRACE, WE COULD HAVE THE HOPE OF RECEIVING [BECOME HEIRS WITH THE HOPE/EXPECTATION OF] THE LIFE THAT NEVER ENDS [ETERNAL LIFE].

Being married doesn't mean our participation in God's Kingdom stops, and it should not stop our participation in the church. As a married couple, being a part of church should be ongoing. Being married should draw us closer to a place of truth and love with God, seeing types of His love and grace extended toward us in our married lives. Just like receiving communion should make us more aware of God's presence and cause us to draw to Him deeper, marriage should do the same for us with God. This means that we should never, ever stop seeking God because we are married. Rather, we should seek Him in a deeper way for the areas of holiness that marriage helps us to develop.

If we are seeking God in a deeper way, we should seek God through the different rites, rituals, and ordinances that we have through the church, namely:

- Water Baptism
- Communion
- Ordination
- Appointments
- Graduation services
- Anointing
- Consecration
- Weddings
- Funerals
- Presentation/Dedication
- Naming

If we pay special attention to the rites, rituals, and ordinances of the church, we notice that many of them revolve around stages of life as well as spiritual life. Water baptism, Communion, ordination, appointments, consecration, services celebrating an anniversary or relevant day, and anointing all relate to different spiritual needs we have and experience as we walk in God's call for us. Weddings, funerals, and presentations/dedications are things that we experience in accord within different stages of life. People who get married have a wedding, funerals memorialize those who have died, and presentation celebrates a new baby or young child becoming a part of God's family, being trained and prepared for new generations. This means that three of the ten rites, rituals, and ordinances relate in a special way to family life, and two of the nine rituals relate directly to our relationship with God as believers.

If you are preparing for marriage, no matter how you desire to live – either with children or without them – you are preparing for a special rite that relates to family life. As you go through your married life, and if you decide to have children and bring them into the fold of spiritual life, you will see the value and importance in these family rites, rituals, and ordinances, and how they relate to spiritual life.

Setting the example for your spouse

I have very seldom met two people who are in the exact same place spiritually when they decide to get married. I don't think that married couples must be the same for marriage to work, and I do think this applies to spiritual levels as much as it does any other level in life. People don't need to be the same to be suited for one another, and if a couple can maintain support, intimacy, and respect for one another, they don't have to be in exactly the same place at the same time. (This is different from being involved with a non-Christian, obviously, which we will discuss more later in this book.)

We all have a different relationship with God and a different walk with God, and not all of us move at the same pace, at the same time, with the same vigor. If you have a spouse who desires to move forward in this walk toward heaven, then it doesn't matter if they are ahead of you, behind you, or somewhere else; it matters they are going where they should, in God's timing and pace. It's the same way as we view remaining in communion with the Body of Christ. Each person in the church universal is walking the path to eternity with God, but we are all at different places. Just because they are ahead of or behind where we may be doesn't nullify where we are or where they are... it just means we are in a different place. Just as we do in the Kingdom, we can do in our marriages: we can be a good example for someone else who needs to or desires to seek God more profoundly.

Psalm 71:7:

I AM AN EXAMPLE [PORTENT] TO MANY PEOPLE, BECAUSE YOU ARE MY STRONG PROTECTION [REFUGE].

John 13:15:

I DID THIS AS AN EXAMPLE [A PATTERN] SO THAT YOU SHOULD DO AS I HAVE DONE FOR YOU.

If you desire your spouse to seek God in a deeper way, then the example for that should be set in your own life and walk. Too often, we start focusing on where someone else is in the faith and don't pay enough attention to where we ourselves may be. I have known many women and men who make their personal prayer and devotional lives center around changing their spouse into the person they hope they will become spiritually. There is a danger in making your spouse the entire focus of your personal prayer life, not to mention a serious spiritual danger in trying to use prayer as a weapon to change other people. Rather than using prayer to try and change others, take a good, long look at yourself. Ask God to show you how you can be a better witness of the Gospel to your spouse, and how you can better reflect the essence of the Christian life. If you feel there is some way that things could be better, take the lead and set the example yourself.

Stop trying to change your spouse

John 21:20-22:

PETER TURNED AND SAW THAT THE FOLLOWER [DISCIPLE] JESUS LOVED [JOHN] WAS WALKING BEHIND THEM [FOLLOWING]. (THIS WAS THE FOLLOWER [DISCIPLE] WHO HAD LEANED AGAINST JESUS AT THE SUPPER AND HAD SAID, "LORD, WHO WILL TURN AGAINST [BETRAY] YOU?" [SEE 13:24–25]) WHEN PETER SAW HIM BEHIND THEM, HE ASKED JESUS, "LORD, WHAT ABOUT HIM?"

JESUS ANSWERED [HIM], "IF I WANT HIM TO LIVE UNTIL I COME BACK, THAT IS NOT YOUR BUSINESS [WHAT IS THAT TO YOU?]. YOU FOLLOW ME."

One of the deepest messages we are called to learn in church is that we are to love people, no matter where they are in their lives. If we love people, we love them as they are. If that means we must keep a distance, or we are not able to be close and personal with them, then that's what it means, but it means that we stop trying to change them. The world is full of different people, different personalities, and yes, different habits that often drive us crazy. When it comes to marriage, we don't have the easy answer of just going off somewhere else and loving our spouse from afar. If we are going to be married to someone, we must take the good with the bad and accept that there will be some things that will be more desirable about that person to live with than other things.

Coupling with what we just discussed in the last section, I know numerous ministers whose entire prayer life and personal spiritual agenda is to make their spouse a minister, in the same way that they are. Or maybe their entire prayer life is about changing their spouse to be something other than they want them to be.

I don't know that I must express how thoroughly unfair such behavior is. This defies the communion principle of unity: despite differences, we can still be one. I recognize that sometimes in marriage, we get in over our heads, and a spouse may demonstrate behavior that is controlling or demonic. I'm not talking about these instances, because nobody should live with these circumstances. I am talking about not accepting your spouse for who they are. If you marry them and you continue to live with them, then they are going to be who they are. If you can't live with someone, then don't stay with them, but don't expect that you are going to change them into someone else.

Ch-ch-changes

I once saw a meme on Facebook that said: "Sometimes the things we cannot change end up changing us." There is some real truth in this statement, because the ultimate end of change comes to us through life. We can't change everything about life. Many things sneak up on us, don't go as planned, and life has a way of changing us. In the principle of communion, we recognize that things change. We remain flexible enough to move through these changes with others, as God is flexible enough to move through our changes with us. Being closed-minded to the changes of your spouse is just as bad as trying to change who they are, because you don't accept something about them.

Ecclesiastes 3:1-8:

THERE IS A TIME [SEASON] FOR EVERYTHING,
*   AND EVERYTHING [EVERY ACTIVITY] ON EARTH [UNDER HEAVEN] HAS*
ITS SPECIAL SEASON [TIME].
THERE IS A TIME TO BE BORN
*   AND A TIME TO DIE.*
THERE IS A TIME TO PLANT
*   AND A TIME TO PULL UP PLANTS [UPROOT WHAT HAS BEEN PLANTED].*
THERE IS A TIME TO KILL

AND A TIME TO HEAL.
THERE IS A TIME TO DESTROY [TEAR DOWN]
    AND A TIME TO BUILD.
THERE IS A TIME TO CRY
    AND A TIME TO LAUGH.
THERE IS A TIME TO BE SAD [MOURN]
    AND A TIME TO DANCE.
THERE IS A TIME TO THROW AWAY STONES
    AND A TIME TO GATHER THEM.
THERE IS A TIME TO HUG [EMBRACE]
    AND A TIME NOT TO HUG [TO REFRAIN FROM EMBRACING].
THERE IS A TIME TO LOOK FOR SOMETHING [SEEK]
    AND A TIME TO STOP LOOKING FOR IT [GIVE UP AS LOST; OR LOSE].
THERE IS A TIME TO KEEP THINGS
    AND A TIME TO THROW THINGS AWAY.
THERE IS A TIME TO TEAR APART
    AND A TIME TO SEW TOGETHER.
THERE IS A TIME TO BE SILENT
    AND A TIME TO SPEAK.
THERE IS A TIME TO LOVE
    AND A TIME TO HATE.
THERE IS A TIME FOR WAR
    AND A TIME FOR PEACE.

As we go along in life, people change. Experiences, age, wisdom, life, and changes around us all change who we are. It's a part of maturing, of getting older, and of experiencing life's changes. In marriage, we need to be flexible enough to change, and also to allow our spouse their room for personal growth and change. This means being respectful of new ideas and thoughts they have, of being open to new visions and things they would like to take on and letting the sky be the limit for them as God does a work in them that none of us could ever imagine.

Spending time together

Psalm 127:1:

IF THE LORD DOESN'T BUILD THE HOUSE,
    THE BUILDERS ARE WORKING FOR NOTHING [IN VAIN; WITHOUT PURPOSE].

The evolution of the "date night" has come about as more people realize how increasingly busy their schedules are and how little time they spend together as a couple. Some of this has to do with the way in which children are raised in modern times. Children are less structured than they used to be, with later bedtimes (if any bedtime at all), parents are more involved in their socialization (such as playdates) and are expected to be more involved in their schooling and other monitored events, such as television watching or surfing the internet. As a result, more of parents' lives revolve around their children, spending money on their children, and doing things for their children than ever before. Instead of seeing child-rearing as training children to be socialized unto adulthood, many parents see their children as little extensions of themselves and feel that it is more important to give children what they want instead of setting boundaries and limits for them.

I am not going to get into extensive details about raising children and what is right or wrong, beyond discussion about the importance of raising them in the faith in a future section. The reason I have raised this point is to look at how the way we do things today causes us to be so busy, we are quickly pulled away from the availability to do what is truly important. Children are a good example of this, but they are not the only example of this. There are many childless couples who are so busy working or climbing career ladders that they seldom, if ever, see their spouses. Some people are so engaged in volunteering, or even ministry work, at times, they are completely devoid of their own relationship with their spouse.

The whole principle of communion is unity and dwelling. In marriage, we need to express our unity and our desire to be with our spouse by being with them. I don't think this should be in an unhealthy or out-of-balance way where we are dominated or overwhelmed by having to spend so much time with someone, that we get to a point where that becomes a task. In life, all of us need time alone, we need time for work and focus, we need time for leisure, and we need time for our spouses. Some people find date nights work for them, but in a larger sense, I think if we have grown so busy that we have to schedule time, we need to look at what we are doing and prune away things that aren't fruitful to make more time in our lives. Spending time with a spouse shouldn't always be about doing something, but should be about being, relaxing, and dwelling together in a peaceful, pleasant setting.

There's room at the table for you

Revelation 3:20:

HERE I AM [LOOK; BEHOLD]! I STAND AT THE DOOR AND KNOCK. IF YOU [ANYONE] HEAR MY VOICE AND OPEN THE DOOR, I WILL COME IN AND EAT WITH YOU, AND YOU WILL EAT WITH ME.

We hear many elaborate theories about the end times and what will happen after Jesus comes back. A largely ignored detail of that end times experience is that when Jesus comes back, we are going to be sitting down with the Lord, and having a wedding supper, i.e., a dinner. Even though it seems like millions throughout history will be present at this banquet, there is still room for one more, just as there is always room for one more person at the banquet of Holy Communion. The same should be true in households when it comes to family meals, because every family meal is a preparation for that great banquet when Jesus returns. It also proves to be a type of communion, teaching children and guests alike about the importance of the spiritual table as well as the family table.

Families should have dinner together, ideally every night. Obviously, there are times when things come up, but that should be the exception, and not the rule. There should be the opportunity to share about the day, to focus on each other as a family, and to do so without the distraction of cell phones, computers, and the internet. Family members should also be encouraged to share the table with guests, inviting others to share meals with the family from time to time, as well.

Raising children in the faith

Deciding to have children is an awesome responsibility. That responsibility increases when you are a Christian couple, deciding to raise a child according to Christian principles. In raising children in the faith, you make the commitment to see your child through the Kingdom process of raising them unto adulthood, where they will, hopefully, choose to follow in the footsteps of their family and pursue the Christian life for themselves. This starts with baby Dedication/presentation and continues all the way through until they are adults.

Proverbs 22:6:

TRAIN CHILDREN TO LIVE THE RIGHT WAY [IN THEIR/OR HIS PATH; REFERRING EITHER TO CHILDREN OR TO GOD], AND WHEN THEY ARE OLD, THEY WILL NOT STRAY [DEPART] FROM IT.

There are many theories on child-rearing from the Christian perspective. It is not my place to debate those here, because how you choose to raise your children is something that you should consider as a couple, over a period of years, prior to having children. Once you have children, the exact way in which you raise them will change as your experience with them changes, as they get older, and as you learn the specific needs and ways of your child.

More than anything, it is most important for children to see their faith as a communion in a way they can understand. Talking to children about God starts from the time they are extremely young and able to realize that God exists, and that He cares about them. Getting a child a good, understandable children's Bible that expounds stories in a way they can understand and helping them to pray and learn prayers are also good ways to help engage them in spiritual things. Most children have unique spiritual awareness and are able to perceive God's presence, even though they might not know what it is. Children should be a part of a church that welcomes and understands their unique needs and recognizes the way they learn. They should attend Sunday School and other children's and youth programs that exist to help aid them in their faith, echoing what they are taught and learning at home from their parents. These programs teach children that church is theirs, too, and make them feel as if they have a part in participation, not just that they are going because their parents are making them.

Children also need to see their parents live their faith. They need to see their parents praying, dedicating and disciplining themselves to the way of the Word, upholding Christian principles, answering questions that they may have about God and faith, and encouraged to develop their spiritual gifts. This means that Christian parents need to know enough to guide, develop, and educate their children, to the best of their ability, so they are duly prepared for the Christian life that lies ahead for them.

Aging

One of the most difficult aspects of a marriage relationship is the aging process. Most people talk about growing old together and are excited at being together that long, for those many years, through that many changes, growth, and ups and downs. There is a true appreciation for genuine communion with a partner as one gets older, and as life typically slows down. The reality of aging with a partner does have that component to it but is often not as glamorous as it sounds. With aging comes many changes: children grow older and move out of the house, people retire, grandchildren come along, and a couple find themselves back alone, as the two-person family where they started. As couples get older still, they face issues of physical ailment, illness, or injury, end-of-life decisions, and, eventually, the end of life.

Isaiah 46:4:

EVEN WHEN YOU ARE OLD, I WILL BE THE SAME [AM HE]. EVEN WHEN YOUR HAIR HAS TURNED GRAY, I WILL TAKE CARE OF [SUSTAIN; CARRY] YOU. I MADE YOU AND WILL CARRY YOU. I WILL TAKE CARE OF [SUSTAIN; CARRY] AND SAVE [RESCUE] YOU.

These things can be scary for individuals, so it is important that couples set out in advance to communicate well and be there for each other, all the way to the end. During their lives, couples need to prepare wills, state end-of-life desires (burial, cremation, termination of life support, etc.) and prepare through retirement and investment for that stage of their lives. There are things that need to be discussed now, because when the time comes, everyone will then be prepared.

Week 11 Assignments

Answer the following questions based on discussions you have had with your future spouse in counseling this week and additionally on your own time and prepare to discuss them at your next counseling session. If you run out of room in a section, finish the answer to your question in your journal.

1. What is Holy Communion? _____

_____

_____

_____

_____

2. How does your church handle Communion services? _____

_____

_____

_____

_____

3. How are unity and communion related? _____

_____

_____

_____

_____

4. How does unity in communion relate to unity in marriage? _____

_____

_____

_____

_____

5. How are respect and communion related? _____

_____

_____

_____

_____

6. How does respect in communion relate to respect in marriage?

_____

_____

_____

_____

7. Are communion and marriage ever designed to end? Why or why
not? _____

_____

_____

_____

8. How should marriage draw us in a deeper way to the rest of the rites, rituals, and ordinances of the church? _____

_____

_____

_____

_____

9. If you desire your spouse to find God in a deeper way, what is the right way to approach this issue? _____

_____

_____

_____

_____

10. Should you try to change your spouse? What should you do instead? _____

_____

_____

_____

_____

11. When a person changes in a relationship, what is the right response to that? _____

_____

_____

_____

_____

12. How will you, as a couple, make sure to spend time together? What are some things you will do when you do spend time together? _____

_____

_____

_____

_____

13. Do you believe family meals are important? Why or why not?

_____

_____

_____

_____

14. Who do you intend to invite over for dinner once you are married? _____

_____

_____

_____

_____

15. How do you intend to raise your children in the Christian faith?

_____

_____

_____

_____

_____

16. Does your church have an active children's ministry? What do they offer? _____

_____

_____

_____

17. What are your end of life wishes? Do you seek cremation or burial? Do you want a funeral? Do you want to remain on life support? Write down and discuss some of your end-of-life beliefs and desires. _____

_____

_____

_____

18. How do you believe the couple in the Song of Solomon expressed their marital communion? _____

_____

_____

_____

_____

19. In reading 1 Corinthians 11:17-34, how do you think the words and requirements as pertain to communion can also relate to many issues that arise in marriages? _____

_____

_____

_____

_____

20. Have your own personal communion experience at your next counseling session, as a couple preparing for marriage. Write about your experience here and speak on how it gave you a new perspective about things relating to communion and the Body of Christ. _____

_____

_____

_____

_____

Week Twelve

When Marriage Doesn't Go as Planned

BUT COMPLETE THE FULL WEEK OF THE MARRIAGE CEREMONY WITH LEAH [THIS ONE], AND I WILL GIVE YOU RACHEL [THE OTHER ONE] TO MARRY ALSO. BUT YOU MUST SERVE ME ANOTHER SEVEN YEARS.
(GENESIS 29:27)

<u>Bible reading:</u> Hosea 1:1-9

<u>Journaling assignments for in-session discussion:</u>

- What are some things that you believe people are unprepared for before they get married?
- Why should we, as believers, have love and mercy for those who are divorced?

We tend to equate long marriages with happy ones. Just because a couple stays married for a long time does not mean that a couple is happy, nor that a marriage is good. Life has a way of changing how we feel about things over time, and marriage is not any different than many of the other things we encounter and experience. For many couples – in fact, for more than half of all couples, if we look at the statistics – the way they change in their perception of marriage becomes so radical, they find themselves unable to live together. It happens more than we'd like to believe, and to more people than we would like to think about. There are many things in life that come our way that hit us, hurt us, and change things forever, including our relationships.

Rather than hammer messages against things, I want us to look at the reason why many of these things happen, and how they affect marital relationships. It's great to be in love and want to get married, and it's awesome to celebrate marital milestones with couples who make it for the duration. There are also instances and signs when a relationship is hurting, and it is better to stop and step back rather than to take further punches. This chapter is for all those who have or who will, one day, must make the difficult decision to step back and let God work in their lives separately, rather than together.

This chapter isn't just about divorce, although we will discuss divorce in it. It is about all those things that starry-eyed couples do not think about, nor anticipate, before they get married. As one of the most difficult chapters and one of the most difficult weeks of pre-counseling you will encounter, take a deep breath and look at those who have gone on these paths differently, all the while understanding more why they made the difficult choices they made to end their marriages.

Marriage as an institution

Galatians 6:2:

BEAR YE ONE ANOTHER'S BURDENS, AND SO FULFIL THE LAW OF CHRIST. (KJV)

I have already spoken on issues pertaining to marriage as an institution, and the way we treat it as such in the church. What we fail to realize is our treatment of marriage in this way has led to more people seeking a way out of the institution rather than trying to resolve issues that arise within it. We are so busy talking against divorce and too busy praying for marriage as an abstract thing that we have forgotten to pray for the people in difficult marriages and offer them the help that they need to get through rough times. In past generations, family, friends, and the church tended to band together and help a family through their hurt, which helped marriages and families to stay together. Now, with people in so many different directions and so many uninterested people, it is far more common to see families fall apart because they don't have the proper support.

I say all this because the reality is that when couples get in trouble, they seldom, if ever, find the true support they need to do what is right for them. People might listen, sometimes leaders even listen, but they are quick to take divorce off the table or start telling couples what, and how, to do this, that, or something else. I believe many marriages would be saved if instead of fighting for an institution, we, as the church, started fighting for the people in the relationship.

If your marriage ever goes through hard times, what you need is the proper support to make decisions for yourselves as a couple and know that the people in your life love and support you, no matter what the decisions may be. Make sure that, as you grow and change and your life circumstances change, those around you have your back and are interested in you as people, rather than just as a marriage institution. This will help safeguard against issues that might arise and help you to feel more supported, loved, and cared about if you go through difficult times.

Getting married for all the wrong reasons

Contrary to popular belief, marriage does not solve all the issues that you have as a couple (or as an individual, for that matter). A marriage license doesn't solve all the issues you have, and it does not turn unhealthy dynamics into healthy ones. If you have unresolved, acknowledged (even if they are only acknowledged within your mind) problems before you get married, you are going to have those problems after you get married.

Proverbs 16:2-3:

YOU MAY BELIEVE YOU ARE DOING RIGHT [ALL PATHS OF PEOPLE ARE PURE IN THEIR EYES],
BUT THE LORD WILL JUDGE YOUR REASONS [MEASURE YOUR MOTIVES; WEIGH THE SPIRITS].

DEPEND ON THE LORD IN WHATEVER YOU DO [COMMIT YOUR ACTS/DEEDS TO THE LORD],
AND YOUR PLANS WILL SUCCEED [BE ESTABLISHED].

It's important that if you are entering into marriage, you are doing it for the right reasons: you love this person and can see yourself in a long-term, committed relationship with them. Any other reason for marriage is wrong and misleading, and will cause serious, if not irreparable, damage to your relationship. Marriage is not a Band-Aid, and it is not a cure-all, for issues you see in someone else. Getting married to someone will not do the following:

- Make them not abusive
- Make them heterosexual or heteronormative if they are homosexual (or queer in some other way)
- Make them stop watching pornography or engaging in other behaviors related to this
- Erase your feelings for someone else (no matter what orientation those feelings might be for or toward)
- Make you better liked or more popular
- Make you a better minister or preacher
- Make them stop drinking or engaging in different detrimental behaviors
- Make your family like you better
- Make you happy
- Make your family drama go away
- Make a traumatic past go away or seem different
- Erase memories
- Help you "find yourself" or figure out who you are

Getting married for any of these reasons will end in divorce. No matter how many years you try to stay together, no matter how much you try to make it work, no matter how much effort you give it, it isn't going to work. Marriage, as a type of Christ and the church, can't survive if the marriage is based on a lie or a deception. Using a spouse to try and escape from something else is wrong, period. It is wrong to use marriage for those purposes, and it is wrong to use the person in marriage for those purposes. For marriages to be healthy, they must be built on honesty. That requires both husband and wife to be honest and upfront about their reasons for marriage and not withholding reasons for marriage that are less than honest.

Prenuptial agreements

Genesis 34:12:

Ask as much as you want for the payment for the bride [bridal payment and gift; traditional payments to the family], and I will give it to you. Just let me marry Dinah [give me the girl as a wife]."

A prenuptial agreement is a contractual document that an engaged couple both sign prior to their marriage that agrees to certain terms and conditions once they are married. Prenuptial agreements tend to involve terms relating to money and distribution of assets during the marriage and in the event a couple may divorce. They typically exist among the very wealthy, but in recent years, prenuptial agreements have been adopted by many average middle-class couples, as well.

People are divided over prenuptial agreements. Some people feel that it takes trust and romance out of a relationship, and others feel like it anticipates divorce before it even starts. The truth is that a prenup, as they are often called, doesn't anticipate divorce. What prenuptial agreements do is establish certain financial regulations within a marriage and establish ownership of certain assets, regardless of marriage or divorce. There are those who feel that prenuptial agreements are a good thing. Marriage is not just about love and romance, but the legal merging of finances, assets, and family ties. Prenuptial agreements make sure that everyone knows where everyone stands, and they offer legal protection to both parties, regardless of what happens during a marriage.

The decision to have a prenuptial agreement is a personal one and depends on the couple. Some people are appalled at the suggestion, while others see it as something that can benefit their marriage. Some find themselves blind-sighted when it comes up, and I have heard of couples breaking up over prenup terms. How you desire to handle your prenup is up to you: either accept, negotiate, or terminate the relationship – but recognize that if you get married with a prenuptial agreement, its terms are binding once you are married.

Marriage to a non-believer

Personally, I don't like the term "unbeliever" because of the way we throw it around. There is a definite implication made in the things we say, that "believers" are implied to be good, and "unbelievers" are implied to be bad. It's worth considering there are plenty of believers whose characteristics don't line up with their faith, and there are many professing Christians who commit adultery, abuse their spouses, mistreat one another, and behave in ways that they shouldn't. This means we must re-think the biases and attitudes we come into this topic with and look at the issue from the perspective of addressing the issues rather than furthering propaganda.

The Bible has mixed perspectives on interfaith marriage. In the Old Testament, interfaith marriage was prohibited by spiritual law. This didn't stop it from happening, however. The prophets compared these "unfaithful marriages" to the greater issue of spiritual adultery: idolatry against God. By the time of the Prophet Malachi, interfaith marriage was so common, temple priests divorced their wives to marry pagan women. Malachi 2:11-16 says:

The people of Judah [Judah] have broken their promises [been unfaithful]. They have done something God hates [an abomination/detestable thing] in Israel and Jerusalem: The people of Judah [Judah] did not respect [desecrated] the Temple [sanctuary; or holy things] that the Lord loves, and the men of Judah married women who worship [the daughter of] foreign gods. Whoever does this might bring offerings to the Lord All-Powerful [Almighty; of Heaven's Armies; of hosts], but the Lord will still cut that person off from the ·community of Israel [tents of Jacob].

This is another thing you do. You cover the Lord's altar with your tears. You cry [weep] and moan, because he does not accept [look with favor on] your offerings and is not pleased with what you bring. You ask, "Why?" It is because the Lord sees how you treated [is the witness between you and] the wife you married when you were young [of your youth]. You broke your promise [have been unfaithful] to her, even though she was your partner and you had an agreement with her [your wife by solemn covenant]. God made [Did not God make... ?] husbands and wives to become one body and one spirit for his purpose—so they would have children who are true to God [godly offspring].

So be careful [guard yourself in your spirit], and do not break your promise [be unfaithful] to the wife you married when you were young [of your youth].

The Lord God of Israel says, "I hate divorce. And I hate the person who [or The one who hates and divorces] does cruel things as easily as he puts on clothes [covers his clothes in violence]," says the Lord All-Powerful [Almighty; of Heaven's Armies; of hosts].

So be careful [on your guard]. And do not break your trust [be unfaithful].

As we've discussed some, marriage in Biblical times wasn't like today. Marriage partners didn't pick their spouses, and arranged marriages meant families sought the most desirable options, not just for a couple, but for the extended family, as well. This means injunctions about marriage to non-believers wasn't for the couple themselves, but for the families who did the "arranging" on their behalf.

By the time we reached the New Testament, interfaith marriage was still discouraged, although not as prohibitive. The rise of Christianity led to new conflicts between couples, especially when one became a believer and the other did not. Couples still didn't choose their mates, which means interfaith marriage became more common. Although often quoted against interfaith marriage, 2 Corinthians 6:14-18 actually doesn't say anything about it:

DO NOT JOIN YOURSELVES TO [BECOME PARTNERS WITH; BE MISMATCHED/UNEVENLY YOKED WITH] UNBELIEVERS. GOOD AND BAD DO NOT BELONG TOGETHER [FOR WHAT PARTNERSHIP HAS RIGHTEOUSNESS AND WICKEDNESS/LAWLESSNESS?]. LIGHT AND DARKNESS CANNOT SHARE

TOGETHER [OR WHAT FELLOWSHIP/PARTNERSHIP CAN LIGHT HAVE WITH DARKNESS?]. HOW CAN CHRIST AND BELIAL [THE DEVIL; SATAN] HAVE ANY AGREEMENT [HARMONY; ACCORD]? WHAT CAN A BELIEVER HAVE TOGETHER [SHARE IN COMMON] WITH A NONBELIEVER? WHAT AGREEMENT [UNION] CAN THE TEMPLE OF GOD HAVE WITH IDOLS? FOR WE ARE THE TEMPLE OF THE LIVING GOD [1 COR. 3:16]. AS GOD SAID: "I WILL LIVE WITH THEM AND WALK WITH THEM. AND I WILL BE THEIR GOD, AND THEY WILL BE MY PEOPLE [LEV. 26:11–12; JER. 32:38; EZEK. 37:27]."

"[THEREFORE] LEAVE THOSE PEOPLE [COME OUT FROM THEIR MIDST],
    AND BE SEPARATE, SAYS THE LORD.
TOUCH NOTHING THAT IS UNCLEAN [POLLUTED, DEFILED],
    AND I WILL ACCEPT [RECEIVE; WELCOME] YOU [IS. 52:11; EZEK. 20:41]."
"I WILL BE YOUR FATHER,
    AND YOU WILL BE MY SONS AND DAUGHTERS,
    SAYS THE LORD ALMIGHTY [2 SAM. 7:14]."

This passage of Scripture is about mixing of worship systems, not marriage. The obvious concern was that Christianity would be tainted by idolatry. Ancient religion wasn't viewed as one part of their lives, but as a thread that wove into every single aspect of their lives. It wasn't as simple as going to church on Sunday and then not mentioning your faith again for an entire week. The businesses, leisure activities, and offerings made were all an extension of how people believed. The "secular" world, as we understand it today, did not exist in the first century (we will discuss this more in a later chapter).

This was true of Christian belief, as well. That is one of the reasons we see so much struggle among early Christians, who were trying to figure out what they believed and how they could live and believe their faith in atmospheres that were so contrary to their understandings. The cultures they lived in espoused different values, and living, working, and day-to-day experiences were a challenge, a temptation against the faith they claimed as their own.

Can some apply this passage to issues an interfaith marriage might encounter? Sure, but that's not the primary purpose of the text. We could look at the advice from a lot of angles and how it applies to marriages, but I believe the Apostle Paul is trying to teach us that the way people believe affects the way people interact in their marriages, families, homes, and churches. Our relationships matter everywhere.

At the same time, we need to consider a few things when we start the debate about having faith in common. The way that we, as people, "work in the field" (i.e., in life) as compared to oxen (in the verse earlier), is, in large part, determined by how we think, feel, and are shaped in our lives. There is more than one way to be "unequally yoked" in a marriage. Just because someone wears the title "Christian" does not mean they believe in or practice their faith in the same exact way as someone else and doesn't automatically make a marriage balanced for life's work. Economic differences, differences in education, differences in tradition, and differences in belief systems can all equate to an unequal yoke. There are many variances in different Christian denominations and churches that cause marital couples to be incompatible if they choose to marry from these different backgrounds. For example: if one partner comes from a tradition that believes women should cover their heads and never wear pants and the other does not, that can cause a lot of strain on a marriage in terms of expectation, presentation, authority, and other issues that will arise through the years. This is just an example of the number of differences couples can have, even if they both claim to be believers. Even though there are many smaller issues that probably shouldn't matter in the way that they do, some of those smaller issues deeply affect the way that people view marriage and the relationships between marital partners and families.

I know many people read the Apostle Paul's words and assume that he is speaking out commands, rather than giving advice. Realistic as the Bible usually is, the Apostle Paul gives additional words as pertain to husbands and wives who are in interfaith relationships. Later in the New Testament, the Apostle Paul makes the following statements:

1 Corinthians 7:12-16:

FOR ALL THE OTHERS [THE REST] I SAY THIS (I AM SAYING THIS, NOT THE LORD [JESUS GAVE NO INSTRUCTION ON THIS, BUT PAUL STILL SPEAKS WITH AUTHORITY AS AN APOSTLE]): IF A CHRISTIAN MAN [BROTHER] HAS A WIFE WHO IS NOT A BELIEVER, AND SHE IS HAPPY [CONTENT; WILLING] TO LIVE WITH HIM, HE MUST NOT DIVORCE [OR LEAVE] HER. AND IF A

CHRISTIAN WOMAN HAS A HUSBAND WHO IS NOT A BELIEVER, AND HE IS HAPPY [CONTENT; WILLING] TO LIVE WITH HER, SHE MUST NOT DIVORCE [OR LEAVE] HIM. THE HUSBAND WHO IS NOT A BELIEVER IS MADE HOLY [SANCTIFIED; TOUCHED BY HOLINESS] THROUGH HIS BELIEVING WIFE. AND THE WIFE WHO IS NOT A BELIEVER IS MADE HOLY [SANCTIFIED; TOUCHED BY HOLINESS] THROUGH HER BELIEVING HUSBAND. IF THIS WERE NOT TRUE, YOUR CHILDREN WOULD NOT BE CLEAN [BE SPIRITUALLY IMPURE; OR BE WITHOUT SPIRITUAL INFLUENCE], BUT NOW YOUR CHILDREN ARE HOLY [SOME CORINTHIANS SAID AN UNBELIEVER DEFILED A CHRISTIAN MARRIAGE; PAUL REVERSES THIS AND SAYS BELIEVERS "SANCTIFY" THE MARRIAGE].

BUT IF THOSE WHO ARE NOT BELIEVERS DECIDE TO LEAVE [OR DIVORCE], LET THEM LEAVE [OR DIVORCE]. WHEN THIS HAPPENS, THE CHRISTIAN MAN [BROTHER] OR WOMAN [SISTER] IS FREE [NOT BOUND; TO THE MARRIAGE COVENANT]. BUT GOD CALLED US TO LIVE IN PEACE [PEACE]. WIFE, YOU DON'T KNOW; MAYBE YOU WILL SAVE YOUR HUSBAND. AND HUSBAND, YOU DON'T KNOW; MAYBE YOU WILL SAVE YOUR WIFE.

The New Testament doesn't say "don't marry a non-believer," but it does give you things to think about if that is something you choose to do. What it does say is that if you do, you need to make sure that you intend to see the commitment through to the end, because more is riding on the relationship. You are also going to be the first witness your non-believing spouse sees, and the way in which that manifests can't be overt. You need to live your faith rather than nag your spouse about believing. Making interfaith marriage work demands a great witness; a great testimony; and a great interaction, day in and day out. Whether or not interfaith marriage or even marriage between people of faith who have differences is a good idea depends on the people in the relationship. It takes more effort to make a relationship with such glaring differences work, and it takes more time and preparation to make sure that those things that are most important to both of you are clarified and clear.

Don't live your life assuming that a concept of abstract love is going to solve everything. There are many people who, in history, have loved their partners deeply and from the heart, but were unable to live with them. Rather than approaching marriage from the perspective that things will be taken care of later, it's important to address issues that need to be addressed, now. If you are marrying someone of a different faith or someone who has different perspectives of faith than you, there are things to sort out now. These things include:

- In what faith will your children be raised?
- How you will handle holiday matters
- Perspectives on male/female/couple relationships
- Keys to running the household
- Ideas each partner has about sex and intimate relationships
- Basic beliefs both hold dear and most important to them about the application of their faith in real life
- How your differences will be worked out
- Ways you can communicate respectfully about your differences

Habits, problems, and issues that hurt marriage

1 Corinthians 15:33:

DO NOT BE FOOLED [DECEIVED; MISLED]: "BAD FRIENDS [COMPANY] WILL RUIN GOOD HABITS [OR CHARACTER; MORALS; A QUOTE FROM THE GREEK POET MENANDER (C. 342–291 BC)]."

I've often described relationships as all the things you are willing to live with in another person. Marriage reflects this. When you choose to get married to someone else, you also inherit their habits, their personal issues, and their flaws. This means that whatever they are going through, you will most likely have to go through them, too. It won't be because you are necessarily engaging in the same behavior, but because their habits, issues, and flaws will either change, or they won't. Either way, you will participate in that journey with them.

There are several habits that are seriously detrimental to marriages. Too often, we encourage people to stay married to help defend the institution of marriage without considering the things that they are going through. We also don't put enough responsibility on the habits and issues of one spouse, encouraging them to change or seek help when these matters arise.

If you are preparing for marriage and you recognize any of these issues within yourself or your future spouse, now is the time to get help and address them. Pretending they don't exist is setting up marriage trouble later as well as personal heartache and stress.

- **Mental illness:** Even though we treat mental illness differently today than we did in years past, having a mental illness still often has a stigma. This means there are many people who do not seek out help or treatment when they are mentally ill. There are also many people who are unaware that they have a mental illness, especially when they have always been the way they are and have never considered that other people do not think or process matters in the way that they do. Marriage to a person with a mental illness is difficult beyond measure, because regular views on matters are distorted and different from normal processing.

- **Substance abuse:** Substance abuse is a dependency upon any chemical substance. Substance abuse can take the form of recreational or chronic use, so any form of using a chemical substance on a regular basis without medical requirement is a form of substance abuse. Substance abuse is a drain on a family in more than one way. It affects families financially, emotionally, physically, and mentally as the addict uses their addiction to control the entire family. Families that live in the chaos of substance abuse often have long-term problems and issues that are not properly resolved without intervention and support.

- **Alcoholism:** Alcoholism is akin to substance abuse, in that it reeks the same kind of havoc on families. Even though alcohol products are legal in most parts of the world, alcohol is just as addictive and just as dangerous to families as illegal drugs. It also is a financial, emotional, physical, and mental drain on the family, and causes unhealthy dynamics to evolve as the family tries to live and accommodate the addiction of the addict.

- **Sex addiction:** Sex addiction is, like other addictions, havoc on family life. Rather than using alcohol or drugs, sex addicts use sex to get their "high." With the promise of romance and endless escapades it can seem exciting at first, but as the sexual high is further sought outside the relationship (whether through pornography or affairs), it becomes trying and unbearable.

- **Gambling:** Gambling not only causes financial hardship; it also causes emotional strain as chronic gamblers display the same behaviors as other addicts: trying to hide the addiction, covering up gambling habits and debts, lying about whereabouts and where money went, and a general loss of trust as the family adjusts to life around the addiction.

- **Wild spending:** Excessive debt, shopping, and irresponsible finances all cause a severe toll on a relationship, just as excessive gambling and alcohol addiction also take their toll. Whenever one partner in a relationship spends large sums of money aimlessly, without discipline and to the detriment of the household, no good can come of it.

- **Absentee relationships:** Being in a relationship by yourself is one of the most difficult things to endure, because it signifies that you are competing with someone or something else that is always going to win out. This is different from having periods where one partner needs to understand that you are doing something important and that it occupies a lot of your time for a period. An absentee relationship is one where your partner is always gone, never has any time, is always out, or is always pursuing something, on a consistent basis, with no end in sight. When you are in an absentee relationship, it eventually turns into a relationship where you adjust to life without your partner, so much so that you are unable to function when you are together.

- **Poor hygiene:** You wouldn't think I'd have to tell people that they should shower, take a bath, wear clean clothes, smell good when they are around other people, comb and cut their hair, and groom themselves, but... we give the message that being in a relationship means letting yourself go, not exercising, being comfortable as you are all the time, and not making any efforts to take care of yourself will lead to conflicts within your relationship. Don't make hygiene, attire, and regular personal care something you do for your spouse – let those be things you do for yourself, that your spouse benefits from. Nobody wants to be around someone who is, just, well... gross.

Unfaithfulness

When one partner is unfaithful to their spouse through adultery, affairs, or in other ways (because there are many ways one partner can be unfaithful to their spouse), the climate of a relationship changes to one of distrust. There are some couples who can move past marital infidelities and become stronger than they were before, but doing so is often rare because it requires both partners of a relationship to examine and deal with why the unfaithfulness happened in the first place. Even though we typically portray affairs as an offender/victim circumstance, that is not always the case. The dirty truth about marital unfaithfulness is that it doesn't start with the actual affair or actual physical unfaithfulness. That is an aspect of unfaithfulness that we often do not want to deal with, nor admit, and that makes recovering from such a situation difficult, if not impossible.

The Bible had a lot to say about adultery, especially in a physical sense. Some passages include:

Exodus 20:14:

YOU MUST NOT BE GUILTY OF [COMMIT] ADULTERY.

Leviticus 20:10:

IF A MAN HAS SEXUAL RELATIONS [COMMITS ADULTERY] WITH HIS NEIGHBOR'S WIFE, BOTH THE MAN AND THE WOMAN ARE GUILTY OF ADULTERY AND [ADULTERER AND THE ADULTERESS] MUST BE PUT TO DEATH [18:20; DEUT. 22:22].

Proverbs 2:16:

IT [WISDOM] WILL SAVE YOU FROM THE UNFAITHFUL WIFE [STRANGE WOMAN] WHO TRIES TO LEAD YOU INTO ADULTERY [FROM THE FOREIGN WOMAN] WITH PLEASING WORDS [FLATTERY; COMPLIMENTS].

Proverbs 6:26:

A PROSTITUTE WILL TREAT YOU LIKE [OR COST YOU] A LOAF OF BREAD, AND [OR BUT] A WOMAN WHO TAKES PART IN ADULTERY [MARRIED WOMAN] MAY COST YOU [HUNTS; STALKS] YOUR LIFE.

Jeremiah 3:9:

AND SHE DIDN'T CARE THAT SHE WAS ACTING LIKE A PROSTITUTE. SO SHE MADE HER COUNTRY UNCLEAN [DEFILED; POLLUTED; IN A RITUAL SENSE] AND WAS GUILTY OF ADULTERY WITH STONE AND WOOD [BY WORSHIPING IDOLS MADE OF THESE MATERIALS].

Jeremiah 23:10:

THE LAND [OF JUDAH] IS FULL OF PEOPLE WHO ARE GUILTY OF ADULTERY. BECAUSE OF THE CURSE THE LAND IS SAD [MOURNS], AND THE PASTURES OF THE DESERT [WILDERNESS] HAVE DRIED UP. THE PEOPLE [THEIR LIVES/ COURSES] ARE EVIL AND THEY USE THEIR POWER IN THE WRONG WAY [THEIR POWER IS NOT RIGHT].

Malachi 3:5:

THE LORD ALL-POWERFUL [ALMIGHTY; OF HEAVEN'S ARMIES; OF HOSTS] SAYS, "THEN I WILL COME TO YOU AND JUDGE YOU. I WILL BE QUICK TO TESTIFY AGAINST THOSE WHO TAKE PART IN EVIL MAGIC [SORCERY], ADULTERY, AND LYING UNDER OATH [PERJURY], THOSE WHO CHEAT WORKERS OF THEIR PAY AND WHO CHEAT WIDOWS AND ORPHANS, THOSE WHO ARE UNFAIR TO [TURN AWAY; DEPRIVE OF JUSTICE] FOREIGNERS [ALIENS; IMMIGRANTS], AND THOSE WHO DO NOT RESPECT [FEAR] ME [PROV. 1:7].

1 Corinthians 6:9-10:

KNOW YE NOT THAT THE UNRIGHTEOUS SHALL NOT INHERIT THE KINGDOM

OF GOD? BE NOT DECEIVED: NEITHER FORNICATORS, NOR IDOLATERS, NOR ADULTERERS, NOR EFFEMINATE, NOR ABUSERS OF THEMSELVES WITH MANKIND, NOR THIEVES, NOR COVETOUS, NOR DRUNKARDS, NOR REVILERS, NOR EXTORTIONERS, SHALL INHERIT THE KINGDOM OF GOD. (KJV)

James 2:11:

[FOR] THE SAME GOD WHO SAID, "YOU MUST NOT BE GUILTY OF [COMMIT] ADULTERY [EX. 20:14; DEUT. 5:18]," ALSO SAID, "YOU MUST NOT MURDER ANYONE [EX. 20:13; DEUT. 5:17]." SO IF YOU DO NOT TAKE PART IN [COMMIT] ADULTERY BUT YOU MURDER SOMEONE, YOU ARE GUILTY OF BREAKING ALL OF GOD'S LAW [YOU HAVE BECOME A BREAKER/TRANSGRESSOR OF THE LAW; MATT. 5:18–19; GAL. 5:3].

Even Jesus cited adultery as grounds for divorce:

Matthew 19:8-9:

JESUS ANSWERED, "MOSES ALLOWED [PERMITTED] YOU TO DIVORCE YOUR WIVES BECAUSE YOU REFUSED TO ACCEPT GOD'S TEACHING [OF YOUR HARD-HEARTEDNESS], BUT DIVORCE WAS NOT ALLOWED IN THE BEGINNING [OR THIS WAS NOT GOD'S INTENTION AT CREATION; FROM THE BEGINNING IT WAS NOT LIKE THIS]. I TELL YOU THAT ANYONE WHO DIVORCES HIS WIFE AND MARRIES ANOTHER WOMAN IS GUILTY OF [COMMITS] ADULTERY. THE ONLY REASON FOR A MAN TO DIVORCE HIS WIFE IS IF HIS WIFE HAS SEXUAL RELATIONS WITH ANOTHER MAN [...EXCEPT IN THE CASE OF SEXUAL IMMORALITY]."

Have you ever wondered why adultery seems to be such a prominent theme in the Scriptures? A large part of it was for all the reasons we've talked about as pertain to historical marriage earlier in time. Women were property, marriage was a property transaction, and men wanted to ensure the children their wives bore were their own. The legal reason adultery was cited as grounds for marital dissolution was simple: sex related deeply to property arrangements, and adultery was regarded as theft, because one man was stealing another man's property. It was more than a moral thing; it also had legal ramifications. If a man or woman chose to commit adultery or have an unlawful (because the relationships were literally illegal) sexual relationship with someone other than their spouse, that confused bloodlines and, thus, had the potential to change property inheritances and transference.

We don't understand marriage and marital infidelity in the same way today. We now can prove DNA, and we view marital relationships differently, because they are not simply property transfers. Even though the reasons for adultery laws weren't necessarily spiritual, that does not mean that marital unfaithfulness does not have spiritual ramifications. Even though they might not have been the driving forces behind what people understood as the law of the land, the spiritual realities behind adultery and unfaithfulness were not lost on those who claimed to be God's spiritual people.

The spiritual principles behind adultery are also found in the Bible and should never be lost on believers. God compares adultery to spiritual unfaithfulness and spiritual adultery. It's because compromising one's marriage and one's integrity – rather than making a choice to be with their mate or not to be with their mate – was parallel to the way in which the Israelites sought out false gods, time and time again, turning their backs on the true God.

Hosea 4:12:

MY PEOPLE ASK WOODEN IDOLS FOR ADVICE [COUNSEL];
    THEY ASK THOSE STICKS OF WOOD [OR DIVINING RODS/STAFFS] TO
ADVISE THEM!
LIKE PROSTITUTES, THEY HAVE CHASED AFTER OTHER GODS [A
SPIRIT/WIND OF PROSTITUTION LEADS/BLOWS THEM ASTRAY]
    AND HAVE LEFT [COMMITTING ADULTERY AGAINST; BEING UNFAITHFUL
TO] THEIR OWN GOD.

In marriage, a couple is supposed to become one. This doesn't mean one person, as we talked about before, but they are supposed to become a unified front. They are supposed to be walking together in the same direction, agreeing on the path they take. This parallels our relationship with God in many ways, as a type of the way we are to regard our relationship with God. We don't become the same being as God, but we do become one with Him, united in His purpose for us. Just as we aren't supposed to be looking for other gods, married couples aren't supposed to be looking for other mates. When they are, it is indicative of other problems and issues in the relationship;

unmet needs and longings for things that their mate can't satisfy. Sometimes it is something within the individual; sometimes it is a conflict with the couple; sometimes it is that their spouse is not able or does not desire to meet their needs. Whatever the reason, unfaithfulness in marriage should be examined carefully, with objectivity and without judgment. It's easy to say "I'll never" or "I won't" when you are not in the situation bringing the relationship breakdown that precedes marital unfaithfulness.

Let's also define adultery and unfaithfulness as more than sexual relationships with someone to whom a spouse is not married. A person can have an affair and be unfaithful with a job, or an ambition, or pursuit of a lifestyle, or with anything that is placed between people in a marriage relationship when it should not be there. In many instances, adultery and unfaithfulness take many forms preceding or sometimes without actual physical adultery taking place. We need to be attentive to the signs and symptoms of these problems so they can be addressed rather than ignored.

Abuse

Domestic violence is described as patterns of behavior existing between a perpetrating partner and a victim, or sometimes mutual perpetrators and mutual victims, in an intimate situation (such as husbands and wives, parents and children, and live-in partners). It is any abusive relationship, including physical abuse, sexual abuse, emotional abuse, financial or economic abuse, spiritual abuse, or verbal abuse. Abusive situations may include one of these forms of abuse, a combination of them, or all of them.

Abuse is an unspoken problem in a large percentage of marriages. Most assume perpetrators are men, but we know for a fact that abusers can take any form, in any relationship: heterosexual, homosexual, queer, and even in situations involving multiple partners. Even though secular statistics cite domestic violence as an issue somewhere around one quarter of all domestic relationships, most domestic violence cases go unreported. This means that, in all reality, domestic violence may be a much, much larger problem than statistics estimate. This is especially true in religious marriages and Christian marriages, where relationships are often regarded as unequal according to gender and women are encouraged to stay with men who batter and abuse them.

Domestic violence operates by cycles of violence that manifest in relationships that seem perfect and ideal in the beginning but quickly get out of control and hit danger zones once the cycles of abuse begin. Domestic violence can occur at any time in a relationship, even if the relationship has been seemingly fine for a long period of time. The cycle of violence may begin by some trigger that may or may not have its origin in the relationship (an example might be a family death, increasing drug and alcohol abuse, or unemployment). Things go from being fine, to tense and not fine, to explosive and dangerous, only to reach a pinnacle once the abuse has occurred to regain a sense of calm and perfection again. The abuser may apologize, promise to do better next time, blame their behavior on a "reacting position" (it is due to something the other person did) and promise to change. They often go overboard in the "perfect" phase, often called the honeymoon period, and the couple seems stronger and more intensely in love than ever before. As with all cycles, things start to begin again, then become abusive and explosive again, and so on and so forth, until one person either leaves the relationship or things become so serious, there is intervention in the relationship.

Malalchi 2:16 makes the following statement:

THE LORD GOD OF ISRAEL SAYS, "I HATE DIVORCE. AND I HATE THE PERSON WHO [OR THE ONE WHO HATES AND DIVORCES] DOES CRUEL THINGS AS EASILY AS HE PUTS ON CLOTHES [COVERS HIS CLOTHES IN VIOLENCE]," SAYS THE LORD ALL-POWERFUL [ALMIGHTY; OF HEAVEN'S ARMIES; OF HOSTS]. SO BE CAREFUL [ON YOUR GUARD]. AND DO NOT BREAK YOUR TRUST [BE UNFAITHFUL].

We can talk about upholding marriage all day long, but the reality is that an abusive situation already breaks and violates the covenant of marriage, even as is found in the Bible. Abuse is not the fault of the victim, but the fault of the perpetrator. If you ever find yourself in an abusive relationship, the only solution to stopping the cycle is to leave. The promises that await at the end of each abusive cycle are never fulfilled, and only more promises result. We know that if God loves us and has created us in His image, living with abuse is not

His will, nor His glory, for us.

Marital unhappiness

I have said before that the purpose of marriage is deeper than happiness; it is holiness. We are going to look at this principle later in this book, in its entirety. That having been said, being unhappy in one's marriage is still something one must look at, because there may be deeper factors in the reason why marital unhappiness has become a regular way of life.

Let's start by realizing that being unhappy from time to time with your spouse or something they have done is completely normal, and no cause for alarm or divorce. None of us are happy, all the time, with other people. Expecting to be happy constantly is one of the reasons why people are so chronically unhappy in marriage. Marriage is a part of life, and with life has occasional unhappiness or disappointment.

Chronic marital unhappiness, however, is not normal and should not be a normal part of married life. Experiencing chronic unrest, dissatisfaction, and wondering if "this is all there is" are not signs of a good marriage. They can reflect problems within an individual, or a bigger problem in the relationship.

James 4:7-10:

SO GIVE YOURSELVES COMPLETELY [SUBMIT] TO GOD. STAND AGAINST [RESIST] THE DEVIL [1 PET. 5:9], AND THE DEVIL WILL RUN [FLEE] FROM YOU. COME NEAR TO GOD, AND GOD WILL COME NEAR TO YOU. YOU SINNERS, CLEAN SIN OUT OF YOUR LIVES [CLEANSE/PURIFY YOUR HANDS; A METAPHOR FOR CLEANING UP YOUR BEHAVIOR]. YOU WHO ARE TRYING TO FOLLOW GOD AND THE WORLD AT THE SAME TIME [YOU DOUBLE-MINDED ONES], MAKE YOUR THINKING PURE [PURIFY YOUR HEARTS; A METAPHOR FOR CLEANING UP YOUR INTERIOR LIFE]. BE SAD [LAMENT], ·CRY [MOURN], AND WEEP! CHANGE YOUR LAUGHTER INTO CRYING [MOURNING] AND YOUR JOY INTO SADNESS [GLOOM; SORROW]. HUMBLE YOURSELF IN THE LORD'S PRESENCE, AND HE WILL HONOR YOU [EXALT YOU; LIFT YOU UP; 1 PET. 5:6].

No matter the cause of marital unhappiness, it should be examined and resolved, if possible. I don't have a laundry list of things to do

What relevance does the marriage laws have for us today?

READING THE OLD TESTAMENT LAWS AS PERTAIN TO MARRIAGE SEEM ARCHAIC TO US TODAY. THEY SEEM INVOLVED AND COMPLICATED, OBSESSED WITH VIRGINITY, MEDDLESOME WHEN IT CAME TO FAMILY INVOLVEMENT, AND QUICK TO STONE PEOPLE FOR A LOT OF REASONS. IN READING THESE COMPLICATED LAWS, WHAT ARE WE SUPPOSED TO LEARN FOR OURSELVES? WHAT RELEVANCE DO THEY HAVE TODAY?

THE MARITAL LAWS OF THE OLD TESTAMENT ARE ARCHAIC AND DON'T HAVE MUCH, IF ANY, LEGAL BEARING ON THE WAY THAT MARRIAGES ARE APPROACHED IN MODERN SOCIETY. WHAT THEY DO SHOW US, HOWEVER, IS THAT MARRIAGE HAS ALWAYS BEEN SOMETHING SERIOUS AND SOMETHING TO BE APPROACHED WITH A LEVEL-HEAD AND SELF-DISCIPLINE. EVEN THOUGH WE MIGHT NOT BE WORRIED ABOUT BLOOD-STAINED SHEETS OR HOW MANY GOATS A MAN CAN GET FOR A TEENAGE GIRL IN THE DOWRY EXCHANGE, THE OLD TESTAMENT LAWS SHOW US THAT GOD CARES ABOUT US AS PEOPLE, EVEN RIGHT DOWN TO SOMETHING AS BASIC, ORDINARY, AND EVERY-DAY AS MARRIAGE AND MARITAL RELATIONSHIPS. IF BLOODLINES AND FAMILY PRESERVATIONS WERE THINGS THAT PEOPLE CARED ABOUT, THEN THE MARITAL LAWS PROVE GOD CARED ABOUT THEM, TOO. EVEN THE LITTLEST DETAILS OF OUR LIVES ARE OF INTEREST AND THOUGHT TO OUR CREATOR.

in this situation, but I do know that God is a good God and He has a way of revealing to us the changes that need to be made. It doesn't mean that we must get divorced if that's not what we seek to do, nor does it mean that we must make huge, drastic life changes. It does mean that if we step back and listen to God, He will help us to address the unhappiness we are experiencing and will show us where exactly it might be in a marriage… and how we can change it.

Family drama

Every one of us has a family member (or sometimes multiple family members) that are what we like to casually call a chronic "mess." Whatever the reason they are messy – baby mamas or baby daddies, drugs or alcohol, bad temperaments or behavior, chronic unemployment, you name it – they are people who thrive on and feed on drama at every turn. They also usually bring about a travesty of people in their wake who also feed on that drama, in one form or another.

The drama that our relatives bring with them may not be noticeable to us, especially because we are used to it and we have grown to live around it. Even if we are embarrassed by it (like normal people are), we have grown accustomed to the dynamics surrounding it and we might handle it in a way that someone else would not. The drama might be particularly noticeable to your spouse, who is not so acclimated to it. It might cause them to be uncomfortable, or to disagree with how to handle it. They may also find themselves awkward or desiring to avoid the messiness, thus causing you to feel uncomfortable with them and the way they want to handle it.

Well, bad news (or good, depending on how you view it): your spouse has every right to feel uncomfortable with a messy relative and to desire to avoid or not involve themselves in that mess. They also have every right to request it not come into their personal space (such as their home or dwelling) and that it does not intrude in your relationship, such as through finances or other things that would put the two of you at a disadvantage. If you want to share with your relatives who thrive on drama, you will have to do it without your spouse, and with consideration that it will not affect your spouse, either.

There's a verse in the Bible that we take very literally, but is trying to teach us something important about marriage and our families:

Genesis 2:24:

So a man will leave his father and mother [in the sense of a new primary loyalty] and be united with his wife, and the two will

BECOME ONE BODY [FLESH].

We know from the history that we spoke of earlier that husbands didn't always leave their families, even though it was customary for brides to do so. The Bible isn't telling us that we can't ever talk to our families, or visit them, or appreciate their input, or even, as need might be for a variety of reasons, live with them some of the time. The Bible is telling us that we need to consider the relationship we have with our spouse as a primary importance and as a familial acceptance all its own. Our spouse deserves the same consideration we would extend to our immediate family, because they become that when we get married.

This means: don't ask your partner to engage in dysfunctional behavior. If something is truly dysfunctional, learn how you can be functional and empowered, and rise above things. If you are uncomfortable with that, then learn how to respect your partner's space and don't expect them to become dysfunctional for you or your family.

Divorce

Divorce is a loaded word in many Christian circles, even today. There are many people who still think divorce is unacceptable, and some think it's unacceptable, regardless of the circumstances. In some denominations, being divorced means you can never remarry, you can never serve in ministry, or that you are unable to hold certain positions.

The Bible doesn't hold a singular position on divorce. Cultures change and attitudes change, and that means that the different positions on divorce changed to accommodate the times, as did marriage customs. These are a general sample of the Bible's words on divorce:

Deuteronomy 22:13-19:

IF A MAN MARRIES A GIRL AND HAS SEXUAL RELATIONS WITH HER BUT THEN DECIDES HE DOES NOT LIKE [HATES] HER, HE MIGHT TALK BADLY ABOUT HER [CHARGE HER WITH WANTON BEHAVIOR] AND GIVE HER A BAD NAME. HE MIGHT SAY, "I MARRIED THIS WOMAN, BUT WHEN I HAD SEXUAL

RELATIONS WITH [APPROACHED] HER, I DID NOT FIND THAT SHE WAS A VIRGIN." THEN THE GIRL'S PARENTS [FATHER AND MOTHER] MUST BRING PROOF [EVIDENCE] THAT SHE WAS A VIRGIN TO THE ELDERS AT THE CITY GATE. THE GIRL'S FATHER WILL SAY TO THE ELDERS, "I GAVE MY DAUGHTER TO THIS MAN TO BE HIS WIFE, BUT NOW HE ·DOES NOT WANT [HATES] HER. THIS MAN HAS TOLD LIES ABOUT MY DAUGHTER [CHARGED MY DAUGHTER WITH WANTON BEHAVIOR]. HE HAS SAID, 'I DID NOT FIND YOUR DAUGHTER TO BE A VIRGIN,' BUT HERE IS THE PROOF [EVIDENCE] THAT MY DAUGHTER WAS A VIRGIN." THEN HER PARENTS ARE TO SHOW THE SHEET [BLOOD-STAINED, SHOWING SHE HAD BEEN A VIRGIN] TO THE ELDERS OF THE CITY, AND THE ELDERS MUST TAKE THE MAN AND PUNISH [DISCIPLINE] HIM. THEY MUST MAKE HIM PAY ABOUT TWO AND ONE-HALF POUNDS [ONE HUNDRED SHEKELS] OF SILVER TO THE GIRL'S FATHER, BECAUSE THE MAN HAS GIVEN AN ISRAELITE VIRGIN A BAD NAME. THE GIRL WILL CONTINUE TO BE THE MAN'S WIFE, AND HE MAY NOT DIVORCE HER AS LONG AS HE LIVES.

Deuteronomy 22:28-29:

IF A MAN MEETS A VIRGIN WHO IS NOT ENGAGED TO BE MARRIED AND FORCES HER TO HAVE SEXUAL RELATIONS WITH HIM [GRABS HER AND LIES WITH HER] AND PEOPLE FIND OUT ABOUT IT [IS DISCOVERED], THE MAN WHO HAD SEXUAL RELATIONS [LAY] WITH HER MUST PAY THE GIRL'S FATHER ABOUT ONE AND ONE-FOURTH POUNDS [FIFTY SHEKELS] OF SILVER. HE MUST ALSO MARRY THE GIRL, BECAUSE HE HAS DISHONORED [HUMILIATED; RAPED] HER, AND HE MAY NEVER DIVORCE HER FOR AS LONG AS HE LIVES [Ex. 22:16–17].

Deuteronomy 24:1-4:

A MAN MIGHT MARRY A WOMAN BUT LATER DECIDE SHE DOESN'T PLEASE HIM [FIND FAVOR IN HIS EYES] BECAUSE HE HAS FOUND SOMETHING BAD [INDECENT; OBJECTIONABLE] ABOUT HER. HE WRITES OUT DIVORCE PAPERS FOR HER, GIVES THEM TO HER [PLACES THEM IN HER HAND], AND SENDS HER AWAY FROM HIS HOUSE. AFTER SHE LEAVES HIS HOUSE, SHE GOES AND MARRIES ANOTHER MAN, BUT HER SECOND HUSBAND DOES NOT LIKE HER EITHER [HATES HER]. SO HE WRITES OUT DIVORCE PAPERS FOR HER, GIVES THEM TO HER [PLACES THEM IN HER HAND], AND SENDS HER AWAY FROM HIS HOUSE. OR THE SECOND HUSBAND MIGHT DIE. IN EITHER CASE, HER FIRST HUSBAND WHO DIVORCED HER MUST NOT MARRY HER AGAIN, BECAUSE SHE HAS BECOME UNCLEAN [IN A RITUAL SENSE]. THE LORD WOULD HATE [DETEST] THIS. DON'T BRING THIS SIN INTO THE LAND THE

LORD YOUR GOD IS GIVING YOU AS YOUR OWN [INHERITANCE; MATT. 5:31–32; 19:3–9].

Malachi 2:16:

THE LORD GOD OF ISRAEL SAYS, "I HATE DIVORCE. AND I HATE THE PERSON WHO [OR THE ONE WHO HATES AND DIVORCES] DOES CRUEL THINGS AS EASILY AS HE PUTS ON CLOTHES [COVERS HIS CLOTHES IN VIOLENCE]," SAYS THE LORD ALL-POWERFUL [ALMIGHTY; OF HEAVEN'S ARMIES; OF HOSTS]. SO BE CAREFUL [ON YOUR GUARD]. AND DO NOT BREAK YOUR TRUST [BE UNFAITHFUL].

Matthew 1:18-19:

THIS IS HOW THE BIRTH OF JESUS CHRIST [THE MESSIAH] CAME ABOUT. HIS MOTHER MARY WAS ENGAGED [PLEDGED; BETROTHED; A FORMAL AGREEMENT BETWEEN FAMILIES THAT REQUIRED A "DIVORCE" TO ANNUL] TO MARRY JOSEPH, BUT BEFORE THEY MARRIED [CAME TO LIVE TOGETHER], SHE LEARNED SHE WAS [OR WAS FOUND/DISCOVERED TO BE] PREGNANT [WITH CHILD] BY THE POWER OF [THROUGH] THE HOLY SPIRIT. BECAUSE MARY'S HUSBAND, JOSEPH, WAS A GOOD [RIGHTEOUS] MAN, HE DID NOT WANT TO DISGRACE HER IN PUBLIC, SO HE PLANNED TO DIVORCE HER [END THE ENGAGEMENT] SECRETLY [PRIVATELY; QUIETLY].

Matthew 5:31-32:

"IT WAS ALSO SAID, 'ANYONE WHO DIVORCES HIS WIFE MUST GIVE HER A WRITTEN DIVORCE PAPER [NOTICE; CERTIFICATE; DEUT. 24:1].' BUT I TELL YOU THAT ANYONE WHO DIVORCES HIS WIFE FORCES [CAUSES; MAKES] HER TO BE GUILTY OF [COMMIT] ADULTERY. THE ONLY REASON FOR A MAN TO DIVORCE HIS WIFE IS IF SHE HAS SEXUAL RELATIONS WITH ANOTHER MAN [...EXCEPT IN THE CASE OF SEXUAL IMMORALITY]. AND ANYONE WHO MARRIES THAT DIVORCED WOMAN IS GUILTY OF [COMMITS] ADULTERY.

Matthew 19:1-9:

AFTER JESUS SAID ALL THESE THINGS [FINISHED THESE WORDS; SEE 7:28], HE LEFT GALILEE AND WENT INTO THE AREA [REGION] OF JUDEA ON THE OTHER SIDE OF [BEYOND] THE JORDAN RIVER. LARGE CROWDS FOLLOWED HIM, AND HE HEALED THEM THERE.

SOME PHARISEES CAME TO JESUS AND TRIED TO TRICK [TO TRAP/TEST] HIM. THEY ASKED, "IS IT RIGHT [LAWFUL; ACCORDING TO THE LAW OF MOSES] FOR A MAN TO DIVORCE HIS WIFE FOR ANY REASON HE CHOOSES?" JESUS ANSWERED, "SURELY YOU HAVE [HAVEN'T YOU… ?] READ IN THE SCRIPTURES: WHEN GOD MADE THE WORLD, 'HE [FROM THE BEGINNING, THE CREATOR] MADE THEM MALE AND FEMALE' [GEN. 1:27; 5:2]. AND GOD SAID, 'SO A MAN WILL LEAVE HIS FATHER AND MOTHER AND BE UNITED WITH [JOINED TO] HIS WIFE, AND THE TWO WILL BECOME ONE BODY [AS THOUGH THEY WERE ONE PERSON; ONE FLESH; GEN. 2:24].' SO THEY ARE NO LONGER TWO, BUT ONE. GOD HAS JOINED THE TWO TOGETHER, SO NO ONE SHOULD SEPARATE THEM."

THE PHARISEES ASKED, "WHY THEN DID MOSES GIVE A COMMAND FOR A MAN TO DIVORCE HIS WIFE BY GIVING HER DIVORCE PAPERS [A CERTIFICATE OF DIVORCE/DISMISSAL; DEUT. 24:1]?"

JESUS ANSWERED, "MOSES ALLOWED [PERMITTED] YOU TO DIVORCE YOUR WIVES BECAUSE YOU REFUSED TO ACCEPT GOD'S TEACHING [L OF YOUR HARD-HEARTEDNESS], BUT DIVORCE WAS NOT ALLOWED IN THE BEGINNING [OR THIS WAS NOT GOD'S INTENTION AT CREATION; FROM THE BEGINNING IT WAS NOT LIKE THIS]. I TELL YOU THAT ANYONE WHO DIVORCES HIS WIFE AND MARRIES ANOTHER WOMAN IS GUILTY OF [COMMITS] ADULTERY. THE ONLY REASON FOR A MAN TO DIVORCE HIS WIFE IS IF HIS WIFE HAS SEXUAL RELATIONS WITH ANOTHER MAN [… EXCEPT IN THE CASE OF SEXUAL IMMORALITY]."

1 Corinthians 7:10-11:

NOW I GIVE THIS COMMAND FOR THE MARRIED PEOPLE. (THE COMMAND IS NOT FROM ME; IT IS FROM THE LORD [JESUS TAUGHT ON DIVORCE; MARK 10:5–12].) A WIFE SHOULD NOT LEAVE [SEPARATE FROM; OR DIVORCE] HER HUSBAND. BUT IF SHE DOES LEAVE [OR DIVORCE], SHE MUST NOT MARRY AGAIN, OR SHE SHOULD MAKE UP [RECONCILE] WITH HER HUSBAND. ALSO THE HUSBAND SHOULD NOT DIVORCE [OR LEAVE] HIS WIFE.

1 Corinthians 7:15-16:

BUT IF THOSE WHO ARE NOT BELIEVERS DECIDE TO LEAVE [OR DIVORCE], LET THEM LEAVE [OR DIVORCE]. WHEN THIS HAPPENS, THE CHRISTIAN MAN [BROTHER] OR WOMAN [SISTER] IS FREE [NOT BOUND; TO THE MARRIAGE COVENANT]. BUT GOD CALLED US TO LIVE IN PEACE [PEACE]. WIFE, YOU DON'T KNOW; MAYBE YOU WILL SAVE YOUR HUSBAND. AND HUSBAND,

I believe that all the things the Bible says can hold truth to them, especially if we consider them in the context of their day and age. It is true that divorce results from hardness of heart, especially in an instance where a divorce is desired for no reason at all, with injustice and lack of feeling. I believe God does hate divorce, because divorce is a hard thing for a couple and a difficult thing for a family. I also believe that when Jesus spoke against divorce in any case except adultery, he was offering protection to families, especially women and children, because men had the right to divorce women for any and all reasons, and men were quick to do so when they wanted another wife or if they were unhappy with the way a woman cooked or cleaned the house. Divorce would give her a sordid reputation, cause her to live in poverty, and prevent her children from justifiable inheritance and support. By raising the bar, Jesus was establishing that divorce is a serious thing, not something to be taken lightly, and that it affects families and children in negative ways.

Divorce, like marriage, related in large part to property acquisitions and the belief that women and children were property. If the woman was displeasing, the man could simply disavow her and refuse to care for her. This was an unjust system that had serious consequences for women in a culture who were not entitled to property rights and, therefore, were lost when abandoned and scorned by angry or unreasonable husbands. It's obvious from looking at these complex passages about divorce that they resulted in sordid reputations and disdain, even when the accusations were not true. Establishing provable adultery as the only cause of divorce in ancient times helped to solidify divorce laws and make it so being divorced was not "his word against hers." It was more than just about adultery or non-adultery or what the people in the relationship did; rather, it was about using a moral and legal avenue to remedy the fact that a marriage didn't go quite the way that someone wanted it to.

Divorce isn't as cut and dry now and does not soil one's moral reputation. It is also not done by the power of a singular (male) party, leaving the wife destitute. The context of divorce has changed, which means that as we review and consider the perspectives of divorced people today, our perspectives should change, as well. Just because God hates divorce doesn't mean that God hates the divorced. It also doesn't mean that there aren't many other justifiable reasons for divorce (aside from legal adultery) as we understand it to exist today. We can't rightly compare the ancient legal systems with those of today, and we can't uphold regulations that pertain to divorce in the same ways, either.

There is hope for people who are divorced. The Bible does not prohibit the divorced from serving in ministry, and if we understand divorce in a modern context rather than an ancient one, it does not prohibit people from seeking God and making the decision to marry again once they are fully and legally removed from their former spouse. This doesn't mean divorce is a desirable or favorable thing, but that people do make mistakes in relationships and that God does not require us to pay for mistakes eternally. If we know and trust that His grace is there for our sins and wrongdoings, that can apply to our relationship misses, as well.

I believe the best way to avoid divorce is to take marriage seriously. We need to stop automatically assuming that because people can live together, they can also be married. We need to stop forcing people to get married because of various things (pregnancy, living together unmarried, age, life changes, etc.). We also must be more understanding about the difficulties that arise in a marriage that cause people to get divorced in the first place. None of us can foresee the strain put on a marriage caused by spousal infidelity, abuse, drifting apart, the death of a child, chronic unemployment, or any other host of issues that arise, causing partners to find themselves incompatible. Rather than punishing the divorced, the divorce process is truly a punishing enough experience to merit compassion and love, especially as they go through their trying issues.

Learning from the divorced and unhappy

This is, arguably, a difficult chapter to pursue through. As wedding preparations are often stressful, thinking about divorce or marital unhappiness is probably the last thing you want to entertain. Even though there is probably a part of you that thinks these things will never happen to you, I am sure that many, many other people in these situations also thought the same thing, once upon a time. I hope that they aren't things that ever come your way, or that you must encounter in your marriage. The reality is, however, that even if you don't deal with these things, people who are divorced and who have experienced difficulty or unhappiness in their marriage often have a lot to offer all married couples about things to watch for, recognize, or think about so their own marriages don't take such negative turns.

There are many who insist they don't want advice from divorced or unhappy people, because they don't feel that they have anything to offer about marriage. They think that only happy couples should give marital advice. The thing they don't consider (because de-nial is more than just a river in Egypt) is that not all couples who claim to be happy truly are, and that people are very good at pretending, especially when it comes to the issue of marriage when in church. The couples who make the best presentation often have the most serious problems that go unresolved. Let's be honest: that isn't the sign of a healthy, happy marriage. If we want to get real, and relate true experience, then we need to consider the fact that divorced and unhappy people have something to tell us about marriage.

Proverbs 19:8:

THOSE WHO GET WISDOM [ACQUIRE HEART] DO THEMSELVES A FAVOR [LOVE THEMSELVES], AND THOSE WHO LOVE LEARNING [GUARD UNDERSTANDING] WILL SUCCEED.

There is wisdom in hearing from people who have failed at or were unhappy in marriage. People who are divorced or unhappy and have worked through the pain, offense, and hurt of the situation are able to see where their relationships went wrong, both in their mates and in themselves. They know the importance and value in looking at oneself first, in examining their own behavior, and that the only people they can change are themselves. Divorced and unhappy people have often gone through long periods of "trying everything," from trying to change their former spouse, to counseling, to praying that their spouse would be different, to resolving to work on their marriage, to taking it to church, only to find that they didn't receive the help and support they needed in the process. Eventually, they realized that the change they needed to make came from within themselves, and with time, the relationship changes to come was its demise. Divorced and unhappy people know the value in seeing signs early, even if they aren't understood or properly discerned early on. They know the truth that divorce is hard…but unhappy and painful marriages are even harder. They also learned "what not to do," and that is as powerful a lesson as what to do, much of the time. If nothing else, they understand the trials of marriage in a way that supposedly happy couples do not, and if you are going through that, identity is a powerful form of healing and a catalyst for needed change.

Week 12 Assignments

Answer the following questions based on discussions you have had with your future spouse in counseling this week and additionally on your own time and prepare to discuss them at your next counseling session. If you run out of room in a section, finish the answer to your question in your journal.

1. If a couple stays married for a long time, does that mean they are happy? What does it mean? _____

_____

_____

_____

_____

2. How does treating marriage as an institution cause problems in people's marriages? _____

_____

_____

_____

_____

3. What are "wrong reasons" to get married? What is the result of getting married for all the wrong reasons? _____

_____

_____

_____

4. What is a prenuptial agreement? How do you feel about prenuptial agreements in marriage? Why do you feel this way?

_____

_____

_____

_____

_____

5. What does the Bible offer on interfaith marriages? _____

_____

_____

_____

_____

6. Where does the term "unequal yoke" come from? How can a couple be "unequally yoked" in different ways? _____

_____

_____

_____

7. Does the Bible outright forbid marriage to a non-believer? What does it teach for these special and unique circumstances? _____

_____

_____

_____

_____

8. What are things that should be considered in an interfaith marriage? _____

_____

_____

_____

9. What are some habits that hurt marriage? Do you see any of these habits in yourself or your future spouse? If so, what are you going to do about them? _____

_____

_____

_____

_____

10. How does marital unfaithfulness start? _____

_____

_____

_____

_____

11. How did adultery relate to legal situations of ancient times?

_____

_____

_____

_____

12. How does adultery relate to spiritual principles? _____

_____

_____

_____

_____

13. Is adultery just a sexual relationship with someone who isn't one's spouse? How else can we understand it in a marriage?

_____

_____

_____

_____

14. Is abuse a proper dynamic for marriage? If someone is in an abusive situation, what should they do? _____

_____

_____

_____

_____

15. Who in your family is a perpetrator of "drama?" How does your future spouse feel about that person and the situations they bring with them? Once you are married, how will you handle this situation as pertains to your spouse? _____

_____

_____

_____

_____

16. What ramifications did divorce have legally in ancient societies? How can we view divorce today that reflects love and mercy on couples? _____

_____

_____

_____

_____

17. What can we learn from people who are divorced or who were unhappy in their marriages? _____

_____

_____

_____

_____

18. What "unplanned" things do you think came up between the couple in the Song of Solomon in the course of their marriage? How do you think they handled it? _____

_____

_____

_____

_____

19. In reading Hosea 1:1-9, how do you think Hosea felt about his marriage to Gomer? Do you think it was the relationship that he hoped he would have in his life? Why or why not? _____

_____

_____

_____

_____

20. What things do you anticipate may become an issue within your own marriage? Write your fears and concerns here, to discuss at your next session with your spiritual leader and your partner. _____

_____

_____

_____

_____

Month Four

SPIRITUALITY IN MARRIAGE

Reading assignments:

- *Discovering The Beauty of Intimacy: A Journey Through the Song of Solomon*: Chapter 5 (The Challenge) and Conclusion (When It's All Been Said and Done)

Week Thirteen

Biblical Marriages

SUPPOSE A MAN FINDS A WOMAN WHO IS NOT PLEDGED [ENGAGED] TO BE
MARRIED AND HAS NEVER HAD SEXUAL RELATIONS WITH A MAN [IS A VIRGIN].
IF HE TRICKS [OR SEDUCES] HER INTO HAVING SEXUAL RELATIONS WITH HIM, HE
MUST GIVE HER FAMILY THE PAYMENT TO MARRY [THE BRIDE-PRICE FOR] HER,
AND SHE WILL BECOME HIS WIFE.
(EXODUS 22:16)

Bible reading: Psalm 45:1-17

Journaling assignments for in-session discussion:

- What is your perspective on Biblical marriages?
- Why do you believe God gives us such diverse examples of marriage in the Bible?

Ah, Bible marriages. Jacob loved Rachel so much, that he worked for her for 14 years… right? Ruth and Boaz were the picture-perfect love story… right? Mary and Joseph rode off on a donkey into the sunset of a Roman census… right? Hosea and Gomer lived happily ever after… right? If you listen to popular teachings, clichés, and expressions that we seem to hear over and over again today, Biblical marriages sound an awful lot like fairy tales: Girl meets boy, boy chases girl, girl marries boy, girl and boy live together, happily ever after. We are told that if we'll only be very, very good and wait on God, we can have a perfect marriage like those relationships in the Bible.

Well, I hate to burst the fantasy bubble (actually, I don't hate doing it at all, but anyway), but the truth about Biblical marriages is that every single one of them is far from perfect. I have said that while Bible men might have been great men of valor and faith, they were not men I would have wanted to be married to. The Bible doesn't say anywhere that their last names were "Charming." There was no David Charming, or Boaz Charming, or Ahab Charming, or even Joseph Charming. They weren't perfect, nor ideal husbands, and their wives often had moments where they left much to be desired, as well. As much as this seems to scare some, I think it's worth a consideration as to why God has given us these examples for marriage in the Scriptures. They exist and are as they are because they are human beings, people who dealt with and encountered serious problems throughout life and worked to overcome them, sometimes with human means, and sometimes by faith. This needs to tell us that marriage, no matter who we choose to marry, will have its difficulties and challenges, and that even with the best of faith, marriage can still be a complex system to navigate.

Adam and Eve

Genesis 2:7-9:

THEN THE LORD GOD TOOK DUST FROM THE GROUND AND FORMED A MAN FROM IT [THERE IS WORDPLAY BETWEEN "GROUND" (ADAMA) AND "MAN" (ADAM)]. HE BREATHED THE BREATH OF LIFE INTO THE MAN'S NOSE, AND THE MAN BECAME A LIVING PERSON. THEN THE LORD GOD [OR THE LORD GOD HAD] PLANTED A GARDEN IN THE EAST [PROBABLY EAST OF PALESTINE], IN A PLACE CALLED EDEN [RELATED TO A WORD MEANING "LUXURIOUS"], AND PUT THE MAN HE HAD FORMED INTO IT. THE LORD GOD CAUSED EVERY BEAUTIFUL [DESIROUS TO SEE] TREE AND EVERY TREE THAT WAS GOOD FOR FOOD TO GROW OUT OF THE GROUND. IN THE MIDDLE OF THE GARDEN, GOD PUT THE TREE THAT GIVES LIFE [OF LIFE] AND ALSO THE TREE THAT GIVES THE KNOWLEDGE [OF THE KNOWLEDGE] OF GOOD AND EVIL.

Genesis 2:15-3:24

THE LORD GOD [TOOK AND] PUT THE MAN [OR ADAM; 1:27] IN THE GARDEN OF EDEN TO CARE FOR [OR TILL] IT AND WORK [TAKE CARE OF; LOOK AFTER] IT. THE LORD GOD COMMANDED HIM, "YOU MAY EAT THE FRUIT FROM ANY TREE [OR ALL THE TREES] IN THE GARDEN, BUT YOU MUST NOT EAT THE FRUIT FROM THE TREE WHICH GIVES THE [OF THE] KNOWLEDGE OF GOOD AND EVIL [EATING FROM THIS TREE WOULD MAKE ADAM, NOT GOD, THE DETERMINER OF RIGHT AND WRONG]. IF YOU EVER EAT FRUIT FROM THAT TREE, YOU WILL [CERTAINLY] DIE!"

THEN THE LORD GOD SAID, "IT IS NOT GOOD FOR THE MAN TO BE ALONE. I WILL MAKE A HELPER [IN THE SENSE OF A PARTNER OR ALLY; THE WORD DOES NOT IMPLY SUBORDINATE STATUS; SEE PS. 79:9] WHO IS RIGHT FOR [IS SUITABLE FOR; CORRESPONDS WITH] HIM."

FROM THE GROUND GOD FORMED EVERY ·WILD ANIMAL [ANIMAL OF THE FIELD] AND EVERY BIRD IN THE SKY [HEAVENS], AND HE BROUGHT THEM TO THE MAN SO THE MAN COULD NAME THEM [TO SEE WHAT HE WOULD CALL THEM]. WHATEVER THE MAN CALLED EACH LIVING THING, THAT BECAME ITS NAME. THE MAN GAVE NAMES TO ALL THE TAME ANIMALS [BEASTS; LIVESTOCK], TO THE BIRDS IN THE SKY [HEAVENS], AND TO ALL THE WILD ANIMALS [ANIMALS OF THE FIELD]. BUT ADAM [OR THE MAN; 1:27] DID NOT FIND A HELPER THAT WAS RIGHT FOR HIM [2:18]. SO THE LORD GOD CAUSED THE MAN TO SLEEP VERY DEEPLY [A DEEP SLEEP TO FALL ON THE MAN/ADAM], AND WHILE HE WAS ASLEEP, GOD REMOVED ONE OF THE MAN'S RIBS [OR SIDES]. THEN GOD CLOSED UP THE MAN'S SKIN AT THE PLACE WHERE HE TOOK THE RIB [OR SIDE]. THE LORD GOD USED THE RIB [OR SIDE] FROM THE MAN TO MAKE [BUILD; CONSTRUCT] A WOMAN, AND THEN HE BROUGHT THE WOMAN TO THE MAN.

AND THE MAN SAID,

"NOW, THIS IS SOMEONE WHOSE BONES CAME FROM MY BONES,
    WHOSE BODY CAME FROM MY BODY [AT LAST, THIS IS BONE OF MY
BONES AND FLESH OF MY FLESH].
I WILL CALL HER [SHE WILL BE CALLED] 'WOMAN [HEBREW 'ISHSHAH],'
    BECAUSE SHE WAS TAKEN OUT OF MAN [HEBREW 'ISH]."

SO A MAN WILL LEAVE HIS FATHER AND MOTHER [IN THE SENSE OF A NEW PRIMARY LOYALTY] AND BE UNITED WITH HIS WIFE, AND THE TWO WILL BECOME ONE BODY [FLESH].

THE MAN AND HIS WIFE WERE NAKED, BUT THEY WERE NOT ASHAMED.

NOW THE SNAKE [SERPENT] WAS THE MOST CLEVER [SHREWD; CUNNING; CRAFTY] OF ALL THE WILD ANIMALS THE LORD GOD HAD MADE. ONE DAY THE SNAKE SAID TO THE WOMAN, "DID GOD REALLY SAY THAT YOU MUST NOT EAT FRUIT FROM ANY TREE IN THE GARDEN?"

THE WOMAN ANSWERED THE SNAKE [3:1], "WE MAY EAT FRUIT FROM THE TREES IN THE GARDEN. BUT GOD TOLD US, 'YOU MUST NOT EAT FRUIT FROM THE TREE THAT IS IN THE MIDDLE OF THE GARDEN [THE TREE OF THE KNOWLEDGE OF GOOD AND EVIL]. YOU MUST NOT EVEN TOUCH IT [EVE WAS ADDING TO THE DIVINE COMMAND], OR YOU WILL DIE.'"

BUT THE SNAKE [3:1] SAID TO THE WOMAN, "YOU WILL [MOST CERTAINLY] NOT DIE. [FOR] GOD KNOWS THAT IF YOU EAT THE FRUIT FROM THAT TREE [FROM IT], [YOUR EYES WILL BE OPENED AND] YOU WILL LEARN ABOUT [EXPERIENCE; KNOW ABOUT] GOOD AND EVIL AND YOU WILL BE LIKE GOD!"

THE WOMAN SAW THAT THE TREE WAS BEAUTIFUL [PLEASING TO THE EYES], THAT ITS FRUIT WAS GOOD TO EAT [FOR FOOD], AND THAT IT WOULD MAKE HER WISE. SO SHE TOOK SOME OF ITS FRUIT AND ATE IT. SHE ALSO GAVE SOME OF THE FRUIT TO HER HUSBAND WHO WAS WITH HER [APPARENTLY HE WAS PRESENT BUT SILENT WHILE THE WOMAN SPOKE TO THE SNAKE], AND HE ATE IT.

THEN, IT WAS AS IF THEIR EYES [THE EYES OF BOTH OF THEM] WERE OPENED. THEY REALIZED [KNEW] THEY WERE NAKED, SO THEY SEWED FIG LEAVES TOGETHER AND MADE SOMETHING TO COVER [LOINCLOTHS FOR] THEMSELVES [ROM. 5:12–21].

THEN THEY HEARD THE [SOUND OF THE] LORD GOD WALKING IN THE GARDEN DURING THE COOL PART OF THE DAY, AND THE MAN AND HIS WIFE HID FROM THE LORD GOD AMONG THE TREES IN THE GARDEN. BUT THE LORD GOD CALLED TO THE MAN AND SAID, "WHERE ARE YOU?"

THE MAN ANSWERED, "I HEARD YOU WALKING IN THE GARDEN [YOUR VOICE/SOUND], AND I WAS AFRAID BECAUSE I WAS NAKED, SO I HID."

GOD [HE] ASKED, "WHO TOLD YOU THAT YOU WERE NAKED? DID YOU EAT FRUIT FROM THE TREE FROM WHICH I COMMANDED YOU NOT TO EAT?"

THE MAN SAID, "YOU GAVE THIS WOMAN TO ME AND SHE GAVE ME FRUIT FROM THE TREE, SO I ATE IT."

THEN THE LORD GOD SAID TO THE WOMAN, "HOW COULD YOU HAVE DONE SUCH A THING [WHAT IS THIS YOU HAVE DONE]?"

SHE ANSWERED, "THE SNAKE TRICKED [DECEIVED; 1 TIM. 2:14] ME, SO I ATE THE FRUIT."

THE LORD GOD SAID TO THE SNAKE [SERPENT],

"BECAUSE YOU DID THIS,
    A CURSE WILL BE PUT ON YOU.
    YOU WILL BE CURSED AS NO OTHER ANIMAL, TAME [BEASTS; LIVESTOCK] OR WILD [OF THE FIELD], WILL EVER BE.
YOU WILL CRAWL [GO] ON YOUR STOMACH [BELLY],
    AND YOU WILL EAT DUST ALL THE DAYS OF YOUR LIFE.
I WILL MAKE YOU AND THE WOMAN
    ENEMIES TO EACH OTHER [PLACE HOSTILITY/ENMITY BETWEEN YOU AND THE WOMAN].
YOUR DESCENDANTS [SEED] AND HER DESCENDANTS [SEED]
    WILL BE ENEMIES.
ONE OF HER DESCENDANTS [HE] WILL CRUSH YOUR HEAD,
    AND YOU WILL BITE [STRIKE; BRUISE; CRUSH] HIS HEEL [ROM. 16:20; REV. 12:9]."

THEN GOD SAID TO THE WOMAN,
"I WILL CAUSE YOU TO HAVE MUCH TROUBLE [OR INCREASE YOUR PAIN]
    WHEN YOU ARE PREGNANT [IN CHILDBEARING],
AND WHEN YOU GIVE BIRTH TO CHILDREN,
    YOU WILL HAVE GREAT PAIN.
YOU WILL GREATLY DESIRE [THE WORD IMPLIES A DESIRE TO CONTROL; 4:7] YOUR HUSBAND,
    BUT HE WILL RULE OVER YOU."

THEN GOD SAID TO THE MAN [OR ADAM; 1:27], "YOU LISTENED TO WHAT YOUR WIFE SAID, AND YOU ATE FRUIT FROM THE TREE FROM WHICH I COMMANDED YOU NOT TO EAT.

Thought Points

Whose fault was it?

Years ago, I was in a Bible class. My teacher said, "The Bible says we all sin because of Adam. But I don't know, maybe we should be blaming Eve!" Of course, every male in the class - at the ripe, young age we were – was in agreement. They cheered his perspective on and formulated all sorts of theological positions (as if they really had any) to defend their opinions. I remember being very put out at the time but wasn't sure why. The truth was, I didn't know much about the Bible back then and couldn't have formed much of a defense if I had wanted to. All I knew was that if they claimed to be so Biblical, they shouldn't be attempting to undermine the Bible with the eternal battle of the sexes (which, ironically enough, has its origins in the garden).

For many years, we've heard the story about Adam and Eve only from the view of what Eve did wrong. We don't consider Adam's role in things and, as a result, we easily believe what we hear about the topic. The Bible is clear in Romans that we all sin because of Adam's transgression, so where does that leave Eve? Was she just an innocent in what happened?

The truth about Adam and Eve is that they show us two aspects that relate to sin, and we should pay attention to what it is trying to tell us. Adam shows us about sin, because he was the one who disobeyed God. The Bible tells us that God gave Adam the instructions about not eating from the fruit of the tree in the Garden, not that He gave those instructions to Eve. Even though Eve seems to know of those regulations and, thus, should have followed them by proxy, she was not the one who had the responsibility of the rule, and, thus, she was not the one who led into sin. Eve was deceived, and she teaches us that deception can be just as bad as disobedience. Whenever we allow ourselves to be beguiled, to listen to Satan or other voices that turn us away from God, we allow ourselves to walk into a place of deception.

Simply put, it was both Adam and Eve's fault that sin came into the world, just through different measures. Adam sinned, but Eve allowed herself to be deceived. We see both parts of this component here because deception and sin work off of each other, and if someone can convince themselves long enough that something is a good idea, they will eventually do it. Deception nor sin are contingent on gender; men and women alike can be deceived and sinned. The story just uses both characters to illustrate the way that the two work in combination and lead away from the will of God.

"So I will put a curse on [Cursed is] the ground,
and you will have to work very hard [toil; labor] for your

FOOD.
IN PAIN YOU WILL EAT ITS FOOD
ALL THE DAYS OF YOUR LIFE.
THE GROUND WILL PRODUCE THORNS AND WEEDS [THISTLES] FOR YOU,
AND YOU WILL EAT THE PLANTS OF THE FIELD.
YOU WILL SWEAT AND WORK HARD FOR [BY THE SWEAT OF YOUR BROW
YOU WILL EAT] YOUR FOOD.
LATER YOU WILL RETURN TO THE GROUND,
BECAUSE YOU WERE TAKEN FROM IT.
YOU ARE DUST,
AND WHEN YOU DIE, YOU WILL RETURN TO THE DUST [TO DUST YOU WILL
RETURN; 1 COR. 15:21-22, 40–45]."

THE MAN NAMED HIS WIFE EVE [THE NAME DERIVES FROM AN EARLY FORM
OF THE VERB "TO LIVE"], BECAUSE SHE WAS THE MOTHER OF ALL THE
LIVING.

THE LORD GOD MADE CLOTHES FROM ANIMAL SKINS FOR THE MAN [OR
ADAM; 1:27] AND HIS WIFE AND DRESSED THEM. THEN THE LORD GOD
SAID, "HUMANS HAVE BECOME LIKE ONE OF US [REFERRING TO THE
SUPERNATURAL HEAVENLY BEINGS, GOD AND THE ANGELS]; THEY KNOW
GOOD AND EVIL. WE MUST KEEP THEM FROM [PUTTING FORTH THEIR HAND
AND TAKING AND] EATING SOME OF THE FRUIT FROM THE TREE OF LIFE, OR
THEY WILL LIVE FOREVER." SO THE LORD GOD FORCED [EXPELLED] ADAM
OUT OF THE GARDEN OF EDEN TO WORK [TILL; OR CARE FOR; 2:5] THE
GROUND FROM WHICH HE WAS TAKEN. AFTER GOD FORCED [DROVE]
HUMANS OUT OF THE GARDEN, HE PLACED ANGELS [CHERUBIM;
PARTICULARLY POWERFUL SPIRITUAL BEINGS] AND A SWORD OF FIRE THAT
FLASHED AROUND IN EVERY DIRECTION ON ITS EASTERN BORDER. THIS
KEPT PEOPLE FROM GETTING [… TO GUARD THE WAY] TO THE TREE OF LIFE.

Adam and Eve were not married according to our definition of marriage today, or any traditional definition found in history. Their marriage was not arranged by their families, and no dowry exchanged hands. They did not have a marriage license, nor did they really choose their relationship with each other. They never even had a ceremony. (All these things should tell us that it isn't these things that really define an intimate, marriage relationship!) Because the Bible teaches them to be the first people on the planet, they didn't have scores of comparisons by which to decide they didn't desire to be together. Their relationship was unique and (literally) one-of-a-kind, never to be repeated throughout history in the same way between two married people...and they still found a way to screw it up.

Adam and Eve had it all. They lived in paradise. There was no sin to bring them down and no competition for their time or their affections. Adam wasn't sitting around, ogling other women as they walked by, and Eve didn't know the feeling of comparing herself to other women or not feeling like she measured up in Adam's eyes. They enjoyed a closeness, a knowing that they came from one another in a literal sense and experienced a sense of completeness in their marriage.

... So, what happened?

We know from the story that sin entered the world when the knowledge of good and evil came when Adam and Eve ate from the fruit in the garden. Eve had a long conversation with Satan (disguised as a serpent), who deceived her into thinking what she was doing was a good idea. She chose to listen to a voice other than God's, and gave Adam the fruit, as well. The Bible says he freely took it and ate of it; it does not say that Eve forced or tricked him into doing it. The results?

Adam was quick to lay the blame on Eve. Eve was quick to blame the serpent. God was looking for someone to be accountable, and neither one chose to do that. As a result, sin entered the world, causing long, hard complications all the way down the ages. It's wonderful to idealize Adam and Eve, but the reality is that the immediate result of sin was the deterioration of their relationship. No longer did they dwell in perfection, but now they were quick to blame their problems on one another. Doesn't that sound like the deeply antagonistic relationship men and women have today?

Adam and Eve show us the darker side of sin and deception in a marriage. Deception leads to sin, because we have stopped listening to God when we are deceived. Sin in marriage causes more than affairs and unfaithfulness. It also causes misplaced blame, antagonism, and, over time, a deterioration in one's marriage. Adam and Eve's sins carried down to their offspring, also showing the reality that the sins of a couple don't just affect them; it affects their children, and future generations, as well. In Adam and Eve, we see the interconnectedness of all people and all things, and that in marriage, those connections extend to others, as well. Sin doesn't just stay "in house" with a couple.

In marriage, we need not just think about ourselves, but think about others, as well: our spouse, our families, our church families, and our friends to come. Our behavior impacts others, and if God isn't in it, it will affect them negatively. We also need to look at the antagonism that exists in too many marriages. Marriage should not be a blame game or a competition, nor does it exist for one spouse to degrade or demoralize another. Yes, all of us have sinned, but all of us don't have to keep sinning all the time. At some point in time, much of our sin becomes a choice that we make. Through God, let's turn this thing around – and be aware that our sins have consequences.

Abraham and Sarah

Genesis 12:1-5:

THE LORD SAID TO ABRAM, "LEAVE YOUR COUNTRY, YOUR RELATIVES, AND YOUR FATHER'S FAMILY [HOUSE], AND GO TO THE LAND I WILL SHOW YOU [CANAAN, THE PROMISED LAND].

I WILL MAKE YOU A GREAT NATION,
    AND I WILL BLESS YOU.
I WILL MAKE YOU FAMOUS [YOUR NAME GREAT],
    AND [OR SO THAT] YOU WILL BE A BLESSING TO OTHERS.
I WILL BLESS THOSE WHO BLESS YOU,
    AND I WILL PLACE A CURSE ON THOSE WHO HARM [OR CURSE] YOU.
AND ALL THE PEOPLE [FAMILIES; CLANS] ON EARTH
    WILL BE BLESSED THROUGH YOU [THE PROMISES OF THE ABRAHAMIC COVENANT]."

SO ABRAM LEFT HARAN [11:31] AS THE LORD HAD TOLD HIM, AND LOT WENT WITH HIM. AT THIS TIME ABRAM WAS 75 YEARS OLD. HE TOOK HIS WIFE SARAI, HIS NEPHEW [THE SON OF HIS BROTHER] LOT, AND EVERYTHING THEY OWNED, AS WELL AS ALL THE SERVANTS [PEOPLE] THEY HAD GOTTEN IN HARAN. THEY SET OUT FROM HARAN, PLANNING TO GO TO THE LAND OF CANAAN, AND IN TIME THEY ARRIVED THERE.

Genesis 15:1-6:

AFTER THESE THINGS HAPPENED, THE LORD SPOKE HIS WORD TO ABRAM IN A VISION: "ABRAM, DON'T BE AFRAID. I WILL DEFEND [BE A SHIELD TO] YOU, AND I WILL GIVE YOU A GREAT REWARD [YOUR REWARD WILL BE GREAT]."

BUT ABRAM SAID, "LORD GOD [HEBREW ADONAI YAHWEH; COMBINATION OF COVENANT NAME YHWH (2:4) WITH COMMON HEBREW WORD FOR "SIR," "LORD," OR "MASTER"], WHAT CAN YOU GIVE ME? I HAVE NO SON [AM CHILDLESS], SO MY SLAVE [SERVANT] ELIEZER FROM DAMASCUS [A MAJOR CITY IN SYRIA] WILL GET EVERYTHING I OWN AFTER I DIE [BE MY HEIR; A HOUSEHOLD SERVANT WOULD TAKE CARE OF A CHILDLESS COUPLE IN THEIR OLD AGE AND IN TURN INHERIT THEIR POSSESSIONS]." ABRAM SAID, "LOOK, YOU HAVE GIVEN ME NO SON, SO A SLAVE BORN IN MY HOUSE WILL INHERIT EVERYTHING I HAVE [BE MY HEIR]."

THEN THE LORD SPOKE HIS WORD TO ABRAM: "HE WILL NOT BE THE ONE TO INHERIT WHAT YOU HAVE. YOU WILL HAVE A SON OF YOUR OWN WHO WILL INHERIT WHAT YOU HAVE."

THEN GOD LED ABRAM OUTSIDE AND SAID, "LOOK AT THE SKY [HEAVENS]. THERE ARE SO MANY STARS YOU CANNOT COUNT THEM. YOUR DESCENDANTS [SEED] ALSO WILL BE TOO MANY TO COUNT."

ABRAM BELIEVED [PUT HIS TRUST/FAITH IN] THE LORD. AND THE LORD ACCEPTED ABRAM'S FAITH, AND THAT FAITH MADE HIM RIGHT WITH GOD [COUNTED/CREDITED IT AS RIGHTEOUSNESS; ROM. 4:3, 9, 22; GAL. 3:6; JAMES 2:23].

Genesis 16:1-16:

SARAI, ABRAM'S WIFE, HAD NO CHILDREN, BUT SHE HAD A SLAVE GIRL FROM EGYPT NAMED HAGAR. SARAI SAID TO ABRAM, "LOOK, THE LORD HAS NOT ALLOWED ME TO HAVE [PREVENTED/RESTRAINED ME FROM HAVING] CHILDREN, SO HAVE SEXUAL RELATIONS WITH [GO TO] MY SLAVE GIRL. IF SHE HAS A CHILD, MAYBE I CAN HAVE MY OWN FAMILY [REPRODUCE; HAVE A CHILD; BUILD] THROUGH HER [TAKING A SECOND WIFE OR CONCUBINE WAS COMMON FOR A CHILDLESS COUPLE AT THE TIME]."

ABRAM DID WHAT SARAI SAID. IT WAS AFTER HE HAD LIVED TEN YEARS IN CANAAN THAT SARAI GAVE HAGAR TO HER HUSBAND ABRAM AS A WIFE [OR CONCUBINE]. (HAGAR WAS HER SLAVE GIRL FROM EGYPT.)

ABRAM HAD SEXUAL RELATIONS WITH [WENT IN TO] HAGAR, AND SHE BECAME PREGNANT [CONCEIVED]. WHEN HAGAR LEARNED SHE WAS PREGNANT [CONCEIVED], SHE BEGAN TO TREAT [LOOK ON] HER MISTRESS SARAI BADLY [WITH CONTEMPT]. THEN SARAI SAID TO ABRAM, "THIS IS YOUR FAULT [MAY THE WRONG/VIOLENCE DONE TO ME BE ON YOU]. I GAVE MY SLAVE GIRL TO YOU [INTO YOUR EMBRACE; INTO YOUR LAP], AND WHEN SHE BECAME PREGNANT [CONCEIVED], SHE BEGAN TO TREAT [LOOK ON] ME BADLY [WITH CONTEMPT]. LET THE LORD DECIDE WHO IS RIGHT— [JUDGE BETWEEN] YOU OR ME."

BUT ABRAM SAID TO SARAI, "YOU ARE HAGAR'S MISTRESS [YOUR SLAVE GIRL IS IN YOUR HAND/POWER]. DO ANYTHING YOU WANT [WHAT IS GOOD IN YOUR EYES] TO HER." THEN SARAI WAS HARD ON [AFFLICTED; ABUSED] HAGAR, AND HAGAR RAN AWAY [FLED FROM HER PRESENCE].

THE ANGEL [MESSENGER] OF THE LORD [THE ANGEL OF THE LORD WAS EITHER A REPRESENTATIVE OF THE LORD OR THE LORD HIMSELF; V. 13; JUDG. 6:11, 14] FOUND HAGAR BESIDE A SPRING OF WATER IN THE DESERT [WILDERNESS], BY THE ROAD TO SHUR [LIKELY A LOCATION IN SOUTHERN CANAAN; 20:1; 25:18; EX. 15:22; 1 SAM. 15:7]. THE ANGEL [HE] SAID, "HAGAR, SARAI'S SLAVE GIRL, WHERE HAVE YOU COME FROM? WHERE ARE YOU GOING?"

HAGAR ANSWERED, "I AM RUNNING AWAY [FLEEING] FROM MY MISTRESS SARAI."

THE ANGEL [MESSENGER] OF THE LORD [16:7] SAID TO HER, "GO HOME TO YOUR MISTRESS AND OBEY [SUBMIT TO] HER." THE ANGEL OF THE LORD ALSO SAID, "I WILL GIVE YOU SO MANY DESCENDANTS [GREATLY MULTIPLY YOUR SEED SO THAT] THEY CANNOT BE COUNTED."

THE ANGEL [MESSENGER] ADDED,
"YOU ARE NOW PREGNANT [HAVE CONCEIVED],
    AND YOU WILL HAVE [GIVE BIRTH TO] A SON.
YOU WILL NAME HIM ISHMAEL [SOUNDS LIKE THE VERB "TO HEAR"],
    BECAUSE THE LORD HAS HEARD YOUR CRIES [OF YOUR AFFLICTION].
ISHMAEL WILL BE LIKE A WILD DONKEY [A WILD DONKEY/ASS OF A MAN].
    HE [HIS HAND] WILL BE AGAINST EVERYONE,

AND EVERYONE [EVERYONE'S HAND] WILL BE AGAINST HIM.
HE WILL ATTACK [DWELL AGAINST] ALL HIS BROTHERS."

THE SLAVE GIRL GAVE A NAME TO THE LORD WHO SPOKE TO HER: "YOU ARE 'GOD WHO SEES ME [OR GOD OF SEEING; HEBREW EL-ROI]' " BECAUSE SHE SAID TO HERSELF, "HAVE I REALLY SEEN GOD WHO SEES ME?" SO THE WELL THERE, BETWEEN KADESH [ALSO KNOWN AS KADESH BARNEA IN NORTHEAST SINAI] AND BERED [LOCATION UNKNOWN], WAS CALLED BEER LAHAI ROI [THE WELL OF THE LIVING ONE WHO SEES ME].

HAGAR GAVE BIRTH TO A SON FOR ABRAM, AND ABRAM NAMED HIM [HIS SON WHICH HAGAR BORE HIM] ISHMAEL. ABRAM WAS EIGHTY-SIX YEARS OLD WHEN HAGAR GAVE BIRTH TO ISHMAEL.

Genesis 18:10-15:

THEN THE LORD [HE] SAID, "I WILL CERTAINLY RETURN TO YOU ABOUT THIS TIME A YEAR FROM NOW [OR IN DUE TIME; ABOUT THE LIVING TIME]. AT THAT TIME YOUR WIFE SARAH WILL HAVE A SON."

SARAH WAS LISTENING AT THE ENTRANCE OF THE TENT WHICH WAS BEHIND HIM. ABRAHAM AND SARAH WERE VERY OLD. SINCE SARAH WAS PAST THE AGE WHEN WOMEN NORMALLY HAVE CHILDREN [IT HAD STOPPED BEING WITH SARAH AFTER THE MANNER OF WOMEN; SHE HAD REACHED MENOPAUSE], SHE LAUGHED TO HERSELF [INWARDLY], "MY HUSBAND AND I ARE TOO OLD [I AM WORN OUT AND MY HUSBAND IS TOO OLD] TO HAVE A BABY [PLEASURE]."

THEN THE LORD SAID TO ABRAHAM, "WHY DID SARAH LAUGH? WHY DID SHE SAY, 'I AM TOO OLD TO HAVE A BABY'? IS ANYTHING TOO HARD FOR THE LORD? NO! I WILL RETURN TO YOU ·AT THE RIGHT TIME A YEAR FROM NOW [OR IN DUE TIME; ABOUT THE LIVING TIME], AND SARAH WILL HAVE A SON."
SARAH WAS AFRAID, SO SHE LIED [DENIED IT] AND SAID, "I DIDN'T LAUGH." BUT THE LORD SAID, "NO. YOU DID LAUGH."

Genesis 21:1-21:

THE LORD CARED FOR [VISITED] SARAH AS HE HAD SAID AND DID FOR HER WHAT HE HAD PROMISED. SARAH BECAME PREGNANT [CONCEIVED] AND GAVE BIRTH TO A SON FOR ABRAHAM IN HIS OLD AGE. EVERYTHING HAPPENED AT THE TIME GOD HAD SAID IT WOULD. ABRAHAM NAMED HIS

SON ISAAC, THE SON SARAH GAVE BIRTH TO. HE CIRCUMCISED [17:10] ISAAC WHEN HE WAS EIGHT DAYS OLD AS GOD HAD COMMANDED.

ABRAHAM WAS ONE HUNDRED YEARS OLD WHEN HIS SON ISAAC WAS BORN. AND SARAH SAID, "GOD HAS MADE ME LAUGH [THE NAME ISAAC IS RELATED TO A HEBREW WORD MEANING "LAUGH"]. EVERYONE WHO HEARS ABOUT THIS WILL LAUGH WITH [OR AT] ME. NO ONE THOUGHT THAT I WOULD BE ABLE TO HAVE ABRAHAM'S CHILD [SUCKLE/NURSE CHILDREN], BUT EVEN THOUGH ABRAHAM IS OLD I HAVE GIVEN HIM A SON."

ISAAC GREW, AND WHEN HE BECAME OLD ENOUGH TO EAT FOOD [WAS WEANED], ABRAHAM GAVE A GREAT FEAST [ON THE DAY OF HIS WEANING]. BUT SARAH SAW ISHMAEL [THE SON OF HAGAR THE EGYPTIAN] MAKING FUN OF ISAAC [LAUGHING; OR PLAYING]. SO SARAH SAID TO ABRAHAM, "THROW [DRIVE] OUT THIS SLAVE WOMAN AND HER SON. HER SON SHOULD NOT INHERIT ANYTHING; MY SON ISAAC SHOULD RECEIVE IT ALL [GAL. 4:21—5:1]."

THIS TROUBLED [DISTRESSED; UPSET] ABRAHAM VERY MUCH BECAUSE ISHMAEL WAS ALSO HIS SON. BUT GOD SAID TO ABRAHAM, "DON'T BE TROUBLED [DISTRESSED; UPSET] ABOUT THE BOY AND THE SLAVE WOMAN. DO WHATEVER [ALL] SARAH TELLS YOU. THE DESCENDANTS I PROMISED YOU WILL BE FROM [THE SEED WILL BE NAMED FOR YOU THROUGH] ISAAC. I WILL ALSO MAKE THE ·DESCENDANTS OF ISHMAEL [THE SON OF YOUR SLAVE WOMAN] INTO A GREAT NATION BECAUSE HE IS YOUR SON [SEED], TOO."

EARLY THE NEXT MORNING ABRAHAM [GOT UP AND] TOOK SOME FOOD AND A LEATHER BAG FULL [SKIN] OF WATER. HE GAVE THEM TO HAGAR AND SENT HER AWAY. CARRYING THESE THINGS AND HER SON [ON HER SHOULDER], HAGAR WENT AND WANDERED [THE VERB MAY IMPLY MOVING AIMLESSLY AND WITHOUT HOPE] IN THE DESERT [WILDERNESS] OF BEERSHEBA [AN AREA IN THE NORTHERN PART OF THE NEGEV, SOUTHERN CANAAN].

LATER, WHEN ALL THE WATER WAS GONE [FINISHED] FROM THE BAG [SKIN], HAGAR PUT HER SON UNDER A BUSH. THEN SHE WENT A GOOD WAY OFF, THE DISTANCE OF A BOWSHOT, AND SAT DOWN ACROSS FROM HIM. SHE THOUGHT, "MY SON WILL DIE, AND I CANNOT WATCH THIS HAPPEN." SHE SAT THERE ACROSS FROM HIM AND BEGAN TO CRY.

GOD HEARD THE BOY CRYING [SOUND/VOICE OF THE BOY], AND GOD'S ANGEL [MESSENGER; 16:7] CALLED TO HAGAR FROM HEAVEN. HE SAID, "WHAT IS WRONG, HAGAR? DON'T BE AFRAID! GOD HAS HEARD THE BOY CRYING [THE SOUND/VOICE OF THE BOY] THERE. HELP [GET UP AND LIFT] HIM UP AND TAKE HIM BY THE HAND. I WILL MAKE HIS DESCENDANTS [HIM] INTO A GREAT NATION." [ISHMAEL IS CONSIDERED THE ANCESTOR OF THE ARAB PEOPLE.]

THEN GOD [OPENED HER EYES AND] SHOWED HAGAR A WELL OF WATER. SO SHE WENT TO THE WELL AND FILLED HER BAG [SKIN] WITH WATER AND GAVE THE BOY A DRINK.

GOD WAS WITH THE BOY AS HE GREW UP. ISHMAEL LIVED IN THE DESERT [WILDERNESS] AND BECAME AN ARCHER. HE LIVED IN THE DESERT OF PARAN [A REGION IN THE EASTERN SINAI PENINSULA], AND HIS MOTHER FOUND A WIFE FOR HIM IN EGYPT [HAGAR'S ORIGINAL HOMELAND].

To properly understand Abraham and Sarah, we need to first look at and understand Abram and Sarai, the people behind the promises and the prophecies. Abram and Sarai were two people, minding their own business, when one day, God appeared to Abram and told him to leave his home – the place he had lived throughout his entire life – and go to a place where God would send him. Abram wasn't a Jewish man; he was a pagan man, living a customarily pagan life, not expecting anything out of the ordinary to happen. He and his wife were an older, barren couple, had no natural hope of having children.

Enter God, and His magnificent promise to Abram to make his name great and his descendants as numerous as the stars. Not realizing the spiritual promise made to him, Abram could only focus on the fact that he did not have a natural heir. Thus, God promised him that he would have a natural heir, one from his own body and with his own genetics, and Abram believed. His name was changed to Abraham, which means father of many nations, and everything was hunky dory, right?

Well... not exactly. Abram, who is now Abraham, and Sarai, who is now Sarah, didn't "believe" consistently in the way they needed to do so. Sarah, in fact downright laughed at the idea she would ever have a baby of her own. God promised them a child, and child they did have... ten years later. In the meantime, Abraham and

Sarah waivered greatly in their faith. They went as far as to try and "help God out," with Sarah offering Abraham her slave girl, Hagar, as a concubine so they could conceive a child and then Abraham and Sarah raise the baby as their own. Their concoction resulted in Sarah finding herself jealous of Hagar, abusing Hagar, Hagar fleeing, and the ultimate issue being the child Ishmael. This matter became far more complicated when Sarah did indeed give birth to a son, named Isaac, and Ishmael and Isaac started displaying classic child rivalries and stepsibling issues.

Talk about a mess.

There's no question that Abraham and Sarah must have both had faith in their lives to obey God in the way that they did. They left everything that was familiar to them and forged a new life. Even though God spoke directly to Sarah, we don't see Sarah protesting about God's orders. After all, what God told Abraham to do affected her life, as well, and she could have chosen to stick around and refuse to leave her home and everything that was familiar to her. They show fidelity, faithfulness when one partner in a marriage receives the call of God and the way that call can affect both people in the relationship, and a true stick-to-itness even when things got difficult or questionable. They show a resolve and dedication to each other that is admirable, because it is obvious that their attitude of faith extended far beyond just believing in God beyond what they understood – it also extended to their belief and trust in each other.

Abraham and Sarah, however, also reveal to us our weak points as people, and how those weak points become weaknesses in a relationship. Both Abraham and Sarah saw themselves as flawed because they didn't have children. This flaw, this impression they had of themselves led to poor and improper judgment in their marriage. It led Sarah, in her desperation, to offer another human being to her husband so she could have this child that she thought she wanted and needed. Abraham went along with the plan because he wanted that child, too. They wanted to have a baby, an heir, more than they wanted to have good sense, good reason, and a happy marriage. That baby they sought more than anything in the world became their idol, and it made it so life wasn't quite so simple anymore.

Ishmael represents everything that becomes so much of an idol to us, we decide to get a bright idea and help God out with bringing it to pass. No matter how much we might like to see them go away, God doesn't let us out of things that easily. Just because God's promise does indeed come to pass and we don't want to deal with the thing we created in disobedience doesn't mean God lets us forsake our duty to see that thing through until the end. Complicated or not, regretful or not...Ishmael is there to stay. Our duty to our Ishmaels remains through our married life. Even though Abraham and Sarah tried to get rid of Ishmael, God always made sure Ishmael was sent back. Ishmael changed the face of their relationship and required both of them to make sacrifices to ensure Ishmael received care.

We can make the following parallel for marriages: bringing in other mates, threesomes, concubines, even additional sexual partners or cohabitating partners is always a bad idea. They complicate a relationship, and doing so doesn't make the relationship better. We can also see the powerful role that idolatry often plays in having children. If you are unable to have children, there are many, many ways to handle it...but accepting the situation as it is goes a long way to contentment rather than desperation. Lastly, Ishmael proves that kids sired from other relationships do not get ignored when you get married again. You still have an obligation to pay for child support or care for those children, see them and be a part of their lives, even if you have moved on to another relationship or mate.

Jacob, Leah and Rachel

Genesis 29:9-30:24:

WHILE JACOB [HE] WAS TALKING WITH THE SHEPHERDS [THEM], RACHEL CAME WITH HER FATHER'S SHEEP, BECAUSE IT WAS HER JOB TO CARE FOR THE SHEEP [SHE WAS A SHEPHERDESS]. WHEN JACOB SAW LABAN'S DAUGHTER RACHEL AND LABAN'S SHEEP, HE WENT TO THE WELL AND ROLLED THE STONE FROM ITS MOUTH AND WATERED LABAN'S SHEEP. NOW LABAN WAS THE BROTHER OF REBEKAH, JACOB'S MOTHER. THEN JACOB KISSED RACHEL AND [LIFTED HIS VOICE AND] CRIED. HE TOLD HER THAT HE WAS FROM HER FATHER'S FAMILY AND THAT HE WAS THE SON OF REBEKAH. SO RACHEL RAN HOME AND TOLD HER FATHER.

When Laban heard the news about his sister's son Jacob, he ran to meet him. Laban hugged him and kissed him and brought him to his house, where Jacob told Laban everything that had happened.

Then Laban said, "You are my own flesh and blood [bone and flesh]."

Jacob stayed there a month. Then Laban said to Jacob, "You are my relative, but it is not right for you to work for me without pay [should you serve me for nothing?]. What would you like me to pay you [will your wages be]?"

Now Laban had two daughters. The older was Leah, and the younger was Rachel. Leah had weak eyes [frail/tender eyes; likely means unattractive], but Rachel was very beautiful. Jacob loved Rachel, so he said to Laban, "Let me marry your younger daughter Rachel. If you will, I will work seven years for you [I will work for seven years for your younger daughter Rachel]."

Laban said, "It would be better for her to marry you [me to give her to you] than someone else, so stay here with me." So Jacob worked for Laban seven years so he could marry Rachel. But they seemed like just a few days to him because he loved Rachel very much.

After seven years Jacob said to Laban, "Give me Rachel [my woman/wife] so that I may marry [go to] her. The time I promised to work for you is over [My days are fulfilled]."

So Laban gave a feast [banquet] for all the people there. That evening he brought his daughter Leah to Jacob, and they had sexual relations [he (Jacob) went into her]. (Laban gave his slave girl Zilpah to his daughter to be her servant [slave girl].) In the morning when Jacob saw that he had had sexual relations with [it was] Leah, he said to Laban, "What have you done to me? I worked hard for you so that I could marry Rachel! Why did you trick [deceive; defraud] me?"

Laban said, "In our country [place] we do not allow the younger daughter to marry before the older daughter [firstborn]. But complete the full week of the marriage ceremony with Leah [this

ONE], AND I WILL GIVE YOU RACHEL [THE OTHER ONE] TO MARRY ALSO.
BUT YOU MUST SERVE ME ANOTHER SEVEN YEARS."

SO JACOB DID THIS, AND WHEN HE HAD COMPLETED THE WEEK WITH LEAH
[OF THIS ONE], LABAN GAVE HIM HIS DAUGHTER RACHEL AS A
WIFE. (LABAN GAVE HIS SLAVE GIRL BILHAH TO HIS DAUGHTER RACHEL TO
BE HER SERVANT [SLAVE GIRL].) SO JACOB HAD SEXUAL RELATIONS WITH
[WENT TO] RACHEL ALSO, AND JACOB LOVED RACHEL MORE THAN LEAH.
JACOB WORKED FOR LABAN FOR ANOTHER SEVEN YEARS.

WHEN THE LORD SAW THAT JACOB LOVED RACHEL MORE THAN LEAH
[LEAH WAS UNLOVED/HATED], HE MADE IT POSSIBLE FOR LEAH TO HAVE
CHILDREN [OPENED UP HER WOMB], BUT NOT RACHEL [RACHEL WAS
BARREN]. LEAH BECAME PREGNANT [CONCEIVED] AND GAVE BIRTH TO A
SON. SHE NAMED HIM REUBEN [SOUNDS LIKE "SEEN MY TROUBLES" IN
HEBREW], BECAUSE SHE SAID, "THE LORD HAS SEEN MY TROUBLES
[DISTRESS]. SURELY NOW MY HUSBAND WILL LOVE ME."

LEAH BECAME PREGNANT [CONCEIVED] AGAIN AND GAVE BIRTH TO
ANOTHER SON. SHE NAMED HIM SIMEON [SOUNDS LIKE "HAS HEARD" IN
HEBREW] AND SAID, "THE LORD HAS HEARD THAT I AM NOT LOVED [OR
HATED], SO HE HAS GIVEN ME THIS SON."

LEAH BECAME PREGNANT [CONCEIVED] AGAIN AND GAVE BIRTH TO
ANOTHER SON. SHE NAMED HIM LEVI [SOUNDS LIKE "BE CLOSE TO" IN
HEBREW] AND SAID, "NOW, SURELY MY HUSBAND WILL BE CLOSE
[BIND/ATTACH HIMSELF] TO ME, BECAUSE I HAVE GIVEN HIM THREE SONS."

THEN LEAH GAVE BIRTH TO ANOTHER SON. SHE NAMED HIM JUDAH
[SOUNDS LIKE "PRAISE" IN HEBREW], BECAUSE SHE SAID, "NOW I WILL
PRAISE THE LORD." THEN LEAH STOPPED HAVING CHILDREN.

WHEN RACHEL SAW THAT SHE WAS NOT HAVING CHILDREN FOR JACOB,
SHE ENVIED [WAS JEALOUS OF] HER SISTER LEAH. SHE SAID TO JACOB,
"GIVE ME CHILDREN, OR I'LL DIE!" JACOB BECAME ANGRY WITH HER AND
SAID, "CAN I DO WHAT ONLY GOD CAN DO [AM I IN THE PLACE OF GOD]?
HE IS THE ONE WHO HAS KEPT YOU FROM HAVING CHILDREN [HAS
WITHHELD THE FRUIT OF YOUR WOMB]."

THEN RACHEL SAID, "HERE IS MY SLAVE GIRL BILHAH. HAVE SEXUAL
RELATIONS WITH [GO TO] HER SO SHE CAN GIVE BIRTH TO A CHILD FOR ME

[BEAR A CHILD ON MY KNEES]. THEN I CAN HAVE MY OWN FAMILY [BE BUILT UP] THROUGH HER."

SO RACHEL GAVE BILHAH, HER SLAVE GIRL, TO JACOB AS A WIFE [OR CONCUBINE], AND HE HAD SEXUAL RELATIONS WITH [WENT TO] HER. BILHAH BECAME PREGNANT [CONCEIVED] AND GAVE JACOB A SON. RACHEL SAID, "GOD HAS JUDGED ME INNOCENT [VINDICATED ME]. HE HAS LISTENED TO MY PRAYER AND HAS GIVEN ME A SON," SO SHE NAMED HIM DAN [SOUNDS LIKE "HE HAS JUDGED" IN HEBREW].

BILHAH BECAME PREGNANT [CONCEIVED] AGAIN AND GAVE JACOB A SECOND SON. RACHEL SAID, "I HAVE STRUGGLED [OR WRESTLED] HARD WITH MY SISTER, AND I HAVE WON." SO SHE NAMED THAT SON NAPHTALI [SOUNDS LIKE "MY STRUGGLE/WRESTLING" IN HEBREW].

LEAH SAW THAT SHE HAD STOPPED HAVING CHILDREN, SO SHE GAVE HER SLAVE GIRL ZILPAH TO JACOB AS A WIFE [OR CONCUBINE]. WHEN ZILPAH, THE SLAVE GIRL OF LEAH, GOT PREGNANT [CONCEIVED] AND HAD A SON, LEAH SAID, "I AM LUCKY [GOOD FORTUNE]," SO SHE NAMED HIM GAD [SOUNDS LIKE "LUCKY" IN HEBREW]. ZILPAH, THE SLAVE GIRL OF LEAH, GAVE BIRTH TO ANOTHER SON, AND LEAH SAID, "I AM VERY HAPPY [OR BLESSED]! NOW WOMEN WILL CALL ME HAPPY [OR BLESSED]," SO SHE NAMED HIM ASHER [SOUNDS LIKE "HAPPY/BLESSED" IN HEBREW].

DURING THE WHEAT HARVEST REUBEN WENT INTO THE FIELD AND FOUND SOME MANDRAKE PLANTS [AN APHRODISIAC, ALSO THOUGHT TO INCREASE FERTILITY] AND BROUGHT THEM TO HIS MOTHER LEAH. BUT RACHEL SAID TO LEAH, "PLEASE GIVE ME SOME OF YOUR SON'S MANDRAKES."

LEAH ANSWERED, "YOU HAVE ALREADY [IS IT A MINOR MATTER THAT YOU HAVE] TAKEN AWAY MY HUSBAND, AND NOW YOU ARE TRYING TO TAKE AWAY MY SON'S MANDRAKES."

BUT RACHEL ANSWERED, "IF YOU WILL GIVE ME YOUR SON'S MANDRAKES, YOU MAY SLEEP [LIE] WITH JACOB TONIGHT."

WHEN JACOB CAME IN FROM THE FIELD THAT NIGHT [IN THE EVENING], LEAH WENT OUT TO MEET HIM. SHE SAID, "YOU WILL HAVE SEXUAL RELATIONS WITH [COME TO] ME TONIGHT BECAUSE I HAVE PAID FOR [BOUGHT; HIRED] YOU WITH MY SON'S MANDRAKES." SO JACOB SLEPT [LAY] WITH HER THAT NIGHT.

THEN GOD ANSWERED LEAH'S PRAYER [HEARD LEAH], AND SHE BECAME PREGNANT [CONCEIVED] AGAIN. SHE GAVE BIRTH TO A FIFTH SON AND SAID, "GOD HAS GIVEN ME WHAT I PAID FOR [BOUGHT; HIRED], BECAUSE I GAVE MY SLAVE GIRL TO MY HUSBAND." SO LEAH NAMED HER SON ISSACHAR [SOUNDS LIKE "PAID FOR" IN HEBREW].

LEAH BECAME PREGNANT [CONCEIVED] AGAIN AND GAVE BIRTH TO A SIXTH SON. SHE [LEAH] SAID, "GOD HAS GIVEN ME A FINE GIFT [DOWRY]. NOW SURELY JACOB WILL HONOR [EXALT] ME, BECAUSE I HAVE GIVEN HIM SIX SONS," SO SHE NAMED HIM ZEBULUN [SOUNDS LIKE "HONOR" IN HEBREW]. LATER LEAH GAVE BIRTH TO A DAUGHTER AND NAMED HER DINAH [CH. 34].

THEN GOD REMEMBERED RACHEL AND ANSWERED HER PRAYER [HEARD HER], MAKING IT POSSIBLE FOR HER TO HAVE CHILDREN [AND OPENED HER WOMB]. WHEN SHE BECAME PREGNANT [CONCEIVED] AND GAVE BIRTH TO A SON, SHE SAID, "GOD HAS TAKEN AWAY MY SHAME [REPROACH]," AND SHE NAMED HIM JOSEPH [SOUNDS LIKE "HE ADDS" IN HEBREW]. RACHEL SAID, "I WISH THE LORD WOULD GIVE [ADD TO] ME ANOTHER SON."

Jacob, Leah, and Rachel is one of the most complicated triads we have in Bible history. It is further complicated that Jacob didn't just have two wives; he also had two concubines, meaning that he was involved with four women at one time. This is the reason he was able to have 12 children, no questions asked. The story of Jacob is, on the most basic level, a good example of how poorly polygamy works, no matter how organized, structured, or efficient one may be at household management. With relationships that involve multiple partners at once, you always have hard feelings, emotions, and a competitive nature that doesn't go away because you believe firmly in what you are doing or how much you try to get the situation to work out.

Jacob's situation was even more complicated because he wasn't just married to two women: he was married to two sisters, who were also his cousins (doesn't that make their story of fighting over him that much weirder?). Anyone who has had a sister (or more than one, at that) knows that sisters already tend to be competitive with each other. Marrying two sisters would seem like a bad idea to any normal person, right?

Jacob's situation wasn't quite that simple. Jacob married Leah and Rachel because he was tricked into marrying Leah. We all know from reading the Bible that Jacob wasn't of the best moral fiber at points of his life. He was comfortable deceiving other people, without a second thought. His mother even helped him with his deceptions, which makes the fact that Laban was his mother's brother most interesting (he was deceived by the brother of his most infamous partner in crime). The ultimate revenge? Jacob is deceived, working for years so he could marry Rachel, only to find out the day after his wedding that he was married to Leah. In turn, Jacob's father-in-law, Laban, required him to work another seven years, so he could also marry Rachel.

We tend to read the ultimate love story into Jacob's relationship with Rachel. By modern standards, being expected to work seven years to marry someone sounds strange, even odd, but working for several years to pay toward a dowry wasn't that uncommon in ancient times. We also read a little too much into our English translation of the word "love" in Genesis 29:18. The word "love" in verse 18 is the word *'ahab* in Hebrew, and it has a variety of meanings: "to love, human love for another, includes family, and sexual, human appetite for objects such as food, drink, sleep, wisdom, lovely (participle); to like." (#0157) The word refers to the entire expanse of human affection, including love, familial ties, appetites, liking someone, finding someone to be physically attractive, and being sexually attracted to someone. In verse 17, the Bible clearly states the physical appearances of the girls: Leah was most likely rather plain and unattractive, while Rachel was physically shapely and physically beautiful. Given the fact that the Bible speaks about physical appearances, Jacob's interest in Rachel wasn't "love" like we talk about in an *agape* sense or in being interested in her as a person, but he was attracted to her and interested in her sexually. How do I know this? Because if Jacob really cared about Rachel, he wouldn't have married her. He was a deceiver at this point in his life, he was dishonest, and he already married her sister – and good, bad, or indifferent – Jacob would have wanted better for Rachel than to marry her and have her spend her entire life competing and fighting with her sister. He interfered in her relationship with her sister, her father, and then Jacob spent the rest of his life in the middle of that complicated mess. We can see throughout the relationship, however, that the deceiver was still a deceiver, and he spent the course of the marriage deceiving the two women, pitting them against each other as they fought over him and who bore him the most children. It sounds more complicated than some of the soap operas on television.

In this extremely complicated marriage, we see many important things about self-identity in marriage and about the dangers of getting married for the wrong reasons. Leah spent her entire married life feeling inferior. Even though history doesn't support her having much of a say in her father's arrangement of her marriage to Jacob, I am going to venture that based on the way the Bible described her, she probably didn't think she would be able to have another chance to get married. She knew what her father was doing, and she thought that she would be able to get Jacob to love her, if she only could get him to know her. Once they were married, she started having babies, not one or two, but several... and Jacob still did not love her. Leah proves that no amount of having sex with a man or having babies for him will make him love you.

Rachel, on the other hand, proves that attraction and being able to catch the eye of a man does not complete you. As much as she seemed to be the sister who had it all and who was able to get Jacob's attention, she was not able to have children for him with the ease that Leah was able to do so. For all the energy and emphasis we place on physical appearance and being attractive to people with the way we look and carry ourselves, Rachel proves to us that happiness doesn't come from those things. Basing your marriage on the fact that you find your mate attractive doesn't make for a successful marriage, because the whole basis of judging oneself or others on physical attributes has a root of competition. Even though Rachel was the preferred wife, that competitive spirit led to endless issues with her sister, Leah, who was able to do something Rachel couldn't do. Rachel proves that marriage, nor a mate, does not complete you as a person and does not make up for your inner inadequacies.

As Abraham and Sarah also proved, Jacob, Leah, and Rachel prove polygamy, polyandry, and polyamory don't work. They might seem like things that sound fun and like endless opportunities for sex and physical exploration, but that quickly gets old as people argue, squabble, and compete for affection and attention.

Moses and Zipporah

Exodus 2:16-22:

THERE WAS A PRIEST IN MIDIAN [JETHRO; ALSO KNOWN AS REUEL] WHO HAD SEVEN DAUGHTERS. HIS DAUGHTERS WENT TO THAT WELL TO GET [DRAW] WATER TO FILL THE WATER TROUGHS FOR THEIR FATHER'S FLOCK. SOME SHEPHERDS CAME AND CHASED [DROVE] THE GIRLS AWAY, BUT MOSES DEFENDED THE GIRLS AND WATERED THEIR FLOCK.

WHEN THEY WENT BACK TO THEIR FATHER REUEL [ANOTHER NAME FOR JETHRO], HE ASKED THEM, "WHY HAVE YOU COME HOME EARLY TODAY?"

THE GIRLS ANSWERED, "THE SHEPHERDS CHASED US AWAY, BUT AN EGYPTIAN DEFENDED US [AN EGYPTIAN MAN RESCUED US FROM THE HAND OF SHEPHERDS]. HE GOT [DREW] WATER FOR US AND WATERED OUR FLOCK."
HE ASKED HIS DAUGHTERS, "WHERE IS THIS MAN? WHY DID YOU LEAVE [ABANDON; FORSAKE] HIM? INVITE HIM TO EAT WITH US."

MOSES AGREED TO STAY WITH JETHRO, AND HE GAVE HIS DAUGHTER ZIPPORAH TO MOSES TO BE HIS WIFE. SHE GAVE BIRTH TO A SON. MOSES NAMED HIM GERSHOM [SOUNDS LIKE "STRANGER/RESIDENT ALIEN THERE" IN HEBREW], BECAUSE MOSES WAS A STRANGER IN A LAND THAT WAS NOT HIS OWN [FOREIGN LAND].

Exodus 4:19-26:

WHILE MOSES WAS STILL IN MIDIAN, THE LORD SAID TO HIM, "GO BACK TO EGYPT, BECAUSE THE MEN WHO WANTED TO KILL YOU [WERE SEEKING YOUR LIFE] ARE DEAD NOW."

SO MOSES TOOK HIS WIFE AND HIS SONS, PUT THEM ON A DONKEY, AND STARTED BACK TO EGYPT. HE TOOK WITH HIM [IN HIS HAND] THE WALKING STICK [STAFF] OF GOD.

THE LORD SAID TO MOSES, "WHEN YOU GET BACK TO EGYPT, DO ALL THE MIRACLES I HAVE GIVEN YOU THE POWER TO DO [SET IN OUR HAND]. SHOW THEM TO THE KING OF EGYPT [PHARAOH]. BUT I WILL MAKE THE KING VERY STUBBORN [HARDEN HIS HEART], AND HE WILL NOT LET THE PEOPLE GO. THEN SAY TO THE KING [PHARAOH], 'THIS IS WHAT [THUS] THE LORD SAYS:

ISRAEL IS MY FIRSTBORN SON [THE PRIVILEGED CHILD]. I TOLD YOU TO LET MY SON GO SO HE MAY WORSHIP [SERVE] ME. BUT YOU REFUSED TO LET ISRAEL GO, SO I WILL KILL YOUR FIRSTBORN SON [11:1–10].'"

AS MOSES WAS ON HIS WAY TO EGYPT [ON THE WAY], HE STOPPED AT A RESTING PLACE FOR THE NIGHT. THE LORD MET HIM THERE AND TRIED TO KILL HIM. BUT ZIPPORAH TOOK A FLINT KNIFE AND CIRCUMCISED [CUT THE FORESKIN OF] HER SON. TAKING THE SKIN, SHE TOUCHED MOSES' FEET [A EUPHEMISM FOR HIS GENITALIA] WITH IT AND SAID TO HIM, "YOU ARE A BRIDEGROOM OF BLOOD TO ME." SHE SAID, "YOU ARE A BRIDEGROOM OF BLOOD," BECAUSE SHE HAD TO CIRCUMCISE HER SON [BY CIRCUMCISION]. SO THE LORD LET MOSES ALONE [THIS EVENT IS DIFFICULT TO INTERPRET, BUT SHOWS THAT CIRCUMCISION IS IMPORTANT TO GOD].

It is unclear according to the Bible as to whether Moses had more than one wife at once. Some traditions teach he had one wife; some traditions teach that he had two. If he had more than one wife, we do not have the name or formal record of that woman. The record of a wife that we do have is that of Zipporah, a woman who is only mentioned in the Bible by name about three times. Moses met Zipporah when her father, Jethro, gave her in marriage to Moses while he was in Midian. Zipporah had seven sisters, and they were involved in Jethro's shepherding work, where Moses worked for him.

We don't know much about the marriage of Zipporah and Moses. It does appear Moses was on good terms with his father-in-law, although it seems in other places that Miriam and Aaron might not always have cared for her. There is one specific incident where we see Zipporah stand up and intervene on Moses' behalf, and that is found in the passage above, in Exodus 4. The details of what exactly this incident alludes to and what it all means aren't clear, and historians disagree about its exact nature. What I do see in it, however, is the fact that Zipporah was there for Moses in a special way, in a way that Aaron and Miram were not. Spouses should be there for each other, looking out for one another and caring about each other, not trying to outdo or compete. Zipporah was completely comfortable with the work Moses had to do, and she knew when he was in trouble, how to help.

Ruth and Boaz

Ruth 3:1-4:17

THEN NAOMI, RUTH'S MOTHER-IN-LAW, SAID TO HER, "MY DAUGHTER, I MUST [SHOULD I NOT… ?] FIND A SUITABLE HOME [REST; A HUSBAND AND A HOME TO PROVIDE SECURITY] FOR YOU, ONE THAT WILL BE GOOD FOR YOU [OR SO YOU WILL BE SECURE; THAT IT WILL GO/BE WELL FOR YOU]. NOW BOAZ, WHOSE YOUNG WOMEN [FEMALE SERVANTS] YOU WORKED WITH, IS OUR CLOSE RELATIVE [AND SO AN APPROPRIATE GUARDIAN/KINSMAN-REDEEMER TO MARRY RUTH; 2:20]. [LOOK; BEHOLD] TONIGHT HE WILL BE WORKING [WINNOWING BARLEY] AT THE THRESHING FLOOR. WASH YOURSELF, PUT ON PERFUME, CHANGE YOUR CLOTHES [OR GET DRESSED UP; OR PUT ON YOUR CLOAK], AND GO DOWN TO THE THRESHING FLOOR. BUT DON'T LET HIM KNOW YOU'RE THERE UNTIL HE HAS FINISHED HIS DINNER [EATING AND DRINKING]. WATCH HIM SO YOU WILL KNOW WHERE HE LIES DOWN TO SLEEP. WHEN HE LIES DOWN, GO AND LIFT THE COVER OFF [UNCOVER] HIS FEET [OR LEGS; EVIDENTLY AN APPEAL FOR MARRIAGE] AND LIE DOWN. HE WILL TELL YOU WHAT YOU SHOULD DO."

THEN RUTH ANSWERED, "I WILL DO EVERYTHING YOU SAY."

SO RUTH WENT DOWN TO THE THRESHING FLOOR AND DID ALL HER MOTHER-IN-LAW TOLD [INSTRUCTED; COMMANDED] HER TO DO. AFTER HIS EVENING MEAL [HE HAD EATEN AND DRUNK], BOAZ FELT GOOD [[L] HIS HEART WAS GOOD/PLEASED] AND WENT TO SLEEP LYING BESIDE [AT THE END OF] THE PILE OF GRAIN. RUTH WENT TO HIM QUIETLY AND LIFTED THE COVER FROM HIS FEET AND LAY DOWN.

ABOUT MIDNIGHT BOAZ WAS STARTLED [OR SHUDDERED] AND ROLLED OVER. [AND LOOK/BEHOLD] THERE WAS A WOMAN LYING NEAR HIS FEET! BOAZ ASKED, "WHO ARE YOU?"

SHE SAID, "I AM RUTH, YOUR SERVANT GIRL. SPREAD YOUR COVER [OR THE CORNER OF YOUR GARMENT; OR YOUR WINGS; 2:12] OVER ME [A REQUEST FOR THE PROVISION AND PROTECTION OF MARRIAGE], BECAUSE YOU ARE A RELATIVE WHO IS SUPPOSED TO TAKE CARE OF ME [GUARDIAN; KINSMAN-REDEEMER; 2:20]."

THEN BOAZ SAID, "THE LORD BLESS YOU, MY DAUGHTER. THIS [SECOND; LAST] ACT OF KINDNESS IS GREATER THAN THE KINDNESS YOU SHOWED TO

NAOMI IN THE BEGINNING [FIRST]. YOU DIDN'T LOOK FOR A YOUNG MAN TO MARRY, EITHER RICH OR POOR. NOW, MY DAUGHTER, DON'T BE AFRAID. I WILL DO EVERYTHING YOU ASK, BECAUSE ALL THE PEOPLE IN OUR TOWN KNOW YOU ARE A GOOD [WORTHY; NOBLE] WOMAN [PROV. 31:10]. IT IS TRUE THAT I AM A RELATIVE WHO IS TO TAKE CARE OF YOU [GUARDIAN; KINSMEN-REDEEMER; 2:20], BUT YOU HAVE A CLOSER RELATIVE THAN I. STAY HERE TONIGHT, AND IN THE MORNING WE WILL SEE IF HE WILL TAKE CARE OF [BE A GUARDIAN FOR; REDEEM] YOU. IF HE DECIDES TO TAKE CARE OF [BE A GUARDIAN FOR; REDEEM] YOU, THAT IS FINE. BUT IF HE REFUSES, I WILL TAKE CARE OF [BE A GUARDIAN FOR; REDEEM] YOU MYSELF, AS SURELY AS THE LORD LIVES. SO STAY HERE [LIE DOWN] UNTIL MORNING."

SO RUTH STAYED NEAR HIS FEET UNTIL MORNING BUT GOT UP WHILE IT WAS STILL TOO DARK TO RECOGNIZE ANYONE. BOAZ THOUGHT, "PEOPLE IN TOWN MUST NOT KNOW THAT THE WOMAN CAME HERE TO THE THRESHING FLOOR." SO BOAZ SAID TO RUTH, "BRING ME YOUR SHAWL [CLOAK] AND HOLD IT OPEN."

SO RUTH HELD HER SHAWL [CLOAK] OPEN, AND BOAZ POURED SIX PORTIONS OF BARLEY INTO IT. BOAZ THEN PUT IT ON HER HEAD [OR HER BACK; HER] AND WENT BACK TO THE CITY.

WHEN RUTH WENT BACK TO HER MOTHER-IN-LAW, NAOMI ASKED, "HOW DID YOU DO [THINGS GO], MY DAUGHTER?"

RUTH TOLD NAOMI EVERYTHING THAT BOAZ [THE MAN] DID FOR HER. SHE SAID, "BOAZ GAVE ME THESE SIX PORTIONS OF BARLEY, SAYING, 'YOU MUST NOT GO HOME WITHOUT A GIFT FOR [EMPTY TO] YOUR MOTHER-IN-LAW.'"

NAOMI ANSWERED, "WAIT [STAY HERE; OR BE PATIENT], MY DAUGHTER, UNTIL YOU SEE WHAT HAPPENS. BOAZ [THE MAN] WILL NOT REST UNTIL HE HAS FINISHED DOING WHAT HE SHOULD DO TODAY."

BOAZ WENT TO THE CITY GATE [THE HUB OF THE TOWN FOR JUDICIAL, BUSINESS, AND SOCIAL INTERACTION] AND SAT THERE UNTIL THE CLOSE RELATIVE [GUARDIAN; KINSMAN-REDEEMER; 2:20] HE HAD MENTIONED PASSED BY. BOAZ CALLED TO HIM, "COME HERE [TURN ASIDE], FRIEND [OR SO-AND-SO; THE MAN IS NOT NAMED, PERHAPS IRONICALLY BECAUSE HE REFUSED TO PRESERVE NAOMI'S FAMILY NAME], AND SIT DOWN." SO THE MAN CAME OVER [TURNED ASIDE] AND SAT DOWN. BOAZ GATHERED TEN OF

THE ELDERS OF THE CITY AND TOLD THEM, "SIT DOWN HERE!" SO THEY SAT
DOWN.

THEN BOAZ SAID TO THE CLOSE RELATIVE [GUARDIAN; KINSMAN-
REDEEMER], "NAOMI, WHO HAS COME BACK FROM THE COUNTRY OF
MOAB, WANTS TO SELL [IS SELLING] THE PIECE OF LAND THAT BELONGED
TO OUR RELATIVE ELIMELECH [IT WAS IMPORTANT IN ISRAEL TO KEEP
PROPERTY IN THE FAMILY]. SO I DECIDED [OR THOUGHT IT MY OBLIGATION]
TO TELL YOU ABOUT IT: IF YOU WANT TO BUY BACK THE LAND [REDEEM IT],
THEN BUY IT [REDEEM] IN FRONT OF THE PEOPLE WHO ARE SITTING HERE
AND IN FRONT OF THE ELDERS OF MY PEOPLE. BUT IF YOU DON'T WANT TO
BUY IT, TELL ME, BECAUSE YOU ARE THE ONLY ONE [OR FIRST IN LINE] WHO
CAN BUY IT, AND I AM NEXT AFTER YOU."

THE CLOSE RELATIVE ANSWERED, "I WILL BUY BACK THE LAND [REDEEM
IT]."

THEN BOAZ EXPLAINED, "WHEN YOU BUY [ACQUIRE] THE LAND FROM [THE
HAND OF] NAOMI, YOU MUST ALSO MARRY [ACQUIRE] RUTH, THE
MOABITE, THE DEAD MAN'S WIFE. THAT WAY, THE LAND WILL STAY IN THE
DEAD MAN'S NAME [… TO RAISE UP A NAME FOR THE DEAD MAN UPON HIS
INHERITANCE]."

THE CLOSE RELATIVE [GUARDIAN; KINSMAN-REDEEMER] ANSWERED, "I
CAN'T BUY BACK THE LAND [REDEEM IT]. IF I DID, I MIGHT HARM
[DESTROY; ENDANGER; PUT IN JEOPARDY] WHAT I CAN PASS ON TO MY OWN
SONS [MY INHERITANCE]. I CANNOT BUY THE LAND BACK [REDEEM IT], SO
BUY IT [REDEEM IT FOR] YOURSELF."

LONG AGO IN ISRAEL WHEN PEOPLE TRADED OR BOUGHT BACK [FOR THE
REDEMPTION AND TRANSFER OF] SOMETHING, ONE PERSON TOOK OFF HIS
SANDAL AND GAVE IT TO THE OTHER PERSON. THIS WAS THE PROOF OF
OWNERSHIP [OR VALIDATION OF THE TRANSACTION] IN ISRAEL.

SO THE CLOSE RELATIVE [GUARDIAN; KINSMAN-REDEEMER] SAID TO BOAZ,
"BUY THE LAND YOURSELF," AND HE TOOK OFF HIS SANDAL.

THEN BOAZ SAID TO THE ELDERS AND TO ALL THE PEOPLE, "YOU ARE
WITNESSES TODAY. I AM BUYING [HAVE BOUGHT] FROM NAOMI
EVERYTHING THAT BELONGED TO ELIMELECH AND KILION AND MAHLON. I
AM ALSO TAKING [HAVE ALSO ACQUIRED] RUTH, THE MOABITE, WHO WAS
THE WIFE OF MAHLON, AS MY WIFE. I AM DOING THIS SO HER DEAD

HUSBAND'S PROPERTY WILL STAY IN HIS NAME AND HIS NAME WILL NOT BE SEPARATED [… SO THAT HIS NAME WILL NOT BE CUT OFF] FROM HIS FAMILY [BROTHERS] AND HIS HOMETOWN [THE GATE OF HIS PLACE]. YOU ARE WITNESSES TODAY."

SO ALL THE PEOPLE AND ELDERS WHO WERE AT THE CITY GATE SAID, "WE ARE WITNESSES. MAY THE LORD MAKE THIS WOMAN, WHO IS COMING INTO YOUR HOME, LIKE RACHEL AND LEAH, WHO TOGETHER BUILT UP THE PEOPLE [HOUSE] OF ISRAEL [THE TWELVE SONS OF ISRAEL WERE BORN TO LEAH, RACHEL AND THEIR SERVANT GIRLS; GEN. 29:31—30:24]. MAY YOU BECOME POWERFUL [OR WEALTHY; OR RENOWNED] IN THE DISTRICT OF EPHRATHAH AND FAMOUS [RENOWNED] IN BETHLEHEM. AS TAMAR GAVE BIRTH TO JUDAH'S SON PEREZ [AN ANCESTOR OF BOAZ (V. 18) WHOSE BIRTH RESULTED FROM A LEVIRATE UNION (2:20; GEN. 38:27–30; DEUT. 25:5–10) AND SO WAS PARALLEL TO THIS SITUATION], MAY THE LORD GIVE YOU MANY CHILDREN THROUGH RUTH. MAY YOUR FAMILY BE GREAT LIKE HIS."

SO BOAZ TOOK RUTH HOME AS HIS WIFE AND HAD SEXUAL RELATIONS WITH [WENT IN TO] HER. THE LORD LET HER BECOME PREGNANT, AND SHE GAVE BIRTH TO A SON. THE WOMEN TOLD NAOMI, "PRAISE [BLESSED BE] THE LORD WHO GAVE YOU THIS GRANDSON [HAS NOT LEFT YOU TODAY WITHOUT A GUARDIAN/KINSMAN-REDEEMER]. MAY HE [HIS NAME] BECOME FAMOUS [RENOWNED] IN ISRAEL. HE WILL GIVE YOU NEW [RESTORE/RENEW YOUR] LIFE AND WILL TAKE CARE OF YOU IN YOUR OLD AGE BECAUSE OF YOUR DAUGHTER-IN-LAW WHO LOVES YOU. SHE IS BETTER FOR YOU THAN SEVEN SONS, BECAUSE SHE HAS GIVEN BIRTH TO YOUR GRANDSON [HIM]."

NAOMI TOOK THE BOY, HELD HIM IN HER ARMS [OR PUT HIM ON HER LAP; OR TOOK HIM TO HER BREAST], AND CARED FOR HIM [OR BECAME HIS NURSE/CAREGIVER]. THE NEIGHBORS GAVE THE BOY HIS NAME, SAYING, "THIS BOY WAS [A SON HAS BEEN] BORN FOR NAOMI." THEY NAMED HIM OBED ["SERVANT"]. OBED WAS THE FATHER OF JESSE, AND JESSE WAS THE FATHER OF DAVID [ISRAEL'S GREATEST KING, THROUGH WHOM THE MESSIAH WOULD COME; 2 SAM. 7:11–17; MATT. 1:1, 5–6; LUKE 3:32].

Perhaps the most romanticized of all Bible couples, Ruth and Boaz are one of the most misunderstood couples in the entire Bible. We've turned their experiences into the love story, when the reality is that Ruth and Boaz didn't meet and instantly fall in love. In fact, they spent a good period avoiding any possibility of intimate relationship with each other. Had it not been for Naomi's intervention, the infamous Ruth and Boaz never would have gotten together!

Ruth and Orprah were the daughters-in-law of Naomi, a Hebrew woman who migrated to Moab with her husband and sons during a period of famine. They settled there and both sons married Moabite women (Ruth and Orprah). After disaster struck, Naomi's husband and two sons all died, leaving her, Ruth, and Orprah as widows. For a period, the three women stuck together, with Ruth and Orprah supporting and caring for Naomi. When Naomi encouraged the two women to return to their own families so they could find husbands and remarry, Orprah left and returned home, while Ruth refused to leave Naomi. The two women travelled to Bethlehem, right around the time of the barley harvest.

Naomi was a widow who lost her two sons, and she probably wasn't a lot of fun to be around. She was bitter and angry, and felt as if God had taken away every good thing from her life. Ruth, a young woman, had to work hard and labor in the fields to provide for her and her mother-in-law their all carb-diet, consisting of barley. In the process, Ruth wound up in Boaz's field, and Boaz regarded her kindly because of her love and devotion to her mother-in-law.

Naomi recognized Boaz to be a relative. With time, she realized he could serve as a kinsman-redeemer for them, making sure they were able to receive and inherit property. The marriage wasn't about love and romance but was about making sure both women were able to survive. Naomi suggested that Ruth take some initiative, and Ruth risked her life to go down to the threshing floor at night and surrender herself at Boaz's feet. Through their discourse, Ruth made every move and proposed to Boaz, because Boaz was not willing to make any of the moves. Even then, he still tried to find someone else to do the job – a relative who was closer to Ruth's age – and only agreed to marry her once the other guy refused!

Doesn't sound like a love story for the ages, does it?

Boaz and Ruth teach us a lot about how our attitudes prior to marriage prepare us for marriage. Neither one of them was looking for a husband or a wife, they were just living their lives. They got up, went to work, stayed the course God had for them, and did what they were supposed to do. Ruth and Boaz knew how to live their lives, and do what was right in God's sight. Ruth and Boaz went on to be very happy in their marriage from what we can see, and they never forgot about Naomi, who was given the blessing of a grandson through their union, even though they didn't get off to the most obvious of starts in their relationship. They show how important wise counsel is, and what a blessing extended family can be. In looking to Ruth and Boaz as examples for marriage dynamics, however, I think that Boaz reminds us that we should be careful with what we pray for. People are quick to say they want a Boaz, then when they get a man who drags his feet and doesn't want to get married, they don't understand what is going on. Boaz did not come into his life with the intent to rescue Naomi and Ruth, and he did not view Ruth from the perspective of a romantic partner. He was also not a man to make the first moves or take initiative. While Ruth and Boaz might have wound up in a good marriage, they got to that place thanks to Naomi's intervention and Ruth's quick thinking...not because he was ready, willing, and able to take himself a wife.

David and Bathsheba

2 Samuel 11:1-12:25

IN THE SPRING, WHEN THE KINGS NORMALLY WENT OUT TO WAR, DAVID SENT OUT JOAB, HIS SERVANTS [OFFICERS; ARMY], AND ALL THE ISRAELITES. THEY DESTROYED [MASSACRED; RAVAGED] THE AMMONITES AND ATTACKED [BESIEGED] THE CITY OF RABBAH. BUT DAVID STAYED IN JERUSALEM. ONE EVENING [AFTERNOON] DAVID GOT UP FROM HIS BED [MIDDAY REST] AND WALKED AROUND ON THE ROOF [THE FLAT ROOFS OF ISRAELITE HOUSES WERE USED FOR LIVING SPACE] OF HIS PALACE [THE KING'S HOUSE]. WHILE HE WAS ON THE ROOF, HE SAW A WOMAN BATHING. SHE WAS VERY BEAUTIFUL. SO DAVID SENT HIS SERVANTS TO FIND OUT WHO SHE WAS. A SERVANT ANSWERED, "THAT WOMAN IS BATHSHEBA DAUGHTER OF ELIAM. SHE IS THE WIFE OF URIAH THE HITTITE [HITTITES WERE FOREIGNERS, BUT HE JOINED THE ISRAELITE CAUSE]." SO DAVID SENT MESSENGERS TO BRING BATHSHEBA TO HIM. WHEN SHE CAME TO HIM, HE HAD SEXUAL RELATIONS [LAY] WITH HER. (NOW BATHSHEBA HAD PURIFIED HERSELF FROM HER MONTHLY PERIOD [UNCLEANNESS; LEV. 15:19–24].) THEN SHE WENT BACK TO HER HOUSE. BUT BATHSHEBA

BECAME PREGNANT [CONCEIVED] AND SENT WORD TO DAVID, SAYING, "I AM PREGNANT."

SO DAVID SENT A MESSAGE TO JOAB: "SEND URIAH THE HITTITE TO ME." AND JOAB SENT URIAH TO DAVID. WHEN URIAH CAME TO HIM, DAVID ASKED HIM HOW JOAB WAS, HOW THE SOLDIERS WERE, AND HOW THE WAR WAS GOING. THEN DAVID SAID TO URIAH, "GO HOME AND REST [WASH YOUR FEET; PERHAPS A EUPHEMISM FOR SEX]."

SO URIAH LEFT THE PALACE [KING'S HOUSE], AND THE KING SENT A GIFT TO HIM. BUT URIAH DID NOT GO HOME. INSTEAD, HE SLEPT OUTSIDE THE DOOR OF THE PALACE AS ALL THE KING'S OFFICERS [GUARD; SERVANTS] DID.

THE OFFICERS TOLD DAVID, "URIAH DID NOT GO HOME."

THEN DAVID SAID TO URIAH, "YOU CAME FROM A LONG TRIP. WHY DIDN'T YOU GO HOME?"

URIAH SAID TO HIM, "THE ARK AND THE SOLDIERS OF ISRAEL AND JUDAH ARE STAYING IN TENTS [BOOTHS; TEMPORARY SHELTERS]. MY MASTER [LORD; COMMANDER] JOAB AND HIS OFFICERS ARE CAMPING OUT IN THE FIELDS. IT ISN'T RIGHT FOR ME TO [HOW CAN I... ?] GO HOME TO EAT AND DRINK AND HAVE SEXUAL RELATIONS [LIE] WITH MY WIFE [THUS RENDERING HIMSELF RITUALLY UNCLEAN AND UNABLE TO GO INTO THE PRESENCE OF THE ARK; LEV. 15:16–18]!"

DAVID SAID TO URIAH, "STAY HERE TODAY. TOMORROW I'LL SEND YOU BACK TO THE BATTLE." SO URIAH STAYED IN JERUSALEM THAT DAY AND THE NEXT. THEN DAVID CALLED URIAH TO COME TO SEE HIM, SO URIAH ATE AND DRANK WITH DAVID. DAVID MADE URIAH DRUNK, BUT HE STILL DID NOT GO HOME. THAT EVENING URIAH AGAIN SLEPT WITH THE KING'S OFFICERS [GUARD; SERVANTS].

THE NEXT MORNING DAVID WROTE A LETTER TO JOAB AND SENT IT BY URIAH. IN THE LETTER DAVID WROTE, "PUT URIAH ON THE FRONT LINES WHERE THE FIGHTING IS WORST [FIERCEST; HARDEST] AND LEAVE HIM THERE ALONE [THEN PULL BACK/WITHDRAW]. LET HIM BE KILLED IN BATTLE [STRUCK DOWN AND DIE]."

JOAB WATCHED [OR BESIEGED] THE CITY AND SAW WHERE ITS STRONGEST DEFENDERS [VALIANT MEN] WERE AND PUT URIAH THERE. WHEN THE MEN

OF THE CITY CAME OUT TO FIGHT AGAINST JOAB, SOME OF DAVID'S MEN WERE KILLED [FELL]. AND URIAH THE HITTITE WAS ONE OF THEM.

THEN JOAB SENT DAVID A COMPLETE ACCOUNT [REPORT] OF THE WAR [BATTLE; FIGHTING]. JOAB TOLD THE MESSENGER, "TELL KING DAVID WHAT HAPPENED IN THE WAR [BATTLE; FIGHTING]. AFTER YOU FINISH, THE KING MAY BE ANGRY AND ASK, 'WHY DID YOU GO SO NEAR THE CITY TO FIGHT? DIDN'T YOU KNOW THEY WOULD SHOOT ARROWS FROM THE CITY WALL? DO YOU REMEMBER WHO KILLED ABIMELECH SON OF JERUB-BESHETH [ANOTHER NAME FOR GIDEON]? IT WAS A WOMAN ON THE CITY WALL. SHE THREW A LARGE STONE FOR GRINDING GRAIN ON ABIMELECH AND KILLED HIM THERE IN THEBEZ [JUDG. 9:50–57]. WHY DID YOU GO SO NEAR THE WALL?' IF KING DAVID ASKS THAT, TELL HIM, 'YOUR SERVANT URIAH THE HITTITE ALSO DIED.'"

THE MESSENGER LEFT AND WENT TO DAVID AND TOLD HIM EVERYTHING JOAB HAD TOLD HIM TO SAY. THE MESSENGER TOLD DAVID, "THE MEN OF AMMON WERE WINNING [GAINING AN ADVANTAGE OVER US]. THEY CAME OUT AND ATTACKED US IN THE FIELD, BUT WE FOUGHT [DROVE; CHASED] THEM BACK TO THE CITY GATE. THE ARCHERS ON THE CITY WALL SHOT AT YOUR SERVANTS, AND SOME OF YOUR MEN [THE KING'S SERVANTS] WERE KILLED. YOUR SERVANT URIAH THE HITTITE ALSO DIED."

DAVID SAID TO THE MESSENGER, "SAY THIS TO JOAB: 'DON'T BE UPSET [DISCOURAGED; TROUBLED] ABOUT THIS. THE SWORD KILLS EVERYONE THE SAME [DEVOURS FIRST ONE AND THEN ANOTHER]. MAKE A STRONGER ATTACK [FIGHT HARDER; PRESS YOUR ATTACK] AGAINST THE CITY AND CAPTURE IT.' ENCOURAGE JOAB WITH THESE WORDS."

WHEN BATHSHEBA [THE WIFE OF URIAH] HEARD THAT HER HUSBAND WAS DEAD, SHE CRIED [MOURNED] FOR HIM. AFTER SHE FINISHED HER TIME OF SADNESS [MOURNING], DAVID SENT SERVANTS TO BRING HER TO HIS HOUSE. SHE BECAME DAVID'S WIFE AND GAVE BIRTH TO HIS SON, BUT THE LORD WAS DISPLEASED WITH WHAT DAVID HAD DONE.

THE LORD SENT NATHAN [A PROPHET WHO WAS IN THE KING'S COURT; 7:2–17] TO DAVID. WHEN HE CAME TO DAVID, HE SAID, "THERE WERE TWO MEN IN A CITY. ONE WAS RICH, BUT THE OTHER WAS POOR. THE RICH MAN HAD MANY SHEEP [FLOCKS] AND CATTLE [HERDS]. BUT THE POOR MAN HAD NOTHING EXCEPT ONE LITTLE FEMALE [EWE] LAMB HE HAD BOUGHT. THE POOR MAN FED THE LAMB, AND IT GREW UP WITH HIM AND HIS CHILDREN. IT SHARED HIS FOOD [ATE FROM HIS PLATE] AND DRANK

FROM HIS CUP AND SLEPT IN HIS ARMS [BOSOM]. THE LAMB WAS LIKE A DAUGHTER TO HIM.

"THEN A TRAVELER STOPPED TO VISIT THE RICH MAN. THE RICH MAN WANTED TO FEED THE TRAVELER, BUT HE DIDN'T WANT [WAS UNWILLING/LOATH] TO TAKE ONE OF HIS OWN SHEEP OR CATTLE [FROM HIS OWN FLOCK OR HERD]. INSTEAD, HE TOOK THE LAMB FROM THE POOR MAN AND COOKED [PREPARED] IT FOR HIS VISITOR."

DAVID BECAME VERY ANGRY AT [BURNED WITH ANGER AGAINST] THE RICH MAN. HE SAID TO NATHAN, "AS SURELY AS THE LORD LIVES, THE MAN WHO DID THIS SHOULD [DESERVES TO] DIE! HE MUST PAY FOR THE LAMB FOUR TIMES [REPAY FOUR LAMBS] FOR DOING SUCH A THING [EX. 22:1]. HE HAD NO MERCY [PITY; COMPASSION]!"

THEN NATHAN SAID TO DAVID, "YOU ARE THE [THAT] MAN! THIS IS WHAT THE LORD, THE GOD OF ISRAEL, SAYS: 'I APPOINTED [ANOINTED] YOU KING OF ISRAEL AND [I] SAVED [RESCUED; DELIVERED] YOU FROM [THE HAND OF] SAUL. I GAVE YOU HIS KINGDOM [YOUR MASTER'S HOUSE] AND HIS WIVES [INTO YOUR ARMS/BOSOM]. AND I MADE YOU KING [GAVE YOU THE HOUSE] OF ISRAEL AND JUDAH. AND IF THAT HAD NOT BEEN ENOUGH, I WOULD HAVE GIVEN YOU EVEN [MUCH] MORE. SO WHY DID YOU IGNORE THE LORD'S COMMAND [DESPISE THE WORD OF THE LORD]? WHY DID YOU DO WHAT HE SAYS IS WRONG [IS EVIL IN HIS SIGHT/EYES]? YOU KILLED [STRUCK DOWN] URIAH THE HITTITE WITH THE SWORD OF THE AMMONITES AND TOOK HIS WIFE TO BE YOUR WIFE! NOW [THEREFORE] ·THERE WILL ALWAYS BE PEOPLE IN YOUR FAMILY WHO WILL DIE BY A SWORD [THE SWORD WILL NEVER DEPART FROM YOUR HOUSE], BECAUSE YOU DID NOT RESPECT [HAVE DESPISED] ME; YOU TOOK THE WIFE OF URIAH THE HITTITE FOR YOURSELF!'

"THIS IS WHAT THE LORD SAYS: 'I AM BRINGING TROUBLE TO [RAISING UP EVIL AGAINST] YOU FROM YOUR OWN FAMILY [HOUSE]. WHILE YOU WATCH [BEFORE YOUR EYES], I WILL TAKE YOUR WIVES FROM YOU AND GIVE THEM TO SOMEONE WHO IS VERY CLOSE TO YOU [YOUR NEIGHBOR]. HE WILL HAVE SEXUAL RELATIONS [LIE] WITH YOUR WIVES, AND EVERYONE WILL KNOW IT [IN BROAD DAYLIGHT]. YOU HAD SEXUAL RELATIONS WITH BATHSHEBA [DID IT] IN SECRET, BUT I WILL DO THIS SO ALL THE PEOPLE OF ISRAEL CAN SEE IT [BEFORE ALL ISRAEL IN BROAD DAYLIGHT; 16:21–22].'"

THEN DAVID SAID TO NATHAN, "I HAVE SINNED AGAINST THE LORD." NATHAN ANSWERED, "THE LORD HAS TAKEN AWAY [FORGIVEN] YOUR SIN.

YOU WILL NOT DIE [PS. 51]. BUT WHAT YOU DID CAUSED THE LORD'S ENEMIES TO LOSE ALL RESPECT FOR HIM [OR HAS SHOWN UTTER CONTEMPT/SCORN FOR THE LORD]. FOR THIS REASON THE SON [CHILD] WHO WAS BORN TO YOU WILL DIE."

THEN NATHAN WENT HOME. AND THE LORD CAUSED THE SON [STRUCK THE CHILD] OF DAVID AND BATHSHEBA, URIAH'S WIDOW, TO BE [AND HE BECAME] VERY SICK. DAVID PRAYED TO [PLEADED WITH; BEGGED; INQUIRED OF] GOD FOR THE BABY. DAVID FASTED AND WENT INTO HIS HOUSE AND STAYED THERE, LYING ON THE GROUND ALL NIGHT. THE ELDERS OF DAVID'S FAMILY [HOUSE] CAME TO [STOOD AROUND] HIM AND TRIED TO PULL HIM UP FROM THE GROUND, BUT HE REFUSED TO GET UP OR TO EAT FOOD WITH THEM.

ON THE SEVENTH DAY THE BABY DIED. DAVID'S SERVANTS [ADVISERS] WERE AFRAID TO TELL HIM THAT THE BABY WAS DEAD. THEY SAID, "LOOK, WE TRIED TO TALK TO DAVID WHILE THE BABY WAS ALIVE, BUT HE REFUSED TO LISTEN TO US [REASON]. IF WE TELL HIM THE BABY IS DEAD, HE MAY DO SOMETHING AWFUL [SOMETHING DESPERATE; HIMSELF HARM]."

WHEN DAVID SAW HIS SERVANTS [ADVISERS] WHISPERING, HE KNEW THAT THE BABY WAS DEAD. SO HE ASKED THEM, "IS THE BABY [CHILD] DEAD?" THEY ANSWERED, "YES, HE IS DEAD."

THEN DAVID GOT UP FROM THE FLOOR [GROUND], WASHED HIMSELF, PUT LOTIONS ON [ANOINTED HIMSELF], AND CHANGED HIS CLOTHES. THEN HE WENT INTO THE LORD'S HOUSE [THE TABERNACLE; HIS HOUSE] TO WORSHIP. AFTER THAT, HE WENT HOME AND ASKED FOR SOMETHING TO EAT. HIS SERVANTS GAVE HIM SOME FOOD, AND HE ATE.

DAVID'S SERVANTS [ADVISERS] SAID TO HIM, "WHY ARE YOU DOING [BEHAVING LIKE] THIS? WHEN THE BABY [CHILD] WAS STILL ALIVE, YOU FASTED AND YOU CRIED. NOW THAT THE BABY [CHILD] IS DEAD, YOU GET UP AND EAT FOOD."

DAVID SAID, "WHILE THE BABY [CHILD] WAS STILL ALIVE, I FASTED, AND I CRIED. I THOUGHT, 'WHO KNOWS? MAYBE THE LORD WILL FEEL SORRY FOR [BE GRACIOUS TO] ME AND LET THE BABY [CHILD] LIVE.' BUT NOW THAT THE BABY [CHILD] IS DEAD, WHY SHOULD I FAST? I CAN'T [CAN I... ?] BRING HIM BACK TO LIFE. SOMEDAY I WILL GO TO HIM, BUT HE CANNOT COME BACK TO ME."

THEN DAVID COMFORTED [CONSOLED] BATHSHEBA HIS WIFE. HE SLEPT WITH [WENT IN TO] HER AND HAD SEXUAL RELATIONS [LAY] WITH HER. SHE BECAME PREGNANT AGAIN [CONCEIVED] AND HAD ANOTHER [GAVE BIRTH TO A] SON, WHOM DAVID [OR SHE; THEY] NAMED SOLOMON. THE LORD LOVED SOLOMON. THE LORD SENT WORD THROUGH NATHAN THE PROPHET TO NAME THE BABY JEDIDIAH ["LOVED BY THE LORD"], BECAUSE THE LORD LOVED THE CHILD [FOR THE LORD'S SAKE].

David and Bathsheba didn't have the most ideal marriage. According to the Bible, David had many wives, but we only have the names of eight of those women. One of those women was Bathsheba, a Hittite (Gentile) woman that David saw bathing and decided he wanted to have her, at all costs. When she became pregnant, he called for her husband, Uriah, to come forth into the palace and tried to find ways to get him out of the picture. When Uriah didn't go away so graciously, David put her husband on the front lines of battle and had him killed, so he could marry her without anyone asking too many questions as to the circumstances surrounding their union. David should have known better, though, because God knew what happened and made sure to send him a word through the prophet. Nathan told David of God's displeasure and made it clear that evil would come upon the house of David. David's family would suffer from war and tumult. He would lose some of his wives and they would be taken by a neighbor, who would do to David what David did to Uriah. The firstborn son of David and Bathsheba also died. David repented, he moved on, and then he and Bathsheba had his son, Solomon, who we all know became a powerful and important king over Israel.

In ancient times, kings were polygamous for political reasons. Marriages signified political alliances between nations, they ensured the bloodline of the king would continue if one queen died or was unable to bear children, and they made for good appearances, causing the nation to look healthy and prosperous. These were further complications to an already complex situation, as their relationship started with dishonesty and lust of the eyes.

If David had many wives, then he didn't need another one. Bathsheba was not the daughter of a king, which means there were no political ties or justifications for it. The adulterous affair he had with her had no blessing, and no good could come out of it. What David and Bathsheba show us about marriage is that how we go into marriage is just as important as where we are at once we get married. Marriages that start in adultery or in less than honorable circumstances come with a host of issues and often end in divorce. Repentance is key from every dishonorable start as God promises us marital hope and promise if we truly make the effort to be honorable once we have repented and fully turned from the place we started.

Jezebel and Ahab

1 Kings 16:29-33:

AHAB SON OF OMRI BECAME KING OF ISRAEL DURING ASA'S THIRTY-EIGHTH YEAR AS KING OF JUDAH, AND AHAB RULED [REIGNED OVER] ISRAEL IN THE CITY OF SAMARIA FOR TWENTY-TWO YEARS. MORE THAN ANY KING BEFORE HIM, AHAB SON OF OMRI DID MANY THINGS THE LORD SAID WERE WRONG [EVIL IN THE EYES/SIGHT OF THE LORD]. HE SINNED IN THE SAME WAYS AS [WALKED IN THE WAYS/PATHS OF] JEROBOAM SON OF NEBAT, BUT HE DID EVEN WORSE THINGS [AS THOUGH IT WERE A LIGHT/TRIVIAL THING]. HE MARRIED JEZEBEL DAUGHTER OF ETHBAAL, THE KING OF SIDON. THEN AHAB BEGAN TO SERVE BAAL AND WORSHIP HIM. HE BUILT A TEMPLE [HOUSE] IN SAMARIA FOR WORSHIPING BAAL AND PUT AN ALTAR THERE FOR BAAL. AHAB ALSO MADE AN IDOL FOR WORSHIPING ASHERAH [SET UP AN ASHERAH POLE; 14:15]. HE DID MORE THINGS TO PROVOKE [AROUSE] THE LORD, THE GOD OF ISRAEL, TO ANGER THAN ALL THE OTHER KINGS BEFORE HIM.

1 Kings 21:1-19:

AFTER THESE THINGS HAD HAPPENED, THIS IS WHAT FOLLOWED. A MAN NAMED NABOTH OWNED A VINEYARD IN JEZREEL, NEAR THE PALACE OF AHAB KING OF ISRAEL. ONE DAY AHAB SAID TO NABOTH, "GIVE ME YOUR VINEYARD. IT IS NEAR MY PALACE, AND I WANT TO MAKE IT INTO A VEGETABLE GARDEN. I WILL GIVE YOU A BETTER VINEYARD IN ITS PLACE, OR, IF YOU PREFER, I WILL PAY YOU WHAT IT IS WORTH."

NABOTH ANSWERED, "MAY THE LORD KEEP ME FROM EVER GIVING MY LAND TO YOU. IT BELONGS TO MY FAMILY [THE LORD FORBID THAT I SHOULD GIVE YOU THE INHERITANCE OF MY FATHERS/ANCESTORS]."

AHAB WENT HOME ANGRY AND UPSET [RESENTFUL AND SULLEN], BECAUSE HE DID NOT LIKE WHAT NABOTH FROM JEZREEL HAD SAID. (NABOTH HAD SAID, "I WILL NOT GIVE YOU MY FAMILY'S LAND [THE INHERITANCE OF MY FATHERS/ANCESTORS].") AHAB LAY DOWN ON HIS BED, TURNED HIS FACE TO THE WALL, AND REFUSED TO EAT.

HIS WIFE, JEZEBEL, CAME IN AND ASKED HIM, "WHY ARE YOU SO UPSET [SULLEN; DEPRESSED] THAT YOU REFUSE TO EAT?"

AHAB ANSWERED, "I TALKED TO NABOTH, THE MAN FROM JEZREEL. I SAID, 'SELL ME YOUR VINEYARD, OR, IF YOU PREFER, I WILL GIVE YOU ANOTHER VINEYARD FOR IT.' BUT NABOTH REFUSED."

JEZEBEL ANSWERED, "IS THIS HOW YOU RULE AS KING [REIGN] OVER ISRAEL? GET UP, EAT SOMETHING, AND CHEER UP. I WILL GET NABOTH'S VINEYARD FOR YOU."

SO JEZEBEL WROTE SOME LETTERS, SIGNED AHAB'S NAME TO THEM, AND USED HIS OWN SEAL TO SEAL THEM. THEN SHE SENT THEM TO THE ELDERS AND IMPORTANT MEN [NOBLES] WHO LIVED IN NABOTH'S TOWN. THE LETTER SHE WROTE SAID: "DECLARE A DAY DURING WHICH THE PEOPLE ARE TO FAST. CALL THE PEOPLE TOGETHER, AND GIVE NABOTH A PLACE OF HONOR AMONG THEM. SEAT TWO TROUBLEMAKERS [SCOUNDRELS] ACROSS FROM HIM, AND HAVE THEM SAY THEY HEARD NABOTH SPEAK AGAINST ["YOU CURSED… "] GOD AND THE KING. THEN TAKE NABOTH OUT OF THE CITY AND KILL HIM WITH STONES [STONE HIM TO DEATH]."

THE ELDERS AND IMPORTANT MEN OF JEZREEL OBEYED JEZEBEL'S COMMAND, JUST AS SHE WROTE IN THE LETTERS. THEY DECLARED A SPECIAL DAY ON WHICH THE PEOPLE WERE TO FAST [FAST]. AND THEY PUT NABOTH IN A PLACE OF HONOR BEFORE THE PEOPLE. TWO TROUBLEMAKERS [SCOUNDRELS] SAT ACROSS FROM NABOTH AND SAID IN FRONT OF EVERYBODY THAT THEY HAD HEARD HIM SPEAK AGAINST ["YOU CURSED… "] GOD AND THE KING. SO THE PEOPLE CARRIED NABOTH OUT OF THE CITY AND KILLED HIM WITH STONES [STONED HIM TO DEATH]. THEN THE LEADERS SENT A MESSAGE TO JEZEBEL, SAYING, "NABOTH HAS BEEN ·KILLED [STONED AND IS DEAD]."

WHEN JEZEBEL HEARD THAT NABOTH HAD BEEN KILLED [STONED AND WAS DEAD], SHE TOLD AHAB, "NABOTH OF JEZREEL IS NO LONGER ALIVE; HE'S DEAD. NOW YOU MAY GO AND TAKE FOR YOURSELF THE VINEYARD HE WOULD NOT SELL TO YOU." WHEN AHAB HEARD THAT NABOTH OF JEZREEL

WAS DEAD, HE GOT UP AND WENT TO THE VINEYARD TO TAKE IT FOR HIS OWN [POSSESSION OF IT].

AT THIS TIME THE LORD SPOKE HIS WORD [WORD OF THE LORD CAME] TO THE PROPHET ELIJAH THE TISHBITE. THE LORD SAID, "GO TO AHAB KING OF ISRAEL IN SAMARIA. HE IS AT NABOTH'S VINEYARD, WHERE HE HAS GONE TO TAKE IT AS HIS OWN [POSSESSION OF IT]. TELL AHAB THAT I, THE LORD, SAY TO HIM, 'YOU HAVE [ᴸ HAVE YOU NOT... ?] MURDERED NABOTH AND TAKEN HIS LAND. SO I TELL YOU THIS: IN THE SAME PLACE THE DOGS LICKED UP NABOTH'S BLOOD, THEY WILL ALSO LICK UP YOUR BLOOD [1 KIN. 22:37–38]!'"

I already know that some of you wonder why I have included Ahab and Jezebel in this chapter on Biblical marriages. They weren't godly people, they went after God's people with a vengeance, and they weren't moral rulers. Surely, they don't have a marriage to emulate! Well, several of the marriages we have looked at aren't necessarily marriages we want to emulate, regardless of who was in them. Jezebel and Ahab made the list because they had a marriage with very visible dynamics that many marriages display, even though they should not.

Ahab was king of Israel for 22 years. The Bible tells us that he specifically sought out Jezebel for marriage, because she was an idolater. He wanted to defy God, and there was no better way to do so than bring a woman into the palace who had no reverence for Him. Even though many people act as if Jezebel was a constant manipulator and Ahab was just a weak victim, the Bible's examination of the two of them could not be further from the truth. Ahab knew exactly what he was doing, trying to irk God with Jezebel's presence and to get her to do the things that he didn't want to do himself.

2 Kings 10:1 also reveals an additional relationship about Ahab and Jezebel's marriage:

Ahab had seventy sons in Samaria [the city, not the region]...

There's no way Jezebel had all those children by herself. Whether wives or, more than likely, concubines, or a combination of both, Ahab and Jezebel had a highly controversial – and complicated – relationship.

Ahab and Jezebel had a dysfunctional dynamic in their marriage known as co-dependency. This means that they knew how to work each other for their own advantage to survive, but they are dependent on that relationship and that dysfunctional dynamic to survive. Ahab knew what to say, how loudly to whine, and how to work Jezebel up so she would do his dirty work. Jezebel, motivated by her own feelings (she probably felt she could do a better job of ruling because her impression of Ahab was far different than that of his subjects and his enemies) and her own desires for power and control, used Ahab's manipulation to manipulate situations.

This endless dynamic by which Ahab and Jezebel played off each other for their own gain is, unfortunately, anything but uncommon. Many couples have unhealthy dynamics in their own marriages, where they don't want to be accountable and don't want to do the right thing, so they defer the responsibility to their mate. Motivated by their own sense of things, they do what needs to be done, taking the heat for it, as well.

All relationships are based on certain dynamics at their core, and those dynamics can be either healthy or unhealthy. Co-dependence in marriage is a dangerous thing, and it leads to many troublesome issues as the marriage goes on. One of the most important principles in marriage is accountability. Don't use your mate to do what you want to do but don't want responsibility for and don't use your mate's weaknesses to get a sense of power and control.

Hosea and Gomer

Hosea 1:2-8:

WHEN THE LORD BEGAN SPEAKING THROUGH HOSEA, THE LORD SAID TO HIM, "GO, AND MARRY [TAKE FOR YOURSELF] AN UNFAITHFUL WOMAN [OR PROSTITUTE; WOMAN/WIFE OF PROSTITUTION/HARLOTRIES] AND HAVE UNFAITHFUL CHILDREN [CHILDREN OF PROSTITUTION/HARLOTRIES], BECAUSE THE PEOPLE IN THIS COUNTRY [THIS LAND] HAVE BEEN COMPLETELY UNFAITHFUL TO [PRACTICED PROSTITUTION/HARLOTRY AGAINST] THE LORD [THEY HAVE BEEN SPIRITUALLY UNFAITHFUL; GOMER MAY HAVE BEEN A PROSTITUTE OR PROMISCUOUS WOMAN BEFORE THE MARRIAGE, OR ONLY AFTERWARD]." SO HOSEA MARRIED [WENT AND TOOK] GOMER DAUGHTER OF DIBLAIM, AND SHE BECAME PREGNANT [CONCEIVED] AND GAVE BIRTH TO HOSEA'S SON.

THE LORD SAID TO HOSEA, "NAME HIM JEZREEL [HEBREW: "GOD SOWS"], BECAUSE SOON I WILL PUNISH THE FAMILY [HOUSE] OF JEHU FOR THE PEOPLE THEY KILLED AT [BLOOD OF] JEZREEL [JEHU SLAUGHTERED THE FAMILY OF KING AHAB; 2 KIN. 9:7—10:28]. IN THE FUTURE [THAT DAY] I WILL PUT AN END TO THE KINGDOM OF [THE HOUSE OF] ISRAEL AND BREAK THE POWER OF ISRAEL'S ARMY [BOW OF ISRAEL] IN THE VALLEY OF JEZREEL."

GOMER BECAME PREGNANT [CONCEIVED] AGAIN AND GAVE BIRTH TO A DAUGHTER. THE LORD SAID TO HOSEA, "NAME HER LO-RUHAMAH [HEBREW: "NO PITY/MERCY" OR "NOT LOVED"], BECAUSE I WILL NOT PITY [HAVE MERCY ON; SHOW LOVE TO] ISRAEL ANYMORE, NOR WILL I FORGIVE THEM. BUT I WILL SHOW PITY [MERCY; LOVE] TO THE PEOPLE OF JUDAH. I WILL SAVE THEM, BUT NOT BY USING BOWS OR SWORDS, HORSES OR HORSEMEN, OR WEAPONS OF WAR [OR BATTLE; WAR]. I, THE LORD THEIR GOD, WILL SAVE THEM."

AFTER GOMER HAD STOPPED NURSING LO-RUHAMAH, SHE BECAME PREGNANT [CONCEIVED] AGAIN AND GAVE BIRTH TO ANOTHER SON. THE LORD SAID, "NAME HIM LO-AMMI ["NOT MY PEOPLE"], BECAUSE YOU ARE NOT MY PEOPLE, AND I AM NOT YOUR GOD.

Hosea 3:1-5:

THE LORD SAID TO ME AGAIN, "GO, SHOW YOUR LOVE TO A WOMAN [PROBABLY GOMER (1:3), WHO HAS SINCE DESERTED HIM] LOVED BY [OR WHO LOVES] SOMEONE ELSE, WHO HAS BEEN UNFAITHFUL TO YOU [IS COMMITTING ADULTERY]. IN THE SAME WAY THE LORD LOVES THE PEOPLE [SONS; CHILDREN] OF ISRAEL, EVEN THOUGH THEY WORSHIP [TURN TO] OTHER GODS AND LOVE TO EAT THE RAISIN CAKES [FOOD EATEN AT PAGAN TEMPLES]."

SO I BOUGHT HER FOR SIX OUNCES OF SILVER [SHEKELS] AND TEN BUSHELS [A HOMER AND A LETHEK; A HOMER WAS 5–6 BUSHELS; A LETHEK WAS ABOUT HALF THAT] OF BARLEY. THEN I TOLD HER, "YOU MUST WAIT FOR [OR LIVE WITH] ME FOR MANY DAYS. YOU MUST NOT BE A PROSTITUTE, AND YOU MUST NOT HAVE SEXUAL RELATIONS WITH ANY OTHER MAN. I WILL ACT THE SAME WAY TOWARD YOU."

IN THE SAME WAY THE PEOPLE [SONS; CHILDREN] OF ISRAEL WILL LIVE MANY DAYS WITHOUT A KING OR LEADER [PRINCE], WITHOUT SACRIFICES OR HOLY STONE PILLARS [USED IN PAGAN WORSHIP; 2 KIN. 3:2; 10:26–28;

17:10], AND WITHOUT THE HOLY VEST [EPHOD; EX. 28:6–14; JUDG. 8:27] OR AN IDOL [HOUSEHOLD IDOLS; TERAPHIM; GEN. 31:19]. AFTER THIS, THE PEOPLE OF ISRAEL WILL RETURN AND FOLLOW [SEEK] THE LORD THEIR GOD AND THE KING FROM DAVID'S FAMILY [DAVID THEIR KING; AN HEIR FROM DAVID'S LINE]. IN THE LAST DAYS THEY WILL TURN IN FEAR [COME IN REVERENCE/AWE] TO THE LORD, AND HE WILL BLESS THEM.

When we talk about Hosea and Gomer, we immediately go to the spiritual reality that their living type was to demonstrate: the broken relationship between God and Israel. God was the dedicated, pursuant Hosea, who refused to give up on his wayward, prostitute wife, Gomer, who typified Israel. Reading the book of Hosea has an eloquent ring to it, one that almost sounds poetic as God gives Hosea command after command to have children that reflect His rejection of Israel's behavior, go out and find his wife who is living as a prostitute, and bring her home, in love.

We read words like this, and we get caught up in the incredible love God has for us, and rightly so. God wants us to read Hosea and hear His love for us and return to Him from any sin we have committed. We don't consider how difficult it is to live as a type of God, illustrating something on this level, and how invasive this type was to Hosea, Gomer, and their family.

The story of Hosea and Gomer was anything but romantic. I highly doubt that, as a prophet, Hosea envisioned himself marrying a prostitute. That was something that would have been frowned upon, not to mention something that would have caused him to have a sordid reputation. Having children with a prostitute would have also created legal complications, because there was no way to guarantee they were his children from a genetic standpoint. They were a family scorned and talked about, hushed in whispers. There were probably many people who questioned Hosea's calling, whether or not he was really hearing from God, and who downright questioned his sanity.

The tender love that Hosea expressed to Gomer is one that should exist in a marriage, even if the other person in the relationship is not a Christian or living as they should. We assume that Hosea and Gomer lived happily ever after, but the Bible doesn't tell us this. We don't know what happened after the prophetic message was delivered and the type was then over. Just like Hosea and Gomer, we don't know where people's marriages end up, or why they end up where they do. Some marriages are not, according to God's purpose for that couple, meant to live happily ever after. There are still people that God calls to teach things through marriage and navigate the difficult waters that pertain to His relationship with us, and our relationships with one another. These marriages, which exist to develop deep holiness in those who experience them and give them the ability to teach spiritual things through them, are prophetic messages in and of themselves. When in this type of marriage, at least one, if not both partners, recognize and learn deep truths about themselves and experience personal wrestling that requires support, rather than strange looks, from those who know them.

Mary and Joseph

Matthew 1:18-25:

THIS IS HOW THE BIRTH OF JESUS CHRIST [THE MESSIAH] CAME ABOUT. HIS MOTHER MARY WAS ENGAGED [PLEDGED; BETROTHED; A FORMAL AGREEMENT BETWEEN FAMILIES THAT REQUIRED A "DIVORCE" TO ANNUL] TO MARRY JOSEPH, BUT BEFORE THEY MARRIED [CAME TO LIVE TOGETHER], SHE LEARNED SHE WAS [OR WAS FOUND/DISCOVERED TO BE] PREGNANT [WITH CHILD] BY THE POWER OF [THROUGH] THE HOLY SPIRIT. BECAUSE MARY'S HUSBAND, JOSEPH, WAS A GOOD [RIGHTEOUS] MAN, HE DID NOT WANT TO DISGRACE HER IN PUBLIC, SO HE PLANNED TO DIVORCE HER [END THE ENGAGEMENT] SECRETLY [PRIVATELY; QUIETLY].

WHILE JOSEPH THOUGHT ABOUT [CONSIDERED; DECIDED; RESOLVED TO DO] THESE THINGS, [LOOK; BEHOLD] AN ANGEL OF THE LORD CAME [APPEARED] TO HIM IN A DREAM. THE ANGEL SAID, "JOSEPH, DESCENDANT [SON] OF DAVID, DON'T BE AFRAID TO TAKE MARY AS YOUR WIFE, BECAUSE THE BABY [WHAT IS CONCEIVED] IN HER IS FROM THE HOLY SPIRIT. SHE WILL GIVE BIRTH TO A SON, AND YOU WILL NAME HIM JESUS, BECAUSE HE WILL SAVE HIS PEOPLE FROM THEIR SINS [THE NAME JESUS MEANS "THE LORD SAVES"]."

ALL THIS HAPPENED TO BRING ABOUT [FULFILL] WHAT THE LORD HAD SAID [SPOKEN] THROUGH THE PROPHET: "[LOOK; BEHOLD] THE VIRGIN WILL BE PREGNANT [CONCEIVE IN HER WOMB; Is. 7:14]. SHE WILL HAVE [GIVE

BIRTH TO] A SON, AND THEY WILL NAME HIM IMMANUEL," WHICH [IN HEBREW] MEANS "GOD IS WITH US."

WHEN JOSEPH WOKE UP, HE DID WHAT THE LORD'S ANGEL HAD TOLD [COMMANDED] HIM TO DO. JOSEPH TOOK MARY AS HIS WIFE, BUT HE DID NOT HAVE SEXUAL RELATIONS WITH HER UNTIL SHE GAVE BIRTH TO A SON. AND JOSEPH [HE] NAMED HIM JESUS.

Christmas cards give us the impression that there was no holier, more complete couple in the Bible than Mary and Joseph. They appear to just glow as they sit around and stare at the baby Jesus (Who also glows, of course). Our re-telling of the Christmas story makes Mary and Joseph sound ideal, like everything was just perfect and they both fell into God's hands at the exact right time... or something like that.

When the angel Gabriel appeared to Mary, she wasn't expecting her life to be anything out of the ordinary. I have known Christians who pray and invoke God to make something special or supernatural happen to them, but that wasn't who Mary was. She was somewhere between twelve and fourteen years old, preparing to get married, to a man that she did not choose for herself. Her life was to be Joseph's wife and a mother and maintain her reputation. Well, one day, an angel comes along, tells her that she is going to be the mother of the Savior of the world, and that was that. So much for ordinary, everyday life. Mary's whole world was going to revolve around this singular calling that she had to answer, and it was going to change her marriage, radically.

We see that Joseph intended to call off the wedding to Mary, because he assumed that she was pregnant by another man, as much as everyone else probably thought the same thing. It required an intervention of God, a message sent via an angel, to get Joseph on board with this virgin birth thing. Even then, given the time in which Jesus was born, I am sure that Mary and Joseph had their issues. Joseph was expected to raise a child that was not his in a culture that prided exclusive procreation, and I am sure the fact that Jesus was not Joseph's child never escaped his mind. The experience must have been difficult for both Joseph and Mary at times, because raising a child with promise is never an easy task.

At the same time, I think that Joseph and Mary show us far more than just fortitude through hardship. Joseph and Mary show us, as did Moses and Zipporah, the power of a spouse recognizing an extraordinary calling on their partner. As hard as it was for Joseph, he had to submit himself to the gift that was present in Mary's life. When a spouse marries someone extraordinary, they must take a few for the team, as the expression goes, and make sure that the spiritual flow is present to facilitate that gift within their spouse. It means sacrifice and that things don't always go their way, but recognizing the calling and gifts on one's spouse – and allowing those gifts and calling to flourish – is what makes a marriage powerfully meaningful and successful when one partner in a marriage is called to do something great for God.

Peter and his wife

Matthew 8:14-15:

WHEN JESUS WENT TO PETER'S HOUSE, HE SAW THAT PETER'S MOTHER-IN-LAW WAS SICK IN BED [LYING DOWN] WITH A FEVER. JESUS TOUCHED HER HAND, AND THE FEVER LEFT HER. THEN SHE STOOD UP AND BEGAN TO SERVE [WAITING ON] JESUS.

We know the Apostle Peter was married because the Bible mentions his mother-in-law. We don't know much about Peter's wife, except that she had a mother, and church tradition supports the fact that Peter also had a daughter who was in ministry. The fact that the Apostle Peter had such an active role in the early church and had a family shows that it can be done, and that it is done as one submits to the gift that God has placed on the one who is called (as we spoke of with Mary and Joseph earlier). The fact that the Bible speaks of the Apostle Peter's mother-in-law and the fact that Jesus came to heal her speaks volumes to the regard that the Apostle Peter had for her.

We live in a world of mother-in-law jokes, scorn for in-laws, and general disregard for extended family. The fact that Jesus healed her and she saw fit to minister and serve unto Him tells us just how important extended family can be in a marital life, and how much we should respect and regard the families that our spouse came from.

Ananias and Sapphira

Acts 5:1-11:

BUT A MAN NAMED ANANIAS AND HIS WIFE SAPPHIRA SOLD SOME LAND [A PIECE OF PROPERTY]. HE KEPT BACK [PILFERED; SKIMMED OFF] PART OF THE MONEY [PROCEEDS; PRICE] FOR HIMSELF; HIS WIFE KNEW ABOUT THIS AND AGREED TO IT. BUT HE BROUGHT THE REST OF THE MONEY AND GAVE IT TO [LAID IT AT THE FEET OF] THE APOSTLES. PETER SAID, "ANANIAS, WHY DID YOU LET SATAN RULE YOUR THOUGHTS [FILL YOUR HEART] TO LIE TO THE HOLY SPIRIT AND TO KEEP [PILFER; SKIM OFF] FOR YOURSELF PART OF THE MONEY [PROCEEDS] YOU RECEIVED FOR THE LAND? BEFORE YOU SOLD THE LAND, IT BELONGED TO YOU. AND EVEN AFTER YOU SOLD IT, YOU COULD HAVE USED THE MONEY [PROCEEDS] ANY WAY YOU WANTED. WHY DID YOU THINK OF DOING THIS? YOU LIED TO GOD, NOT TO US!" WHEN ANANIAS HEARD THIS, HE FELL DOWN AND DIED. SOME YOUNG MEN CAME IN, WRAPPED UP HIS BODY, CARRIED IT OUT, AND BURIED IT. AND EVERYONE WHO HEARD ABOUT THIS WAS FILLED WITH FEAR.

ABOUT THREE HOURS LATER HIS WIFE CAME IN, BUT SHE DID NOT KNOW WHAT HAD HAPPENED. PETER SAID TO HER, "TELL ME, WAS THE MONEY [PAYMENT] YOU GOT FOR YOUR FIELD THIS MUCH?"

SAPPHIRA ANSWERED, "YES, THAT WAS THE PRICE."

PETER SAID TO HER, "WHY DID YOU AND YOUR HUSBAND AGREE [CONSPIRE] TO TEST THE SPIRIT OF THE LORD [GAL. 6:7–8]? LOOK! THE MEN [FEET OF THOSE] WHO BURIED YOUR HUSBAND ARE AT THE DOOR, AND THEY WILL CARRY YOU OUT." AT THAT MOMENT [INSTANTLY] SAPPHIRA FELL DOWN BY HIS FEET AND DIED. WHEN THE YOUNG MEN CAME IN AND SAW [DISCOVERED; FOUND] THAT SHE WAS DEAD, THEY CARRIED HER OUT AND BURIED HER BESIDE HER HUSBAND. THE WHOLE CHURCH AND ALL THE OTHERS WHO HEARD ABOUT THESE THINGS WERE FILLED WITH FEAR [TERROR; AWE].

I am ending this chapter with a look at an infamous bad duo: Ananias and Sapphira, the couple who will forever be known to history as trying to withhold promised funds from God... who got caught. Ananias and Sapphira sold some property that they owned, and Ananias kept back part of the money for himself. We learn that she knew about it, too; she was complicit in the act. When Ananias went to lay the remainder of the money at the apostles' feet, they got caught. The Apostle Peter reprimanded him, called out their sin, and then God knocked him dead, right then and there. A few hours later, Sapphira came in, not knowing that Ananias had died. When the Apostle Peter confronted her about the money and asked if they brought the whole amount, she lied and said that they had given the full price to them. She, too, was reprimanded, called out in her sin, and knocked dead, on the spot. The two of them were buried next to each other, and the story of their death caused fear and awe throughout the church.

There are many people today who believe that wives and husbands have a moral obligation to lie for each other. Some people teach that if a husband tells a wife to do something, even if it is immoral or illegal, she must do it to be pleasing before God. There are others who teach that if a man really loves a woman, he should be willing to lie and cover up her sin. The story of Ananias and Sapphira proves that any form of conspiracy that seeks to cover up sin and remain complicit within it is sinful in and of itself, and God does not endorse, nor condone it. When confronted with a situation where a spouse asks us to lie or cover for them, we must do as the apostles spoke and obey God rather than men. Going all the way back to Adam and Eve, God desires people to be accountable. That is a repeated theme in relationships, all the way down to the present day. Marriage is not a place to cover for someone else, but to help build one another unto principles of godliness and holiness.

Week 13 Assignments

Answer the following questions based on discussions you have had with your future spouse in counseling this week and additionally on your own time and prepare to discuss them at your next counseling session. If you run out of room in a section, finish the answer to your question in your journal.

1. What do you believe we can learn from Biblical couples? _____

_____

_____

_____

_____

2. Why does God give us examples of real-life marriages in the Bible? _____

_____

_____

_____

_____

3. Were Adam and Eve married according to traditional or modern concepts of marriage? What does this tell us? _____

_____

_____

_____

_____

4. What does Adam and Eve show us about sin in a marriage? _____

_____

_____

_____

_____

5. What can we learn from the relationship that Abraham and Sarah had? _____

_____

_____

_____

_____

6. Why was Jacob's marital situation complicated? What does it teach us about relationships with multiple partners at once? _____

_____

_____

_____

7. What can we learn from Leah about marriage? What can we learn from Rachel? _____

_____

_____

_____

_____

8. What do Moses and Zipporah tell us about marriage? _____

_____

_____

_____

_____

9. Did Ruth and Boaz meet and instantly fall in love? What circumstances surrounded Ruth and Boaz's relationship? _____

_____

_____

_____

_____

10. When someone says they are "waiting for Boaz," what kind of a situation will they likely encounter? _____

_____

_____

_____

11. What did David's quest for Bathsheba show about his own character? _____

_____

_____

_____

_____

12. What can we learn from David and Bathsheba? _____

_____

_____

_____

_____

13. What is co-dependency and how was Ahab and Jezebel's relationship dysfunctional? _____

_____

_____

_____

_____

14. How did Hosea's marriage affect his own reputation? Do you believe that marital "types" still exist today? What do you think life is like for people in those relationships? _____

_____

_____

_____

15. What vital and important precept do we see in Mary and Joseph's marriage? What other things can we see in their relationship? _____

_____

_____

_____

16. What does mention of Peter's mother-in-law in the New Testament tell us about marriage? _____

_____

_____

_____

17. Are couples Biblically commanded to lie for one another? What does the story of Ananias and Sapphira tell us about this kind of behavior? _____

_____

_____

_____

18. How do you think knowing the history of their ancestors impacted the relationship of the couple in the Song of Solomon?

_____

_____

_____

_____

_____

19. In reading Psalm 45:1-17, why do you think royal weddings were special? As people who are sons and daughters of the King, how are our own weddings and marriages special? _____

_____

_____

_____

_____

20. Write down your own thoughts and reflections on a Bible couple, even one that is not mentioned in this chapter. What do you learn from them? What do they teach you? How do they prepare you for the marriage you plan on having? _____

_____

_____

_____

_____

Week Fourteen

Marriage, Christ and the Church

TURN, O BACKSLIDING CHILDREN, SAITH THE LORD; FOR I AM MARRIED UNTO
YOU: AND I WILL TAKE YOU ONE OF A CITY, AND TWO OF A FAMILY, AND I WILL
BRING YOU TO ZION.
(JEREMIAH 3:14, KJV)

Bible reading: Ephesians 5:21-33

Journaling assignments for in-session discussion:

- How do marriages display the love Christ has for the church,
  and the church for Christ?
- Where do you think we, as a church, can do better on showing
  our relationship with Christ?

We've all heard of terms such as "God is married to the
backslider" and that "Christ is married to the church."
You probably also know from reading this book that
marriage is a type – something that points to a greater spiritual
reality – of the relationship Christ has with the church. It sounds
nice and it sounds eloquent to the ear, but what does that mean for
marriages, and what does that mean for the church? What does that
mean for us, as His people?

Seeing God as "married to His people" and we as "married" to

Him gives us a great perspective about the relationship we are supposed to have with God, and the kind of relationship we are supposed to have in marriage. By looking at marriage, we are better able to see what God intends for us as people with Him, how we are to interact with Him, and how we are to also interact as married people.

There is a special promise and hope found in every marriage that is dedicated to God. When two people come together to form one life, they show the world that love is real, and family can work. They also show people that God is real, in a way that many do not expect, and have not considered. In this section, we are going to learn how all these things are interconnected, and why those things are vitally important.

Marriage and spiritual understandings present in ancient religions

Hosea 2:16-20:

THE LORD SAYS, "IN THE FUTURE SHE WILL CALL ME 'MY HUSBAND';
NO LONGER WILL SHE CALL ME 'MY BAAL ["BAAL" CAN MEAN "HUSBAND," "MASTER," OR "BAAL" (THE CANAANITE GOD); IN THIS WORDPLAY, ISRAEL HAS REPLACED ONE HUSBAND (THE LORD) WITH ANOTHER (BAAL)].'
I WILL NEVER LET HER SAY [REMOVE FROM HER LIPS] THE NAMES OF BAAL AGAIN;
PEOPLE WON'T USE [UTTER; INVOKE; OR REMEMBER] THEIR NAMES ANYMORE.
AT THAT TIME I WILL MAKE AN AGREEMENT [COVENANT; TREATY] FOR THEM
WITH THE WILD ANIMALS [BEASTS OF THE FIELD], THE BIRDS [BIRDS OF THE SKY/HEAVENS], AND THE CRAWLING THINGS [CREEPING THINGS OF THE GROUND].
I WILL SMASH [SHATTER; ABOLISH] FROM THE LAND
THE BOW AND THE SWORD AND THE WEAPONS OF WAR [OR WAR; BATTLE],
SO MY PEOPLE WILL LIVE [LIE DOWN] IN SAFETY.
AND I WILL MAKE YOU MY PROMISED BRIDE [BETROTH YOU TO ME] FOREVER.
I WILL BE GOOD AND FAIR [BETROTH YOU IN RIGHTEOUSNESS AND JUSTICE];
I WILL SHOW YOU MY LOVE [LOYALTY; UNFAILING LOVE;

LOVINGKINDNESS] AND MERCY.
I WILL BE TRUE TO YOU AS MY PROMISED BRIDE [BETROTH YOU IN
FAITHFULNESS],
*   AND YOU WILL KNOW [OR ACKNOWLEDGE ME AS] THE LORD.*

In modern society, the idea of being "married" to God might sound strange or shocking to some. The imagery of being married to a god or the gods in ancient religion, however, was not a foreign concept. In fact, one particular god that seemed to be of serious idolatry temptation for the ancient Israelites, Ba'al, had a name that meant, by extension, "husband." This is in large part why God would often speak of being a true husband for the Israelites, and also why their idolatry was compared to adultery.

Ancient theology was a little different than we understand theology today, and the way the ancients understood spirituality was also different. Today, we look at spirituality in terms of choices and relationships, and even though we often use terminology that the ancients used to express their love and devotion to God, we don't always mean it in the same way. We often believe the world to be both sacred and secular, and that the sacred or spiritual aspects of our lives are separate from the secular aspects of the things that we do. Even though this is not really the best way to view our relationship with God or our spirituality, it is how most people understand life, and that separation affects their relationship with God. Many people see their relationship with God as reserved for certain times and places, and see their spirituality as different from the secular, or non-spiritual things, they might want to do.

In the ancient world, people saw themselves as being bound and committed to their gods in more of a literal sense. They believed and recognized their presence to transcend their lives, permeating every aspect of them. There was no such thing as "secular" culture; everything was an extension of the spiritual, and they believed their spiritual deities to be present in everything they did. Whether it was work or worship, it was all the same to them. Their gods had an eternal presence and they, too had to respond to and acknowledge that presence in all things. They were constantly doing for and in communication with their gods, and everything became an extension of that relationship.

This understanding was a part of the life of the ancient Hebrews, as well. Their relationship with God was designed to permeate every aspect of their lives. They were governed by, bound to, and connected to God in their daily living, and that governance and bond affected all their movements and decisions. Thus, following false gods was a serious offense. It was forsaking the God to Whom they were bound in the closest possible way for someone else that looked more desirable at that moment. Doing so hurt God, and it also hurt the Hebrews. God was not just their friend, or their buddy, but He was their spouse, and they, His people.

God is married to His people

In Sunday School, one of the first questions children have about God is, "Why isn't God married?" Many of them think it must be lonely to be God, sitting up in heaven without a wife. Some are confused at how God can have a Son and not have a wife. Their questions are good, because they are asking some very deep, probing theological things that we, as adults in our faith, should think about. We might try to answer the questions in a way that they will understand, but the questions kids ask about God have answers to take seriously.

The truth about God is that God is married. God is married to His people, those who follow His precepts and walk in His ways. When we decide to make the commitment to Him, we are married to Him. Because we often talk about God as Father or speak of Him in other terms that do not have the same connotation as "married," we forget that God is married... to us.

Isaiah 62:4:

YOU WILL NEVER AGAIN BE CALLED THE PEOPLE THAT GOD LEFT [ABANDONED; DESERTED], NOR YOUR LAND THE LAND THAT GOD DESTROYED [DESOLATE]. YOU WILL BE CALLED THE PEOPLE GOD LOVES [MY DELIGHT IS IN HER; HEPHZIBAH; A PROPER NAME], AND YOUR LAND WILL BE CALLED THE BRIDE OF GOD [MARRIED; BEULAH; A PROPER NAME], BECAUSE THE LORD LOVES YOU [TAKES DELIGHT IN YOU]. AND YOUR LAND WILL BELONG TO HIM AS A BRIDE BELONGS TO HER HUSBAND [BE MARRIED].

The reason we speak of being married to God is because there is a certain commitment implied in the relationship. It is designed to be exclusive, to be for life, it involves communication, and it involves respect and honor. Marriage is also the imagery used because it associates a certain level of intimacy, or personal knowledge, within its understanding. It is God's desire that we are one with Him, that our purposes are the same for our lives as His purposes for us. It is God's will that we know Him, spend time with Him, and come before Him, unashamed because we will be found in Him. It's not spoken in this language to sound weird or spooky. By describing God as our spouse and us as married to Him, it immediately explains who He is to us, and who we are to Him.

The church is the Bride of Christ

In the New Testament, we see Christ referred to as the "bridegroom" and the church alluded to be the Bride of Christ. This is the same imagery as the Old Testament, but it was stepped up in its language in keeping with New Testament culture. In Jesus' death, He paid the price for sin and death. Through His blood, He bought us – redeemed us – and takes us as His own.

John 3:29:

THE BRIDE BELONGS ONLY TO THE BRIDEGROOM. BUT THE FRIEND WHO HELPS THE BRIDEGROOM [OR THE BEST MAN] STANDS BY AND LISTENS TO HIM. HE IS THRILLED [REJOICES GREATLY] THAT HE GETS TO HEAR THE BRIDEGROOM'S VOICE. IN THE SAME WAY, I AM REALLY HAPPY [MY JOY IS FULFILLED; IN THIS ANALOGY, JOHN IS THE BEST MAN AND JESUS IS THE BRIDEGROOM].

Mark 2:19:

JESUS ANSWERED, "THE FRIENDS OF THE BRIDEGROOM [OR WEDDING GUESTS; CHILDREN OF THE WEDDING HALL] DO NOT FAST WHILE THE BRIDEGROOM IS STILL WITH THEM [JESUS IS REFERRING TO HIMSELF; JOHN 3:29; REV. 19:7]. AS LONG AS THE BRIDEGROOM IS WITH THEM, THEY CANNOT FAST.

Ephesians 5:25-33:

HUSBANDS, LOVE YOUR WIVES AS CHRIST LOVED THE CHURCH [COL. 3:19; 1 PET. 3:7] AND GAVE HIMSELF FOR HER TO MAKE HER HOLY [SANCTIFY HER], CLEANSING HER IN THE WASHING OF WATER BY THE WORD [THE "WASHING" MAY BE (1) BAPTISM, (2) SPIRITUAL CLEANSING (TITUS 3:5), OR (3) AN ANALOGY DRAWN FROM THE JEWISH PRENUPTIAL BATH (EZEK. 16:8–14); THE "WORD" MAY BE (1) THE GOSPEL, (2) A BAPTISMAL FORMULA, OR (3) THE CONFESSION OF THE ONE BAPTIZED]. HE DID THIS SO THAT HE COULD PRESENT THE CHURCH TO HIMSELF LIKE A BRIDE IN ALL HER BEAUTY [IN SPLENDOR; GLORIOUS], WITH NO EVIL OR SIN [STAIN OR WRINKLE] OR ANY OTHER WRONG THING IN IT [SUCH THING], BUT PURE [HOLY] AND WITHOUT FAULT [BLAMELESS]. IN THE SAME WAY, HUSBANDS SHOULD LOVE THEIR WIVES AS THEY LOVE THEIR OWN BODIES. THE MAN WHO LOVES HIS WIFE LOVES HIMSELF. [FOR] NO ONE EVER HATES HIS OWN BODY [FLESH], BUT FEEDS AND TAKES CARE OF IT. AND THAT IS WHAT CHRIST DOES FOR THE CHURCH, BECAUSE WE ARE PARTS [MEMBERS] OF HIS BODY. THE SCRIPTURE SAYS, "SO [FOR THIS REASON] A MAN WILL LEAVE HIS FATHER AND MOTHER AND BE UNITED [JOINED] WITH HIS WIFE, AND THE TWO WILL BECOME ONE BODY [FLESH; GEN. 2:24]." THIS SECRET [MYSTERY] IS VERY IMPORTANT [OR GREAT; PROFOUND]—I AM TALKING ABOUT CHRIST AND THE CHURCH. BUT [HOWEVER; IN ANY CASE; OR TO SUM UP] EACH ONE OF YOU MUST LOVE HIS WIFE AS HE LOVES HIMSELF, AND A WIFE MUST RESPECT [REVERENCE; V. 21] HER HUSBAND.

Revelation 21:9-10:

THEN ONE OF THE SEVEN ANGELS WHO HAD THE SEVEN BOWLS FULL OF THE SEVEN LAST TROUBLES [PLAGUES] CAME TO ME, SAYING, "COME WITH ME [COME], AND I WILL SHOW YOU THE BRIDE, THE WIFE OF THE LAMB [THE CHURCH; EPH. 5:27–29]." AND THE ANGEL CARRIED ME AWAY BY THE SPIRIT [OR IN THE SPIRIT] TO A VERY LARGE AND HIGH MOUNTAIN. HE SHOWED ME THE HOLY CITY, JERUSALEM, COMING DOWN OUT OF HEAVEN FROM GOD.

Revelation 22:17:

THE SPIRIT AND THE BRIDE SAY, "COME!" LET THE ONE WHO HEARS THIS SAY, "COME!" LET WHOEVER IS THIRSTY COME; WHOEVER WISHES MAY HAVE [TAKE; RECEIVE] THE WATER OF LIFE AS A FREE GIFT [FREELY].

For Christ to be spoken of as having "bought" us refers to the bridal dowry that we spoke of earlier in this book. By His blood, we are His, those He has redeemed. We, as His church, have come into His presence, and become one with Him. We respect, honor, and cherish Him, await His return with anticipation, and rejoice as a people who can now also say they are married to God, through Christ. Being a part of the church gives us a new outlook on life, one where we are committed, concerned, and now also a part of the extended family of Christianity, found all throughout the world.

How wedding ceremonies are symbolic of our relationship with God

In my book, *Sacred Ceremonies: The Who, What, Where, When, Why, and How of Christian Ordinances, Rites, and Rituals*, I say the following:

The church exists in covenant with God, which is illustrated throughout the Bible as a marriage relationship between God and His people. As was stated above, weddings are a type of the wedding to come when Jesus returns. This special symbolism reminds the participants of four very important spiritual principles that relate to our faith and our walk of faith:

- **Honor:** Are we honoring the Lord as we should? Most of the church would agree honor is an issue in the church, but believe it is someone else's problem. Spouses are called to honor and respect one another, just as the church is called to honor and respect Christ. Honor is an action, brought about in how we speak of the Lord, if we obey the Lord's commands to us, and our general interaction with Him in our everyday spiritual walk. Weddings remind us of our command to honor the Lord and that such honor is not grievous or burdensome — it is what we do because we love and respect the Lord.

- **Love:** We use the word "love" on a regular basis in our culture. We say we love everything from coffee to reality shows and then come into church and say we love Jesus. This casual disconnect from understanding true love means we do not know how to uphold true love in our lives. Love is an action. It is something we do that reflects everything we are. True love is shown. Husbands and wives are called to love one another, and to display that love in their conduct. Love of the Lord is also a spiritual principle shown through action. Jesus summarized the call to love best in John 14:15:

IF YE LOVE ME, KEEP MY COMMANDMENTS. (KJV)

Do you say you love Jesus? If so, how do you show it?

- **Faithfulness:** The concept of being faithful is often regarded as outdated. In a world that changes at the drop of a hat, remaining faithful to anything is unheard of. Even though infidelity rates are high, God still calls those marriage partners whom He has called together to remain faithful to one another throughout their marital relationship. This faithfulness is more than a sexual fidelity; it is also a call to support and encourage one another and remain the biggest advocate of the other that could ever exist this side of heaven. We too are called to be faithful in our spiritual walk, because God is faithful toward us. Whether God has given us a ministry call, commitment, assignment, job, or life, we are called to remain faithful to that, no matter what we go through, as we work out our salvation with fear and trembling (Philippians 2:12). As believers in Christ, we see through our commitment to God unto the end.

- **Holiness:** Marriage is a call to holiness for both man and woman who choose to enter into the married life. As each partner comes into the relationship with issues, hurts, and areas in need of healing, both are given the opportunity to strive toward greater holiness as marriage provides love and healing. Marriage is an excellent reminder to the call of holiness, the pursuit of holiness, and the walk of holiness in our daily lives.

Weddings are also important because they celebrate the life and bond of human love. It's an awesome experience to stand and walk with couples into their marital experience. Marriage can be a wonderful thing when the relationship is God-ordained and can bring each person closer to their God-ordained purpose. It is an opportunity for the Body to come together in unity to uphold the dignity and beauty of what God creates in and between His people.

Does the world not need a great reminder that love is real and marriage can be a great thing? We hear so much negativity about love, about spirituality, about marriage in general, and sometimes even about God, the glass that people see through darkly tends to get dimmed in a dark slant, one that rejects hope. The reason God has given us different rites, rituals, and ordinances is so that we can, as people have hope. We can participate in eternity through all the things God has commissioned for us to do: wash feet, break bread and wine, go down into the waters of baptism, separate ourselves for consecration, celebrate that someone has gone home to be with the Lord, the laying on of hands in ordination, appointing someone to one of the appointment works, presenting a child for dedication, anointing the sick, and yes, what this book is specifically about, the celebration of a wedding, as two people join together for marriage. Marriage has the awesome opportunity to inspire and call us back to honor, love, faithfulness, and holiness as we open ourselves up to God's possibilities present in the beauty of all God offers to us.

Song of Solomon 4:8-9:

COME WITH ME FROM LEBANON, MY BRIDE.
   COME WITH ME FROM LEBANON,
FROM THE TOP OF MOUNT AMANA,
   FROM THE TOPS OF MOUNT SENIR AND MOUNT HERMON.
COME FROM THE LIONS' DENS
   AND FROM THE LEOPARDS' HILLS [APART FROM HIM SHE IS IN A
DANGEROUS PLACE].
MY SISTER [AN ANCIENT TERM OF ENDEARMENT], MY BRIDE,
   YOU HAVE THRILLED MY HEART [DRIVE ME CRAZY];
YOU HAVE THRILLED MY HEART [DRIVE ME CRAZY]
   WITH A [ONE] GLANCE OF YOUR EYES,
   WITH ONE SPARKLE [JEWEL] FROM YOUR NECKLACE.

This might all sound like a mouthful, but there is some real truth in the reality that weddings show the joining of two people in important and essential principles. Weddings also type and show us many important principles that we should have in our relationship with God, as well. Honor, love, faithfulness, and holiness are all things that we, as believers, need to look at in our lives. If we are married to God, that means we should reflect that. If we are married to someone else, we should reflect our relationship with God in that marriage.

Understanding covenant

"Covenant" is an older term for an arrangement or an agreement. Most people understand it to be an ancient understanding of a contract. This is true, with one exception. Most ancient understandings of covenant were far more permanent than contracts as we understand them now, as most contracts contain both a start date and an end date. They also typically involved a sacrifice, usually of an animal, and symbolism that showed the two individuals or families to be permanently joined for life or for many, many years. In a Biblical understanding, covenants were designed to last for generations, centuries, and in some cases, all the way into eternity.

Genesis 9:8-11:

THEN GOD SAID TO NOAH AND HIS SONS, "NOW [OR LOOK] I AM MAKING MY AGREEMENT [COVENANT; TREATY; 6:18] WITH YOU AND YOUR PEOPLE [SEED] WHO WILL LIVE AFTER YOU [AFTER YOU], AND WITH EVERY LIVING THING THAT IS WITH YOU—THE BIRDS, THE TAME [LIVESTOCK; CATTLE] AND THE WILD ANIMALS, AND WITH EVERYTHING THAT CAME OUT OF THE BOAT [ARK] WITH YOU—WITH EVERY LIVING THING ON EARTH. I MAKE [ESTABLISH] THIS AGREEMENT [COVENANT; TREATY; 6:18] WITH YOU: I WILL NEVER AGAIN DESTROY ALL LIVING THINGS BY A FLOOD [A FLOOD WILL NEVER AGAIN CUT OFF ALL FLESH]. A FLOOD WILL NEVER AGAIN DESTROY THE EARTH."

Mark 14:22-25:

WHILE THEY WERE EATING, JESUS TOOK SOME BREAD AND THANKED GOD FOR [BLESSED] IT AND BROKE IT. THEN HE GAVE IT TO HIS FOLLOWERS [DISCIPLES] AND SAID, "TAKE IT; THIS IS MY BODY."

THEN JESUS TOOK A CUP AND THANKED GOD FOR IT [GAVE THANKS] AND GAVE IT TO THE FOLLOWERS [THE DISCIPLES; THEM], AND THEY ALL DRANK FROM THE CUP.

THEN JESUS SAID, "THIS IS MY BLOOD WHICH IS THE NEW AGREEMENT THAT GOD MAKES WITH HIS PEOPLE [OR WHICH CONFIRMS/ESTABLISHES THE NEW COVENANT; OF THE NEW COVENANT; EX. 24:8. JER. 31:31–34]. THIS BLOOD IS POURED OUT FOR MANY [IS. 53:12]. I TELL YOU THE TRUTH, I WILL NOT DRINK OF THIS FRUIT OF THE VINE [WINE] AGAIN UNTIL THAT DAY WHEN I DRINK IT NEW IN THE KINGDOM OF GOD.

Acts 3:25-26:

YOU ARE DESCENDANTS [CHILDREN; SONS] OF THE PROPHETS. YOU HAVE RECEIVED THE AGREEMENT [COVENANT; TREATY] GOD MADE WITH YOUR

ANCESTORS [FATHERS; PATRIARCHS]. HE SAID TO YOUR FATHER ABRAHAM, 'THROUGH YOUR DESCENDANTS [HEIRS; SEED] ALL THE NATIONS [OR FAMILIES] ON THE EARTH WILL BE BLESSED [GEN. 22:18; 26:4].' GOD HAS RAISED UP HIS SERVANT [OR CHILD] JESUS AND SENT HIM TO YOU FIRST [THE JEWS WERE TO RECEIVE THE BLESSING FIRST, AND THROUGH THEM GOD WOULD BLESS ALL NATIONS] TO BLESS YOU BY TURNING EACH OF YOU AWAY FROM DOING EVIL [YOUR WICKED WAYS].

Acts 7:8:

GOD MADE AN AGREEMENT [COVENANT; A TREATY-LIKE RELATIONSHIP] WITH ABRAHAM, THE SIGN OF WHICH WAS CIRCUMCISION [GEN. 17:9–14]. AND SO WHEN ABRAHAM HAD HIS SON [BECAME THE FATHER OF; BEGAT] ISAAC, ABRAHAM CIRCUMCISED HIM WHEN HE WAS EIGHT DAYS OLD. ISAAC ALSO CIRCUMCISED HIS SON JACOB [OR BECAME THE FATHER OF JACOB], AND JACOB DID THE SAME FOR HIS SONS, [OR BECAME THE FATHER OF] THE TWELVE ANCESTORS OF OUR PEOPLE [PATRIARCHS; THE TWELVE SONS OF JACOB WHO WERE THE "FATHERS" OF THE TWELVE TRIBES OF ISRAEL].

Our relationship with God is designed to be a covenant:

- It is something we mutually agree with God about.
- It has binding terms.
- Both parties have responsibilities to meet in the arrangement.
- It is designed to be permanent.
- It involved the sacrifice of Jesus Christ for our sins.
- It is designed to last for eternity.
- God has given us great symbolism through rites, rituals, and ordinances to celebrate and acknowledge our covenant.
- He has confirmed His covenant by the Holy Ghost.

Matthew 19:3-6:

SOME PHARISEES CAME TO JESUS AND TRIED TO TRICK [TO TRAP/TEST] HIM. THEY ASKED, "IS IT RIGHT [LAWFUL; ACCORDING TO THE LAW OF MOSES] FOR A MAN TO DIVORCE HIS WIFE FOR ANY REASON HE CHOOSES?"

JESUS ANSWERED, "SURELY YOU HAVE [HAVEN'T YOU... ?] READ IN THE SCRIPTURES: WHEN GOD MADE THE WORLD, 'HE [FROM THE BEGINNING,

THE CREATOR] MADE THEM MALE AND FEMALE' [GEN. 1:27; 5:2]. AND GOD SAID, 'SO A MAN WILL LEAVE HIS FATHER AND MOTHER AND BE UNITED WITH [JOINED TO] HIS WIFE, AND THE TWO WILL BECOME ONE BODY [AS THOUGH THEY WERE ONE PERSON; ONE FLESH; GEN. 2:24].' SO THEY ARE NO LONGER TWO, BUT ONE. GOD HAS JOINED THE TWO TOGETHER, SO NO ONE SHOULD SEPARATE THEM."

Marriage is taught by many to be a covenant, because in ancient times, covenant often related to the joining of tribes, clans, and groups together through marriage. To forge protection, identity, and alliances, covenants were used to join not just a couple in marriage, but families, as well. Thus, marriage, even as we understand it today, echoes many principles that relate to covenant:

- It is something mutually agreed upon, either by the couple or by their families.
- It has binding terms.
- Both parties have responsibilities to meet in the arrangement.
- It is designed to be permanent.
- It involves a certain level of sacrifice, as both parties die to themselves.
- It is a symbol of God as well as containing symbols, such as rings, that display the commitment of both parties.
- It is a type of the relationship that Christ has with the church.

The type and the reality

The passage of Scripture that is required reading is often quoted for several different reasons. We are going to look at it here, and at parts of it again in the next chapter.

Ephesians 5:21-33:

YIELD [SUBMIT; BE SUBJECT; ... YIELDING/SUBMITTING; GRAMMATICALLY LINKED TO THE PREVIOUS SENTENCE, AND SO PART OF BEING FILLED WITH THE SPIRIT] TO EACH OTHER OUT OF REVERENCE [RESPECT; FEAR; AWE] FOR CHRIST.

WIVES, YIELD TO [SUBMIT TO; BE SUBJECT TO; TO] YOUR HUSBANDS, AS YOU DO TO THE LORD, BECAUSE THE HUSBAND IS THE HEAD OF THE WIFE,

AS CHRIST IS THE HEAD OF THE CHURCH. AND HE IS THE SAVIOR OF THE BODY, WHICH IS THE CHURCH. AS THE CHURCH YIELDS [SUBMITS; IS SUBJECT] TO CHRIST, SO YOU WIVES SHOULD YIELD [SUBMIT; BE SUBJECT] TO YOUR HUSBANDS IN EVERYTHING [COL. 3:18; 1 PET. 3:1–6].

HUSBANDS, LOVE YOUR WIVES AS CHRIST LOVED THE CHURCH [COL. 3:19; 1 PET. 3:7] AND GAVE HIMSELF FOR HER TO MAKE HER HOLY [SANCTIFY HER], CLEANSING HER IN THE WASHING OF WATER BY THE WORD [THE "WASHING" MAY BE (1) BAPTISM, (2) SPIRITUAL CLEANSING (TITUS 3:5), OR (3) AN ANALOGY DRAWN FROM THE JEWISH PRENUPTIAL BATH (EZEK. 16:8–14); THE "WORD" MAY BE (1) THE GOSPEL, (2) A BAPTISMAL FORMULA, OR (3) THE CONFESSION OF THE ONE BAPTIZED]. HE DID THIS SO THAT HE COULD PRESENT THE CHURCH TO HIMSELF LIKE A BRIDE IN ALL HER BEAUTY [IN SPLENDOR; GLORIOUS], WITH NO EVIL OR SIN [STAIN OR WRINKLE] OR ANY OTHER WRONG THING IN IT [SUCH THING], BUT PURE [HOLY] AND WITHOUT FAULT [BLAMELESS]. IN THE SAME WAY, HUSBANDS SHOULD LOVE THEIR WIVES AS THEY LOVE THEIR OWN BODIES. THE MAN WHO LOVES HIS WIFE LOVES HIMSELF. [FOR] NO ONE EVER HATES HIS OWN BODY [FLESH], BUT FEEDS AND TAKES CARE OF IT. AND THAT IS WHAT CHRIST DOES FOR THE CHURCH, BECAUSE WE ARE PARTS [MEMBERS] OF HIS BODY. THE SCRIPTURE SAYS, "SO [FOR THIS REASON] A MAN WILL LEAVE HIS FATHER AND MOTHER AND BE UNITED [JOINED] WITH HIS WIFE, AND THE TWO WILL BECOME ONE BODY [FLESH; GEN. 2:24]." THIS SECRET [MYSTERY] IS VERY IMPORTANT [OR GREAT; PROFOUND]—I AM TALKING ABOUT CHRIST AND THE CHURCH. BUT [HOWEVER; IN ANY CASE; OR TO SUM UP] EACH ONE OF YOU MUST LOVE HIS WIFE AS HE LOVES HIMSELF, AND A WIFE MUST RESPECT [REVERENCE; V. 21] HER HUSBAND.

This passage of Ephesians is speaking of the power of covenant in a way that I don't think our natural minds properly comprehend. The evidence of this is in the way that we try to use this passage to regulate roles and subordination in a marriage relationship. That is not what the Apostle Paul was trying to teach us, not by a long shot. The passage isn't about who makes more money than who or who stays home with the kids while who works (we'll talk about that more in the next chapter). The Apostle Paul was using marriage to teach us of the great mystery of Christ and the church, which is called a "great mystery" because it is something that, no matter how much we might try, we will only understand in types and shadows this side of heaven. That doesn't mean we shouldn't try, but it does mean that it is something so unfathomable, it is beyond our full comprehension.

By using the example of marriages of His day, the Apostle Paul shows the things that happened in marriage and the things that happen between Christ and the church:

- Mutual submission of one to another
- A spirit of reverence
- A yielding Spirit to our Head, Christ
- A willingness to serve one another
- Love as Christ loved the church
- Washing in baptism
- Glory and splendor without evil, sin, or any wrong thing in it
- Loving as we love our own bodies (as ourselves)
- Becoming one

All these things are commands not just for married people, but for the church as well. When married couples approach marriage with the right attitude, which is addressed here – walking in love, yielding to Christ and to one another, serving one another, striving to become one, and striving to live together without sin between you – we see the type active, a relationship that reflects Christian precept and the values that He desires us to have one to another, and with Him.

Extended family

Intimately involved in covenant is the concept of merging two unlike beings or groups of people together as one unit.

Ephesians 2:11-22:

[THEREFORE] REMEMBER THAT YOU WERE BORN AS GENTILES [ARE GENTILES IN THE FLESH], THE ONES CALLED "UNCIRCUMCISED" BY THOSE WHO CALL THEMSELVES "CIRCUMCISED." (THEIR CIRCUMCISION IS ONLY SOMETHING THEY THEMSELVES DO ON THEIR BODIES [... PERFORMED IN THE FLESH BY HANDS].) REMEMBER THAT IN THE PAST [AT THAT TIME/SEASON] YOU WERE WITHOUT CHRIST [THE MESSIAH]. YOU WERE NOT CITIZENS [EXCLUDED FROM THE CITIZENSHIP] OF ISRAEL, AND YOU HAD NO PART IN [WERE ALIENS/STRANGERS TO] THE AGREEMENTS WITH THE PROMISE THAT

GOD MADE TO HIS PEOPLE [COVENANTS OF PROMISE; THE ABRAHAMIC (GEN. 12:1–3), MOSAIC (EX. 19—24), AND DAVIDIC (2 SAM. 7) COVENANTS.] YOU HAD NO HOPE, AND YOU DID NOT KNOW GOD. BUT NOW IN CHRIST JESUS, YOU WHO WERE FAR AWAY FROM GOD ARE BROUGHT NEAR THROUGH THE BLOOD OF CHRIST'S DEATH [CHRIST; BLOOD SYMBOLIZING HIS SACRIFICIAL DEATH]. CHRIST HIMSELF IS OUR PEACE. HE MADE BOTH JEWS AND GENTILES ONE PEOPLE [BOTH ONE], AND BROKE DOWN THE WALL OF HATE [HOSTILITY; ENMITY] THAT DIVIDED THEM [THE WALL BEYOND WHICH GENTILES COULD NOT PASS IN THE JERUSALEM TEMPLE, OR THE LAW OF MOSES THAT DISTINGUISHED JEW FROM GENTILE (SEE V. 15)] BY GIVING HIS OWN BODY [IN HIS FLESH; THIS PHRASE MAY GO WITH THE FOLLOWING SENTENCE]. HE DID THIS BY ENDING [SETTING ASIDE; NULLIFYING] THE LAW OF COMMANDS AND RULES BY GIVING HIS OWN BODY [IN HIS FLESH; THIS PHRASE MAY GO WITH THE PREVIOUS SENTENCE]. HIS PURPOSE WAS TO MAKE THE TWO GROUPS OF PEOPLE BECOME ONE NEW PEOPLE [HUMANITY; PERSON; MAN] IN HIM AND IN THIS WAY MAKE PEACE. IT WAS ALSO CHRIST'S PURPOSE TO END [PUT TO DEATH; KILL] THE HATRED [HOSTILITY; ENMITY] BETWEEN THE TWO GROUPS, TO MAKE THEM INTO ONE BODY, AND TO BRING THEM BACK [RECONCILE THEM] TO GOD. CHRIST DID ALL THIS WITH HIS DEATH ON THE CROSS [… THROUGH THE CROSS]. CHRIST CAME AND PREACHED [PROCLAIMED THE GOOD NEWS OF] PEACE [IS. 52:7] TO YOU WHO WERE FAR AWAY FROM GOD [FAR AWAY/OFF], AND TO THOSE WHO WERE NEAR TO GOD [NEAR; IS. 57:19]. YES, IT IS [FOR; OR SO THAT] THROUGH CHRIST WE ALL HAVE THE RIGHT TO COME [FREE ACCESS] TO THE FATHER IN [BY] ONE SPIRIT.

NOW YOU GENTILES ARE NOT FOREIGNERS OR STRANGERS ANY LONGER, BUT ARE CITIZENS TOGETHER WITH GOD'S HOLY PEOPLE [THE SAINTS]. YOU BELONG TO GOD'S FAMILY [HOUSEHOLD]. YOU ARE LIKE A BUILDING THAT WAS BUILT [… HAVING BEEN BUILT] ON THE FOUNDATION OF THE APOSTLES AND PROPHETS. CHRIST JESUS HIMSELF IS THE MOST IMPORTANT STONE [CORNERSTONE; OR CAPSTONE; IS. 28:16; 1 COR. 3:11] IN THAT BUILDING, AND THAT WHOLE BUILDING IS JOINED TOGETHER IN CHRIST. HE MAKES IT GROW AND BECOME A HOLY TEMPLE IN THE LORD. AND IN CHRIST YOU, TOO, ARE BEING BUILT TOGETHER WITH THE JEWS [BUILT TOGETHER] INTO A PLACE WHERE GOD LIVES THROUGH THE SPIRIT.

The whole concept of extended family is a difficult one, as we have addressed in several places throughout this book. The odds of liking everyone in your future spouse's family is highly unlikely, and you will most likely deal with different familial pressures at points in time to do or be something other than what you are. There will also probably be at least one relative who loves drama, and you desire to avoid. It is never acceptable for someone to try and morph you into their own image, and it is perfectly acceptable to want to avoid someone or avoid unnecessary drama or unkindness in your life. The reality, however, is that through marriage, you and your spouse have joined two families. They may be two different types of families, they may not have much in common, and they might not always particularly care for one another, but through the virtue of marriage, those two families – and the families that joined in marriage before them – and those before them – and so on – have now all become a part of the same family.

The same is true in the church, as we can see above. God not only uses marriage to bring families together; He also uses the work of Christ. As people who were once far from God, God used Christ to bring us to Him and Christ to bring us to each other. If you think about the church as one large family, all over the world, completely different from one another, speaking different languages, and all worshipping one God, it sounds impossible... yet that's exactly what God has done. It's an incredible thing to think of all the church joined together, as one Body, in Him.

Sadly, we don't tend to think of "church" as extended family, but that's exactly what church is. Often, we think of the church as competing for immediate family time, and we think that if we take our families to church instead of "spending" time together doing something else, that will hurt our family. Just like in marriage we need to make time for our extended families, we need to go to church, assembling ourselves together, to see and interact with our spiritual family. It is a part of spiritual health as well as family help.

Putting a misguided concept of family above the church – always making family time more of a priority than spiritual connection – gives members of that family the message that the church, spiritual things, and the world at large revolves around them. This is a dangerous message that causes people to be self-centered, self-absorbed, and uninterested in what is going on with other people. The family is a type of God's family and is a smaller portion of that family. Our families should never be isolated, nor pitted against the church or seen as a competitive thing. There is enough time in the week to spend with the immediate family and to spend at church. There is also plenty of room to view going to church as seeing family, rather than treating one as more important than the other. It's all part of the same puzzle, just different pieces.

Bible study

We can't say that we know and love God if we don't learn more about Him. As part of our relationship with Him, we should always be studying the Scriptures. Within the covers of the Bible, we learn more about how people have interacted with God throughout history and the ways that they have also interacted with each other.

Bible study helps to unite couples as well as unite us to the Body of believers, the church. It unites us to our great cloud of witnesses, of believers past who had issues much like we do, today. In reading, we are united to that covenant, that great purpose of the ages and even greater promises to come.

2 Timothy 3:16-17:

ALL SCRIPTURE IS INSPIRED BY GOD [BREATHED OUT BY GOD; GOD-BREATHED] AND IS USEFUL FOR TEACHING, FOR SHOWING PEOPLE WHAT IS WRONG IN THEIR LIVES [REFUTING ERROR; REBUKING], FOR CORRECTING FAULTS, AND FOR TEACHING HOW TO LIVE RIGHT [TRAINING IN RIGHTEOUSNESS]. USING THE SCRIPTURES, [… SO THAT] THE PERSON WHO SERVES GOD [GOD'S PERSON] WILL BE CAPABLE [COMPETENT], HAVING ALL THAT IS NEEDED [FULLY EQUIPPED] TO DO EVERY GOOD WORK.

The biggest part of the marriage covenant is that it is bigger than we are. Our lives, our purposes, our families are bigger than just us, with or without children, walking through our lives that have no meaning. Seeing your marriage as a covenant enriches it, because it always reminds you that you are living out a type that as you love your spouse, so too does Christ love you.

Week 14 Assignments

Answer the following questions based on discussions you have had with your future spouse in counseling this week and additionally on your own time and prepare to discuss them at your next counseling session. If you run out of room in a section, finish the answer to your question in your journal.

1. How did ancient people understand spirituality? _____

_____

_____

_____

_____

2. How did this understanding affect their view of being married "spiritually" to God or to the gods? _____

_____

_____

_____

_____

3. What does it mean to say that "God is married to His people?"

_____

_____

_____

_____

_____

4. What does it mean to say that the church is the "Bride of Christ?"

_____

_____

_____

_____

5. When you think of your own relationship with God, what characteristics does it have that remind you of a marriage? _____

_____

_____

_____

6. What are four very important spiritual principles that we see present in weddings? _____

_____

_____

_____

7. How are weddings and marriages a great reminder that spiritual things are real? _____

_____

_____

_____

_____

8. What is a covenant? _____

_____

_____

_____

_____

9. In what ways is our relationship with God designed to be a covenant? _____

_____

_____

_____

_____

10. In what ways is marriage a covenant? _____

_____

_____

_____

_____

11. In what ways is marriage a type of Christ and the church?

_____

_____

_____

_____

_____

12. Why is it so important that marriage is approached with the right attitude? _____

_____

_____

_____

_____

13. How do two families become one through marriage? _____

_____

_____

_____

_____

14. How does the church become one family through Christ? _____

_____

_____

_____

15. Is church an example of extended family? How so? _____

_____

_____

_____

_____

16. What happens when we have a misguided sense of family and start putting immediate family above the church? _____

_____

_____

_____

_____

17. Why is Bible study so important in the lives of married couples?

_____

_____

_____

_____

18. What do you think the couple in the Song of Solomon believed about covenant? _____

_____

_____

_____

_____

19. In reading Ephesians 5:21-33, why do you think God chose marriage to serve as a type of the relationship between Christ and the church? _____

_____

_____

_____

_____

20. How does preparing for your own marriage give you a new perspective on being married to God through the church? Write your own thoughts on this and then discuss at your next session.

_____

_____

_____

_____

_____

Week Fifteen

Walking in Intimacy

GOD MADE [DID NOT GOD MAKE... ?] HUSBANDS AND WIVES TO BECOME ONE BODY AND ONE SPIRIT FOR HIS PURPOSE—SO THEY WOULD HAVE CHILDREN WHO ARE TRUE TO GOD [GODLY OFFSPRING]. SO BE CAREFUL [GUARD YOURSELF IN YOUR SPIRIT], AND DO NOT BREAK YOUR PROMISE [BE UNFAITHFUL] TO THE WIFE YOU MARRIED WHEN YOU WERE YOUNG [OF YOUR YOUTH].
(MALACHI 2:15)

<u>Bible reading:</u> 1 John 4:7-21

<u>Journaling assignments for in-session discussion:</u>

- How is it possible to truly know another human being?
- How do you understand it when we talk about "intimacy with God?"?

When we talk about marriage, it's common to discuss love and concepts of love, but it is uncommon to hear discussion about intimacy. As this workbook goes along with the book, *Discovering Intimacy: A Journey Through the Song of Solomon*, you have been reading and studying about intimacy as a part of this process. There are probably many things that have been realized and many ideas that have changed as you've gone through that book. Like many other people, you might have associated sex with intimacy or thought that intimacy was something that all people shared, all the time. As you are now at the conclusion of (if not near the conclusion of) that book, you are probably thinking about intimacy, especially as it relates to the relationship you will have in your marriage.

This week there will be a little review of what you've read in the textbook as well as some additional learning and insight into the world of intimacy. As a people who are called to an intimate relationship with God and with our spouses, it's important we develop the necessary insight into intimacy to make sure we are walking it out in our lives. Intimacy should not be ever, ever lost on us, lost on our understanding or alien to our operations. As Christians, we should be people, day in and day out, who see the important connection between love and inter-personal connection that is present in intimacy and intimate relationships.

Love is from God

Love is the universal theme for every wedding under the sun. There is something special about weddings that inspires us all to think about and consider the love that we have in our lives and, by extension, love in general. How good are we at loving our neighbor? How good are we about loving God? How good are we about receiving God's love? How good are we about receiving the love that other people extend toward us in life?

John 3:16-17:

[FOR] GOD LOVED THE WORLD SO MUCH THAT HE GAVE HIS ONE AND ONLY [ONLY; UNIQUE; ONLY BEGOTTEN; 1:14, 18] SON SO THAT WHOEVER BELIEVES IN HIM MAY NOT BE LOST [PERISH], BUT HAVE ETERNAL LIFE. [FOR; INDEED] GOD DID NOT SEND HIS SON INTO THE WORLD TO JUDGE THE WORLD GUILTY [CONDEMN THE WORLD], BUT TO SAVE THE WORLD THROUGH HIM.

If we are Christians, then we recognize that God is love. This means that love is a spiritual principle, something that is interwoven in the relationship between heaven and earth. It reflects God's presence, everywhere, and in all situations and all things. We know that God is omnipresent, and love is one of the most powerful ways that the omnipresence of God is proven. From eternity past to eternity future, people have walked in a sense of love, and a sense of relationship, with the divine and with other people, even though they might never have had the first understanding of what this whole "love: thing was about.

Our ultimate purpose in walking in love is to show other people that God is in us, we are His children, and that we have overcome the world. Whenever we love another person, we are proving that God is real, a part of our lives, and that He cares about us.

Then the question becomes, what is love? We talk about love all the time as if it is some sort of emotion or vague concept, something that we "feel," but that proves to us that we don't know what love is. As I said earlier, love is a spiritual principle. It is an outlook, an attitude, and a way of handling things that expresses what God wants for us in everything that we do. When we walk in love, we show grace and mercy in our interactions with others. It doesn't mean that we do not allow for the results of consequences for behavior or that we aren't people who believe in being upfront or disciplining children, but it does mean that the way in which we handle people and handle situations comes from something other than our anger and emotions all the time. Our emotions are quick to change and often different from one moment to the other, but when we walk in love, we see the value in what we need to do, how to do it, and how to interact properly with other human beings, who we recognize are created in the image of God.

Intimacy, which is a principle of relationship, is a part of love. We can't rightly say that we share an intimate closeness with someone if we don't love them. We might be able to interact with them, do all sorts of physical things with them, or even have them as basic acquaintances, but if we don't really love them, we cannot say that we have been in a place of intimacy with them. If God is not a part of our interactions with them and not a part of our relationship as a unit, that further makes intimacy a difficult principle to understand and abide by. Love may not mean all the warm, fuzzy, cartoonish things we try to make it out to be, but it does mean something powerful and world-changing if we think about it. It gives us the ability to love each other, to love God, and to, yes, love our spouse.

How God knows us, and we know God

Psalm 139:1-4:

*LORD, YOU HAVE EXAMINED [INVESTIGATED; SEARCHED] ME
    AND KNOW ALL ABOUT ME.
YOU KNOW WHEN I SIT DOWN AND WHEN I GET UP [RISE].
    YOU KNOW [UNDERSTAND] MY THOUGHTS BEFORE I THINK THEM [FROM
AFAR].
YOU KNOW [MEASURE] WHERE I GO [MY PATH] AND WHERE I LIE DOWN
[MY LYING DOWN].
    YOU KNOW [ARE FAMILIAR WITH] EVERYTHING I DO [ALL MY PATH].
LORD, EVEN BEFORE I SAY A WORD [WHEN NO WORD IS ON MY TONGUE],
    YOU ALREADY KNOW IT [ALL OF IT].*

The Bible tells us that before we were ever born, God knew us. He knew us in His thoughts, He knew us as spiritual beings, and He knows us now, as the people He created. It only makes sense to consider that God, as our Creator, knows us, His creation. When we are created by such perfect design, that means God put every thought, purpose, and effort into who we are and into our attributes.

God knows us better than any other person on this earth ever will or ever can know us. As our Creator, it is His desire that we come before Him, to know Him, as well. It's not God's purpose for us to be far off, but for us to be connected in a special way, in a way that echoes the intimate way that He knows us, as well. Through our relationship with Him, we can know Him better, learn about His operations in our lives, and discover His will for us. Coming to this place brings us to a blessed place in Him for worship, of meditative focus on Him, of praise, and of the beauty of living out our lives in love. If our Creator, our Father, our spiritual husband in the church is love, then we, too, should be love, as well.

Romans 8:15:

*THE SPIRIT YOU RECEIVED DOES NOT MAKE YOU SLAVES AGAIN TO FEAR
[OR YOU DID NOT RECEIVE THE SPIRIT OF SLAVERY, LEADING TO FEAR];
INSTEAD, YOU RECEIVED THE SPIRIT WHO ADOPTS YOU AS GOD'S*

CHILDREN [OF ADOPTION]. WITH [THROUGH] THAT SPIRIT WE CRY OUT, "ABBA [ARAMAIC FOR "FATHER"; MARK 14:36], FATHER."

Galatians 4:6:

SINCE YOU ARE GOD'S CHILDREN [OR SONS], GOD SENT THE SPIRIT OF HIS SON INTO YOUR HEARTS, AND THE SPIRIT CRIES OUT, "ABBA [ARAMAIC FOR "FATHER," A TERM OF INTIMACY], FATHER."

In speaking of the intimate way that God knows us, we see that He encourages us to know Him in that intimate way, as well. The term "Abba" is a term of intimacy, one that indicates closeness and familiarity. At the end of the day, that is all intimacy really is: closeness. It is the way that people interact with each other when they are close to each other and familiar with one another, knowing likes, dislikes, respecting personal space, and communicating with one another about the things that are most important to them as they go along in this journey of life. When we are intimate with God, it makes it easier to be intimate with others, and to refrain from the fear of getting hurt that often comes from distrust and abuse.

Walking with one another

The walk that we have in this life is not singular. Whether someone decides to be married or single, they are still in this world with other people. If we choose to walk in love, it makes getting along with others much easier. If we resist love and resist walking in love, it makes relationships with all people much more difficult. This is especially true when it comes to marriage, and when in marriage, it comes to living with another person.

Micah 6:8:

THE LORD HAS TOLD YOU, HUMAN [O MAN], WHAT IS GOOD; HE HAS TOLD YOU WHAT HE WANTS [THE LORD REQUIRES] FROM YOU: TO DO WHAT IS RIGHT TO OTHER PEOPLE [JUST], LOVE BEING KIND TO OTHERS [MERCY; LOVINGKINDNESS], AND LIVE HUMBLY, OBEYING [WALK HUMBLY WITH] YOUR GOD.

Just like we have to walk out love and show it to others, we must

Should family or church come first?

A LOT OF CHURCH TEACHING TODAY TALKS ABOUT FAMILY AND EMPHASIZES FAMILY TIME. THIS HAS LED MANY CHRISTIANS TO ADOPT THE ATTITUDE THAT THEIR FAMILIES ARE THE MOST IMPORTANT THINGS IN THE WORLD, AND THAT THEIR CHILDREN SHOULD TAKE PRIORITY OVER EVERY OTHER ASPECT OF THEIR LIVES. INSTEAD OF TITHING OR GIVING TO THE CHURCH, FAMILIES ARE PERVERTING THE CHURCH'S MESSAGES AND SAVING FOR FAMILY VACATIONS, BIGGER HOUSES, THINGS FOR THEIR CHILDREN, AND AVOIDING CHURCH ACTIVITIES BECAUSE IT MEANS THEY WILL BE UNABLE TO HAVE "FAMILY TIME." I MEET TOO MANY PEOPLE WHO CAN'T ATTEND PRAYER MEETINGS, BIBLE STUDY, SEVERAL CHURCH SERVICES PER MONTH, OR ANY TYPE OF CONFERENCES OR SPECIAL EVENTS BECAUSE IT WILL SOMEHOW INTERFERE IN THEIR "FAMILY TIME" AND THEY WILL MISS SOMETHING THEY PERCEIVE TO BE IMPORTANT IN THEIR CHILDREN'S LIVES. CHILDREN NEED TO RECOGNIZE THAT THEY ARE A PART OF A FAMILY, THAT IS ALSO A PART OF GOD'S FAMILY, WHICH IS THE CHURCH. THE MORE A FAMILY PUTS THEIR KIDS OR THEIR FAMILY AS A WHOLE FIRST, THE MORE THE KIDS LEARN THAT THE FAMILY REVOLVES AROUND THEM, AND CHURCH SHOULD EXIST AS A CONVENIENCE WHEN THEY ARE DONE WITH THEIR ACTIVITIES. THERE IS NOTHING WRONG WITH CHILDREN BEING INVOLVED IN THINGS AT SCHOOL, SUCH AS SPORTS OR CLUBS, BUT THERE IS SOMETHING WRONG WITH PARENTS ACCOMMODATING TOO MANY ACTIVITIES AND INTERESTS TO THE DETRIMENT OF A FAMILY'S SPIRITUAL DEVELOPMENT. INSTEAD OF LEARNING THAT BEING A PART OF CHURCH IS A PART OF YOUR RELATIONSHIP WITH GOD AND BEING INTERESTED IN THE THINGS THAT ARE GOING ON WITH OTHER PEOPLE, TOO MANY ARE GETTING THE MESSAGE THAT EVERYTHING SHOULD, ALL THE TIME, BE ABOUT THEM – AND THAT GOD SAYS THIS IS ALL RIGHT, BECAUSE IT'S ABOUT FAMILY.

CHURCH AND FAMILY SHOULD NOT BE IN COMPETITION WITH EACH OTHER. FAMILIES SHOULD SEE CHURCH INVOLVEMENT AS A PART OF THEIR FAITH LIFE AND THEIR FAMILY LIFE. FROM A YOUNG AGE, CHILDREN SHOULD BE IN CHURCHES THAT HELP THEM LEARN ABOUT GOD AND MEET THEIR SPECIFIC SPIRITUAL NEEDS. AS THEY GET OLDER, THEY SHOULD BE PARTICIPATING AND VOLUNTEERING IN CHURCH, SO THEY UNDERSTAND AND SEE THEMSELVES AS A PART OF THE LARGER CHURCH COMMUNITY.

PUTTING FAMILY BEFORE GOD IS A SIGN OF IDOLATRY. IT DOESN'T MATTER THAT IT IS FAMILY; IT'S STILL IDOLATRY. MAKE SURE THAT YOUR KIDS SEE YOU AS AN EXAMPLE OF FAITH AND FELLOWSHIP, AND THAT THEY, TOO, SEE THEMSELVES AS A PART OF GOD'S CHURCH.

walk out intimacy. If we are constantly self-centered or too busy for our spouses, then we are avoiding intimacy and intimate communication with them. Our intimate walk is shown in time shared, in the quality of that time, and in the nature of the way that we interact with our spouse. If we don't desire to be with our spouse in a balanced way (in the general course of living and intimate life), then that says a lot about how we feel about our spouse and about our relationship, in general. When we decide to get married, we do so with the understanding that we are going to be walking with someone, not against them or ahead of them, for a good portion of our lives. The foundation for this intimacy starts early in marriage, and as the relationship goes through many changes and grows over the years, it helps it to sustain on its own, as the couple learns the joys and blessings of walking together instead of apart.

Time and early care in marriage

In the Old Testament law pertaining to war regulations, we find a few verses about the early years of marriage sandwiched in between other passages that pertain to legal regulations.

Deuteronomy 20:5-9:

THE OFFICERS [OR SCRIBES] SHOULD SAY TO THE ARMY, "HAS ANYONE [WHO HAS] BUILT A NEW HOUSE BUT NOT GIVEN IT TO GOD [DEDICATED IT]? HE MAY GO HOME, BECAUSE HE MIGHT DIE IN BATTLE AND SOMEONE ELSE WOULD GET TO GIVE HIS HOUSE TO GOD [DEDICATE IT]. HAS ANYONE [WHO HAS] PLANTED A VINEYARD AND NOT BEGUN TO ENJOY IT? HE MAY GO HOME, BECAUSE HE MIGHT DIE IN BATTLE AND SOMEONE ELSE WOULD ENJOY HIS VINEYARD. IS ANY MAN [WHO IS] ENGAGED TO A WOMAN AND NOT YET MARRIED TO HER? HE MAY GO HOME, BECAUSE HE MIGHT DIE IN BATTLE AND SOMEONE ELSE WOULD MARRY HER." THEN THE OFFICERS [OR SCRIBES] SHOULD ALSO SAY, "IS ANYONE HERE AFRAID? HAS ANYONE LOST HIS COURAGE [HEART]? HE MAY GO HOME SO THAT HE WILL NOT CAUSE OTHERS TO LOSE THEIR COURAGE, TOO [MELT THE HEARTS OF HIS RELATIVES/BROTHERS LIKE HIS HEART]." WHEN THE OFFICERS [SCRIBES] FINISH SPEAKING TO THE ARMY, THEY SHOULD APPOINT COMMANDERS TO LEAD IT.

Deuteronomy 24:5:

A MAN WHO HAS JUST MARRIED MUST NOT BE SENT TO WAR [WITH THE ARMY] OR BE GIVEN ANY OTHER DUTY. HE SHOULD BE FREE TO STAY HOME FOR A YEAR TO MAKE HIS NEW WIFE HAPPY [20:7].

Some historians find these regulations about war and marriage unusual, but in terms of ancient cultures, it was not that strange. There is the obvious reason of contracts and covenants that we spoke of earlier, and the way in which the death of a newly married husband could affect the dowries and arranged marriages that have recently taken place. Another motive, especially in times of war, was the continuation of the nation. If a young husband was at home attending to his wife, there was a far more likely chance of her becoming pregnant and the family lineage continuing than if he was out on the battlefield. There was probably also the issue of distraction. If a man was off fighting and he missed his young wife or wondered what was going on at home, he was not going to be focused on the battle at hand, which was fighting whatever enemy needed address at that time.

Beyond the practical reasons for these regulations, God knew and recognized that newly married people needed time to themselves. In taking this time, they develop the necessary intimate connections to know each other and live together for the duration. It wasn't practical to develop a truly intimate relationship if a husband or a wife was off somewhere else, having to devote time, attention, and focus on anything except for their marriage.

Couples today must cover household expenses and provide for themselves, and this often means that extended honeymoon vacations or long trips without working are often unreasonable. Note, however, that the Bible doesn't say that these things are required for a couple to develop the early intimate skills and knowing of one another to become a truly intimate couple. The Word of the Lord was for the husband to go home, not for the husband and wife to spend money on a trip. The intimacy that comes in marriage comes from knowing your partner, not from having to keep up with the Joneses. This means that some couples, especially those who are thinking that married life requires such grand gestures, need to look at what is truly important in their relationships, and in their lives. For the foundation of your marriage to be right, it requires early time and effort to be spent as the couple learns to respect – and regard – the other one, their differences and individuality, as they learn how to live together.

Sex in marriage

In my commentary on the Song of Solomon, I have an entire chapter devoted to sex and desire. Without reiterating everything in that chapter in this book, there are a couple of basics that I want to outline here as pertain to sex and pertain to sex within marriage:

- Sex is a part of the intimacy of most marriages, although there are intimate relationships in life (friends, family) that do not involve sex. In some relationships (such as those that are asexual), sex might not be a primary intimacy, or one at all.
- Sex is an expression of the intimacy between partners in most marriages, but it is not the only source.
- If sex is part of a marriage, it is something both partners should look forward to and should meet both of their physical pleasure needs.
- Both partners in the relationship should discuss likes and dislikes and feel comfortable exploring those likes within the confines of their relationship.
- Either spouse should feel comfortable initiating sex or sexual relations if such is part of their relationship.
- There is no big, long "should" or "should not" list when it comes to sex and sexual preferences, likes, and dislikes. There is only the matter of sexual preference, and whether someone feels comfortable doing something. Preferences should be discussed prior to marriage. If someone is uncomfortable with something, they should under no circumstances be forced into doing it.
- Sex should not ever violate either party.

1 Corinthians 7:1-7

NOW I WILL DISCUSS [CONCERNING] THE THINGS YOU WROTE ME ABOUT [IN A LETTER FROM THE CORINTHIANS; SEE 8:1; 12:1; 16:1]. IT IS GOOD FOR A

MAN NOT TO HAVE SEXUAL RELATIONS WITH [TOUCH; A EUPHEMISM FOR SEX] A WOMAN [PROBABLY ANOTHER SLOGAN (6:12; 8:1, 4; 10:23) ASSERTING THAT A CELIBATE LIFESTYLE WAS SPIRITUALLY SUPERIOR]. BUT BECAUSE SEXUAL SIN IS A DANGER [OF SEXUAL TEMPTATIONS; OF SEXUAL SINS], EACH MAN SHOULD HAVE [OR HAVE SEXUAL RELATIONS WITH] HIS OWN WIFE, AND EACH WOMAN SHOULD HAVE [OR HAVE SEXUAL RELATIONS WITH] HER OWN HUSBAND. THE HUSBAND SHOULD GIVE HIS WIFE ALL THAT HE OWES HER AS HIS WIFE [MEET HER SEXUAL NEEDS]. AND THE WIFE SHOULD GIVE HER HUSBAND ALL THAT SHE OWES HIM AS HER HUSBAND [MEET HIS SEXUAL NEEDS]. THE WIFE DOES NOT HAVE FULL RIGHTS [AUTHORITY] OVER HER OWN BODY; HER HUSBAND SHARES THEM. AND THE HUSBAND DOES NOT HAVE FULL RIGHTS [AUTHORITY] OVER HIS OWN BODY; HIS WIFE SHARES THEM [REVOLUTIONARY TEACHING IN THE FIRST CENTURY, WHEN WIVES WERE GENERALLY VIEWED AS THE POSSESSION OF THEIR HUSBANDS]. DO NOT REFUSE TO GIVE YOUR BODIES TO [REFUSE SEX TO; DEPRIVE] EACH OTHER, UNLESS YOU BOTH AGREE TO STAY AWAY FROM SEXUAL RELATIONS FOR A TIME SO YOU CAN GIVE YOUR TIME [DEVOTE YOURSELVES] TO PRAYER. THEN COME TOGETHER AGAIN [RESUME YOUR SEXUAL RELATIONSHIP] SO SATAN CANNOT TEMPT YOU BECAUSE OF A LACK OF SELF-CONTROL. I SAY THIS TO GIVE YOU PERMISSION TO STAY AWAY FROM SEXUAL RELATIONS FOR A TIME [AS A CONCESSION/ALLOWANCE]. IT IS NOT A COMMAND TO DO SO. I WISH THAT EVERYONE WERE LIKE ME [UNMARRIED], BUT EACH PERSON HAS HIS OWN GIFT FROM GOD. ONE HAS ONE GIFT, ANOTHER HAS ANOTHER GIFT.*

Even though there are people who have devoted entire books to sex in marriage, the Bible doesn't devote that much time to things like techniques, interests, and the who, what, where, when, and why of how it should be done. I believe that the advice the Apostle Paul gives in 1 Corinthians 7 above applies to marriage and applies to marriage in an important way. Even though we are going to look at this passage again in the next chapter in a slightly different way, I feel that the facts of this passage apply about sex in the marriage as much as about mutual fasting and self-control in marriage. When we become married, intimate partners with someone else, there is a point in our lives where we end, and they begin. It doesn't mean that we stop being our own, unique, individual people, but that we agree when we become married to become a part of each other. The Apostle Paul's words weren't the erasing of consent in sex or that people should have sex if they are sick, in pain, tired, or doing something else at that moment. It was the concept that if we are married, we seek to give ourselves to each other in sex. There is no reason to get deep in marriage and resolve to have a sexless relationship or to swing to extremes, unless such is desired due to asexuality. In a marriage relationship, the key is to find what works for the two of you: your own pace, your own interests, and your own expressions of a physical relationship with one another.

Mutual submission

We can't talk about sex and the Song of Solomon and not discuss the issue of submission, which may, upon first glance, seem to be misplaced. It's not misplaced, not at all, and picks up on many of the themes we have discussed in this chapter and the last one, as well.

Ephesians 5:21-33:

YIELD [SUBMIT; BE SUBJECT; ... YIELDING/SUBMITTING; GRAMMATICALLY LINKED TO THE PREVIOUS SENTENCE, AND SO PART OF BEING FILLED WITH THE SPIRIT] TO EACH OTHER OUT OF REVERENCE [RESPECT; FEAR; AWE] FOR CHRIST.

WIVES, YIELD TO [SUBMIT TO; BE SUBJECT TO; TO] YOUR HUSBANDS, AS YOU DO TO THE LORD, BECAUSE THE HUSBAND IS THE HEAD OF THE WIFE, AS CHRIST IS THE HEAD OF THE CHURCH. AND HE IS THE SAVIOR OF THE BODY, WHICH IS THE CHURCH. AS THE CHURCH YIELDS [SUBMITS; IS SUBJECT] TO CHRIST, SO YOU WIVES SHOULD YIELD [SUBMIT; BE SUBJECT] TO YOUR HUSBANDS IN EVERYTHING [COL. 3:18; 1 PET. 3:1–6].

HUSBANDS, LOVE YOUR WIVES AS CHRIST LOVED THE CHURCH [COL. 3:19; 1 PET. 3:7] AND GAVE HIMSELF FOR HER TO MAKE HER HOLY [SANCTIFY HER], CLEANSING HER IN THE WASHING OF WATER BY THE WORD [THE "WASHING" MAY BE (1) BAPTISM, (2) SPIRITUAL CLEANSING (TITUS 3:5), OR (3) AN ANALOGY DRAWN FROM THE JEWISH PRENUPTIAL BATH (EZEK. 16:8–14); THE "WORD" MAY BE (1) THE GOSPEL, (2) A BAPTISMAL FORMULA, OR (3) THE CONFESSION OF THE ONE BAPTIZED]. HE DID THIS SO THAT HE COULD PRESENT THE CHURCH TO HIMSELF LIKE A BRIDE IN ALL HER BEAUTY [IN SPLENDOR; GLORIOUS], WITH NO EVIL OR SIN [STAIN OR WRINKLE] OR ANY OTHER WRONG THING IN IT [SUCH THING], BUT PURE [HOLY] AND WITHOUT FAULT [BLAMELESS]. IN THE SAME WAY, HUSBANDS SHOULD LOVE THEIR WIVES AS THEY LOVE THEIR OWN BODIES. THE MAN

WHO LOVES HIS WIFE LOVES HIMSELF. [FOR] NO ONE EVER HATES HIS OWN BODY [FLESH], BUT FEEDS AND TAKES CARE OF IT. AND THAT IS WHAT CHRIST DOES FOR THE CHURCH, BECAUSE WE ARE PARTS [MEMBERS] OF HIS BODY. THE SCRIPTURE SAYS, "SO [FOR THIS REASON] A MAN WILL LEAVE HIS FATHER AND MOTHER AND BE UNITED [JOINED] WITH HIS WIFE, AND THE TWO WILL BECOME ONE BODY [FLESH; GEN. 2:24]." THIS SECRET [MYSTERY] IS VERY IMPORTANT [OR GREAT; PROFOUND]—I AM TALKING ABOUT CHRIST AND THE CHURCH. BUT [HOWEVER; IN ANY CASE; OR TO SUM UP] EACH ONE OF YOU MUST LOVE HIS WIFE AS HE LOVES HIMSELF, AND A WIFE MUST RESPECT [REVERENCE; V. 21] HER HUSBAND.

In the last chapter, we discussed Ephesians 5:21-33 as an illustration of covenant. Through marriage, the Apostle Paul was trying to teach us about our relationship with Christ through the church. Unfortunately, through the years, we have focused so much on only one side of view pertaining to this passage that we have completely mis-stepped what was being taught to us.

The teachings on Biblical submission are often taught through the lens of patriarchal culture: men are the head of the household, women and children are the property of the men, and women are, by extension, subordinate to men in all possible ways. The passage is seen as endorsing traditions of power and control, and women are seen as inferior to men. No matter how much people who endorse a traditional understanding of this passage might try to talk around what I just said, that is the root of the understanding. They do not see the beauty of what is spoken of here between Christ and the church, nor do they consider that Christ does not force anyone to be a part of His church, nor does He lead us with abuse and a dominant spirit. What Christ did for the church was die for it, submit His life to the Father's will and surrender Himself that humanity might be saved. Christ performed the ultimate act of submission, not the ultimate act of control.

That is the essence of what is wrong with the way people interpret Ephesians 5:21-33. They teach that women should allow their husbands to abuse their bodies, to constantly make themselves available for sex even if they are in pain or physically incapacitated, that they should have no voice in marriages, and that they should blindly follow and do whatever their husbands want, whether it is right. It should be obvious now, by this point in the book, that's not what God is saying to us, at all, in this passage. If anything, I believe it is reinforcing a principle of mutual submission and also teaching us that submission is not static.

Marriage is not a one-dimensional experience where one fulfills one constant role and another a different one. In fact, marriage is extremely multi-dimensional. There isn't one situation where one person always defers to the will of another one, because that destroys the concept of working together and walking in agreement. If you are truly submitting yourself to God, that makes you a servant, not a boss. If we are standing before God as honorable people, and submitting to Christ, Who is the true Head of every church and every household, then we are learning how to walk in love, and love one another. That means that there will be times when a wife will need to yield to her husband's situation or position, and there will be times when a husband will have to yield to his wife's position. When a husband is told by God that his position is to love his wife as Christ loved the church, that is an act of submission, of dying to himself, to love her rightly and properly. This means that both partners in the marriage need to submit themselves to the other. They need to look at themselves first, respect one another, and care enough about their marriage to realize it isn't all about them. This is how we continue to uphold Christian values in a marriage, without it becoming about power and control.

This all relates to sex and the commentary on the Song of Solomon because we saw in the Song of Solomon just how forward the woman was about the nature of her desires and her sexual intentions. We would be foolish to think that her forward nature ended with sex and that she wasn't forward in other areas of her life, as well. Having a forward partner – one who speaks their mind (and does so with a right spirit, of course), one who you know where you stand – is an open door to intimacy because they are able to reveal themselves to their partners. Having someone who is timid, afraid, uncertain, or unclear about who they are makes intimacy that much more of a challenge.

Role reversals

When I talk about "role reversals" I am not talking about male/female role reversals, although those can obviously apply to what we are going to discuss here. What I am talking about here are occasional shifts in the typical roles that each partner in a relationship plays. For example, if one partner typically does the vacuuming and one partner always does the dishes, there should be times when each partner shifts their duties and does what the other partner typically does.

As I spoke of in the last sections, submission is a flexible thing, something that changes through time. One of the ways that submission plays heavily in marriage is the ability to do what needs to be done, when it needs to be done, whether it is specifically someone's "job" or not. Role reversals are an example of the fact that a relationship should be flexible, and not static. They move with the tides of intimacy in the relationship. There may be many situations by which one partner is incapacitated or unable to do the jobs they typically do, and the other partner will need to take over.

Galatians 3:26-29:

[FOR] YOU ARE ALL CHILDREN OF GOD THROUGH FAITH IN CHRIST JESUS [OR IN CHRIST JESUS YOU ARE ALL CHILDREN/SONS OF GOD THROUGH FAITH]. [FOR] ALL OF YOU WHO WERE BAPTIZED INTO CHRIST HAVE CLOTHED YOURSELVES WITH CHRIST. IN CHRIST, THERE IS NO DIFFERENCE BETWEEN JEW AND GREEK [NEITHER JEW NOR GREEK], SLAVE AND FREE PERSON, MALE AND FEMALE. YOU ARE ALL THE SAME [OR UNITED; ONE] IN CHRIST JESUS. YOU [IF YOU...] BELONG TO CHRIST, SO YOU ARE ABRAHAM'S DESCENDANTS [SEED]. YOU WILL INHERIT ALL OF GOD'S BLESSINGS BECAUSE OF THE PROMISE GOD MADE TO ABRAHAM [...HEIRS ACCORDING TO THE PROMISE].

All throughout history, people have assigned duties to one singular person in the relationship, but this type of thinking is not Biblical. We have seen both partners in relationships cross duties and do different jobs and also experience the purpose of role reversals in their relationships. This is another aspect of intimacy, and one that we should embrace not just in the traditional sense, but in any sort of role reversal that we demonstrate in our own relationships.

Trust

In intimacy, marriages need to be places of trust. Stories of domestic violence, of wild and out of control spouses, of disrespect, and of degradation within marriages fill our news feeds online, our newspapers, and the different photos that go viral. Our world is full of people who entered an intimate relationship with someone only to have them hurt or violate them.

There can't be intimacy without love, and there certainly can't be intimacy without trust. Trust is the way that intimacy is conveyed. While we talk about the many ways that trust is violated, we don't talk nearly enough about the ways that we make ourselves trustworthy.

Genesis 39:3-6:

POTIPHAR SAW THAT THE LORD WAS WITH JOSEPH AND THAT THE LORD MADE JOSEPH SUCCESSFUL [PROSPEROUS] IN EVERYTHING HE DID. SO POTIPHAR WAS VERY HAPPY WITH JOSEPH [JOSEPH FOUND GRACE/FAVOR IN HIS EYES] AND ALLOWED HIM TO BE HIS PERSONAL SERVANT [ATTEND HIM]. HE PUT JOSEPH IN CHARGE OF THE HOUSE, TRUSTING HIM WITH EVERYTHING HE OWNED. WHEN JOSEPH WAS PUT IN CHARGE OF THE HOUSE AND EVERYTHING POTIPHAR OWNED, THE LORD BLESSED THE PEOPLE IN POTIPHAR'S [THE EGYPTIAN'S] HOUSE BECAUSE OF JOSEPH. AND THE LORD BLESSED EVERYTHING THAT BELONGED TO POTIPHAR, BOTH IN THE HOUSE AND IN THE FIELD. SO POTIPHAR LEFT JOSEPH IN CHARGE OF EVERYTHING HE OWNED AND WAS NOT CONCERNED ABOUT ANYTHING EXCEPT THE FOOD HE ATE.

Joseph wasn't just a great dream interpreter or someone who people could come to for business deals. Joseph reached his position with the king of Egypt because he was trustworthy. In looking at him, let's see what the characteristics of trust look like.

- **Trust knows how to be a servant:** Service keeps coming up repeatedly, especially in marriage. If you are trustworthy, you know how to be of service to your spouse: how to help them out and how to be there for them when it matters.

- **Trust understands the principles of good stewardship:** In marriage, if you can't be trusted to keep your word, keep control of your habits, keep control of your spending, and use your time wisely, you are going to have a hard time being trustworthy in your marriage. Good stewardship recognizes people shouldn't have to be baby-sat and that couples should be able to enjoy each other rather than always worrying about what one or both are doing.

- **It doesn't matter what is given to a trustworthy person; they will take care of it:** No matter how big or small, whether the job is praised to the sky, or not, whether anyone notices, or not, trust gets the job done. Not only is it done, but it's also done well.

- **If it's not theirs, you can trust a trustworthy person with it:** Couples shouldn't worry that their most important possessions will wind up in a pawn shop or that something of theirs will be stolen or missing. This applies to their lives, as well. When lives are shared in a marriage, they should be shared equally, not taken advantage of, nor mistreated or abused.

- **They are not abusive of power:** Trustworthy people aren't in it for the power trip. They do not lord authority over people, and they don't do things to deliberately abuse or threaten others through force of power.

- **Trust makes it so people do not have to worry about things in their lives:** We spend so much time worrying about things in our lives: what we are going to do, where we are going to go, and how we are going to do it. In the face of intimacy, these concerns should cease. If one partner can do one thing another can't, then that concern is taken care of. In intimacy, the struggle ends.

Ceasing power struggles

The last thing we are going to look at this week is the call to cease in the face of strife. Conventional advice tells us to "fight fair" when we are married, which means don't hit the weaknesses or sensitivities of your spouse that will cause them the most pain. The problem with this advice is that there is no such thing as "fighting fair" because the whole point of fighting is for someone to win. People don't fight so that they can be fair and equitable to each other, they fight so that their position will overpower someone else's. This basic precept of fighting means that behind every fight is a power struggle, and within that struggle is the need for both parties to step back and look at the real struggle behind the fight.

It is not God's will that we fight each other. We are told that we are in a spiritual battle and to recognize the forces of evil that we are supposed to fight, but we are not supposed to be in strife and anger with one another. The Bible acknowledges that people do fight, and when emotions get the better of us and anger rises, we must handle it properly. Intimacy is not a place for strife. While we acknowledge that sometimes it comes up because people get in the flesh, in intimacy, we should realize when we are wrong and learn the power of proper apology and communication.

Ephesians 4:26-29:

WHEN YOU ARE ANGRY, [OR BE ANGRY, AND] DO NOT SIN [PS. 4:4; THERE IS A TIME FOR RIGHTEOUS ANGER, BUT IT MUST NOT RESULT IN SIN], AND BE SURE TO STOP BEING ANGRY BEFORE THE END OF THE DAY [DON'T LET THE SUN SET ON YOUR ANGER]. DO NOT GIVE THE DEVIL A WAY TO DEFEAT YOU [FOOTHOLD; OPPORTUNITY]. THOSE WHO ARE STEALING MUST STOP STEALING AND START WORKING. THEY SHOULD EARN AN HONEST LIVING FOR THEMSELVES [DO SOMETHING GOOD/USEFUL WITH THEIR HANDS]. THEN THEY WILL HAVE SOMETHING TO SHARE WITH THOSE WHO ARE POOR [HAVE NEED].

DON'T SAY ANYTHING THAT WILL HURT OTHERS [LET ANY ROTTEN/UNHEALTHY WORD COME FROM YOUR MOUTH], BUT ONLY SAY WHAT IS HELPFUL [GOOD] TO MAKE OTHERS STRONGER [BUILD OTHERS UP] AND MEET [ACCORDING TO] THEIR NEEDS. THEN WHAT YOU SAY WILL DO GOOD [GIVE GRACE; BE A GIFT] TO THOSE WHO LISTEN TO YOU.

- Do not sin in anger.
- Do not let anger fester from day to day; work out your issues without letting them harbor overnight.
- Don't allow your emotions to give the enemy a foothold in your life.
- Make sure there is productivity in all that you do; work so your household is supported.
- Watch your mouth and make sure that you are careful to speak

properly to your spouse.

Ephesians 4:31:

DO NOT BE BITTER OR ANGRY OR MAD [RAGING]. NEVER SHOUT ANGRILY OR SAY THINGS TO HURT [SLANDER; INSULT] OTHERS. NEVER DO ANYTHING [GET RID OF ALL KINDS OF] EVIL.

- Get rid of bitterness, rage, anger, brawling, slander, and malice. Do not allow those things to become a part of your marriage.

James 1:19-20:

MY DEAR [BELOVED] BROTHERS AND SISTERS [FELLOW BELIEVERS], [UNDER-STAND/KNOW THIS:] ALWAYS BE WILLING TO LISTEN AND SLOW TO SPEAK. DO NOT BECOME ANGRY EASILY [BE QUICK TO LISTEN, SLOW TO SPEAK, SLOW TO ANGER; PROV. 17:28], BECAUSE ANGER WILL NOT HELP YOU LIVE THE RIGHT KIND OF LIFE GOD WANTS [BECAUSE HUMAN ANGER DOES NOT PRODUCE GOD'S RIGHTEOUSNESS].

- Be quick to listen. Listen to your spouse when they are talking and hear them out when they have something to discuss.
- Be slow to speak. Don't have to have the first word or the last word all the time.
- Be slow to become angry. Give your spouse the benefit of the doubt, knowing that you love them.
- Righteousness is not brought about by anger. While there is righteous anger, being angry all the time and so caught up in emotion doesn't lead to a righteous life.

Proverbs 29:11:

FOOLISH PEOPLE LOSE THEIR TEMPERS [OR LET NOTHING GO UNEXPRESSED; LET ALL THEIR SPIRIT OUT],
BUT WISE PEOPLE CONTROL THEIRS [QUIET THINGS DOWN AFTERWARD].

- Avoid the need to "vent" all the time.
- Keep yourself under control.

Week 15 Assignments

Answer the following questions based on discussions you have had with your future spouse in counseling this week and additionally on your own time and prepare to discuss them at your next counseling session. If you run out of room in a section, finish the answer to your question in your journal.

1. What is love? How does it apply as a spiritual principle? _____

_____

_____

_____

_____

2. How is intimacy related to love? _____

_____

_____

_____

_____

3. What does it mean to say that "God is married to His people?"

_____

_____

_____

_____

_____

4. How does God know us? _____

_____

_____

_____

5. How do we know God? How does God desire that we know Him? _____

_____

_____

_____

6. How does intimacy work when couples are trying to walk through life together? _____

_____

_____

_____

7. What are some of the practical reasons why the Old Testament relieved newly married soldiers from duty? _____

_____

_____

_____

_____

8. What are some of the spiritual reasons for these regulations?

_____

_____

_____

_____

9. What are some basics that pertain to sex within a marriage? _____

_____

_____

_____

10. When we are in an intimate relationship in marriage, what advice exists as pertains to sex and sexual boundaries? _____

_____

_____

_____

11. What lens are the teachings on marital submission often taught through? Is this helpful or harmful? _____

_____

_____

_____

_____

12. How is submission mutual in a marriage? Why is this principle so important? _____

_____

_____

_____

13. Is there room for a forward partner in a marriage? Why or why not? _____

_____

_____

_____

_____

14. Why are "role reversals" important? _____

_____

_____

_____

15. How do "role reversals" demonstrate the intimacy in a marriage? _____

_____

_____

_____

16. How is trust a part of intimacy? _____

_____

_____

_____

17. How do we cease our power struggles in marriage? What does the Bible tell us about the way that we fight? _____

_____

_____

_____

18. What do you think the couple in the Song of Solomon argued about? What do you think they did after they stopped fighting?

_____

_____

_____

_____

_____

19. In reading 1 John 4:7-21, why do you think that of all the things God could reveal Himself to be, He chose love? What does this tell us about marriage? _____

_____

_____

_____

_____

20. How do you feel about sex and sexual intimacies? What are your likes and dislikes? Write them down and then discuss these issues with your partner. If you run into any conflicts in the process, discuss them with your spiritual leader at your next session.

_____

_____

_____

_____

_____

Holiness in Marriage

MARRIAGE SHOULD BE HONORED BY EVERYONE, AND HUSBAND AND WIFE
SHOULD KEEP THEIR MARRIAGE [THE MARRIAGE BED SHOULD BE KEPT] PURE
[UNDEFILED]. GOD WILL JUDGE AS GUILTY [JUDGE] THOSE WHO TAKE PART IN
SEXUAL SINS [THE SEXUALLY IMMORAL AND ADULTERERS].
(HEBREWS 13:4)

Bible reading: Hebrews 12:10-24

Journaling assignments for in-session discussion:

- What is your concept of holiness?
- Do you believe it is possible to live holy and be married?
  Why or why not?

Your sessions for pre-marital counseling are winding up. Discussion of your workbook answers for this week will be a part of your last session. It is almost time for you to get married. You are probably experiencing a range of emotions, from nervousness to excitement. There may even be a little stress in there, especially as final things need to get done. You're probably thinking about the wedding, your life after the wedding, maybe even a honeymoon trip, and the things you need to pack. So, for one more week, I ask for your attention, because we are going to talk about something very important and vital for this last session. Here, in this chapter, we are going to talk about holiness and its role in marriage.

Marriage is an important catalyst for holiness in most individuals, which is why it is a very foundational building block, even acknowledged among the most spiritual. While the Apostle Paul might not have wanted to be married himself, he couldn't deny that the single life was not for everybody. For most people, married life is an important part of holiness development. It's not a wild free-for-all, as most people teach, nor is it a big spiritual compromise on God's part to make sure children have legal parents. Holiness comes in a powerful way from marriage because marriage causes us to see ourselves as people. It gets us to look at us and our own flaws and consider the things within us that still need change. Unfortunately, we often do the opposite in marriage and start looking at everything that we want to change in our partner. If we want to be people who are truly of God, we need to start seeing marriage as a means by which we can change and grow as people and become the people God desires us to be.

Is it possible to be holy and be married?

1 Corinthians 7:1-2:

NOW I WILL DISCUSS [CONCERNING] THE THINGS YOU WROTE ME ABOUT [IN A LETTER FROM THE CORINTHIANS; SEE 8:1; 12:1; 16:1]. IT IS GOOD FOR A MAN NOT TO HAVE SEXUAL RELATIONS WITH [TOUCH; A EUPHEMISM FOR SEX] A WOMAN [PROBABLY ANOTHER SLOGAN (6:12; 8:1, 4; 10:23) ASSERTING THAT A CELIBATE LIFESTYLE WAS SPIRITUALLY SUPERIOR]. BUT BECAUSE SEXUAL SIN IS A DANGER [OF SEXUAL TEMPTATIONS; OF SEXUAL SINS], EACH MAN SHOULD HAVE [OR HAVE SEXUAL RELATIONS WITH] HIS OWN WIFE, AND EACH WOMAN SHOULD HAVE [OR HAVE SEXUAL RELATIONS WITH] HER OWN HUSBAND.

Church history has often suggested that the only way to live a truly holy life is to be single – and celibate. People have justified this belief by misinterpreting the Apostle Paul's words and turning them into rules rather than seeing he was stating his own perspective about the issue. It's an unfortunate fact that through much of Christian history, people have associated all types of sex with sin and believed it was impossible to be holy and married or sexual as a being. This has led to all sorts of strange marriage situations throughout the ages, including married couples who forsook all sexual activity or who became monks and nuns, renouncing their wedding vows.

This probably sounds strange (and even impossible) by modern standards. It sounds odd that married couples would forsake their own marriage to live a different type of life because they believed God was displeased with their marriage. Even though we generally accept that married life is acceptable in the sight of God, we still seem to think that marriage is some sort of divine compromise and that being married is a lesser spiritual form than single life.

The truth is that I do believe the single life is difficult for most people, even those who are wired for it by orientation or called to it for the sake of purpose (or both). They forsake everything that seems "natural" to most of the world: marriage, companionship, (often) sex, children, and family. Some do it well and some don't, but those who do it walk a whole different life of purpose and platonic companionship. I think it is a serious misnomer, however, to say that it is a higher spiritual calling than married life. In the single life, those who are called to be single find their call to holiness in that specific lifestyle. The things that help them to develop their spiritual call are found in what they are called to do and how they are called to live. The same is true for married people. If you are a person called to be married (which most people are), then the attributes you need to acquire to develop a deeper holiness will come out through marriage. Most people need the opportunity to work through their holiness with other people in an intimate setting. We need to see ourselves, what we are made of, the ways that we treat others, and we need daily opportunities to work through those things in a setting of trust and honesty.

So, not only is it possible to be "set apart" and different in marriage, but it is also one of the primary settings where most people acquire the skills to become even more dedicated and purposed for the Lord. Marriage gives those who enter its covenant the ability to learn more about what it means to be set apart, while remaining in the world and experiencing the challenges and pitfalls of this world. It offers instant support when circumstances are right and provides a safe place to develop deeper holiness when the walk is difficult or challenging.

Getting to know true love

Marriage doesn't work without true love. I am talking about real love, not early infatuations and attractions that a couple experience. While those feelings are certainly real, they are often fleeting. They last right up until the point in a relationship where holiness needs to start. We don't usually think of holiness as a component of marriage, but the truth about marriage is that it brings with it a lot of opportunities to fail and fall into sin. The world is tempting, and things such as adultery, infidelity, social and work ambitions, pornography, and even some leading advice tends to make the grass look greener somewhere other than your marriage. The reality of married life is that it seldom, if ever, goes the way that people plan. Couples face loss of family members, short or long-term illness, disabilities, personal or emotional difficulties, and stress factors that change the way a person may feel about themselves and about their relationship.

1 Corinthians 13:4-7:

LOVE IS PATIENT AND KIND. LOVE IS NOT JEALOUS [ENVIOUS], IT DOES NOT BRAG, AND IT IS NOT PROUD [ARROGANT; CONCEITED; PUFFED UP]. LOVE IS NOT RUDE [DISRESPECTFUL], IS NOT SELFISH [SELF-SERVING], AND DOES NOT GET UPSET WITH OTHERS [IS NOT EASILY PROVOKED/ANGERED]. LOVE DOES NOT COUNT UP [KEEP A RECORD OF] WRONGS THAT HAVE BEEN DONE. LOVE TAKES NO PLEASURE [DOES NOT REJOICE] IN EVIL [WRONGDOING; INJUSTICE] BUT REJOICES OVER THE TRUTH. LOVE PATIENTLY ACCEPTS ALL THINGS [BEARS ALL THINGS; OR ALWAYS PROTECTS], ALWAYS TRUSTS [BELIEVES ALL THINGS], ALWAYS HOPES [HOPES ALL THINGS], AND ALWAYS ENDURES [ENDURES ALL THINGS].

At a certain point in every relationship, a couple must see their marriage for more than just an opportunity to have sex without question or being in it because they think their mate looks really good. Marriage needs to become about a deeper love, one that sees the true potential in a mate and wishes the best for them. While *eros*, or attraction (sometimes translated as love in the Bible) is something that keeps the human species going, it is not the main thing that keeps couples together. If couples don't ever gain a sense of *agape* (sometimes translated as charity, other times benevolence, usually love) which is the love spoken of in 1 Corinthians 13. If a marriage is going to survive and thrive, it needs to become about the attributes spoken of here:

- Patient
- Kind
- Not jealous
- Not bragging
- Not proud
- not rude
- not selfish
- not easily provoked
- not keeping a record of wrongs
- not rejoicing in wrong
- rejoicing in truth
- accepting all things
- always trusting
- always hoping
- Always enduring

Every single one of the things we are supposed to do – and refraining from the things we are not supposed to do – are not just about love, they are also expressions of holiness. They prove to the world (and to our mates in a more immediate sense) that we are a different kind of people. It means that we don't bail on our mates when life gets hard and that we persevere through the difficult things that other people give up on. We believe in our mates, but we also believe in God, Who gives us the strength to endure through life's ups and downs.

Marriage is about more than happiness

We've been led to believe that marriage is all about our happiness, and the second that marriage becomes uncomfortable or fails to make us happy, we shouldn't stay married anymore. The truth about marriage is that it's not about being happy all the time, and it isn't your spouse's job to make you happy. In a spiritual sense, marriage is about the development of deeper holiness, as we have been

Thought Points

The Bible on love

New Testament writers didn't use just one word for the word we translate in English as "love." Rather, they echoed Greek culture and embellished on four different words, each used to describe a different type of love or affection for someone or something. These four terms are *EROS*, *PHILEO*, *STORGAY*, and *AGAPE*.

EROS – This term is found in the Greek translation of the Old Testament (the Septuagint). It is often found (although not exclusively) in the Song of Solomon. It is used to describe sexual attraction, desire, interest, or that sexual interest in connection. The word is always used in a sexual context and seeks gratification and pleasure in a sexual way. (It's how a man or a woman can say, "I love my wife/husband, but I am not in love with her/him." They are saying that even though they might love them as a person, they are not physically attracted to them anymore.) Personally, I think *EROS* is better translated to be "attraction" or "physical desire."

PHILEO – This term indicates "brotherly love" or a strong affection for somebody else. It's more than just being a casual acquaintance of someone, but it is not sexual or romantic in nature. It's a loving friendship, one based on a bond where a friend is "closer than a brother" (Proverbs 18:24).

STORGAY – This term defines love for one's family or relatives, especially in the context of a bond. It's basically "familial honor."

AGAPE – *Agape* defines the highest form of love. Whenever the Bible speaks of loving God, loving our neighbor, or displaying the love of God to one another, it always speaks of *agape*. It is considered to be the divine love, completely spiritual in nature, that seeks the greatest good for everyone involved and is the completeness of unselfish love.

Even in Biblical terminology, love is understood in many different ways because love is based on relationship. Saying that we "love" someone is complicated. It's not always easy to define, or to understand, because it is personal to how people see it. Most, if not all people, will walk in *EROS*, *PHILEO* and *STORGAY* in their lives, both giving and receiving them. *Agape*, however, is a different matter. As the highest form of love, it should be at the foundation of all of our relationships, the foundation of our interactions with others, and the very thing that transforms our relationship with God.

discussing. Your happiness, your personal sense of security, your well-being, and your self-esteem should all be things that your partner mirrors to you, but they should not be things that you find from them. Things happen, whether good or bad; marriages fail, people die, life changes, but your inner securities and sense of self-worth should not change.

Psalm 5:11:

BUT LET EVERYONE WHO TRUSTS [FINDS REFUGE IN] YOU BE HAPPY [REJOICE]; LET THEM SING GLAD SONGS FOREVER. PROTECT [SPREAD YOUR PROTECTION ON] THOSE WHO LOVE YOU AND WHO ARE HAPPY BECAUSE OF YOU [LET THOSE WHO LOVE YOUR NAME REJOICE IN YOU].

Being married shows us what we are made of, because marriage either makes or breaks many people. If we look at current statistics, it breaks a lot of people. Some remarry, only to find the same issues, while some are strong at their broken places and make their second marriages work. People who make their marriages work do so by two factors: being married to a compatible person and refusing to walk away when life is challenging. The best marriages consist of people who don't rely on their mates to be happy, who know how to do well all by themselves but prefer to do so with their partners, who recognize their marriages to be a choice, and who allow their true holy character to come through as they share their lives with a partner.

Forgiveness

Ah... forgiveness. That topic we love to hear about in terms of receiving it from God but hate it when we are supposed to be forgiving with other people. It sounds great when we are absolved of our own sins, but forgiving other people of theirs, letting things go, and moving forward doesn't sound like quite as much fun. When someone else wrongs us, we want to hold on to it. Marriage is a perfect catalyst for forgiveness, both giving it and receiving it.

I know it might sound hard to believe, but spouses have a way of getting on each other's nerves. When you spend as much personal time with someone as you do with your spouse, it's not uncommon to see things that they do cause offense or hurt. It may very well be unintentional, but that doesn't make it feel better, much of the time. In fact, being married to the person who caused the offense might make it feel worse.

Causing offense, being offended, sinning against someone, and feeling the sting of sin are all a part of living with other people in this life. It's great to think that marriage is going to make these things go away, but it doesn't. Actually, I think that marriage tends to bring these things out more, so we can deal with them and work them out. If we are doing things that are offensive to our spouse, odds are good that we are doing them to other people, as well.

How do we handle these issues in marriage? The same way we are supposed to approach forgiveness, period.

Ephesians 4:29-32:

DON'T SAY ANYTHING THAT WILL HURT OTHERS [LET ANY ROTTEN/UNHEALTHY WORD COME FROM YOUR MOUTH], BUT ONLY SAY WHAT IS HELPFUL [GOOD] TO MAKE OTHERS STRONGER [BUILD OTHERS UP] AND MEET [ACCORDING TO] THEIR NEEDS. THEN WHAT YOU SAY WILL DO GOOD [GIVE GRACE; BE A GIFT] TO THOSE WHO LISTEN TO YOU. AND DO NOT MAKE THE HOLY SPIRIT SAD [GRIEVE/BRING SORROW TO THE HOLY SPIRIT]. THE SPIRIT IS GOD'S PROOF THAT YOU BELONG TO HIM AND HE WILL MAKE YOU FREE WHEN THE FINAL DAY COMES [...BY WHOM YOU WERE SEALED FOR THE DAY OF REDEMPTION]. DO NOT BE BITTER OR ANGRY OR MAD [RAGING]. NEVER SHOUT ANGRILY OR SAY THINGS TO HURT [SLANDER; INSULT] OTHERS. NEVER DO ANYTHING [GET RID OF ALL KINDS OF] EVIL. BE KIND AND LOVING [COMPASSIONATE; TENDERHEARTED] TO EACH OTHER, AND FORGIVE EACH OTHER JUST AS GOD FORGAVE YOU IN CHRIST.

In marriage, forgiveness is an essential for a long and successful relationship. Problems will arise, and forgiveness needs to be the answer. Forgiveness doesn't make an action right. It doesn't say that what someone did was acceptable and invite them to do it repeatedly. What it does is give the opportunity for healing and acceptance, so people can move forward from a situation. In forgiveness, we acknowledge that we don't always do things right ourselves and recognize that forgiveness is required for a relationship to be healthy and for both people to start over, without bitterness or resentment, when things come up.

This means that marriage partners need to be able to communicate their hurts and offenses to one another. Apologies should go with wrongdoing, and "I forgive you" should go with repentance. Couples should recognize the way in which they wound one another and should make that much more of an effort not to engage in such speech or conduct again.

Sacrifice

Sacrifice is one of those words that makes people cringe. I know growing up, the church I attended encouraged us to manufacture sacrifices. We were taught that our sacrifices completed Christ's sacrifice and somehow attributed to our own personal salvation. While I don't believe that we should be deliberately seeking to make ourselves suffer and I certainly don't believe that we need to suffer in and of ourselves for our own salvation, I do believe that sacrifice is a part of life. In this life, we live with other people, we encounter others, and due to the sins and behaviors of other people (and, yes, sometimes even our own choices), we experience suffering. Our sacrifices become a type, or an illustration, and literally only a part, of what Jesus went through for us. In this regard, that makes us look at our own thoughts, understand in a deeper way about Jesus' sacrifice for us, and gain a greater spiritual perspective on the atonement.

Sacrifice is the principle that to have something, something else must be given up. It means that we often must put ourselves aside and do what is best for another person or is in the best interest of those involved in a situation (as is the case with marriage). There are many, many ways that marriage often requires sacrifice. When we want to pursue something or do something in this life, there are sacrifices that go with it. Marriage is no different than any other thing that we might like to pursue or do in this life that requires our efforts.

For example: if you are married and your job wants to promote you, but it is going to mean that your work schedule will interfere with your spouse's job or your spouse's ministry calling, that promotion needs to be weighed in the light of all those different things. If you have the opportunity to be promoted but you will have to do your job in another city and then commute several days a week, you need to think about how that will impact your marriage or your time with family. If you want to buy a new car but it will make it so there is no money for anything else in your household: it will short groceries and bills, then the wants that you have need to be considered in the light of the realities that doing what you want will cause.

Mark 8:34:

THEN JESUS CALLED THE CROWD TO HIM, ALONG WITH HIS FOLLOWERS [DISCIPLES]. HE SAID, "IF PEOPLE [ANYONE WANTS] WANT TO FOLLOW ME, THEY MUST GIVE UP THE THINGS THEY WANT [DENY THEMSELVES; SET ASIDE THEIR OWN INTERESTS]. THEY MUST BE WILLING EVEN TO GIVE UP THEIR LIVES TO [TAKE UP THEIR CROSS AND] FOLLOW ME."

Conventional wisdom tells us that "It takes work to make a marriage work." This is very true (and it is different from having to work for a marriage, which means nothing is there and you keep trying to fabricate something). If being married is important to you, it needs to be important enough to make the effort toward making your partner important in your life and avoiding idolatrous and selfish temptations to put yourself first. Sometimes sacrifices need to be made to keep a family together and thriving. I won't promise that God will give you what you want in the end, but having the love and support of your spouse is far more rewarding than pursuing the things that you want for yourself.

Dying to self

John 12:24-26:

I TELL YOU THE TRUTH [TRULY, TRULY I SAY TO YOU], A GRAIN OF WHEAT MUST FALL TO THE GROUND AND DIE TO MAKE MANY SEEDS [MUCH FRUIT]. BUT IF IT NEVER DIES, IT REMAINS ONLY A SINGLE SEED [GRAIN]. THOSE WHO [THE ONE WHO...] LOVE THEIR LIVES WILL LOSE THEM, BUT THOSE WHO HATE THEIR LIVES IN THIS WORLD WILL KEEP [GUARD; PRESERVE] TRUE LIFE FOREVER [IT FOR ETERNAL LIFE]. WHOEVER SERVES ME MUST FOLLOW ME. THEN MY SERVANT WILL BE WITH ME EVERYWHERE I AM. MY FATHER WILL HONOR ANYONE WHO SERVES ME.

Every Christian is called to deep self-examination and to die to the things within them that keep them from God. We usually refer to this as the "flesh," or the things that tie us and connect us to our wants and desires that relate to selfishness and unholy conduct. It's the part of us that wants to put ourselves first, have our own way, be served instead of serving, and have the entire world generally revolve around us. Even though most people probably wouldn't describe themselves as being "that bad" or "that extreme," every single one of us has a part of us that wants their own way. None of us like to be confronted with being wrong, or inflated, or arrogant, or difficult... or... or... or... so on and so forth. Whether or not we like it, every one of us has this nature within us, and doesn't like being confronted with it. We like to hear that God loves us and that He accepts us as we are, but we don't like dealing with the call to change.

Whether we are married or not, we are called to die to that nature and to rise to greater things in Christ. Still, marriage has a way of bringing to light every dark, hidden way that we are still surrendering to the flesh in our lives. As we go along in the Christian life, we should be displaying more of God's nature in us, and less of the fleshly selfishness. There sits marriage, revealing all the areas of our lives, where we need to make changes... and so conveniently... do not want to. Living with someone, seeing things that bother us about them, seeing things that bother them about us, seeing our responses to things, and monitoring our own behavior helps us to see – and confront – exactly where we are problematic within ourselves as we walk daily through the issues of life present in marriage.

Service

Nobody likes the idea of being "a servant." Even in Christianity, that is supposed to be centered around Christ, Who is the ultimate servant, we hear things like, "You're the head, and not the tail!" (Yes, this is in the Bible, but it is taken out of context.) We're given the idea that being in God means being "top dog," not having to be a servant. Even the word itself sounds unpleasant, like something you are not going to want to do.

Luke 22:24-30:

THE APOSTLES ALSO BEGAN TO ARGUE [THEN AN ARGUMENT/DISPUTE OCCURRED AMONG THEM] ABOUT WHICH ONE OF THEM WAS THE MOST IMPORTANT [GREATEST]. BUT JESUS SAID TO THEM, "THE KINGS OF THE GENTILES RULE [LORD IT] OVER THEM, AND THOSE WHO HAVE AUTHORITY OVER OTHERS LIKE TO BE CALLED 'FRIENDS OF THE PEOPLE' ['BENEFACTORS']. BUT YOU MUST NOT BE LIKE THAT. INSTEAD, THE GREATEST AMONG YOU SHOULD BE LIKE THE YOUNGEST, AND THE LEADER SHOULD BE LIKE THE SERVANT. [FOR] WHO IS MORE IMPORTANT: THE ONE SITTING AT THE TABLE [RECLINING] OR THE ONE SERVING? IS IT NOT THE ONE SITTING AT THE TABLE [RECLINING]? BUT I AM LIKE A SERVANT AMONG YOU.

"YOU [BUT YOU ARE THE ONES WHO] HAVE STAYED WITH ME THROUGH MY STRUGGLES [TRIALS]. JUST AS MY FATHER HAS GIVEN [GRANTED; CONFERRED ON] ME A KINGDOM, I ALSO GIVE [GRANT; CONFER ON] YOU A KINGDOM SO YOU MAY EAT AND DRINK AT MY TABLE IN MY KINGDOM. AND YOU WILL SIT ON THRONES, JUDGING THE TWELVE TRIBES OF ISRAEL.

When we think of being a servant, we think of slaves abused by their masters and forced into the most menial of jobs. God does not ask us to be abused by other people, but He does command that we are people who don't seek attention for what we do and we are willing to do what needs to be done, no matter how big or small that job might be. If you are a Christian, you are called to serve. If you are a married Christian, male or female, you are called to serve your spouse. This is about far more than just doing a few chores around the house and calling it done. Service is an attitude, a way of anticipating need and meeting needs and wants through your relationship. When we are people of service, we are concerned about what our partners need rather than our own. We can't do enough to make sure that they have what they need or that they are comfortable, even if it means maybe we do without something or don't get something for a while. When both partners assume a position of servanthood toward each other, it makes marriage much more pleasurable and that much more enjoyable.

Avoiding contention

In my book, *Fruit of the Vine: Study and Commentary on the Fruit of the Spirit*, I discuss the connection between patience and contention. The truth is that the answer to contention is not at all about pacifying difficult people, nor is it about becoming contentious yourself. The truth is that we should be neither contentious, nor constantly overlooking frustration, in our lives.

Different translations of the Bible translate the word "contention" or "contentious" differently. Some of these terms include "self-seeking" (New International Version 1984), "quarrelsome and nagging" (New International Version 2011), "selfishly ambitious" (New American Standard Bible), "cross and petulant" (The Message Bible), "factious" (American Standard Version) and "self-willed" (Weymouth New Testament). We can see from these different descriptions that someone who is "contentious" is deliberately willful, trying to get attention with their negative, annoying and vexing behavior. They control other people by being deliberately argumentative, irritating, and frustrating to other people.

Proverbs 21:19:

IT IS BETTER TO DWELL IN THE WILDERNESS, THAN WITH A CONTENTIOUS AND AN ANGRY WOMAN. (KJV)

Proverbs 26:21:

AS COALS ARE TO BURNING COALS, AND WOOD TO FIRE; SO IS A CONTENTIOUS MAN TO KINDLE STRIFE. (KJV)

Proverbs 27:15:

A CONTINUAL DROPPING IN A VERY RAINY DAY AND A CONTENTIOUS WOMAN ARE ALIKE. (KJV)

Romans 2:8:

BUT UNTO THEM THAT ARE CONTENTIOUS, AND DO NOT OBEY THE TRUTH, BUT OBEY UNRIGHTEOUSNESS, INDIGNATION AND WRATH... (KJV)

Who in the world wants to live with someone like this? The Bible is clear that men and women alike can be contentious, and that this is not a characteristic that is virtuous or beneficial to the believer. It is particularly damaging to a marriage, because it shows a total lack of disregard for the other person's feelings and their personage.

Galatians 2:16-21:

YET WE KNOW THAT A PERSON IS MADE RIGHT WITH GOD [JUSTIFIED; DECLARED RIGHTEOUS] NOT BY FOLLOWING [THE WORKS OF] THE LAW, BUT BY TRUSTING IN [FAITH IN; OR THE FAITHFULNESS OF] JESUS CHRIST. SO WE, TOO, HAVE PUT OUR FAITH IN CHRIST JESUS, THAT WE MIGHT BE MADE RIGHT WITH GOD [JUSTIFIED; DECLARED RIGHTEOUS] BECAUSE WE TRUSTED IN [THROUGH FAITH IN; OR BECAUSE OF THE FAITHFULNESS OF] CHRIST. IT IS NOT BECAUSE WE FOLLOWED [BY THE WORKS OF] THE LAW, BECAUSE NO ONE [HUMAN BEING; FLESH] CAN BE MADE RIGHT WITH GOD [JUSTIFIED; DECLARED RIGHTEOUS] BY FOLLOWING [THE WORKS OF] THE LAW.

WE JEWS CAME TO CHRIST, TRYING TO BE MADE RIGHT WITH GOD, AND IT BECAME CLEAR THAT WE ARE SINNERS, TOO [OR BUT IF WE OURSELVES, ALSO, BY SEEKING TO BE JUSTIFIED IN CHRIST, WERE FOUND TO BE SINNERS...]. DOES THIS MEAN THAT CHRIST ENCOURAGES [IS A SERVANT/MINISTER OF] SIN? NO [ABSOLUTELY NOT; MAY IT NEVER BE]! BUT I WOULD REALLY BE WRONG [OR PROVE MYSELF TO BE A LAWBREAKER/SINNER] TO BEGIN TEACHING AGAIN THOSE THINGS THAT I GAVE UP [IF I REBUILD THOSE THINGS I TORE DOWN; DEPENDENCE ON THE LAW FOR SALVATION]. IT WAS THE LAW THAT PUT ME TO DEATH [OR TRYING TO KEEP THE LAW CONDEMNED ME TO DEATH; FOR THROUGH THE LAW I DIED TO THE LAW], AND I DIED TO THE LAW SO THAT I CAN NOW LIVE FOR GOD [NO LONGER DEPENDING ON THE LAW FOR SALVATION, PAUL NOW DEPENDS ON GOD'S GRACE]. I WAS PUT TO DEATH ON THE CROSS [HAVE BEEN CRUCIFIED] WITH CHRIST, AND I DO NOT LIVE ANYMORE—IT IS CHRIST WHO LIVES IN ME. I STILL LIVE IN MY BODY [FLESH], BUT I LIVE BY FAITH IN [OR BECAUSE OF THE FAITHFULNESS OF] THE SON OF GOD WHO LOVED ME AND GAVE HIMSELF TO SAVE ME [FOR ME; ON MY BEHALF]. BY SAYING THESE THINGS I AM NOT GOING AGAINST [DO NOT SET ASIDE/NULLIFY] GOD'S GRACE. JUST THE OPPOSITE [FOR...], IF THE LAW COULD MAKE US RIGHT WITH GOD, THEN CHRIST'S DEATH WOULD BE USELESS [IN VAIN; FOR NOTHING].

Every one of us needs the reminder that we are not saved by ourselves, nor of the law, or our ideas about the law, or even our own re-created, reincarnated ideas of the way in which we try to apply the law today. In marriage, I think keeping sight of these concepts is most helpful. We are quick to run off about everything we think in marriage today, without any regard to what our attitude and presentation of our thoughts might do to our spouse.

In terms of contentious people, we are constantly dealing with people who think they "know best" about whatever it is they spout off, and we need to be careful that we don't adopt the same attitudes when it comes to our own marriages (and life outlooks, at that). We live in a world full of casual scholars, who think they read a few paragraphs on something online and now they know more than everyone else does. This has caused contention to soar sky-high and has left us square in the middle of a world full of extremes. We see one end of "dos and don'ts," and another extreme of people who just don't obey God in the least, no matter what they may claim. What we need to see is that both are equally frustrating to God and are a frustration of His grace to us. Grace has not been given to us as an excuse for us to disobey what God is saying to us, nor is it an excuse to just modify our relationship with Him to suit our own personal need to be self-righteous and personally glorified. As with all things in the Father, God calls us to seek the balance - the middle ground - between these two excessive extremes. When we find balance, we are grounded in a place that ceases to frustrate His grace.

Just as we can frustrate God's grace, we can frustrate our spouse because they find us vexing. We love to talk about patience, love, grace, and forgiveness in marriage if it's not about what we do, but we are people who can be vexing and difficult, even to the most patient of spouses at times. If you recognize this behavior in yourself, it's time to learn about the grace of being quiet and respectful with your spouse. You do not have to scream, yell, or speak in a nasty or demeaning tone to get your point across. Rather than being contentious, behave with maturity and wisdom, and know your partner well enough to know the best way to convey important messages and feelings without behaving in a messy or contentious way.

Self-control in marriage

It might seem odd to talk about marriage and self-control, but if we look at much of what is taught as pertains to marriage today, we're almost given the message that marriage is an avenue to live without self-control. If the single life is all about being self-controlled, married life is taught to be the total opposite. There are marital courses that make marriage sound like it is a free-for-all between husband and wife, where endless sex is available and both partners need to, more or less, "put up or shut up." Marriage is not taught to be decent or ordered, we do not learn about propriety or disciplines in the marriage relationship, and we don't learn the very important role that self-control plays in every marriage action, from the bedroom to daily interactions in life.

There's one main reason why self-control is such an important concept in the Bible. Personal governance and ability to rule one's impulses and desires are a must if we are going to master any major goal in our lives, both spiritual and natural. If our lives are spent pursuing lust, physical desires, desires for power, wants disguised as needs, and vague emotional pursuits, we don't have the focus and disciplines we need to accomplish.

1 Corinthians 7:1-7:

NOW I WILL DISCUSS [CONCERNING] THE THINGS YOU WROTE ME ABOUT [IN A LETTER FROM THE CORINTHIANS; SEE 8:1; 12:1; 16:1]. IT IS GOOD FOR A MAN NOT TO HAVE SEXUAL RELATIONS WITH [TOUCH; A EUPHEMISM FOR SEX] A WOMAN [PROBABLY ANOTHER SLOGAN (6:12; 8:1, 4; 10:23) ASSERTING THAT A CELIBATE LIFESTYLE WAS SPIRITUALLY SUPERIOR]. BUT BECAUSE SEXUAL SIN IS A DANGER [OF SEXUAL TEMPTATIONS; OF SEXUAL SINS], EACH MAN SHOULD HAVE [OR HAVE SEXUAL RELATIONS WITH] HIS OWN WIFE, AND EACH WOMAN SHOULD HAVE [OR HAVE SEXUAL RELATIONS WITH] HER OWN HUSBAND. THE HUSBAND SHOULD GIVE HIS WIFE ALL THAT HE OWES HER AS HIS WIFE [MEET HER SEXUAL NEEDS]. AND THE WIFE SHOULD GIVE HER HUSBAND ALL THAT SHE OWES HIM AS HER HUSBAND [MEET HIS SEXUAL NEEDS]. THE WIFE DOES NOT HAVE FULL RIGHTS [AUTHORITY] OVER HER OWN BODY; HER HUSBAND SHARES THEM. AND THE HUSBAND DOES NOT HAVE FULL RIGHTS [AUTHORITY] OVER HIS OWN BODY; HIS WIFE SHARES THEM [REVOLUTIONARY TEACHING IN THE FIRST CENTURY, WHEN WIVES WERE GENERALLY VIEWED AS THE POSSESSION OF

THEIR HUSBANDS]. DO NOT REFUSE TO GIVE YOUR BODIES TO [REFUSE SEX TO; DEPRIVE] EACH OTHER, UNLESS YOU BOTH AGREE TO STAY AWAY FROM SEXUAL RELATIONS FOR A TIME SO YOU CAN GIVE YOUR TIME [DEVOTE YOURSELVES] TO PRAYER. THEN COME TOGETHER AGAIN [RESUME YOUR SEXUAL RELATIONSHIP] SO SATAN CANNOT TEMPT YOU BECAUSE OF A LACK OF SELF-CONTROL. I SAY THIS TO GIVE YOU PERMISSION TO STAY AWAY FROM SEXUAL RELATIONS FOR A TIME [AS A CONCESSION/ALLOWANCE]. IT IS NOT A COMMAND TO DO SO. I WISH THAT EVERYONE WERE LIKE ME [UNMARRIED], BUT EACH PERSON HAS HIS OWN GIFT FROM GOD. ONE HAS ONE GIFT, ANOTHER HAS ANOTHER GIFT.

I said in the last chapter that we were going to look at this passage here, only a little differently. The reason we are looking at this here, again, is because the Bible is endorsing and encouraging self-control in marriage through this passage. Rather than treating marriage as a free-for-all, it is a coming together of two consensual adults who agree to trust and respect the bodies and boundaries of one another. Contrary to what many do teach, there is such a thing as rape in marriage. If a husband or a wife does not agree to the sexual act that is performed on them, then they are being sexually violated. Sex is not supposed to be something done by force, by physical violation, with intimidation, or just for the satisfaction of one party. If sex isn't consensual, it's not pleasing before God.

We need to recognize that it might seem like sex will be one of those things that people are automatically compatible on prior to marriage, but once you are in the marriage, things that pertain to sex will seem different. There will be times when your partner is tired, ill, in physical discomfort, or generally unable to engage in sexual relations. There is nothing wrong, nor abnormal with this. What is wrong is when a marital partner doesn't respect or care enough about their partner to put their own needs aside and care about their mate. When one partner is not in a sexual place, for whatever reason, their spouse should respect that. If it goes on for long periods of time, that should definitely be discussed and investigated, but periodic sexless periods are completely within the range of personal boundaries and space.

There will also be times when couples will mutually agree to refrain from sexual activity while they focus on other pursuits. Whether it is specifically for prayer and fasting, spending time doing something spiritual or practical, or due to a partner's absence, sexual abstinence is an occasional part of marriage. There are also circumstances where a partner is somehow ill, incapacitated, or otherwise unable to engage in sexual activity, whereby sexual abstinence will also be required. These are all opportunities for self-control, and to show your spouse that you love and care about them beyond sexual desires.

People have different "sexual paces." Some people desire sex frequently; others are not interested in it as often. Self-control in marriage arises with a compromise, ensuring that both partners have their needs met. Each partner's needs, their likes and dislikes, and their attention should also be respected.

Marital privacy

Hebrews 13:4:

MARRIAGE SHOULD BE HONORED BY EVERYONE, AND HUSBAND AND WIFE SHOULD KEEP THEIR MARRIAGE [THE MARRIAGE BED SHOULD BE KEPT] PURE [UNDEFILED]. GOD WILL JUDGE AS GUILTY [JUDGE] THOSE WHO TAKE PART IN SEXUAL SINS [THE SEXUALLY IMMORAL AND ADULTERERS].

When it comes to marriage, the problems that you have, and the things that you do, some things need to remain in the house, between the marriage partners. It doesn't take much for information to wind up in the wrong hands, and some things need to remain in your marriage. Sexual preferences and habits, physical issues that you or your partner may have, even some of the personal things about disagreements or behaviors that your spouse has should remain among the two of you. This not only shows respect, but it also shows a great sense for the sanctity of the relationship.

Supporting your mate and their calling

The very last section of this week's work is on one of the most important aspects of marriage, and that is support. We have tapped on it a little bit in the past, but supporting your mate and their calling also deeply relates to us as a set apart, holy people. In the world, we aren't taught to support other people. This is a message that transcends worldly marital arrangements. One person is taught to give, and the other is taught to demand. We don't see a lot of balance in marriages in the world (or in the church, for that matter). When we see marriage in church, we hear a lot of conflicting advice and often deep confusion as one side says one thing, and the other says something else.

What we do hear a lot about, both in the world and the church respectively, is how important it is to communicate with your spouse and how essential it is that the marital unit remain intact. It is a lot easier to communicate and remain a couple, avoiding the temptations and pitfalls that come along in life, when you know that your spouse cares about you and considers you as a person, a human being.

When it comes to calling, we recognize that God has placed that within us and it's not something we can turn off and shut off at whim. Callings can be inconvenient in a marriage, because they demand something of both parties that sometimes one or both are not willing to give. This attitude, however, does not reflect service. If you have decided to marry someone, you are deciding to marry all of them, regardless of where God is going to take them in their lives. By being married, you are open to the possibility that their calling may develop deeper, that more may be asked of you than is required right now, and that you are the person who can give them the support that's needed through the developments and changes that are to come.

Ecclesiastes 4:9-11:

TWO PEOPLE ARE BETTER THAN ONE,
*   BECAUSE THEY GET MORE DONE BY WORKING TOGETHER [A GOOD*
RETURN FOR THEIR HARD WORK/TOIL].
IF ONE FALLS DOWN,
*   THE OTHER CAN HELP HIM [HIS COLLEAGUE] UP.*
BUT IT IS BAD [A PITY] FOR THE PERSON WHO IS ALONE AND FALLS,
*   BECAUSE NO ONE IS THERE TO HELP.*
IF TWO LIE DOWN TOGETHER, THEY WILL BE WARM,
*   BUT A PERSON ALONE WILL NOT BE WARM.*

Song of Solomon 8:6-7:

PUT [SET] ME LIKE A SEAL [LEAVING AN IMPRESSION ON CLAY, SHOWING

OWNERSHIP] ON YOUR HEART [INSIDE],
 LIKE A SEAL ON YOUR ARM [OUTSIDE].
LOVE IS AS STRONG AS DEATH;
 JEALOUSY [OR PASSION] IS AS STRONG [TENACIOUS] AS THE GRAVE.
LOVE BURSTS INTO FLAMES [ITS FLAME IS AN INTENSE FIRE]
 AND BURNS LIKE A HOT FIRE [OR A GODLIKE FLAME].
EVEN MUCH WATER CANNOT PUT OUT THE FLAME OF LOVE;
 FLOODS CANNOT DROWN [FLOOD] LOVE.
IF A MAN OFFERED EVERYTHING [ALL THE WEALTH] IN HIS HOUSE FOR LOVE,
 PEOPLE WOULD TOTALLY REJECT IT [OR HE WOULD BE COMPLETELY DESPISED].

Being there for your mate is about more than money. It's also about making sure that you encourage them, that you are there when they have a hard time, and that you are there when it counts. Every couple's specific needs are different, because everyone's lives and callings are each a little different. As you go through your marriage, remember the foundations we have laid here, through this program. Some things are real clear to do, and others will be trickier, but remember – you are working through holiness, and your marriage is helping you to do that. As you go along, you will have the support and tools to figure out what works for you.

Week 16 Assignments

Answer the following questions based on discussions you have had with your future spouse in counseling this week and additionally on your own time and prepare to discuss them at your next counseling session. If you run out of room in a section, finish the answer to your question in your journal.

1. Do you think it is possible to be holy and be married? How do you think marriage can help holiness? _____

_____

_____

_____

_____

2. Does marriage work without love? Why or why not? _____

_____

_____

_____

_____

3. What is the difference between *eros* and *agape*? _____

_____

_____

_____

_____

4. What are the attributes of true love? _____

_____

_____

_____

_____

5. Is marriage about more than personal happiness? Who is responsible for your happiness? _____

_____

_____

_____

_____

6. How is forgiveness important in a marriage? _____

_____

_____

_____

_____

7. How does sacrifice relate to marriage? _____

_____

_____

_____

8. What are some examples of sacrifices that exist in marriage?

_____

_____

_____

_____

_____

9. When it comes to "dying to self," why is this an important precept in a marriage? _____

_____

_____

_____

_____

10. Are all Christians called to service? How does this apply to a marriage? _____

_____

_____

_____

_____

11. What are some examples of ways you can be of service to your future spouse? _____

_____

_____

_____

_____

12. What is contention? What are some different terms for contention? _____

_____

_____

_____

_____

13. Where do you think contention comes from? _____

_____

_____

_____

_____

14. How can you avoid contention in your own marriage? _____

_____

_____

_____

_____

15. Why is self-control such an important component of a marriage?

_____

_____

_____

_____

_____

16. What are some examples of having self-control in marriage? Why is privacy important? _____

_____

_____

_____

17. How do you intend to support your future spouse in their calling? _____

_____

_____

_____

18. How do you think the couple in the Song of Solomon viewed their marriage? Do you think they saw it as an opportunity for deeper holiness? Why or why not? _____

_____

_____

_____

_____

19. In reading Hebrews 12:10-24, why do you think God chose marriage to help so many people grow and develop holiness in their lives? _____

_____

_____

_____

_____

20. Who do you believe God is calling you to be? How is marriage going to help you to develop that calling? How is it going to benefit your future spouse? Write below and in your journal, if needed, and discuss at your final counseling session. _____

_____

_____

_____

_____

A Pre-Wedding Prayer

Father, we thank You for being the One Who proves Himself faithful to us in our marriages. We are blessed in knowing that You have brought this together, and that nobody can come along and tear it apart. We declare that by the power of the Spirit, we shall grow holy in our marriage. We will allow You to move through our marriage and through us as people, which will change our outlook and perspective on relationships. We pray for the ability to submit to You, and to submit to one another. We stand as part of the Body of Christ and commit to remain a part of Your church, connected through our local churches. We embrace our families, our extended families, and our family yet to come. We stand upon Your Word, and upon Your revelation to us. Help us, Lord, through the good times and the bad. Help us to always lift one another up unto life, and to live life. Allow us the blessing and beauty of developing deeper holiness and righteousness in this relationship, as we seek a greater sense of Your truth. Let us focus on the good, the noble, the right, the beautiful, and the honorable. Whatever is ahead for us, we are ready, because we trust You. Bless our marriage, Father, with Your Spirit in the way that only You can.

In Jesus' Name,

Amen

Dr. Lee Ann B. Marino, Ph.D., D.Min., D.D.

THESE THAT HAVE TURNED THE WORLD UPSIDE DOWN ARE COME HITHER ALSO.
(ACTS 17:6, KJV)

DR. LEE ANN B. MARINO, PH.D., D.MIN., D.D. (she/her) is "everyone's favorite theologian" leading Gen X, Millennials, and Gen Z with expertise in leadership training, queer and feminist theology, general religion, and apostolic theology. She has served in ministry since 1998 and was ordained as a pastor in 2002 and an apostle in 2010. She founded what is now Sanctuary Apostolic Fellowship Empowerment (SAFE) Ministries in 2004. Under her ministry heading Dr. Marino is founder and Overseer of Sanctuary International Fellowship Tabernacle (SIFT) (the original home of National Coming Out Sunday) and The Sanctuary Network, and Chancellor of Apostolic Covenant Theological Seminary (ACTS).

Affectionately nicknamed "the Spitfire," Dr. Marino has spent over two decades as an "apostle, preacher, and teacher" (2 Timothy 1:11), exercising her personal mandate to become "all things to all people" (1 Corinthians 9:22). Her embrace of spiritual issues (both technical and intimate) has found its home among both seekers and believers, those who desire spiritual answers to today's issues.

Dr. Marino has preached throughout the United States, Puerto Rico, and Europe in hundreds of religious services and experiences throughout the years. A history maker in her own right, she has spent over two decades in advocacy, education, and work for and within minority spiritual communities (including African American, Hispanic, and LGBTQ+). She has also served as the first woman on all-male synods, councils, and panels, as well as the first preacher or speaker welcomed of a different race, sexual orientation, or identity among diverse communities. Today, Dr. Marino's work extends to over 150 countries as she hosts the popular *Kingdom Now* podcast, which is in the top 20 percentile of all podcasts worldwide. She is also the author of over 35 books and the popular Patheos column, *Leadership on Fire*. To date, she has had five bestselling titles within their subject matter: *Understanding Demonology, Spiritual Warfare, Healing, and Deliverance: A Manual for the Christian Minister*; *Ministry School Boot Camp: Training for Helps Ministries, Appointments, and Beyond*; *Discovering Intimacy: A Journey Through the Song of Solomon*; *Fruit of the Vine: Study and Commentary on the Fruit of the Spirit*; and *Ministering to LGBTQ+ (and Those Who Love Them): A Primer for Queer Theology* (and its accompanying workbook).

As a public icon and social media influencer, Dr. Marino advocates healthy body image (curvy/full-figured), representation as a demisexual/aromantic, and albinism awareness as a model. Known to those she works with, she is a spiritual mom, teacher, leader, professor, confidant, and friend. She continues to transform, receiving new teaching, revelation, and insight in this thing we call "ministry." Through years of spiritual growth and maturity, Dr. Marino stands as herself, here to present what God has given to her for any who have an ear to hear.

For more information, visit her website at kingdompowernow.org.

www.ingramcontent.com/pod-product-compliance
Lightning Source LLC
Chambersburg PA
CBHW080603270326
41928CB00016B/2909